The Architect in Practice

The Architect in Practice

Tenth Edition

David Chappell

Andrew Willis

WILEY-BLACKWELL

A John Wiley & Sons, Ltd., Publication

This edition first published 2010
© 2010 and 2005 David Chappell and Andrew Willis

Blackwell Publishing was acquired by John Wiley & Sons in February 2007. Blackwell's publishing programme has been merged with Wiley's global Scientific, Technical, and Medical business to form Wiley-Blackwell.

Registered office
John Wiley & Sons Ltd, The Atrium, Southern Gate, Chichester, West Sussex, PO19 8SQ, United Kingdom

Editorial offices
9600 Garsington Road, Oxford, OX4 2DQ, United Kingdom
2121 State Avenue, Ames, Iowa 50014-8300, USA

For details of our global editorial offices, for customer services and for information about how to apply for permission to reuse the copyright material in this book please see our website at www.wiley.com/wiley-blackwell.

The right of the authors to be identified as the authors of this work has been asserted in accordance with the Copyright, Designs and Patents Act 1988.

Wiley also publishes its books in a variety of electronic formats. Some content that appears in print may not be available in electronic books.

Designations used by companies to distinguish their products are often claimed as trademarks. All brand names and product names used in this book are trade names, service marks, trademarks or registered trademarks of their respective owners. The publisher is not associated with any product or vendor mentioned in this book. This publication is designed to provide accurate and authoritative information in regard to the subject matter covered. It is sold on the understanding that the publisher is not engaged in rendering professional services. If professional advice or other expert assistance is required, the services of a competent professional should be sought.

Library of Congress Cataloging-in-Publication Data

Chappell, David (David M.)
    The architect in practice / David Chappell, Andrew Willis.—10th ed.
        p. cm.
    Includes bibliographical references and index.
    ISBN 978-1-4051-9852-3 (pbk. : alk. paper)   1. Architectural practice—United States.   I. Willis, Andrew.   II. Title.
    NA1996.C47 2010
    720.68—dc22

                                                                    2010001843

A catalogue record for this book is available from the British Library.

Set in 10 on 12.5pt Minion by Toppan Best-set Premedia Limited
Printed in Singapore by Ho Printing Singapore Pte Ltd

2   2011

The Inspiration

From a pseudonymous letter of a quantity surveyor to
the *Builder*, 9 March 1951

'I have great admiration for an architect who does his job well, because he has one of the
most difficult jobs in the world. He must be an artist but at the same time in his
administration of a building contract be a business man, and in interpreting it even
something of a lawyer.'

The Dedication

To Arthur Willis, Christopher Willis and Bruce George
and
To the architectural profession
in the hope that the book may encourage that co-operation of which its joint authorship is
a symbol.

Contents

Preface

It is often said that architects are poor at business. We suspect that, if true, it is because they enjoy what they do so much. It is not unusual to find architects continuing to work in order to see their buildings constructed long after disputes about fees and other things would have persuaded other professionals to walk away. Architecture is undoubtedly one of the professions that can be enjoyed. It offers a wealth of interest in a variety of fields which few other professions can match, and provides an emotional satisfaction which only the other arts can stimulate. In order to derive the fullest pleasure from it, architects must devote themselves completely to its study and practice. The more proficient they become and the greater mastery they can acquire, the more complete will be their enjoyment.

Ability to design and skill in draftsmanship or in using computer-aided design equipment will not alone make an architect. Architects should bring the same skill to all sides of their profession, whether it is the initial building survey, feasibility studies, concept design, production information or the giving of professional advice and undertaking the administration of the construction contract. In common with other professions, architects owe a duty of care to their clients but they have a greater responsibility than most in that the buildings and environments that they create affect the population at large.

The purpose of this book is to present to architectural students, and perhaps the less experienced practitioners, some indication of the practice and procedure with which they must be acquainted if they are to follow their profession with success. They must find clients to employ them, they must be able to manage an office and be responsible for a good deal of administrative work in connection with construction contracts, and they must know something of finance, law, the general structure of the construction industry and the organisation and requirements of those authorities who exercise so much control over their day-to-day work. Let the readers, therefore, move away from their CAD equipment, lay aside their thick felt pens and settle down to their desk or armchair to study an aspect of their work which is essential to make them efficient architects.

The architect's work is here looked at mainly from the angle of the private practitioner dealing with the JCT forms of contract, though references are made where appropriate to public service practice and to the government and other forms of contract. Architects in private practice are often commissioned to act for public authorities and they must therefore be able to adapt to the differing conditions which this type of work involves.

The chapters have been arranged in the sequence which the progress of a construction contract makes natural. Part 1 opens with an introduction to the construction industry and is followed by some basic principles of practice, sources of information, legal and administrative matters. Part 2 follows the running of a construction project, the chapters being based on the work stages of the RIBA Plan of Work which has again been revised since the last edition. Part 3 ends the book with what can best be described as management matters, covering finance, insurance, obtaining work and employing staff. Each chapter includes some illustrations, and ends with notes of law cases together with a selected bibliography.

The Architect in Practice was first published over 50 years ago in 1952. It was written by two men, one a quantity surveyor and one an architect, both of whom had a flair for writing and who, after working together for some years, came to the conclusion that a textbook on architectural practice was needed. During that time, through nine editions, it has remained a leading textbook used in the education of architects worldwide.

It is a matter worthy of some note that the mantle of quantity surveying author has passed down through three generations of the Willis family.

The format of the book was radically changed for the seventh edition in order to make it more accessible to the casual reader. The revised format was well received and it has been continued thereafter. While the format changed, the message and philosophy remained and remain the same: here is a book which tries to present to the reader some of the elementary duties that architects owe to their clients and contractors alike and to endorse the adage that of the many responsibilities that are borne by the architect, the greatest is the duty of care.

Architectural practice is now much more complex than was the case 50 years ago. There is now a multitude of forms of building contract to choose from, which would take a lifetime to read. It is not possible to write in any detail on such a wide subject: it warrants a set of textbooks on its own. The most helpful thing that we can do is to point the reader to relevant sources for this and other allied subjects.

As usual, this edition has been brought up to date and some of our commentaries revised where we judged it appropriate to do so. Among other things, the sections on planning and the Building Regulations have been thoroughly revised, changes to the education of architects in the UK have been detailed, the new ARB Architects Code: Standards of Professional Conduct and Practice, which comes into force from January 2010, has been incorporated, reference has been made to the Companies Act 2006 which came completely into force in October 2009, the commentary on the RIBA Standard Form for the Appointment of an Architect 1999 (SFA/99) has been updated and reference has been added to deal with the latest RIBA Standard Agreement 2010 (S-10-A). The Joint Contracts Tribunal has reissued all its contracts as a 2005 suite and two revisions have already been issued. The new contracts have been substantially revised in both structure and detail from the 1998 series and new contracts have been added. All references to JCT contracts in this book have been updated, where appropriate, to refer to the new contracts. We are pleased to know that this book is used in the Republic of Ireland and in this edition, we have included reference to education, registration and CPD requirements of the Royal Institute of the Architects of Ireland.

The Local Democracy, Economic Development and Construction Act 2009 gained Royal Assent on 12 November 2009 after we had finished our work on this book. Part 8 of the Act amends the Housing Grants, Construction and Regeneration Act 1996. No commencement date has been fixed for Part 8 and it is thought that it is not likely to take effect for some months. We have been able to insert a reference to the new Act in Chapter 6, but space does not allow a detailed consideration. Part 8 will not apply to contracts entered into before the commencement date.

Finally we hope that our efforts will assist future generations of architects in the way that Arthur Willis and Bruce George assisted our generations.

David Chappell
Andrew Willis
January 2010

Acknowledgements

We are grateful to Allan Ashworth DUniv (Hon) MSc MRICS and Keith Hogg BSc MRICS PGCE for their agreement to the use in this book of parts of the text of *Willis's Practice and Procedure for the Quantity Surveyor*. We are also grateful to the following for particular assistance as indicated:

> Richard Cobb BA Econ (Hons) DipTP MRTPI, Chartered Town Planner, for continuing to contribute Planning Legislation and Practice in Chapter 9. It has been substantially revised for this edition.
>
> Bob Cooper BEng(Hons) MSc FBEng FRICS, Technical Advisor, Association of Building Engineers, for updating the Building Regulations in Chapter 10.
>
> Crease Strickland Parkins, Architects of York, for the setting out plan in Fig. 15.1.
>
> Caroline M. Dalziel LLB(Hons), Solicitor, for again commenting on company law in Chapter 4 and on employment law in Chapter 18.
>
> Designworks Architects of Northampton, for assistance in various ways.
>
> Jane Johnston MA(Hons) Landscape Architecture Licentiate Member of the Landscape Institute, for a contribution about landscape architecture.
>
> Lawrence J. G. Johnston BSc MSc MCIArb RIBA, for continuing to contribute the whole of Chapter 2.
>
> Space Craft Architects of London, for the provision of various examples at short notice.

The ARB Standards of Conduct and Practice, CPD information, how ARB works, Prescription Procedures and data from the web pages, copyright Architects Registration Board, are reproduced by kind permission of the ARB.

The RIAI Accreditation information, registration, CPD and the summary of the role of the RIAI are reproduced by kind permission of the Royal Institute of the Architects of Ireland.

Extracts from the RIBA Code of Conduct, RIBA membership procedures and the relevant parts of the RIBA website relating to RIBA Services, validation procedures and CPD requirements, copyright Royal Institute of British Architects, are reproduced here by kind permission of the RIBA.

The RIBA Contract Administration Forms are reproduced by kind permission of the copyright owners, the RIBA, and by the publishers, RIBA Publishing. Copies of the forms are available from RIBA Bookshops at www.ribabookshops.com.

The RICS Valuation and Statement of Retention Values forms, reproduced on pages 282 and 286, can be purchased from the RICS at www.ricsbooks.com.

Abbreviations and Acronyms

ABE	Association of Building Engineers
AC	Appeal case
ACA	Association of Consultant Architects
ACAS	Advisory, Conciliation and Arbitration Service
ACE	Architects Council of Europe, Association of Consulting Engineers
All ER	All England Law Reports
APM	Association for Project Managers
ARB	Architects Registration Board
ARCUK	Architects Registration Council of the United Kingdom
BAE	Board of Architectural Education
BBA	British Board of Agrément
BCIS	Building Cost Information Service
BEC	Building Employers Confederation
BLR	Building Law Reports
BPF	British Property Federation
BRE	Building Research Establishment
BSI	British Standards Institute
BSRIA	Building Services Research and Information Association
C-10-A	RIBA Concise Agreement 2010
CABE	Commission for Architecture and the Built Environment
CAD	Computer-aided design
CATS	Credit Award Transfer System
CAWS	Common Arrangement of Work Sections
CC	Construction Confederation
CCPI	Co-ordinating Committee for Project Information
CDM	Construction (Design and Management)
CE/99	RIBA Conditions of Engagement 1999 (2004 update)
CI/SfB	Construction Information/Samarbetskommitten for Byggnadsfragor
CIArb	Chartered Institute of Arbitrators
CIB	Construction Industry Board
CIBSE	Chartered Institution of Building Services Engineers
CIC	Construction Industry Council
CIJC	Construction Industry Joint Council
CIL	Community Infrastructure Levy
CILL	Construction Industry Law Letter

CIOB	Chartered Institute of Building
CIRIA	Construction Industry Research and Information Association
CITB	Construction Industry Training Board
CLD	Construction Law Digest
CLG	Communities and Local Government
ConLR	Construction Law Reports
ConstLJ	Construction Law Journal
CPA	Construction Products Association
CPD	Continuing professional development
CPI	Co-ordinated project information
D-10-A	RIBA Domestic Project Agreement 2010
DB	JCT Design and Build Contract 2005 series
DCLG	Department of Communities and Local Government
DCMS	Department of Culture, Media and Sport
ECTS	European Credit Transfer System
EH	English Heritage
EPIC	Electronic Product Information Co-operation
EU	European Union
GPDO	Town and Country Planning (General Permitted Development) Order 1995
IC	JCT Intermediate Building Contract 2005 series
ICD	JCT Intermediate Building Contract with contractor's design 2005 series
ICE	Institution of Civil Engineers
ICWCI	Institute of Clerks of Works and Construction Inspectorate of Great Britain Inc
IEEE	Institute of Electrical and Electronics Engineers
IFC 98	JCT Intermediate Form of Contract 1998 edition
IMechE	Institute of Mechanical Engineers
IStructE	Institution of Structural Engineers
ISO	International Standards Organisation
JCT	Joint Contracts Tribunal
JCT 98	JCT Standard Form of Building Contract 1998 edition
LDD	Local Development Document
LDF	Local Development Framework
LDS	Local Development Scheme
LI	Landscape Institute
LLP	Limited liability partnership
LPA	Local Planning Authority
MIPPS	Ministerial Interim Planning Policy Statement
MW	JCT Minor Works Building Contract 2005 series
MW 98	JCT Agreement for Minor Building Works
MWD	JCT Minor Works Building Contract with contractors design 2005 series
NBS	National Building Specification

NJCC	National Joint Consultative Committee for Building
NPF	National Planning Framework
PAN	Planning Advice Note
PAYE	Pay as you earn
PD	Permitted development
PFI	Private Finance Initiative
PINS	Planning Inspectorate
PPG	Planning Policy Guidance
PPP	Public Private Partnership
PPS	Planning Policy Statements
PSA	Property Services Agency
RIAI	Royal Institute of the Architects of Ireland
RIAS	Royal Incorporation of Architects in Scotland
RIBA	Royal Institute of British Architects
RICS	Royal Institution of Chartered Surveyors
RPB	Regional planning body
RSAW	Royal Society of Architects in Wales
RSS	Regional Spatial Strategy
RSUA	Royal Society of Ulster Architects
RTPI	Royal Town Planning Institute
S-10-A	RIBA Standard Agreement 2010
SBC	JCT Standard Building Contract 2005 series
SFA/99	RIBA Standard Form of Agreement 1999 (2004 update)
SMM	Standard Method of Measurement for Building Works
SoS	Secretary of State
SPD	Supplementary Planning Document
SPG	Supplementary Planning Guidance
SPP	Scottish Planning Policy
SPV	Special Purposes Vehicle
SW/99	RIBA Small Works appointment 1999 (2004 update)
TAN	Technical Advice Note
TPO	Tree Preservation Order
UCAS	Universities and Colleges Admissions Service
UCO	Town and Country (Use Classes) Order 1987
WLR	Weekly Law Reports

Part 1
Background to Practice

1 The Construction Industry

1.1 Introduction

The construction industry is concerned with the planning, regulation, design, manufacture, fabrication, erection and maintenance of buildings and other structures. It includes the separate areas of activity of building, civil engineering and heavy engineering. Whilst the demarcation between these broad sectors is blurred, the majority of architects are involved on building projects in their various forms.

Project values can vary significantly from minor works costing a few hundred pounds to major building schemes costing tens of million pounds or major transportation and other infrastructure projects costing several billion pounds. Whilst there are certain similarities in the principles of execution of projects, the scale, complexity and organisation vary enormously.

1.2 Significance of the construction industry

The construction industry is an important part of any economy. In the UK it accounts for approximately 8% of the nation's Gross Domestic Product (GDP), although its share of national output has declined over the last 20 years.

There are particular characteristics that distinguish the construction industry from all others including:

- the physical nature of the product
- the product is normally manufactured on the client's premises (i.e. the construction site)
- most of the products are one-off designs
- the traditional arrangement separates design from manufacture
- it produces investment rather than consumer goods
- its activities may be affected by the vagaries of the weather
- its processes include a complex mix of different materials, skills and trades
- typically, throughout the world, it includes a small number of relatively large construction companies and a very large number of small firms.

The construction industry is a major employer of labour, employing approximately 2.3 million people in the UK, from the unskilled through to the highly skilled technology professional. Therefore, due to its significance, the fortunes of the construction industry provide one of the best indicators of a country's economic performance. An active construction industry generally represents a buoyant economy.

1.3   An ever changing industry

As construction is such a significant industry, it is particularly susceptible to trends in both national and international economies, and in particular such issues as:

- uncertainty in business cycles
- levels of employment
- interest rates
- rates of inflation
- manufacturing output
- market economies.

In times of recession, clients are unwilling to invest and this clearly has a direct influence on the industry as a result of reduced expenditure on capital projects.

The industry also needs to continually adapt, to respond to technological advancements, changes in government policy and initiatives and new methods of procurement; this has particularly been the case over recent years.

As a result of privatisation over the last 25 years, the levels of public sector spending as a proportion of the whole have reduced significantly. Furthermore, as the construction industry moved into the 21st century, the balance between publicly and privately funded projects changed still further when there were significant developments in how public sector works are procured and increased public/private sector collaboration being encouraged (e.g. private finance initiatives (PFIs) and public-private partnerships (PPPs).

The demand for improvements in performance is ever increasing and cannot be ignored. Reviews carried out during the 1990s highlighted the dissatisfaction amongst major clients due to the unpredictability of projects in terms of delivery to time, within budgets and to the standards of quality expected. The Latham Report[1] identified that this was due to the fragmentation and confrontation that exist. More recently, *Rethinking Construction*[2] again recognised the level of dissatisfaction and put forward proposals for improving performance across the industry as a whole, centred around five key drivers: committed leadership; customer focus; integrated processes and teams; drive for quality; commitment to people. The task force behind the report considered that these drivers, together with the application of performance targets, provided the focus for considerable improvements within the industry.

Subsequently, in 1999, the government, recognising the need for improvement in the procurement of government construction projects, launched the Achieving Excellence in Construction initiative, and put in place a strategy for sustained improvement in procurement and achieving whole-life value for money.

Particular focus was given to the use of partnering and developing long-term relationships, reducing financial and decision-making approval chains and improving skills development. The increased use of performance measurement indicators, value and risk management techniques and whole-life costing was also encouraged. Whilst this was a public sector initiative, major private sector clients have similar objectives.

A parallel initiative by Constructing Excellence aimed to achieve a step change in construction productivity through continuous improvement, focusing particularly on innovation, productivity and communicating knowledge of best practice, this being encouraged through promoting net-working, collaboration and demonstration projects, and benchmarking performance.

Many of these aims were reflected in a subsequent review by the National Audit Office, *Modernising Construction*, in 2001, which also highlighted the need to address more effectively the operational efficiency of completed buildings.

More recently, the need to continue to improve the levels of safety within the industry was reinforced by the introduction of the Construction (Design and Management) Regulations 2007. Also, the sustainable agenda has become more and more a central factor in all developments both large and small, with the need for a sustainable approach to planning, design and construction processes, sustainable supply chains and the need to measure carbon foot-prints. This is leading to more extensive consideration of the whole-life cost equation of developments in both the public and private sector, which has an impact on both the design and procurement processes.

These and other developments and initiatives clearly show that there is a drive for continued improvement in the construction processes (although the results have been mixed) which, together with the ever more sophisticated developments in information technology and communications, means that the roles, responsibilities and relationships of all those involved in the industry will continue to change. Thus architects, along with all others in the industry, need to keep abreast of all such developments and tailor their approach and services in order to respond.

1.4   Clients

The building team comprises the designers and the constructors both working at the behest of the client, who is the customer and the most important team member. The client is responsible for commissioning the design in the first place and ultimately for the construction.

Clients appear in many guises. They are the clients of the professionals; they are the 'employer' under the standard building contracts (SBC) and they are the ultimate owners of the building until such time as they dispose of it. It is the client who in the long run pays the bill and in that respect calls the tune; this is something which must never be forgotten.

Architects, like most other professionals, must have clients before they can practise. Unlike the painter, the author or the poet, they are not at liberty to choose their own subject. They may, of course, be their own clients as, for instance, when they design their own houses but otherwise they are dependent on commissions from others. This applies whether architects are principals or assistants in private practice or are salaried officials in government or local government, in which case their clients will be the council or committee they serve.

Relationships with the client are of prime importance; an architect must not only embark on a process of design (which is a personal thing) but must also attempt to interpret the client's needs and provide a product that is wanted.

An architect acts as the client's agent in spending sums of money, which may be substantial; the amount the client will eventually have to spend may well depend on the skill and efficiency of the architect. It is therefore essential that client and architect should have confidence in each other, particularly as the architect also has certain responsibilities towards the contractor. The old adage that a good building requires a good client as well as a good architect is as true today as it ever was.

How then does a client choose the architect? It may be in one of several ways.

- The client may have approached RIBA Client Services and been given a shortlist of suitable architects, from which a choice can be made.
- The client may have searched the Chartered Practice area on the RIBA website (see Chapter 19, section 19.1.1).
- The client may have seen a building or photograph of a building that is liked and finds out the name of the architect.
- The architect may be recommended by a mutual acquaintance.
- The architect may specialise in designing a particular building type.
- It may be through success in an open competition for a particular building or project.
- Via an entry in a directory or by commissioning external public relations consultants (who themselves must not infringe the Code of Professional Conduct).
- It may be in response, by the architect, to an advertisement in the official journal of the European Union.

1.5 Contractors

The building contractor, the second party to the building contract with the employer, is the constructor, whose operations are at the hub of the complex construction industry. Contracting firms vary greatly in their size and capabilities. Many are small firms whose work may vary from one or two houses and some jobbing work to individual contracts of perhaps £250,000 in value. However, the bulk, in value, of construction work is in the hands of a comparatively small number of larger firms, often with several regional offices, and many carrying out work overseas. Most firms are limited companies, a number are public companies, but some of the very small contractors still operate as partnerships (see also Chapter 4, section 4.2).

Traditionally, the contractor was chosen by competitive tender, having priced either a specification and drawings or a bill of quantities. Alternatively, work was negotiated with a chosen contractor. Today, the procurement processes and the contractual arrangements that are entered into are many and varied. The role of architects when working for a contractor is described in Chapter 3 and their relationship with the contractor regarding procurement procedures, programming and construction is covered in Chapters 7–13.

Sub-contractors, as their name suggests, are companies to whom work is sub-let. When work is sub-let, it is delegated; however, the contractor is still liable to the employer for any defects in such work.

The work will be sub-let for one of two reasons. It may be the specific wish of the architect that a certain parcel of work be carried out by a particular company. Under previous editions of the standard contract, this was addressed through the nominated sub-contractor provisions. However, these were considered somewhat cumbersome and tended to obscure issues of responsibility, and have been omitted in the SBC.

The standard contracts make provision for the contractor to select from a list of not less than three names provided by the architect whose duties and responsibilities do not extend beyond naming (SBC clause 3.8) and the naming procedures contained in IC (clause 3.7). The sub-contractor then becomes 'domestic' (see below) and neither the main nor sub-contractor enjoys many of the contractual rights they would previously had under the nomination process, although the situation becomes complex if the sub-contractor's employment is terminated or the contract repudiated.

Alternatively, it will be the sole choice of the contractor to whom it sub-lets work, in which case the sub-contractor is known as a 'domestic' sub-contractor. The architect's powers are limited to approving or otherwise the names put forward by the contractor

1.6   Consultants

1.6.1   Architects

Architects are the designers of the building project and have the difficult task of translating their client's ideas into an acceptable design and then into working drawings. It should be noted that the profession of architect is, subject to an Act of Parliament,[3] a registered profession. For business purposes no one can call him or herself an architect in the United Kingdom unless they are on the register maintained by the Architects' Registration Board (ARB). Only those qualified in accordance with these regulations can be admitted to the register. However, it is only the name 'architect' that is protected; anyone can carry out the role as long as the name is not used.

As the name implies, the architect should be the master-builder – the leader of the building industry team referred to above (the word 'architect' is derived from the Greek root *arch* meaning 'chief' and the word *teckton* meaning 'carpenter or builder'). Architects are qualified to design and administer the erection of buildings, and must possess both theoretical and practical knowledge. Their work is a science as well as an art, for they must produce a structure as well as create form, and must combine aesthetic effect with practical considerations. They must visualise the interior as well as the exterior of the building and must ensure that the accommodation is properly related to the requirements of owners and occupiers, that the form and construction are appropriate to the function of the building and its setting, and the design is developed within the budget set by the client.

Like playwrights, architects are dependent on other people to interpret their designs, and their involvement during the erection of a building is as important to its ultimate success as are the directions given by the producer and stage manager for a play.

The list of duties set out by Hudson in the last edition (1926) of *Hudson's Building Contracts* to be edited by him is still considered to remain fairly comprehensive today.[4]

'(i)   To advise and consult with the employer (not as a lawyer) as to any limitation which may exist as to the use of the land to be built on, either *(inter alia)* by restrictive covenants or by the rights of adjoining owners or the public over the land, or by statutes and by-laws affecting the works to be executed.

(ii)   To examine the site, sub-soil and surroundings.

(iii)   To consult with and advise the employer as to the proposed work.

(iv)   To prepare sketch plans and a specification having regard to all the conditions which exist and to submit them to the employer for approval, with an estimate of the probable cost, if requested.

(v)   To elaborate and, if necessary, modify or amend the sketch plans as he may be instructed and prepare working drawings and a specification or specifications.

(vi)   To consult with and advise the employer as to obtaining tenders, whether by invitation or by advertisement, and as to the necessity or otherwise of employing a quantity surveyor. (Engineers do not so often employ a quantity surveyor.)

(vii)   To supply the builder with copies of the contract drawings and specification, supply such further drawings and give such instructions as may be necessary, supervise the work, and see that the contractor performs the contract, and advise the employer if he commits any serious breach thereof.

(viii)   To perform his duties to his employer as defined by any contract with his employer or by the contract with the builder, and generally to act as the employer's agent in all matters connected with the work and the contract, except where otherwise prescribed by the contract with the builder, as, for instance, in cases where he has under the contract to act as arbitrator or quasi-arbitrator.'

It should be noted that architects inspect, rather than supervise, work, something which the courts now understand. It has been established for nearly 40 years that the architect never acts as a quasi-arbitrator under any of the JCT standard contracts.

Architects must have a good, practical knowledge of building and allied trades and must have at least a working knowledge of the more specialised aspects of building, such as mechanical and electrical engineering services. Above all, they must be creative and dedicated to solving the client's problems as expressed in the brief.

The various aspects of the role of the architect are explained in detail in the following chapters.

1.6.2   Quantity surveyors/cost managers

The work and services provided by the quantity surveyor today might be described as the financial management of the project, whether it be on behalf of the client or the contractor. The term 'quantity surveyor' does not now reflect the services that are provided, since these have been extended during the past 30 years to cover what might be more appropriately termed *project cost management*.

Traditionally, certainly during the early part of the last century, quantity surveyors were employed as preparers of bills of quantities for building projects. Their role was constrained to a limited but important part of the development process. This role was quickly extended to include the preparation of valuations for interim certificates and the agreement of final accounts with the contractor.

During the 1960s the quantity surveyor's role was enlarged to include design cost planning in an attempt to provide the client with some form of value for money and cost-effectiveness (see Chapter 9, section 9.3). In more recent times greater emphasis has been placed on the need to examine construction costs in terms of their life cycle rather than solely in terms of initial costs.

The work of the quantity surveyor today can be summarised briefly as follows.

- Preliminary cost advice
- Cost planning, including investment appraisal and whole-life costing
- Value management
- Risk analysis
- Procurement and tendering procedures
- Contract documentation

- Tender evaluation
- Cash flow forecasting, financial reporting and interim payments
- Final accounting and the settlement of contractual disputes
- Cost advice during use by the client
- Insolvency services
- Technical auditing

It is advantageous for the quantity surveyor to become fully involved at the outset of a project's development. Although lip service has been paid to this in the past, the designer has often completed this stage of the development process relying only on a very limited input from the quantity surveyor. It is during this stage that the type and size of the project are largely determined and these two factors alone commit a considerable proportion of the total cost. Quantity surveyors can therefore provide a proper and sizeable contribution during the process of strategic planning and, by becoming familiar with the special needs of the client, they can properly evaluate the options that are under consideration.

1.6.3   Other consultants

The other members of the design team who will be involved can include the following.

- Structural engineers
- Building services engineers
- Landscape consultants
- Specialist consultants

Structural engineers

The structural engineer's function is to advise on structural design from foundations to roof, including advice on ground conditions on projects where such services are required. The structural stability of the building will be their responsibility, which will include advice, specification, design and supervision of the works in progress. They should be an early appointment, as their advice will greatly influence the outcome of the ultimate design, which in many cases cannot be furthered without the basic structural information being available. Some structural engineers will offer drainage and other infrastructure advice. Alternatively, design input on these issues may be provided by an engineer specialising solely in this type of work.

Building services engineers

Services both mechanical and electrical today form a major part of most projects. Building services engineers provide advice, specification and schematic or detailed drawings and are sometimes responsible for obtaining tenders from specialist firms. Again, they should be an early appointment and should be closely involved in ensuring the proper integration of services into the design.

Failure to achieve such integration is a frequent cause of delay and disruption on construction sites, leading to acrimony, costs and, at worst, litigation.

Landscape consultants

With the current emphasis on environmental aspects of construction projects, it is not unusual for architects specialising in landscape work or specialist consultants to be involved in the design and supervision of what are traditionally known as the external works. Ground formations, planting and arboreal work are the finishing touches which can make or break the external aesthetics of a new or refurbished building.

Specialist consultants

On certain projects there is a need for other specialist consultants. These can include:

- *acoustic engineers,* where concert halls, theatres and the like are involved
- *theatre consultants* for all types of theatre work
- *curtain walling engineers* for special cladding work
- *information technology consultants* for complex data and communications installations
- *interior or furniture designers* where the client wishes to use a special interior designer.

This list of specialist consultants is not exhaustive but as buildings become ever more complex, more and more such specialists tend to be required. This needs to be addressed when preparing fee budgets for a client who will need to be advised of the services required and the benefits their involvement can bring.

CDM co-ordinator

Under the Construction (Design and Management) Regulations 2007, where a project is notifiable, the client needs to appoint a CDM co-ordinator to advise and assist the client with their duties and in particular co-ordinate health and safety aspects of design work, liaise with the principal contractor and prepare the health and safety file.

1.7 Clerk of works

The clerk of works is sometimes employed as the client's inspector on the construction site, either directly by the client or through the architect.[5] Clerks of works are responsible for checking that the materials and workmanship conform to the specification outlined in the contract documents. They may, albeit rarely, be authorised to issue instructions to the contractor but under JCT forms of contract their powers are more limited.

While architects are required to give adequate inspection to check that a building is erected generally in accordance with the provisions of the contract, their terms of appointment rarely require them to make constant inspections. There is, however, often a need for such constant attention: hence the employment of a clerk of works. An architect has to act impartially between the client and the contractor, but the clerk of works is only responsible to the client. The architect must therefore maintain a delicate balance in dealing with the clerk of works and contractor and, whilst preserving the authority of the clerk of works, the risk of unfair dictation to the contractor must be guarded against.

The clerk of works' duties and limitations should be clearly understood, and it is the responsibility of the architect to see that they are properly instructed. Good clerks of works can be of the greatest assistance to the architect, who should make a point of getting to know them well and gaining their confidence at the earliest stage. They are usually persons of considerable practical experience who have graduated from a particular trade and the architect should not hesitate to take their advice on practical matters when the occasion demands.

The primary duty of the clerk of works is, as already mentioned, to ensure that the work is carried out in strict accordance with the drawings and specification. Their authority is therefore limited to ensuring that the standard required under the terms of the contract is maintained and they can condemn any work or materials that fall short of this standard. The clerk of works must be on site throughout the hours that the contractor's operatives are there (unless only employed on a part-time basis) and, furthermore, must endeavour to be everywhere at once! It is a most difficult job to do well, and requires both tact and knowledge. The architect should recognise this and do all that is possible to help.

The clerk of works can also be of considerable assistance by keeping, for instance, a record of any work that is likely to be covered up so that correct measurements can be taken. This applies particularly to foundations and other items subject to remeasurement or required for 'as built' record purposes.

Besides these duties, there are a variety of other records which the clerk of works should keep. Daywork sheets will be submitted when works may need to be valued on a daywork basis and it will be necessary to certify that the time and materials are correct. Records of operatives on site and what they are doing, visitors, weather records and the like can prove invaluable later on. Altogether a most important role.

1.8   Construction industry bodies

1.8.1   Professional organisations

Members of the building team all have their professional organisations that act as learned societies with library, research facilities and internet websites for members and in some cases provide recognised educational qualifications as well. In the interests of the general public, they are responsible for overseeing the conduct of members and practice generally. They also provide a central source for social activities and for the general dissemination of information by way of journals, lectures, etc. The major such bodies are as follows.

- *Architects*
  Royal Institute of British Architects (RIBA) (www.architecture.com)
  Royal Incorporation of Architects in Scotland (RIAS) (www.rias.org.uk)
  Royal Society of Ulster Architects (RSUA) (www.rsua.org.uk)
  Royal Institute of the Architects of Ireland (RIAI) (www.riai.ie)
  Association of Consultant Architects (ACA) (www.acarchitects.co.uk)

- *Clerks of works*
  Institute of Clerks of Works and Construction Inspectorate of Great Britain Inc. (ICWCI) (www.icwgb.org)

- *Construction professionals*
  Chartered Institute of Building (CIOB) (www.ciob.org.uk)

- *Engineers*
  Institution of Civil Engineers (ICE) (www.ice.org.uk)
  Chartered Institution of Building Services Engineers (CIBSE)
    (www.cibse.org)
  Institute of Electrical and Electronics Engineers (IEEE) (www.ieee.org)
  Institute of Mechanical Engineers (IMechE) (www.imeche.org.uk)
  Institution of Structural Engineers (IStructE) (www.istructe.org.uk)
  Association of Building Engineers (ABE) (www.abe.org.uk)

- *Landscape*
  Landscape Institute (LI) (www.landscapeinstitute.org.uk)

- *Planners*
  Royal Town Planning Institute (RTPI) (www.rtpi.org.uk)

- *Project managers*
  Association for Project Management (APM) (www.apm.org.uk)

- *Surveyors*
  Royal Institution of Chartered Surveyors (RICS) (www.rics.org.uk)

1.8.2 Contractor organisations

Contractor organisations also have bodies that look after their members and represent their interests, in particular in national and regional negotiations on such matters as wages, working rules and contract conditions. These bodies formally came together under the umbrella organisation of the Construction Confederation, however this body has recently been disbanded. Its function is now fulfilled, in part, by the Contractors Legal Group, formed to represent the common interests of contractors on contractual and legal matters.

1.8.3 Manufacturers trade associations

There are a number of associations representing manufacturers from whom useful information and advice can be obtained as to the use of materials that their members manufacture or use. Amongst these may be mentioned:

- Council for Aluminium in Building
- Brick Development Association
- British Constructional Steelwork Association Ltd
- British Precast Concrete Federation Ltd
- British Woodworking Federation
- British Cement Association
- Clay Pipe Development Association Ltd
- Copper Development Association
- Lead Development Association
- Mastic Asphalt Council
- Timber Research and Development Association
- Zinc Development Association.

In fact, nearly all manufacturers have some sort of publicity organisation for their particular trade.

1.8.4   Other organisations

Other organisations exist which further the work of the industry in many ways. A selection of the more important of these is described below.

Association for Consulting and Engineering (ACE) (www.acenet.co.uk)

This association represents the business interests of the consulting and engineering businesses in the UK, promoting the contribution that engineers and consultants make to construction and other industries.

British Board of Agrément (BBA) (www.bbacerts.co.uk)

This is an official body for the assessment of new building products for which certificates are issued. Since its formation, the scope has widened to include traditional construction products which have an export potential. The Board works in conjunction with the European Organisation for Technical Approvals.

British Property Federation (BPF) (www.bpf.propertymall.com)

This is a body which represents the interests of the property-owning and investment industry. A key feature of its activity is to persuade the government, through lobbying, of the importance of the property industry to the overall economy.

British Standards Institution (BSI) (www.bsigroup.co.uk)

This institute has a scope much wider than that of the construction industry alone. It is the recognised authority in the UK for the preparation of national standards covering specifications for dimensions, preferred sizes, quality, performance, methods of testing, terms, definitions and symbols, and codes of practice. All publications are listed and available through the BSI website. A large number of standards apply to the construction industry. Committees responsible for framing the standards have representation from contractors, architects, engineers and surveyors as well as experts in the manufacture of the material concerned. British Standards are widely adopted in the Commonwealth countries. The BSI also has an obligation to publish British versions of European Standards (these are referenced BS EN), and withdraw any conflicting British Standards or parts thereof.

Building Centre (www.buildingcentre.co.uk)

This organisation is backed and supported by manufacturers of all types of building products. It maintains a permanent exhibition where samples of a wide variety of materials can be seen. It is an agency from which names and addresses and often leaflets of manufacturers can be obtained, and is particularly useful when only the branded name of a material is known.

Building Cost Information Service (BCIS) (www.bcis.co.uk)

The Building Cost Information Service is the Royal Institution of Chartered Surveyors' cost information service formulated originally for quantity surveyors, to contribute cost and other information in accordance with the reciprocal basis of the service. Its information is now available through online application, data licensing and publications.

Building Research Establishment (BRE) (www.bre.co.uk)

The BRE's main establishment is at Garston near Watford. It undertakes research on building materials and advises on difficulties within its sphere of work. A large proportion of its annual budget is spent on research, with the remainder on information activities. It is engaged in research across a wide spectrum of activities associated with building and often presents the results of research in publications, details of which are available through its website.

Commission for Architecture and the Built Environment (CABE) (www.cabe.org.uk)

This organisation is a statutory body funded by the Department for Culture, Media and Sport as well as communities and local government. It is the government's advisor on architecture, urban design and public space. It works with clients, designers, users and policy makers to advise on how to get better value out of better design.

Constructing Excellence (www.constructingexcellence.org.uk)

This cross-sector, cross-supply chain organisation is charged with driving the change agenda in construction to improve industry performance to produce a better built environment.

Construction Industry Council (CIC) (www.cic.org.uk)

The Construction Industry Council was established in 1988 with five members. Since then, it has grown in size and influence and is now the largest body concerned with all aspects of the built environment. It is the forum for the industry's professional bodies, research organisations and specialist trade associations and speaks as a single body on behalf of the industry.

Construction Industry Research and Information Association (CIRIA) (www.ciria.org.uk)

The Construction Industry Research and Information Association operates across market sectors and disciplines to deliver a programme of business improvement services and research activities for its members and those engaged in the delivery and operation of the built environment. The CIRIA is an independent member-based, not-for-profit association.

Construction Skills (www.cskills.org.uk)

The Construction Industry Training Board (CITB) was established under the Industrial Training Act in July 1964. This Act intended to secure an improvement in the quality and efficiency of industrial training, and to make sure that an adequate supply of people are properly trained for all levels of operation within the industry. Construction Skills is now the Sector Skills Council and Industry Training Board for the construction industry. The Industry Training Board is funded by raising a levy on contracting firms based on the number of employees. In return, it is able to offer grants to employers who undertake their courses. A network of advisors is available to provide advice to contracting employers as to how to get the best from their workforce.

Joint Contracts Tribunal Ltd (JCT) (www.jctltd.co.uk)

This organisation is composed of representatives of clients, architects, surveyors, contractors and sub-contractors. The constituent bodies are as follows.

- British Property Federation
- Contractors Legal Group
- Local Government Association
- National Specialist Contractors Council Ltd
- Royal Institute of British Architects

- Royal Institution of Chartered Surveyors
- Scottish Building Contract Committee Ltd

It is responsible for drafting the various JCT Forms of Building Contract, for their periodic revision and the issue of practice notes for clarification purposes. Its work also includes considering questions raised by and through the representative members on the forms of contract.

Construction Products Association (CPA) (www.constructionproducts.org.uk)

This association (formerly the National Council of Building Material Producers) was originally constituted to represent the collective interests of its members to government, the Commission of the European Communities, the EDC, CBI, BSI and other trade and professional organisations. It seeks to promote increased collaboration between building material producers. It nominates representatives on government and other committees, and seeks to promote trade both at home and overseas. The Council is also able to provide advice on legislation, technical matters, contracts and commercial matters appropriate to its interests. It provides an annual report and weekly information in addition to other technical literature.

Construction Industry Joint Council (CIJC)

The CIJC is the body comprising unions and employer organisations which determines the wages and conditions for the industry on a national basis. It also on occasion arranges negotiations between employers and operatives for the settlement of disputes.

References

1. Latham, M. (1994) *Constructing The Team*, HMSO.
2. DETR (1988) *Rethinking Construction: the Report of the Construction Task Force*, Department of the Environment, Transport and the Regions.
3. Architects Act 1997 as amended.
4. Furst, S. & Ramsey, V. (2006) *Keating on Buildings Contracts*, 8th edn, Sweet & Maxwell.
5. Institute of Clerks of Works (2006) *Clerk of Works and Site Inspector Handbook*, RIBA Publishing.

2 Basics

2.1 Introduction

This chapter describes the journey through architectural education, the existence of the European 'Qualifications' Directive, the Architects Registration Board (UK), the Royal Institute of British Architects and associated bodies and regions (UK), and the Royal Institute of the Architects of Ireland. It outlines the route travelled to become a qualified architect. It sets out the requirements for registration, the respective professional codes and standards of each authority, and the requirements to maintain 'continued professional development' as a practitioner architect.

2.2 From education to registration and beyond

To become an architect, with the ability, knowledge and competence to undertake architectural practice, is a process which combines academic education and professional training. In common with several vocational disciplines, the process is lengthy and demands a commitment by the individual embarking upon the challenge. Despite the hard work and the complexity of learning programmes, most students engaged in architectural education find it exciting, stimulating and eventually a fulfilment of their personal endeavours.

The scope and range of methods of practice mean that architects can operate across a wide variety of activities covering the entire process, including design, construction, maintenance, repair and conservation of buildings. Whether the architect is engaged in urban master planning or the detailed design of a building, problem solving is a key activity and, together with delivering a professional service, can be a rewarding occupation (see Chapter 3).

Within the UK and Ireland the normal pattern is the successful completion of all the stages of architectural education and the required periods of professional training and the successful achievement of the professional qualification examination, enabling the individual in the UK to apply to join the Register of Architects administered by the Architects Registration Board (ARB) (UK). This progression provides eligibility to apply to become a 'chartered architect' with the Royal Institute of British Architects (RIBA). The RIBA is the professional body for all the UK. For architects in Scotland, the Royal Incorporation of Architects in Scotland (RIAS) represents and serves their interests. In Wales, the Royal Society of Architects in Wales (RSAW) represents and serves the profession and in Northern Ireland the Royal Society of Ulster Architects (RSUA) is the regional body. In Ireland, the professional and registration body is the Royal Institute of the Architects of Ireland (RIAI). The RIAI, in 2008, under the Building Control Act, became the body responsible for maintaining the Register for Architects.

2.3   Routes through architectural education and training

There exist two identifiable routes to achieve the necessary skills and knowledge to become a qualified architect practitioner:

- full-time education and training programmes offered by universities and, in Ireland, by Institutes of Technology also
- office-based education and training (UK only).

Currently the majority of students engaged in secondary-level education choose to apply to enter tertiary-level academic programmes of architectural education which are centred in schools of architecture. Those students will be studying a range of subjects at secondary level, which can range from arts-based topics through to science topics. For the assistance of potential applicants, each school of architecture publishes its undergraduate entry requirements, and the RIBA compiles a list of the schools and a brief outline of programmes offered.[1] Figure 2.1 shows the patterns of sequential full-time education and training programme. An enrolled student progresses through the sequence as illustrated, and finally presents for the professional qualification examination. The time period for completion of this route can be a total of 7–8 years.

The route to enter a programme of architectural education requires the student to achieve the necessary secondary level assessments; GCSEs, AS levels, A levels, Scottish Highers, Irish Leaving Cert or GNVQs, B/Tech Diploma, which the receiving school of architecture will accept as meeting its entry criteria. For students living in the UK, this process is normally managed by the Universities and Colleges Admissions Service (UCAS).[2] In Ireland a similar process is managed by the Central Applications Office (CAO).[3]

An alternative route, which some students find more suitable or attractive to follow, is a combination of office 'practice'-based learning with short academic programmes; often this is distance learning relating to part-time activities offered by some schools of architecture. This route suits students who cannot engage in full-time education and who find that their learning is best supported in the work environment.

One disadvantage of this route is its duration. In order to cover all the necessary contents of the RIBA/ARB criteria, more time is needed than in the full-time route, and students may expect to add more years to their commitment to qualify. However, a clear advantage is the income from salaried employment during that period. This, together with the workplace experience, is a context

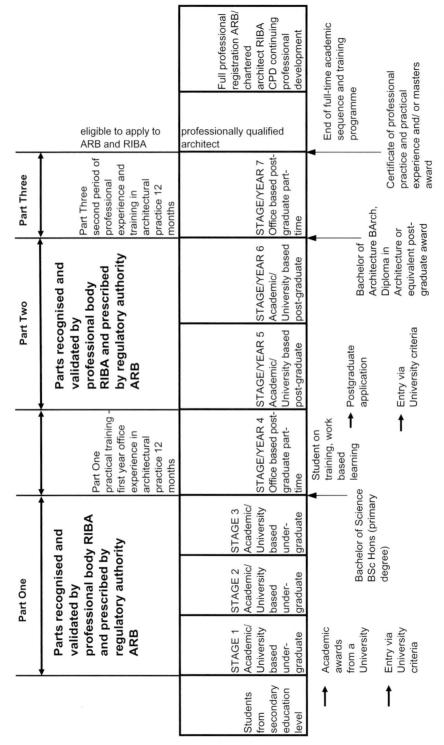

Fig. 2.1 Typical arrangement of a full-time architectural programme of academic education and professional training in the UK.

which an academic-based course cannot simulate. Several schools of architecture operate these part-time programmes and they can be sourced via the RIBA. The RIBA offers guidance on this route and its own RIBA examination in Architecture for Office-based Candidates.[4] Currently this runs jointly under a partnership with Oxford Brookes University.

2.4   European Directive, content/structure of architecture programmes, modes of learning, credits/CATS/ECTS

2.4.1   Introduction

When a university-based school of architecture wishes to offer a validated or prescribed or accredited architecture programme, it must satisfy the educational and professional training requirements published by the RIBA and ARB or, as appropriate, the RIAI.

The European Recognition of Professional Qualifications Directive 2005/36/EC[5] is the central basis for the qualification of architects. Formerly known as the Architects Directive produced by the EEC in 1985 (85/384/EEC), this sets out the fundamental requirements for architectural education and training across the member states. The 11 points of the 1985 Directive were reproduced in the Qualifications Directive of 2005 and are the basis for each European member state to establish programmes of architectural education.

'2005/36/EC Article 46:
(a) ability to create architectural designs that satisfy both aesthetic and technical requirements;
(b) adequate knowledge of the history and theories of architecture and the related arts, technologies and human sciences;
(c) knowledge of the fine arts as an influence on the quality of architectural design;
(d) adequate knowledge of urban design, planning and the skills involved in the planning process;
(e) understanding of the relationship between people and buildings, and between buildings and their environment, and of the need to relate buildings and the spaces between them to human needs and scale;
(f) understanding of the profession of architecture and the role of the architect in society, in particular in preparing briefs that take account of social factors;
(g) understanding of the methods of investigation and preparation of the brief for a design project;
(h) understanding of the structural design, construction and engineering problems associated with building design;
(i) adequate knowledge of physical problems and technologies and of the function of buildings so as to provide them with internal conditions of comfort and protection against the climate;

(j)   the necessary design skills to meet building users' requirements within the constraints imposed by cost factors and building regulations;

(k)   adequate knowledge of the industries, organizations, regulations and procedures involved in translating design concepts into buildings and integrating plans into overall planning.'

In the UK the 11 points of the Directive are expanded into more detail via the 'Criteria'. The Criteria are currently under review by the ARB and the RIBA. When the Criteria are adopted, they will be the basis upon which the schools of architecture will formulate their programmes of architectural education.

In Ireland the 11 points of the Directive are embodied in the RIAI Statement of Policy on Architectural Education and the schools of architecture address these points in the formulation of their programmes of architectural education.

Figure 2.1 uses the terms Part One, Part Two and Part Three. This terminology is set out in the Criteria by both the ARB and RIBA in the UK. The terms represent defined levels or thresholds of attainment by the student when engaged in the 7–8-year programme.

Architectural education and training is an incremental and iterative process. The identification of the Parts is a demonstration of that progression. Part One is normally achieved upon the successful completion of the first cycle. The primary degree is the academic award granted by the academic provider.

The Part Two is normally achieved upon successful completion of the second cycle, of advanced architectural studies, which builds upon the skills acquired during Part One. The description of the academic award is decided by the educational institute offering the programme. This Part Two award can be described as a diploma, an advanced diploma or another primary degree descriptor, e.g. Bachelor of Architecture and in some circumstances a Masters, e.g. in Scotland. The Part Three is commonly recognised in the UK as the 'Qualification' examination and has associated courses to support it. The diagram also indicates two designated periods of professional training experience which are required in order to be eligible for the Qualification examination.

The progression by students through the Parts, at the date of writing, is hampered by the lack of work/commissions for the profession. Students with a Part One degree cannot obtain the required period of professional practice experience to prepare them appropriately for a postgraduate Part Two programme. Higher up the professional tree, a Part Two graduate, expecting to acquire the required periods of professional training experience, is also disadvantaged by the lack of suitable employment and projects for documentary submission.

In Ireland, the terminology of Parts is not commonly used. The levels of attainment are represented by academic awards. The structure of the programmes varies from a 5-year full-time course to three plus two and four plus one models. The period of 24 months of postgraduate professional training experience required for the Irish 'Professional Qualification' examination must follow completion of the 5-year programme. Some students opt to take a year out between the third and fourth years of study. This is not a requirement for re-entry to the academic programme, but neither does it count as part of the postgraduate experience.

2.4.2 Bologna Accord

Across Europe the Bologna Accord[6] sets out the structure and framework for third-level/ university-based education and training.

- It was initiated in 1999.
- It became the Bologna Framework in 2005. Ministers of the member states adopted this in Bergen.
- It involves 45 countries.
- All 25 member states are to have Bologna in place by 2010.

Bologna objectives

- To map national qualifications of each country into an international matrix.
- To create international transparency of qualifications.
- To obtain international recognition of qualifications.
- To encourage/enable international mobility of learners and graduates.

Three cycles in the total process

- Primary degree (3–4 years).
- Masters degree (minimum 2 years).
- Doctoral degree (discussion on duration).

2.4.3 Modes of learning

Central to the delivery and processes of architectural education is the 'architectural studio'. Across all the university-based programmes of architectural education, this is the central core, around which supportive and informative lectures, seminars, workshops, field/study trips are arranged. The aim of a 'creative design environment' is pivotal to the studio as a thought-provoking context and problem-solving method of education. Similar activities can be found in allied disciplines such as arts courses.

Progression through Parts One and Two builds upon increasingly complex studio projects which extend from the simple tasks set out in a first-year course to the advanced study of a comprehensive design project undertaken in the final year. Different modes of learning can be identified within this process.

- Academic-based learning
- Studio/project-based learning

- Self-directed learning
- Practice-based learning – the office experience

Academic-based learning is an extension of the methods experienced by students at secondary-level education. Formal lectures cover a range of relevant subjects, e.g. history, theory, arts, structures, environment, technology, social studies, landscape studies. The proportion of subjects reinforces the aims and objectives of each level. Studio- or project-based learning provides opportunities for the student to explore, create designs and critically reflect upon their outputs via the process of critiques (CRITS). CRITS are arranged at intervals across the duration of a project and at the close of the project. The student presents their output to a range of reviewers, including fellow students, tutors and guest critics (often from external sources, e.g. practitioners, specialists). The feedback given at the CRIT is intended to advance the process of problem solving and acquisition of design skills.

Self-directed learning is often overlooked as an important component in architectural education. It involves the student taking charge of the scope and depth of a particular subject or activity. It can include research, reading, observation, investigation and recording data.

With progression through the levels, the proportion of self-directed learning gradually increases, which is part of the preparation for the practice of architecture outside the architectural programme. Practice-based learning is embodied in the required periods of professional training experience, the office experience and the delivery of professional architecture services. A candidate's preparation for the Part Three final qualification examination relies heavily on this level of learning.

2.4.4   Credit allocation and credit transfer systems

The European model

Across Europe, Ireland and the EU member states adopted the European Credit Transfer System – ECTS.

- A primary degree equates to 180 ECTS (normally 60 ECTS for each year of a 3-year degree).
- A secondary degree equated to 120 ECTS (normally 60 ECTS for each of the 2 years of the award).

UK Credit Award Transfer System (CATS)

For various reasons the UK chose not to adopt the EU models, although it still based its system on acquired totals of modules over a specified time period.

- Primary degree (not less than 3 years) equates to 360 CATS.
- Secondary degree (not less than 2 academic years or equivalent time) equates to 240 CATS.

2.4.5   Contents of architecture courses, credit allocation, modularity, CATS

Across all of the UK tertiary education there was a shift 10-15 years ago for all disciplines to adopt this modular and credit system. In operation, it became difficult to apply to the discipline of architecture which evolved as a holistic system of education. Courses became arranged around full modules and fractions of modules, e.g. half modules.

The intention was to introduce flexibility across programmes and academic providers whereby the student could take modules or half modules and be awarded credits for each. Each academic programme provider assembled the contents, subjects and activities in each year of their programme to enable the accumulation of these credits, to reach the totals required at the completion of each cycle.

2.5   Approval of programmes of architectural education

2.5.1   Validation, prescription and accreditation

When an academic provider seeks to gain approval for a programme of architectural education, it can apply for a process of 'Validation' applied by the RIBA, also for 'Prescription' applied by the ARB, and in Ireland 'Accreditation' applied by the RIAI. The RIBA also operates a policy of validation of Parts One and Two outside the UK domain.

Existing courses can apply to have the process renewed following the completion of the period of recognition, normally a 4–5-year cycle. If successful, the programme is then designated and continues to hold approval by the appropriate bodies and authorities.

2.5.2   Validation by the RIBA

At the date of writing the validation procedures operated by the RIBA are under review. Hitherto the process has been one of peer review.

'RIBA validation is a peer review process that monitors compliance with internationally recognised minimum standards in architectural education and encourages excellence and diversity in student achievements.

The RIBA has had a long-standing involvement in promoting high quality and innovative architectural education throughout the world. Through validation, the RIBA identifies courses and examinations which achieve the standards necessary to prepare students for the professional practice of architecture.

Visiting Boards visit schools of architecture to assess the output standard of courses for exemption from the RIBA's examinations in architecture. The Boards are composed of practising architects, academics, architecture students and construction team co-professionals.

From September 2003 the RIBA assumed sole responsibility for Visiting Boards in the United Kingdom.[7]

The complete list of architecture programmes holding RIBA validation extends to 40 schools of architecture and can be found on www.architecture.com. The list is updated after each cycle of visits is completed.

2.5.3   Prescription of UK courses by the Architects Registration Board

Under the Architects Act 1997, the Architects Registration Board (ARB) has responsibility for prescribing the qualifications and practical training required for entry onto the UK Register of Architects.

From 2003 the ARB devised a procedure which did not involve physical visits to the education providers. There is no *in situ* inspection of portfolios and no direct assessment of student output. Instead, the ARB undertakes a document-based assessment system across a very thorough analysis of identified requirements. With this process, which is separate from the one undertaken by the RIBA, schools are invited to apply for prescription, following a step-by-step sequence of documentary submissions. This information includes:

■ mapping documents which demonstrate how and where the Parts One, Two and Three meet the requirements of the Criteria[8]
■ reports produced by other bodies – quality assurance, RIBA reports
■ reports by external examiners for Parts One, Two and Three, for each year completed under the prescription cycle
■ student numbers on each Part, statistics on student progression, pass/fail rates and dropouts from programmes
■ description of accommodation facilities, staff resourcing and capital expenditure assurances to secure the operation of programmes to an acceptable level of quality
■ assurances from the senior management of the academic provider which establishes continued financial support for the subject/school across the period of prescription.

Upon receipt of all the documented information required, the application is considered by the ARB Prescription Committee. The ARB can and does ask for further and better information and clarification on the evidence submitted initially with the application. Once the process is completed, the Prescription Committee makes recommendations to the Board for final decisions.

The ARB process can prescribe with attached conditions, decline to prescribe and remove Prescription from a programme. An additional ARB requirement is the annual return of information from the academic provider, which normally includes student progression, external examiners' reports, and assurances from senior institutional management on resourcing for the programme.

2.5.4   Accreditation of courses by the RIAI

The RIAI operate a process of accreditation which at the date of writing 'accredits' programmes in architectural education in Ireland. The procedure is being amended in line with the Building Control Act 2007 under which Prescription by a state authority will take place. Currently the RIAI accreditation procedures contain the following stages.

■ Application by an education provider to have a new architecture programme accredited, or for an existing accredited programme to be renewed, or for an existing programme to be accredited for the first time.
■ There follows a sequence of documentary submissions and the appointment of a Visiting Board by the RIAI Board of Architectural Education (BAE).
■ A pattern of visits to the relevant school.
■ Followed by the preparation of a report, which contains recommendations to the BAE.
■ Recommendations cover a range of options in respect of the programme which has been visited, following the application. The following extract is from the RIAI Visiting Board procedures dated 25 January 2008.[9]

'**Section 5.0 Approval**
5.1 Provisional Approval
Having completed its review of a course seeking accreditation for the first time the Visiting Board will recommend to the BAE that the course be accorded or refused Provisional Approval. Provisional Approval is dependent on the Board forming the view that the course if implemented as planned will meet RIAI criteria.

If the Board considers that the course as planned would not meet RIAI criteria, but that with adjustment it might do so, it may issue an Interim Report indicating to the School the areas in which improvements need to be made and steps that might be taken by the School, and may propose a provisional date for a further Visit.

This sequence of Visit and Interim Report may be repeated until such time as the Visiting Board considers that it can make a definitive recommendation to the BAE.

It is the view of the RIAI that Provisional Approval should be in place before the first intake of students into the course.

5.2 Final Approval
A course which has been accorded Provisional Approval will be visited annually by a Visiting Board, at a time to be agreed, until the first cohort of students has completed the course. Where circumstances warrant, such annual visits may be carried out by a reduced Visiting Board.

Following the visit at which the work of the first cohort of graduating students has been reviewed, the Visiting Board will prepare its Final Report and recommend to the BAE that the course be accorded or refused RIAI Approval.

5.3 Continued Approval

A course is normally granted Approved status for a maximum period of 4 years. The academic year during which the next accreditation visit will fall due is indicated in the Visiting Board's Final Report.

An Educational Institution should notify the RIAI of any significant changes in circumstances concerning the course which occur in the intervening period.'

The process of visits can take place in two phases. A Phase One visit is undertaken during the operation of the school at a point where the Visiting Board can observe the school in action and meet with students, staff and senior management of the academic institution. It is the opportunity for the Board to review resources, facilities, library provision and staffing levels.

A Phase Two visit normally occurs upon completion of the academic period when the Board looks at assessed output from the students, obtains feedback from external examiners and can view a range of portfolios across a sequence of academic years, since the previous visit.

Following the completion of the two phases of visits, the Visiting Board prepares a report with recommendations to the BAE. Decisions by the BAE are then presented to RIAI Council, normally for ratification. Accreditation approval normally exists for a specified period of time. Each provider is required to notify the RIAI of any circumstances which may arise during the time period which could materially affect the course provision and quality of output standards.

2.6   Practising architecture in the United Kingdom

2.6.1   Registration

The ARB is the authority established by statute to maintain a Register of Architects, and to regulate the conduct of the architects' profession in the UK. Only persons whose names are on the Register may use the title 'architect' in business or practice. The ARB's duties and functions are defined in the Architects Act 1997. It is the ARB's responsibility to set the standards of education, training and professional conduct required for registration as an architect.

The ARB is also the competent authority in the UK for the implementation and administration of the provisions of the Professional Qualifications Directive 2005/36/EC.[10] At the date of writing, there are three main routes to registration as an architect in the UK. These are categorised under holding of qualifications and the various origins of those qualifications.[11]

Route one

Relates to applicants who hold qualifications obtained within the UK including the successful completion of Part One and Part Two awards, together with the completion of the required period of practical training experience in architecture and the award of a prescribed Part Three qualification in professional practice. This is the normal mainstream acquisition of awards as set out in the diagram and if undertaken consecutively will have a duration of 7–8 years.

Route two

Relates to applicants who hold qualifications obtained outside the UK in a member state of Europe and have certification by that member state that the qualifications held are listed in the 2005/36/EC Directive[12] for the purposes of mutual recognition within Europe and certification of completion of a 2-year period of postgraduate practical training experience subject to certain conditions.

Route three

Relates to holders of qualifications acquired outside the UK, and outside the provisions of the EU Directive 2005/36/EU who are required to pass an Examination for Equivalence to Prescribed Qualifications, appropriate to their level of qualification and professional training experience. All parts of the Examination for Equivalence to Prescribed Qualifications are owned by and administered by the ARB.[13]

2.6.2 The ARB application process

When the applicant has met the requirements for registration via the appropriate route, the process involves completing a registration form from the ARB, submission of documentary evidence, with precise descriptions of awards held, signing of a declaration of truth, plus an initial registration fee. This fee is intended to cover the costs of the admission process. The application is then considered by the Registration Department on a regular basis. Successful applicants are notified once decisions have been made.

The application process can take 6–8 weeks and will depend upon the accuracy of the information submitted. Following successful admission to the Register, architects are required to undertake specified actions and compliances, including:

- payment of an annual registration retention fee
- notification to the ARB of any change in name or address
- compliance with the ARB standards of conduct which include the holding of appropriate indemnity assurance, which again is a confirmation/notification process on a pro-forma produced by the ARB and must be returned annually.

At the date of writing there are 33,260 registered persons on the ARB Register. Changes to the Register occur on a daily basis.[14]

2.6.3   Membership of the RIBA

There are two broad categories of membership of the RIBA, within which there are sub-categories.

Individual membership

There are four types of individual membership.

- RIBA chartered membership for qualified persons, eligible to be on the ARB Register in the UK.
- RIBA associate membership for persons who have been awarded Part One and Part Two but not yet qualified, i.e. have not been awarded Part Three.
- RIBA student membership for persons enrolled on architectural education programmes validated by the RIBA or a relevant Commonwealth Association of Architects (CAA) course.
- RIBA affiliate membership for persons who have a personal or professional interest in architecture, but are not eligible for the other three categories of membership.

Practice membership

There are two types of practice membership.

- The RIBA Chartered Practice Scheme for architectural practices located within the UK.
- International Registered Practices for architectural practices which are based overseas.

At the date of writing, there are 44,105 members of the RIBA. A proportion of this figure includes members who are based outside the UK. Figure 2.2 shows the breakdown of membership from figures provided by the RIBA.

	UK	International	Other	Total
Affiliate	607	95	230	932
Fellow	235	123	0	358
Associate Member	491	75	0	566
Chartered	22,811	4,555	1,926	29,292
Student	12,495	462	0	12,957
Total	36,639	5,310	2,156	44,105

Fig. 2.2 Breakdown of RIBA membership ('Other' is joint RIAS and CIAT affiliates).

2.7   Practising architecture in Ireland

2.7.1   Criteria

'Membership of the Royal Institute of the Architects of Ireland is open to fully qualified architects who meet all of the requirements for independent practice in Ireland, and are eligible for admission to the Register of Architects, established under the Building Control Act 2007.

Under clause 19(2) of the Building Control Act 2007, any person who is a member of the RIAI is eligible for admission to the Register. Similarly, under clause 14(4) all persons on the Register are eligible for membership of the RIAI. Consequently a person may apply for RIAI membership, for registration, or for both. There is one single application process and the admission criteria are identical.'[15]

2.7.2   Admission routes

At the date of writing there are seven routes to registration/RIAI membership. Figure 2.3 sets out the seven routes with explanations for each of them.

Route	Explanation
Member/Register Route A1	People who have a prescribed qualification or an accredited non-EU qualification in architecture and who have already passed a prescribed postgraduate examination in professional practice
Member/Register Route A2	People who have a prescribed qualification or an accredited non-EU qualification in architecture and who are applying to take the RIAI Examination in Professional Practice
Member/Register Route B	People who have a prescribed qualification or an accredited non-EU qualification in architecture and at least 2 years of approved postgraduate practical experience, and have passed a postgraduate professional practice examination in another jurisdiction
Member/Register Route C	People who have a prescribed qualification or an accredited non-EU qualification in architecture and who have acquired 7or more years of postgraduate practical experience
Member/Register Route D	Nationals of EU member states, Iceland, Lichtenstein, Norway and Switzerland with qualifications in architecture from EU member states other than Ireland and who meet the requirements of EU Directive 2005/36/EC on the recognition of professional qualifications
Member/Register Route E	People who have been performing duties commensurate with those of an architect in this state for 10 or more years prior to 1 May 2008 may apply for technical assessment under section 14(2)(h) of the Building Control Act 2007
Member/Register Route F	The Building Control Act 2007 provides for a Register admission examination which can be taken by people who are at least 35 years of age and have at least 7 years of practical experience performing duties commensurate with those of an architect in this state. The examination became available from January 2010

Fig. 2.3   Routes to registration/RIAI membership.

The route chosen depends upon the applicant's qualification, training, juris-diction and relevant experience. It should be noted that in Ireland there are two dedicated admission routes to the RIAI for Architectural Technician mem-bership and one for Architectural Graduate membership.

2.8 Maintenance of standards, regulation, codes of conduct for architects

Each of the authorities and professional bodies involved with architecture devises a set of standards and codes which are intended to maintain a high level of competence and professionalism from architects. The ARB produces *The Architect's Code*, the RIBA produces *A Code of Conduct* and the RIAI pro-duces *A Code of Professional Conduct*. The RIAI document is currently under review through the process of the Building Control Act 2007.

Both the ARB Code and the RIBA Code are set out below, with commentary as appropriate. Architects are advised to consult the actual documents in detail. At the date of writing, the ARB 1997/2002 code has been revised and the new code will be effective from January 2010. The RIBA code, effective from 2005, is still in place with several updates contained in the detailed guidance notes.

2.9 The ARB Code: Standards of Professional Conduct and Practice

2.9.1 Introduction

The Code has a preamble which is essential reading.

'As an architect you are expected to:
1. Be honest and act with integrity
2. Be competent
3. Promote your services honestly and responsibly
4. Manage your business competently
5. Consider the wider impact of your work
6. Carry out your work faithfully and conscientiously
7. Be trustworthy and to look after your clients' money properly
8. Have appropriate insurance arrangements
9. Maintain the reputation of architects
10. Deal with disputes or complaints appropriately
11. Co-operate with regulatory requirements and investigations
12. Have respect for others.'

2.9.2 The standards

'*Standard 1: Honesty and integrity*
1.1   You are expected at all times to act with honesty and integrity and to avoid any action or situations which are inconsistent with your profes-

sional obligations. This standard underpins the Code and will be taken to be required in any consideration of your conduct under any of the other standards.

1.2   You should not make any statement which is contrary to your professional opinion or which you know to be misleading, unfair to others or discreditable to the profession.

1.3   Where a conflict of interest arises you are expected to disclose it in writing and mange it to the satisfaction of all affected parties. You should seek written confirmation that all parties involved give their informed consent to your continuing to act. Where this consent is not received you should cease acting for one or more of the parties.

1.4   Where you make or receive any payment or other inducement for the introduction or referral of work, you should disclose the arrangement to the client or prospective client at the outset.'

This is very similar to principle 1 of the RIBA Code. It requires architects to act with complete honesty at all times and it is to be noted that architects must not make or support statements which are contrary to their professional opinions. This alone would preclude an architect who was instructed by the client to issue (or withhold) a certificate of practical completion from doing so if the architect had a different view. The novation or consultant switching of an architect in a design and build situation is an example of a conflict situation which is only acceptable when both employer and contractor have full knowledge and agreement. It is worth comparing the content of point 1.4 of this Code with the Notes at point 1.6 to Principle 1 of the RIBA Code. Reading the ARB's point 1.4, it appears that 'inducement' is not a breach of the Code, provided all parties are made aware of it. Contrast this with the RIBA note 1.6 which informs members 'not to offer or take bribes'. The word 'bribe' is described in *Collins Dictionary of English* as 'To promise, offer, or give something, usually money (to a person) to procure services or gain influence'.

'*Standard 2: Competence*
2.1   You are expected to be competent to carry out the professional work you undertake to do and if you engage others to do that work you should ensure that they are competent and adequately supervised.

2.2   You are expected to make appropriate arrangements for your professional work in the event of incapacity, death, absence from or inability to work.

2.3   You are expected to ensure that the necessary communication skills and local knowledge are available to you to discharge your responsibilities.

2.4   You are expected to keep your knowledge and skills relevant to your professional work up to date and be aware of the content of any guidelines issued by the Board from time to time.'

This standard is of particular relevance to the sole practitioner who may be tempted to take on commissions which are too large or complex. Such a practitioner may often have a reciprocal arrangement with a similar practitioner for holiday and sickness cover. Special care must be taken that the liability and insurance aspects of such cover are dealt with in a proper agreement.

'*Standard 3: Honest promotion of your services*
3.1   You are expected to promote your professional services in a truthful and responsible manner.
3.2   In advertising and promoting your professional services you should comply with the codes and principles applying to advertising generally. These include those of the Advertising Standards Authority or any other body having oversight of advertising standards in various media.
3.3   The business style of a practice should not be misleading.
3.4   If you are a principal in a practice you are expected to ensure that all architectural work is under the control and management of one or more architects, and that their names are made known to clients and any relevant third party. You should notify your client promptly of any change in the architect responsible for the work.'

It has been said that it is misleading for a sole practitioner architect to be styled 'X and Associates' simply on the strength of occasionally working closely with other disciplines. The point may be debatable, but it would certainly be misleading for a sole practitioner to be styled 'X and Partners'. Difficult questions of control may arise in multidisciplinary offices wishing to offer an architectural service.

'*Standard 4: Competent management of your business*
4.1   You are expected to have effective systems in place to ensure that your practice is run professionally and that projects are regularly monitored and reviewed.
4.2   You should ensure that you are able to provide adequate professional, financial and technical resources when entering into a contract and throughout its duration. You should also, where appropriate, ensure you have sufficient suitably qualified and supervised staff to provide an effective and efficient service to clients.
4.3   You should ensure that adequate security is in place to safeguard both paper and electronic records for your clients, taking full account of data protection legislation, and that clients' confidential information is safeguarded.
4.4   You are expected to ensure that before you undertake any professional work you have entered into a written agreement with the client which adequately covers:
    ■   the contracting parties;
    ■   the scope of the work;
    ■   the fee or method of calculating it;
    ■   who will be responsible for what;
    ■   any constraints or limitations on the responsibilities of the parties;
    ■   the provisions for suspension or termination of the agreement;

- a statement that you have adequate and appropriate insurance cover as specified by the Board;
- your complaints handling procedure (see Standard 11), including details of any special arrangements for resolving disputes (e.g. arbitration).

4.5   Any agreed variations to the written agreement should be recorded in writing.

4.6   You are expected to ensure that your client agreements record that you are registered with the Architects Registration Board and that you are subject to this Code; and that the client can refer a complaint to the Board if your conduct or competence appears to fall short of the standards in the Code.

4.7   You should make clear to the client the extent to which any of your architectural services are being subcontracted.

4.8   At the end of a contract (if requested) or otherwise upon reasonable demand, you should promptly return to a client any papers, plans or property to which the client is legally entitled.'

This standard is considerably expanded in breadth and depth when compared with the previous Standard 4. It embodies much of the content of the previous Standard 11. It sets out very clearly what actions the architect should take.

This standard has an affinity with Principle 3 of the RIBA Code. It sets out very clearly how architects should order their relationships with their clients. Any of the RIBA terms of engagement would satisfy the criteria set out in note 11.1 if properly completed. For architects to let clients know that the Board is the disciplinary body in case of unacceptable professional conduct or serious professional incompetence seems like inviting trouble where some clients are concerned. It may provide support for architects, to insist on a fee payment, from certain clients who have expected the architect to speculate with no charge for professional services at the outset.

'*Standard 5: Considering the wider impact of your work*
5.1   Whilst your primary responsibility is to your clients, you should take into account the environmental impact of your professional activities.'

This standard steps back from the status of the previous Standard 5 which was longer and more definitive. Within the UK, various statutory bodies play a significant role in the environmental impact of development, including Planning and Environment, and Heritage. This standard should be compared with the Code for Landscape Architects: see section 3.9 which is very specific on environmental matters.

'*Standard 6: You should carry out your professional work faithfully and conscientiously and with due regard to relevant technical and professional standards*
6.1   You are expected to carry out your work promptly and with skill and care and in accordance with the terms of your engagement.

6.2 You should carry out your professional work without undue delay and, so far is reasonably practicable, in accordance with any time-scale and cost limits agreed with your client.

6.3 You are expected to keep your client informed of the progress of work undertaken on their behalf and of any issue which may significantly affect its quality or cost.

6.4 You should, when acting between parties or giving advice, exercise impartial and independent professional judgement. If you are to act as both architect and contractor you should make it clear in writing that your advice will no longer be impartial.'

Point 6.4 is a very important clause. Architects can find themselves in questionable circumstances when involved in design and build methods of development and novated to the contractor.

'Standard 7: Trustworthiness and safeguarding clients' money

7.1 You are expected to keep proper records of all money held by you which belongs to a client or other third party, and to account for it at all times.

7.2 You should keep such money in a designated interest-bearing bank account, called a 'client account' which is separate from any personal or business account.

7.3 You are expected to instruct the bank in writing and ensure that all money in the client account is held as clients' money, and that the bank cannot combine it with any other account, or exercise any right of set-off or counterclaim against it.

7.4 You should ensure that money is not withdrawn from a client account to make a payment unless it is made to or on behalf of a client on the client's specific written instructions.

7.5 Unless otherwise agreed by the client, you should arrange for any interest (or other benefit) accruing from a client account to be paid to the client.'

If considering the management of clients' money, architects should take clear professional advice from specialist advisers, skilled in this means of financial operation. Architects would be well advised never to hold money on behalf of others. There is seldom any sufficient reason to do so and the process can be misinterpreted.

'Standard 8: Insurance arrangements

8.1 You are expected to have adequate and appropriate insurance cover for you, your practice and your employees. You should ensure that your insurance is adequate to meet a claim, whenever it is made. You are expected to maintain a minimum level of cover, including run-off cover, in accordance with the Board's guidance.

8.2 The need for cover extends to professional work undertaken outside your main practice or employment.

8.3 If you are an employed architect you should, as far as possible, ensure that insurance cover and/or other appropriate indemnity arrangements are provided by your employer.

8.4 You are expected to provide evidence that you have met the standards expected of this Standard in such form as the Board may require.'

Clauses 8.2 and 8.3 carry 'health' warnings for employed architects who may wish to undertake additional personal work, outside their main activities for their respective employers. The principal duty is laid on architects who are either sole practitioners or employers. They must ensure adequate cover for themselves and employees. The duty extends to employees to ensure, so far as they can, that their employers have professional indemnity insurance cover. Many architects carry on professional services outside their main occupation and they should be covered for every kind of work they may perform. Therefore, architects practising as property surveyors, even as a sideline, must have proper insurance.

Architects working as sole practitioners can face considerable difficulties in satisfying the requirements, because insurance for them may be difficult to obtain or obtainable only at a large premium. The ARB guidelines state that architects should have appropriate run-off cover after ceasing to practise. This can be particularly difficult for a sole practitioner on retirement, because the money to fund the increasing costs of premiums may not be available. The availability of professional indemnity insurance cover and costs of cover are dependent on market forces in the commercial sector of insurance.

'*Standard 9: Maintaining the reputation of architects*
9.1 You should ensure that your professional finances are managed responsibly.

9.2 You are expected to conduct yourself in a way which does not bring either yourself or the profession into disrepute. If you find yourself in a position where you know that you have fallen short of these standards, or that your conduct could reflect badly on the profession, you are expected to report the matter to the Board. For example, you should notify the Registrar within 28 days if you:
- are convicted of a criminal offence;
- are made the subject of a court order disqualifying you from acting as a company director;
- are made the subject of a bankruptcy order;
- are a director of a company which is wound up (other than for amalgamation or reconstruction purposes);
- make an accommodation with creditors (including a voluntary arrangement);
- fail to pay a judgment debt.

The above are examples of acts which may be examined in order to ascertain whether they disclose a wilful disregard of your responsibilities or a lack of integrity; however, this list is not exhaustive.

9.3   In appropriate circumstances, you should report to the Board and/or other public authority another architect whose conduct falls significantly short of the expected standards. If you are in doubt as to whether such a report is required, you should consult the Board for guidance.

9.4   You should not enter into any contract (other than in a settlement of a dispute) the terms of which would prevent any party from reporting an apparent breach of the Code to the Board.

9.5   If you are subject to an investigation by the Board you are expected to use your best endeavours to assist in that investigation.'

This Standard 9 is expanded in depth and breadth when compared with the previous Standard 9. In the current economic climate, financial difficulties may not be in the architect's control, e.g. the immediate and unplanned collapse of financial support from a lender upon which the practice has relied in order to trade.

'Standard 10: Deal with disputes or complaints appropriately

10.1   You are expected to have a written procedure for prompt and courteous handling of complaints which will be in accordance with the Code and provide this to clients. This should include the name of the architect who will respond to complaints.

10.2   Complaints should be handled courteously and promptly at every stage; and as far as practicable in accordance with the following time scales:
    a.   an acknowledgement within 10 working days from the receipt of a complaint; and
    b.   a response addressing the issues raised in the initial letter of complaint within 30 working days from its receipt.

10.3   If appropriate, you should encourage alternative methods of dispute resolution, such as mediation or conciliation.'

This Standard is a key factor in the concept of consumer protection which underpinned the creation of the ARB.

'Standard 11: Co-operation with regulatory requirements and investigations

11.1   You are expected to co-operate fully and promptly with the Board, within any specified timescale, if it asks you to provide information which it needs to carry out its statutory duties, including evidence that you are complying with these Standards.

11.2   You should notify the Board promptly and in writing of any changes in the details held about you on the Register, including your address. Under the Act, architects who do not tell the Board of a change of address may be removed from the Register.'

'Standard 12: Respect for others

12.1   You should treat everyone fairly and in line with the law. You should not discriminate because of disability, age, gender, sexual orientation, ethnicity, or any other inappropriate consideration.'

2.10   RIBA Code of Conduct

2.10.1   Introduction

The RIBA publishes a Code of Conduct which is binding on its members. The current Code has been in force since 1 January 2005. It radically changed the old Code which had been effective for some years. The latest Code is focused on the consumer and the wider society. Undertakings no longer support the three principles. Instead, there are guidance notes with the principles and a further set of detailed guidance notes, which include much of the subject matter in the former Code and undertakings, but much enlarged. However, it is feared that many architects will find the new arrangement confusing. It is clear that the principles need the attached guidance notes. Although the Code has a brief index linking the detailed guidance to the principles, it might have been better if the detailed guidance, excellent as it is in isolation, had been incorporated into the brief guidance notes under the appropriate principle, so that the whole could have been read together.

The Code regulates the actions of members between themselves and in relation to their clients and to the public at large. The Code does more than simply put into words what most clients would expect of their professional advisors. It is more than just a set of rules for fair dealing; it points out the high standard of behaviour which is expected of a professional person in a position of trust.

A member may engage in any activity, whether as proprietor, director, partner, salaried employee, consultant or in any other capacity, provided that the member's conduct complies with the Code. The principles are set out below together with some comments on the brief notes provided as guidance in upholding the principles.

2.10.2   Principle 1: Integrity

'Members shall act with honesty and integrity at all times.'

Where members are acting between parties, they must be impartial. So, for example, they must interpret the building contract fairly between client and contractor. If called upon to decide the line of a boundary between neighbours or any other matter where both sides look to them for expert judgement, they must give an honest opinion. This provision does not, of course, prevent them from representing the client in any such dispute against an opponent. The architect's duty to act fairly will arise only when both sides are relying on his or her judgement. This is related to members' duty not to allow themselves to be influenced by their own or others' self-interest.

Members must undertake not to make or acquiesce to any statement in which they do not believe or which is misleading or unfair or otherwise discreditable to the profession. This undertaking should be a matter of stating the obvious. It should go without saying that a member of any profession should be a model of the highest integrity.

Members' other business interests are covered by this Principle. If they are such as might lead the client or employer to question the architect's integrity because they are or appear to be related to the subject of the commission, the architect is obliged to disclose them in writing before being engaged by the client. Obvious examples of such situations are cases where the architect already acts for a contractor in some other matter and the client may wish to employ the contractor to carry out building work, or if the architect owns land adjacent to the client's property and over which it will be necessary to agree an easement. The architect must withdraw unless the client or employer accepts the situation in writing.

If any potential conflict of personal or professional interest arises which is not specifically covered in the code, the architect must do one of three things:

- withdraw from the situation, or
- remove whatever is causing the conflict of interests, or
- inform the client and anyone else concerned and obtain the agreement of all parties to the architect's continued engagement.

The requirement that members should respect the confidentiality and privacy of others is no more than should be expected of anyone – let alone a professional person.

2.10.3   Principle 2: Competence

'In the performance of their work Members shall act competently, conscientiously and responsibly. Members must be able to provide the knowledge, the ability and the financial and technical resources appropriate for their work.'

A high standard of skill, care and knowledge is expected. Impartiality is again stressed.

Members should make sure that they have the resources to carry out commissions and provide a proper service. Student members should seek guidance from architects if they intend to undertake commissions themselves. Employees are expected to give prior notice to both parties before accepting an engagement elsewhere.

Before entering into an agreement, members must clearly set out the terms including what services will be provided, responsibilities, any limitation of liability, how fees will be calculated, how the agreement may be terminated and adjudication provision. All such agreements should be in writing and it is sensible to use the RIBA terms of engagement, as appropriate, not least because they contain clauses of benefit to the architect.

The onus is placed on members to keep clients informed of project progress and to use their best endeavours to meet agreed time, cost and quality requirements.

2.10.4   Principle 3: Relationships

'Members shall respect the relevant rights and interests of others.'

The guidance to this Principle addresses broader issues such as respect for the beliefs and opinions of others, social diversity and fair dealing. Members should have regard to the effect of their work on the wider community and the environment.

Members are expected to comply with good employment practice and where they take part in a competition, they should ensure that it is reasonable and transparent.

Finally, effective procedures must be in place to deal with complaints.

2.10.5   Detailed guidance on the RIBA Code

As noted above, the detailed notes can be downloaded from the RIBA website: www.architecture.com. The notes go beyond simple guidance and give substantial advice on the following.

Guidance note number	Contents
GN1	Integrity, conflicts of interest, confidentiality and privacy, corruption and bribery
GN2	Competition
GN3	Advertising (including advice on business names, RIBA crest, RIBA affix, etc.) revised in July 2007
GN4	Appointments (including suspension, taking over from a previous architect and fee quotations). Recently updated to take into account the RIBA's new suite of appointment documents
GN5	Insurance
GN6	Continuing professional development
GN7	Relationships (including supplanting or taking over from another architect)
GN8	Employment and equal opportunities
GN9	Complaints and dispute resolution

2.11   Continuing professional development (CPD)

'It's not over until the fat lady sings.'[16]

2.11.1   General

With the attainment of the relevant qualifications, registration and membership of a professional body, architects might consider that they had done enough. However, the world of the professional person is rarely a static, stationary one. It has become widely accepted that any person offering a professional service must maintain the standards of that service through continuing professional development. In architecture, it is a requirement, an obligation upon the architect, and CPD must be undertaken, in order to comply with registration and professional membership.

2.11.2   The ARB and CPD

Standard 2 of the 2010 version of the ARB Code requires of the architect:

'You are expected to keep your knowledge and skills relevant to your professional work up to date, and be aware of the content of any guidelines issued by the Board from time to time.'

A similar requirement is contained in the 2002 edition Standard 6. The ARB defines CPD as:

'the systematic maintenance, improvement and broadening of knowledge and skill and the development of personal qualities necessary for the execution of professional and technical duties throughout the practitioner's working life.'

The ARB has produced its own guidelines which elaborate the way in which architects should approach CPD.

- 'Be informed by a reflection on your work and the identification of areas where further development is needed.
- Relate to your development in the context of your organisation.
- Be informed by the changes occurring in the profession as a whole.
- Recognise the benefits of learning across professional boundaries.

The changing role and responsibilities of the architect, especially in relation to the modern construction industry, and changes in the nature of practice have led to significant changes in the following areas where updating your knowledge and competence might be necessary.

- The nature of the built environment and hence planning policy
- Health and Safety legislation
- Management
- Sustainable development
- Procurement methods
- Working with others in an integrated way
- Enhanced performance measurement
- Urban and neighbourhood regeneration/ urban design
- New technology
- Design
- Construction best practice
- Accessibility
- Building legislation

Suggested topics for updating within these broad areas include: graphics and modelling IT programmes; energy conservation and management; the use of new materials; and management-related legislation such as employment, equal opportunities, and the Working Time Directive.'

The ARB reflects upon the sources of complaints which are received about architects and points out that:

'In general, many of the complaints relate to architects not adhering to Standards 11 and 12 of the Code. These tend to suggest that some architects might benefit from CPD which covers the following areas:
- financial management skills in devising and managing budgets
- business management skills
- project management skills
- communication skills.'

The ARB advises architects to think laterally. It points out that CPD need not be expensive. It identifies suggested topics, general areas for learning and keeping up to date. It also addresses the methods and means of undertaking CPD.

'During the course of practice – on the job learning
Internal discussion meetings
Adviser/consultancy positions
Training another member of staff
Supervising a student's professional practice experience
Secondment to another department
Planning and running an in-house training event

Externally
For those not in teaching, involvement with a school of architecture (as mentor, lecturer or external examiner)
Preparing presentations for colleagues, client, faculty groups
Membership of architecture-related committees/working groups
Membership of groups such as historic building groups
Studying for a further professional qualification or academic award
Undertaking short courses, for example to update computer skills at adult education colleges
Attending conferences, seminars, workshops to enhance a skill or knowledge
Participating in competitions

Self-directed and informal learning
Keeping abreast of new government policies, new technical reports
Research for and writing articles for publication
Reading the architecture press and journals (as long as this is within a structured framework of CPD)
Open and distance learning'

It is worth noting that the ARB emphasises the output of CPD rather than the input in terms of hours spent each year. This approach should be compared with the approach to CPD taken by the RIBA. Further information on CPD and the ARB can be found on the ARB website.[17]

2.11.3 The RIBA and CPD

The RIBA introduced mandatory CPD on 1 April 1999. The RIBA's requirements for CPD for chartered members are established under the RIBA Code and a broad description is contained in Guidance Note 6 – continuing professional development. Paragraph 6.1 states:

> 'Members are expected to continue to develop and update their skills, knowledge and expertise throughout their careers for the benefit of their clients and the quality of the built environment. Learning does not cease on passing Part Three and becoming a chartered member. The Royal Institute therefore requires its practising chartered members to undertake **continuing professional development** (CPD) for as long as they continue in practice (RIBA Byelaw 2.8(a)). This is also an obligation under Standard 6 of the Architects' Code, published by the Architects Registration Board and applicable to members registered in the UK.' (This is a reference to the 2002 Code.)

The RIBA publishes on its web page (www.architecture.com/cpd) detailed information and guidance on CPD and how architects should undertake and record their activities in CPD. The documents are a combination of rules and guidance. The RIBA defines CPD as follows:

> 'CPD (Continuing Professional Development) is the requirement that the members of a profession or organisation undertake training to maintain their competence, knowledge, skills and integrity on a regular, structured basis after they qualify. Dozens of professional organisations – especially in the construction, legal, medical and financial sectors – require CPD of their members.'

Unlike the ARB, the RIBA approach to CPD obliges chartered members to participate in a system that focuses on 'time', 'points' and a 'core curriculum'. The basic requirements are stated as follows.

> 'All chartered members of the RIBA are required to do the following in order to maintain their competence through CPD:
> - 100 points per year
> - 35 hours per year, comprising:
>   - 17.5 hours of the 35 from a set curriculum
>   - At least two hours from the 35 in health and safety CPD
>   - At least 15.5 hours of the 35 in other CPD
> - Half of your CPD should be structured wherever possible
> - Record and plan your CPD, preferably online
>
> This is expected no matter where you practise or what you do. The only exception is for fully retired members.'

The points

The requirement is to accumulate 100 points each year. Each activity attracts between 1 and 4 points. The points are intended to be an indication of what the architect got from the activity, and the extent to which it contributed to the architect's own development. It is the architect's responsibility to assign points and it is not for the CPD provider to stipulate the points value of any activity. The idea of points is to provide a way to enable the individual architect to reflect on his or her activities in comparison with overall goals.

Structured CPD

Structured CPD is any activity done in a classroom or lecture setting, whether with other people in a room or via online lessons, provided there are specific learning outcomes. Examples of structured CPD would be RIBA conferences, RIBA regional seminars, RIBA CPD Providers' Network seminars, training courses, conferences, online or distance learning, certificates, diplomas, relevant additional degrees. The RIBA advises that members should attempt to achieve 50% of CPD via structured methods.

The core curriculum

It is not the intention that architects should simply collect hours or points indiscriminately. The intention is to ensure that architects maintain their competence. With this in mind, the RIBA introduced a mandatory core curriculum. Just over half an architect's yearly CPD hours must be drawn from the core curriculum. As might be expected, the list of subjects is generic, drawn up on the basis of the major skills which every architect requires. As an aid to learning, suggested learning outcomes for each subject are set out.

A useful feature of the website is a frequently asked question and answer section. Topics dealt with include:

- content of the core curriculum
- required knowledge levels
- determining programme of work
- monitoring CPD compliance
- exemptions and personal circumstances
- what counts as CPD and the validity of activities
- RIBA services on CPD
- employer's guidance.

To ensure that CPD is taken seriously, the RIBA selects a random sample of 5% of members each year and calls for evidence of CPD by way of a record sheet. Feedback and advice are offered. As a last resort, members who refuse to co-operate could be expelled from the RIBA. It is anticipated that this would not occur until after a series of warnings had been issued.

2.11.4   The RIAI and CPD

The RIAI defines CPD as:

'The systematic maintenance, improvement and broadening of knowledge and skill and the development of personal qualities necessary for the execution of professional and technical duties throughout the practitioner's working life.'

RIAI policy on CPD

The RIAI Members' Guide to CPD, issued in January 1998, was the Institute's first formal statement of policy on CPD. In September 2009, the RIAI Council ratified a revised policy on CPD and the extracts and information included in this section are taken from that new revised policy. Drafted in compliance with the Building Control Act 2007, the purpose of RIAI CPD is set out as follows.

■ 'To support architects and architectural technologists in the production of high-quality architecture
■ To protect the consumer
■ To protect the public interest
■ To increase client satisfaction
■ To increase effectiveness (for the practice)
■ To increase job satisfaction (for the architect or architectural technologist)
■ To promote career advancement (for the employee)
■ To promote the performance and the reputation of the profession.'

RIAI policy on CPD can be briefly summarised as follows.

'Application
This Policy applies to any person who is registered on the Register for Architects (registrants) and to all members of the RIAI, except those who are no longer professionally active. For those on maternity, parental, carer, or long-term sick leave, not involved in architecture or construction, semi-retired or unemployed it will be deemed sufficient to meet the full requirement through Unstructured CPD including, where possible, relevant online programme provision.

Standards
The RIAI Standards of Knowledge, Skill and Competence for Architects and for Architectural Technicians/Technologists represent the minimum standards required. Any person to whom the Policy applies must take all reasonable steps to maintain an appropriate level of professional skills and, at a minimum, to maintain on a consistent basis the requirements of the relevant RIAI Standard of Knowledge, Skill and Competence.

Requirements
The RIAI requires the following minimum level of CPD involvement.
  1) In the course of each year, each registrant/member must accumulate a total of 40 hours of CPD activity, divided as follows:
     a. 20 hours Structured CPD
     b. 20 hours Unstructured CPD.

Recommendations

Professionals have a duty to ensure that they are capable of providing the services they offer. Within the context of RIAI CPD Requirements it is the responsibility of each registrant/member to judge the best approach to undertaking the CPD activity necessary to:

    a. maintain compliance with the relevant Standard of Knowledge, Skill and Competence, and

    b. acquire and maintain the skills appropriate to their current activities and chosen career path.

Sanctions

Any person failing to meet the requirements will be alerted to the deficiency before the end of the year and at the end of the year given a period of 6 weeks' grace within which to make good.

    If still not compliant at the end of the grace period the registrant/member will be asked to provide an explanation for his/her non-compliance. Unless there is good reason the matter will be referred to the Professional Conduct Committee. Sanctions open to the Professional Conduct Committee include censure, fines, suspension, conditions for continued registration, and removal from the register.'

The policy concludes with advice on confidentiality and the RIAI support mechanisms for CPD.

2.12   Consumer protection

2.12.1   Origins of the ARB

A review of the Architects Registration Council of the United Kingdom (ARCUK)[18] was initiated by the Secretary of State and undertaken Mr John Warne in 1992–93. The ARCUK had been established under the Architects (Registration) Acts 1931–69. Reading the recommendations, which are now 17 years old, the key factors which John Warne highlighted are still pertinent to the ongoing debate about the Architects Registration Board and the Royal Institute of British Architects and consumer protection.

    One of his recommendations was to abandon the existence of a separate body, like the ARCUK, and enable the RIBA to maintain and administer the Register of Architects. Changes would have been necessary within the RIBA, to safeguard the interests of the consumer and to make transparent the operation of complaints and discipline. At the time, these recommendations caused considerable alarm within the established architectural profession. It was considered that the removal of protection of the title 'architect' would diminish the stature of the profession and increase unfair competition from other disciplines in the construction sector.

    In a remarkable turn of events, the RIBA, together with the regional bodies, lobbied the government of the day, to resist many of the recommendations contained in the Warne Report. What followed these events was a temporary measure in 1996, when a hurriedly prepared amendment was added (as Part III) into an existing draft Bill proceeding through the various stages of reading within the Houses of Parliament. This became known as the Housing Grants, Construction and Regeneration Act 1996 (see Chapter 6, section 6.4.2).

Eventually, the principal Act was granted parliamentary approval and was placed on the statute book in 1997. The Architects Registration Board came into existence on 1 April 1997. The Architects Act 1997 was further amended and revised to align with the requirements of the Qualifications Directive EU.2005/361 in 2007–08. The current relevant Statutory Instrument is 2008 No 1331 – The Architects (Recognition of European Qualifications etc and Saving and Transitional Provision) Regulations 2008[19] which came into force on 20 June 2008.

2.12.2   The Powers of the ARB

Under the provisions of the Architects Act 1997 and the Architects Regulations 2008, the ARB was given defined statutory responsibilities.

- Holding and maintaining the UK Register of Architects.
- Regulating the use of the title 'architect' for the benefit of the profession and consumers.
- Acting as the 'competent authority' in the UK for the administration of the European Commission's Architects Directive, 2005/e6 EU.
- Prescribing the qualifications for entry onto the UK Register of Architects.
- Setting standards of conduct and competence of architects in the interests of the consumer and, under codes of conduct and competence, disciplining any architect who fails to meet the stated standards.
- Removing from the register, and thereby preventing an architect from practising, if that architect is found to be guilty of serious professional incompetence or unacceptable professional conduct.
- Initiating criminal proceedings for pursuing any person misusing the title 'architect'. Further information on these matters can be found under the General Rules made by the ARB.[20]

The sponsoring government department for the ARB is the Department of Communities and Local Government. The constituent members of the ARB are as follows.

- Eight members, who are described as lay persons with no professional architectural qualifications, are appointed by the Privy Council after consultation with the Secretary of State and others. These Board members represent the interests of the users of architectural services and the general public.
- Seven remaining members, who are elected in accordance with an electoral scheme made by the Board with the approval of the Privy Council following consultation with bodies which are representative of architects. All registered architects can participate in this election process. These seven architects represent the architectural profession.

Normally a Board member serves for a period of 3 years and can serve for a second consecutive 3-year term if re-elected/renominated. The Board appoints a Chief Executive and Registrar who is charged with the management of the Register and other matters pertaining to the Act, including the education and training of persons applying for entry to the Register, consumer protection and compliance with the Act. The element of protection for consumers was a major difference between the old ARCUK and the new ARB.

2.12.3   The ARB's work

In practical terms of everyday activities, the staff of the ARB, together with advisory committees, subgroups and panels of experts, carry out their duties and responsibilities under three main areas: education (see section 2.5), registration and regulation.

Registration

The staff at the ARB provide detailed information on how to apply for entry onto the Register, including advice on the requirements of education awards in architecture and professional training. A person can be removed from the ARB Register for failing to pay the annual retention fee.

Regulation

When discharging the duties of regulation, the ARB has established a complaints procedure, which provides advice and guidance to clients and persons who have reason to complain about an architect. There is a step-by-step process for investigation of a complaint and the ARB has a Professional Conduct Committee (PCC) to administer this disciplinary aspect of the Act. Serious matters will eventually be dealt with by a PCC hearing. The persons present will usually consist of:

- an independent chairman appointed by the Law Society
- a lay member of the ARB
- an architect member of the ARB.[21]

To assist architects, in 2003 the ARB produced guidance notes on what constitutes serious professional incompetence and unacceptable professional conduct. The introduction to these notes states that they are also of assistance to consumers to enable them to understand how the ARB functions. The guidance notes are extensive, and set out in detail the events, circumstances and contexts of what actions or activities might lead to a breach. They include, among other matters:

- descriptions of unacceptable professional conduct
- the management of an architectural practice

- architects' relationships with clients
- conflicts of interest
- dealing with complaints
- serious professional incompetence
- forms
- regulations
- consents
- project management.

The ARB reports and web pages carry information about persons investigated by the complaints procedure, and persons disciplined. Hearings of the PCC are held in public and defendants are entitled to legal representation. On hearing a case against an architect, the PCC can decide:

- to reprimand and conclude the matter
- to impose a penalty or fine for a sum up to £2500
- to suspend the registration of the named person for up to 2 years
- to strike the named person off the register for 2 years or more
- that there is no case to answer.

There is a right of appeal to the High Court or Court of Session (Scotland) against a decision of the PCC. The PCC does not award costs to any party involved in a hearing, and the costs of defence by the named persons, e.g. solicitors and barristers' fees, fall entirely upon the shoulders of the defendant. Legal costs can be included in the cover of professional indemnity insurance policies, at a price.

2.12.4 Consumer protection and the ARB

This aspect of the ARB is a notable difference from the ARCUK and operates by:

- disciplining architects as previously described
- insisting that architects, when they practise, hold adequate levels of professional indemnity insurance cover
- ensuring that the education and training of architects wishing to apply to enter the Register are of an acceptable level
- prescribing programmes of architectural education and training, and removing prescription, should a programme fall short of the required standard
- requiring architects, under the Code, to have in place a complaints procedure for dealing with a client's dispute relating to the architect's professional services
- pursuing and, if necessary, prosecuting any person using the title 'architect' when they are not lawfully permitted to use the title to so describe themselves[22]
- requiring architects, under the Code, to maintain their standards of competence in professional services by undertaking CPD.

Questions which have been posed in relation to the ARB's role since its inception in 1999 include the following.

- Is the balance between the rights of a client and the rights/honour of the professional equally weighted and set out clearly in the Act?
- Is the pursuit of architects who are in breach of some part of the Acts leading to greater public confidence in the profession or greater scepticism about the body of architects?
- Do some clients vexatiously complain to the ARB to avoid paying professional fees or discharging their requirements under a condition of a contract?
- Does the sheer existence of mandatory professional indemnity insurance encourage claims against the professional?
- The title 'architect' is protected; the function of providing/offering architectural services is not.[23] Does the Act really protect the consumer and prevent misrepresentation by non-architects?

2.12.5 The role of the RIBA

The RIBA was awarded its chartered status in 1837. The remit of the RIBA at that time was 'the general advancement of architecture and the promotion of the acquirement of the knowledge of the arts and science connected herewith'. The RIBA's mission statement published in 2005 is:

> 'To advance architecture by demonstrating benefit to society and promoting excellence in the profession'.

An election process forms the representation on the Council of the RIBA which is the charter body, comprising 65 trustees, the large majority of whom are chartered architects. This election procedure also selects the President. The organisation of the RIBA embraces the RIBA Board which is the group and holding company with an executive structure.

- RIBA Holdings Ltd
- RIBA Professional Services Ltd
- RIBA Enterprises Ltd
- RIBA Trust

To uphold its mission and vision within this overall structure, the work and activities of the RIBA are undertaken through eight main committees:

- Communications Panel
- International Relations Committee
- Practice Committee
- Research Committee
- Education Committee
- Finance Committee
- Membership and Regional Chairs Committee
- Library Committee.

In addition, there are sub-committees:

- Discipline
- Policy and Strategy Task Group
- Client Services and Membership Task Group.

Through its company and committee structure, the RIBA provides, promotes and organises a whole range of initiatives which enhance the built environment, education and training competitions and membership services, including:

- programmes of lectures, exhibitions and events
- works in schools, community architectural projects
- awards programmes, prizes and events to acknowledge excellence
- dialogue with government departments, clients and the construction industry
- awareness and advice for clients
- studies and reports on matters of procurement, energy, conservation, planning
- validates programmes of architectural education and training (see section 2.5.2)
- works with the Joint Contracts Tribunal on forms of building contract
- manages CPD and membership requirements
- curates the British Architectural Library.

2.12.6 The role of the RIAI

The following summary setting out the role and functions of the RIAI has been specially provided by the RIAI. It sets out clearly the operation of the RIAI as both the professional body and the registering body.

'The Royal Institute of the Architects of Ireland (RIAI) was founded in 1839 as the representative body for architects in Ireland. In 2008, with the introduction of registration under the Building Control Act 2007, the RIAI was designated as the registration body for architects and the competent authority under Directive 2005/36/EC on the Recognition of Professional Qualifications. Under the Act any person not on the Register who uses the title 'Architect' or practises under any name, style or title containing the word 'Architect' is guilty of an offence.

As a professional body the RIAI is governed by a 24-member Council elected by the membership. Its objectives are the advancement of architecture and of quality in the built environment, the promotion of high standards of professional conduct and practice, and the development of architectural training and education. In this role it delivers the range of promotional, support and advisory services to members and public usual for a professional body. It is a member of the Architects Council of Europe (ACE) and the International Union of Architects (UIA).

The RIAI carries out its statutory functions under the terms of the Building Control Act 2007, which sets out routes to registration, admission, appeal and disciplinary procedures, fees and penalties. The Admissions and Appeals Boards and the Professional Conduct Committee all have non-architect majorities. The non-architects are Government nominees, as are the Chairs, each of whom is a solicitor, barrister or former judge. A complaint can be brought on the basis of professional misconduct or poor professional performance. Disciplinary sanctions include censure, fines, suspension and/or removal from the Register. Appeals against decisions on admissions or conduct can be brought on procedural or substantive matters and any person adversely affected by a decision of the Appeals Board can appeal to the High Court.

As a competent authority under the Professional Qualifications Directive the RIAI processes applications for registration in accordance with the terms of the Directive and its Code of Conduct for National Administrative Practices under Directive 2005/36/EC. The RIAI was a founding member of the European Network of Architectural Competent Authorities (ENACA), a forum for information exchange and discussion aimed at effective implementation of the Professional Qualifications Directive in relation to architects.'

Check www.RIAI.ie for the current code.

References and notes

1. Courses validated by the RIBA can be found on www.architecture.com.
2. www.ucas.ac.uk. Readers should note that there exist many courses on architecture which do not hold RIBA validation or ARB prescription, and these will not enable the graduate to qualify and register.
3. www.cao.ie.
4. The RIBA Examination in Architecture for Office-based Candidates: www.architecture.com.
5. European Commission: http://ec.europa.eu.
6. Further information on the Bologna Accord and the countries participating in it can be found at: www.accessmasterstour.com.
7. Extract from RIBA website: www.architecture.com validation procedures at 20/08/09.
8. Further information on the ARB and the Criteria can be found at www.arb.org.uk.
9. The full procedures document can be found at: www.riai.ie, section – education.
10. http://ec.europa.com.
11. Extract from the ARB guidance notes *Applying for Registration in the UK*. Hard copy available from the ARB, 8 Weymouth Street, London WIW 5BO, or www.arb.org.uk.
12. From time to time the list of architectural programmes held by the Commission is updated: www.ec.europa.eu/internalmarket/indexenhtm.

13. Further details on registering with the ARB can be obtained at: www.arb.org.uk/registration/applying-for-reg-world.shtml.
14. www.arb.org.uk – registered architects list.
15. Register and member admission routes: www.riai.ie.
16. The catchphrase 'It ain't over till the fat lady sings' essentially means that one should not assume the outcome of some activity until it is actually finished – coined from an opera suite.
17. www.arb.org.uk/education/continuing-professional-development.
18. Warne, E.J.D. (1993) *Review of the Architects (Registration) Acts 1931–1969.* HMSO.
19. The Architects (Recognition of European Qualifications etc and Saving and Transitional Provision) Regulations 2008: www.opsi.gov.uk/si/si2008/uksi20081331.
20. General rules made by ARB December 1999.
21. The full PCC is composed of four architect Board members, three lay Board members and two solicitors appointed by the Law Society. A minimum of one from each of these groups attends any hearing.
22. This duty of the ARB is under section 20 of the Act and the ARB has produced guidance notes to simplify the position.
23. The telephone directories of trades and businesses, known as 'Yellow Pages' in the UK, have coverage of other descriptions.

3 Employment

3.1 Introduction

Fifty years ago, opportunities for employment were fairly clear cut so far as architects were concerned. They were employed either in private practice or in local government. There were a relatively small number of architects who were employed in other areas, but they were the minority. Moreover, architects in private practice tended to be considered 'real' architects while those in the public sector were said to lead a sheltered life in which they were not called upon to exercise the full range of architectural responsibilities.

In the intervening period, things have moved on. Undoubtedly, the kinds of responsibility shouldered by architects in each area of employment are not identical, but if exercised properly, architects' duties call for similar qualities and skills in the public sector situation as in the private sector. Indeed, in recent years, many such public sector offices have effectively been made into self-contained 'private' firms offering their services to a broad spectrum of clients. Moreover, it is generally accepted that a great many opportunities exist for architects outside the traditional fields of employment.

Other areas of employment have always existed, but architects have tended to ignore them in favour of the more traditional architectural work. However, the current uncertain economic situation is forcing many architects to seek work entirely outside the construction industry where their hard-won skills may be of little value. In other cases, architects are looking more seriously at applications of architectural skills within the industry which are not popular. In some of these occupations, the architect is employed largely in a traditional way, in other cases just one facet of the architectural 'package' is used – for example, design, project management, drawing ability and so on. One of the great advantages of an architectural education has always been that, because it is so broadly based, the qualified architect has access to a great many employment possibilities.

The following brief summary is an indication of employment options. It cannot be comprehensive because the range of possible opportunities is as great as individual ingenuity makes it.

3.2 Private practice

Most lay people still think of architects as being employed in private practice. An architect will opt for private practice for many reasons.

Because the type of work is likely to be varied

This is the kind of statement which scarcely bears examination. There are certainly practices both large and small which handle an amazing variety of work, but most practices tend to have certain project types in which they profess particular expertise. Even in a large office handling different project types, the individual architect will often find that he or she is always given a particular kind of work to do.

Because of the particular type of work

There are some private firms which tackle projects which an architect would not encounter elsewhere. These might include very large and prestigious buildings or buildings under the direction of a famous and much sought after signature architect or highly specialised building types. Although many organisations such as banks, media companies, hospitals, railways and airports may have their own property departments, the range of work undertaken may be confined to refurbishments, alterations and extensions. In practice, the design of a new media centre, hospital and so on is rarely left to the 'in-house' architects. Therefore, an architect seeking to gain experience in such specialised buildings usually has to join those private firms which specialise in them.

This is not really the place to enter into a long discussion about whether a client is better advised to engage a private firm which specialises in hotels to design a new hotel or whether a firm which has no previous hotel experience would actually produce a refreshingly different solution to an old problem. In theory, every architect can design any building after going through the appropriate processes of briefing, analysis and synthesis, but in practice, time is money and the architect with previous experience of a particular building type will most likely be asked to design the next such building commission to come into that office.

The opportunity to become involved

This is very closely related to the next reason ...

The opportunity to take responsibility

Certainly, in the small to medium-sized office an architect usually will be encouraged to take responsibility for work, site inspections and even management of staff, provided he or she can demonstrate the appropriate ability. In larger offices, there may be more bureaucracy but even there, an architect prepared to work hard and gifted with ordinary competence can enjoy a fulfilling life. With greater than ordinary competence or a real flair in some field, there is no reason why the architect should not rise to the top of the firm in due course. Although the authors have not seen statistics, many years of observation suggest that it is more likely that a competent hard-working architect will gain worthwhile promotion by staying a number of years in a private office than if the same architect stayed for the same number of years in a public sector office.

The opportunity to advance to principal status

This is closely linked to the last reason. An architect who feels involved in the firm's fortunes, who takes on responsibility above that indicated in the job description (if any), who demonstrates ability and who attracts a following of satisfied clients is almost certain to rise to the top of any private firm. This is because such a firm owes its existence to satisfied clients who return with new commissions. A private firm cannot afford to carry passengers, because they must be paid for out of the income generated by the rest of the staff. A really first-class architect, generating more than his or her fair share of fee income for the firm, attracting and keeping clients, eventually effectively becomes the firm in that if such an architect left, the firm would be hard pressed to survive long afterwards. That scenario is more common among small practices, but the principle holds good in any practice. It is possible for an architect employed in a private practice to become the firm or a very sizeable portion of it.

There are many one-person practices in the country and a few large multi-disciplinary practices employing over 50 staff. Most practices, however, fall into the category of medium to small, employing 3–30 persons. Indeed, in 2008, 53% of all architects worked in practices with 10 staff or less.[1] Some architects prefer the small office because of its friendly atmosphere. It by no means follows that a small office is friendly and a large office unfriendly. Indeed, a clash of personalities which can be absorbed within a firm employing 50 would be disastrous in an office of only five people. The larger office may also offer certain advantages in the form of back-up and benefits which may not be available in a small office. There may be greater freedom in a small office, but there is less flexibility to meet sudden surges in workload. The most notable point about a private office is that there is always the pressure to earn the income to pay the bills. For the architect at the bottom of the hierarchy, the pressure is more noticeable in the smaller firm where the key policy decisions can be readily seen in a fairly crude way. Such pressure gives many people a sense of excitement and a rush of adrenalin. We suspect that this is an important, if perhaps unrecognised, factor in the decision to work in private practice.

Satisfaction

We know of no architects who opt for private practice as a way of ensuring job security. Private practice usually suffers badly whenever there is a recession, because it depends directly on individual clients being prepared to invest money in building work. The public sector is usually thought of as more secure employment, but anecdotal evidence suggests that many architects find public sector employment more stressful than private practice. This may be because working in private practice puts the architect in closer relationship with the client, there is usually less bureaucracy and often a greater sense of achievement.

3.3 Local authority

In 1988, about 10% of all architects were employed in local government or in government departments.[2] That figure had dropped to 8% in 2008.[1] After the 1974 reorganisation of local government, most county councils and district councils appointed an architect as one of the chief officers at the head of a department. The size of department and the precise responsibilities varied with the authority. That was followed by a policy of making the architects' department a entity separate from the other council departments, economically more accountable than before and often able to take on commissions from other organisations. In some instances, a department has been made completely independent and becomes a private practice rather like any other except that its birth took place under unusual circumstances. In other instances, the architects' department has ceased to exist altogether, certainly as an identifiable unit.

The character of local government offices varies greatly and so does the scope of the work. Some operate, as noted above, as large departments under the leadership of a chief officer responsible to the council. In other cases, the department may be part of the surveyor's or engineer's department, or it may be part of the council's building department.

The work of an architect in local government is basically the same as that of the architect in private practice. The council will in effect be the client although the relationship between council and architect will be that of master and servant. In practice, for the day-to-day running of a local authority office, the architects treat individual local authority departments as their clients. This certainly helps to separate duties and allegiances even though both architect and client are employed and paid by the same body. The architect will be governed by the council's standing orders. However, in carrying out duties, the architect must always remember the obligation to behave in a thoroughly professional manner, particularly when called upon to carry out duties under the contract such as certifying or giving extensions of time. Not only should the council not prevent the architect from acting in this way, the council has a positive duty to ensure that the architect carries out his or her duties properly.[3] In dealing with third parties, particularly contractors, architects must be scrupulous to ensure that the contractor is aware that they are not acting as the employer under the building contract, but only as the architects and that actions to be attributable to the employer are carried out by designated persons in a separate department of the local authority.

Architects in local government have certain advantages. If the authority is of reasonable size, they have the authority's other departments, legal, public health, building control, planning and so on, available for advice. In the larger authorities, the architects' departments may contain other specialists such as quantity surveyors, mechanical and electrical engineers, structural engineers, landscape architects and interior designers, although less frequently nowadays than formerly. Architects operating in that kind of office will in effect be in a multidisciplinary environment able to call upon any assistance necessary.

It is sometimes said that local government offices do not offer as much scope as do private practices. The truth, of course, is not quite so simple. Many offices have a high reputation and such offices will tackle all the authority's prestige works. Smaller offices may confine themselves to fairly routine tasks or small-ish projects, handing out the occasional large project to a private firm on a consultancy basis.

Any architect contemplating working in local government must make appropriate enquiries first. It must never be forgotten that not all architects want to design very large and prestigious projects. Many feel more at home working on smaller jobs. A particular feature of working in local government is that architects who put in a number of years service with the same authority will build up an understanding of the philosophies of, and relationships with, the departments who regularly require building work. There is the opportunity to make considerable progress through the development of briefs for particular purposes. Such architects have a unique opportunity to evaluate the perfor-mance of existing buildings and to feed back the information into current design.

There are also many opportunities for architects in the planning depart-ments of local authorities to influence design and planning on a larger scale, perhaps through structure plans or local plans or through involvement in town design, listed buildings, conservation areas and the like.

Very often, such architects are also members of the Royal Town Planning Institute.

Advancement may be slower and along more rigidly defined lines than is the case in private practice, but the staff will be divided into recognised grades. Each has a maximum and minimum salary and regular annual incremental increases. Promotion may be based upon seniority as well as technical and administrative ability. There are well-defined conditions of service which include such matters as holidays, sick leave, pension and hours of service.

3.4   Other public sector organisations

Other public and semi-public organisations such as universities, health author-ities and trusts tend to offer rather specialised experience. Architects are often employed in house, sometimes within a property services department, and these bodies are closer in organisational structure to a local government office than a private practice. They offer a unique opportunity to develop expertise in a particular building type which can be a very satisfying experience. For example, many architects gain enormous satisfaction from a professional lifetime spent in the rapidly developing world of healthcare. The principal disadvantage of such sectors stems from the same root: the difficulty in moving to an office carrying out different kinds of projects unless the particular expertise is required. Another disadvantage is the tendency of such organisations to put major projects in the hands of private firms.

In this category, it is also possible to group retail chains and hotels which very often employ their own architects to deal with minor building works, investigation of defects, maintenance and to liaise with independent consultants. It is possible to gain considerable experience in dealing with a wide variety of building structures in such offices. The buildings can vary from the very old and historic to the brand new.

Ecclesiastical authorities generally entrust new building to private architects. There are limited openings for the post of diocesan surveyor to carry out church inspections and maintenance work. The Church of England has a well-organised system. The Roman Catholic, Methodist and other non-conformist churches have fewer official posts, most work being undertaken on an *ad hoc* basis as required.

Some housing associations have their own architects' departments, but most work is carried out by independent consultants and increasingly on a design-and-build basis by contractors.

3.5   Large companies

Some large companies have their own architects' departments. The work tends to be highly specialised, but it very much depends on the company. The atmosphere is more commercial than in local government but there are similarities, particularly in the way in which the architect works for the employer rather than in an independent capacity for a client. The career structure and conditions of service are also likely to be better defined than in many private offices. Work within one company can vary, i.e. laboratories, warehouses, offices and housing for employees. Sadly, as all companies look for ways of cutting costs, the numbers of in-house architects are certain to fall. Some companies have overseas branches and the chance to travel is attractive to some architects.

3.6   Contractors

There are some large contractors which employ their own architects. The quantity surveyor has always had a place in building contracting and it seems natural that the architect should be involved also. Architects, however, have a poor reputation among building contractors and they are more likely to be employed in a design capacity than in a practical quality control role.

The majority of medium-sized contractors carrying out design-and-build work will engage private firms of architects on a project basis, because it is more cost effective than maintaining an architects' department. Some of the larger contractors, however, do maintain departments of their own and very often, having the facility to inject major capital sums into computer-aided design (CAD) and other expensive equipment, they can create a stimulating and exciting environment in which to work. All contractors suffer from credit squeezes and maintaining an architects' department is not as cost effective in a recession as buying in, probably at cut-price rates, the services of private architects struggling to make ends meet. Therefore, it will become less common for contractors to have their own departments.

Although architectural designs emanating from contractors have aroused adverse comment from time to time, there are many good examples. In addition, there is often a good opportunity for quality control and detailed administration. This is particularly the case because changes to the design are very significant to contractors when it is they who pick up the cost and not, as is usual, the building owner. There are opportunities for architects who are sufficiently flexible. Indeed, there is no reason why an architect should not rise to director level.

Many architects dislike the idea of working for a contractor because they feel a split duty between the contractor, as their employer, and the ultimate purchaser of the building. In practice, this need not be a problem. The contractor's objective is to construct a building which satisfies the requirements as laid down in the contract and to make a reasonable profit. In addition, the contractor wants the purchaser to be happy with the building. Very few contractors are rogues. Some may be hard businessmen but many are just the opposite – hence the large number of bankruptcies in the industry. There are two things to remember.

- A contractor who has architects as employees should not ask them to act contrary to their professional judgement. That is probably why the architect was appointed in the first place.
- An architect employed by a contractor cannot give the contractor's client independent advice.[4] An architect must always make the position clear to the client. It is especially important when it appears that the architect is acting in the capacity of an independent consultant. This can happen, for example, when the contractor undertakes a design-and-build project and the architect is involved in settling the client's brief.

Every architect should spend some time, if possible, working in the office of a medium-sized contractor. Architects rarely understand contractors. They may think that they do, but understanding follows from closely identifying with them on a day-to-day basis. There is much practical experience to be gained, together with an indefinable empathy with the contractor's difficulties which will be useful throughout the architect's career.

3.7   Manufacturers

Product design and development has traditionally had a valuable input from architects. Furniture design is a good example where many architects try their hands. Some classic pieces of furniture are named after the architect who designed them. A less common area of employment is in the field of building components. There is a multitude of products which would, and in some cases do, benefit enormously from architectural input: electrical fittings, ironmongery, floor wall and ceiling tiles and panels, glazing units, doors, windows, etc. In many instances, a relatively common building component might be improved by an experienced architect. The number of architects who work in this field is small and it is usually an interest which develops in the course of performing general architectural services.

3.8 Teaching

There are good opportunities for architects in schools of architecture if they have an interest in teaching. That is the most important thing. Most schools advertising for staff lay stress on skill in design, but they also expect a prospective lecturer to offer one or two other subjects about which they feel confident to lecture. A lecturing post, therefore, will usually involve a number of hours lecturing every week together with studio, workshop and some administrative responsibilities. There are some who regret the emphasis on design skills and argue that while design is the distinguishing architectural skill, every school should have some lecturers whose principal skills lie elsewhere, for example in construction, building procurement, professional practice and building sciences. It is probably important that these people are also qualified architects.

There are also openings for lecturers in other construction disciplines such as surveying or building and besides universities, there are many colleges of building where architects can make a valuable contribution.

Starting salaries are often considered to be low compared with salaries for architects of equivalent experience in other fields, but salaries in the new universities may be higher than in older establishments. It actually varies with the economic climate. As a result, lecturing tends to attract younger members of the profession, because as an architect gains experience outside teaching, he or she cannot afford to take a drop in salary in order to make the move from, say, private practice to teaching. Experience in practice is the great difference between the requirements for a lecturer in architecture and a lecturer in, say, mathematics or history. The budding lecturer should, therefore, gain as much experience as possible before becoming a full-time teacher. Most posts have opportunities for research and consultancy work.

Architects who do not wish to take up lecturing as a full-time career, but who are interested nonetheless, can often contribute useful practical input by doing part-time lecturing. The financial rewards tend to be modest, but there is a great deal of satisfaction to be gained.

3.9 Other specialisations

All professionals tend to specialise in one way or another as they gain experience. This is for the perfectly natural reason that they realise that their own profession is not just doing one activity, but is a collection of activities which are performed to different degrees. There are many opportunities for architects to specialise within the profession. For example, they may specialise in a particular building type. Many architects specialise in housing or schools or hospitals, industrial buildings and so on. They may also specialise in the tasks they do. For example, they may do only design, production drawings, survey work, contract administration, model making, perspectives or information technology. In the early days of CAD, some architects even specialised in putting other architects' designs onto the computer. That has largely vanished now that most architects are expected to have CAD skills.

These are to some extent fairly obvious ways in which architects can specialise. There are other less obvious specialisms: investigating defects, expert witness work, contractual advice, adjudication and arbitration are examples.

Architects, or sometimes persons studying architecture who have completed only part of the course, opt to qualify in another discipline such as planning or landscape architecture. A basic architectural education is an extremely good foundation for either profession. The landscape architect is bound by the Objects of the Landscape Institute, as set out in the Royal Charter of the Landscape Institute paragraph 5(1), 'to protect, conserve and enhance the natural and built environment for the benefit of the public'. The aims of the architect and the landscape architect are very closely related, as one might expect. 'Landscape architecture' is defined by the Landscape Institute Charter in paragraph 5(2) as:

> 'a. The application of intellectual and analytical skills to the assessment and evaluation of the landscape and its character and the resolution of existing and potential conflicts through the organisation of landscape elements, spaces and activities based on sound principles of ecology, horticulture, design, planning, construction and management;
> b. the planning and design of all types of outdoor and enclosed spaces;
> c. the determination of policies and planning for existing and future landscapes;
> d. the appraisal and harmonious integration of development and the built environment into landscapes;
> e. the conservation, modification and continuing management of the landscapes of town and countryside and sustaining their characteristic features and habitats;
> f. the promotion of a greater knowledge and understanding of materials and technology to enhance the appreciation of and resolution of practical landscape issues and problems; and
> g. the promotion of a better understanding of the principles and purposes of natural, biological and physical systems affecting or relating to the landscape.'[5]

Few architects can avoid some degree of specialisation as they gain experience, because the range of skills required of the architect is just too great and each particular skill is becoming so complex. To many architects, however, the most satisfying element in their work is the chance to be involved in so many different ways in the production of a building. These architects will always fight to retain a degree of broad architectural activity within which to practise their specialisms.

3.10   Adjudicator, arbitrator or expert witness

None of the activities in this section can really be pursued as a full-time occupation. Architects sometimes combine all three roles and manage to make a reasonable living, because they are good and in demand. For most architects, however, these particular activities will be undertaken alongside practice in the more traditional architectural role.

Following the coming into force of the Housing Grants, Construction and Regeneration Act 1996 and Construction Contracts (Northern Ireland) Order 1997, adjudication has become very popular as a dispute resolution mechanism and it has largely replaced arbitration as the dispute resolution procedure of choice for contractors. It appears that the number of adjudications may have peaked but there are currently about 1600 nominations a year, having dropped from a high of over 2000. Although in theory any architect can be an adjudicator, in practice adjudicators must have certain qualities. They must have experience in the construction industry sufficient to make them wise in the ways of the people they are likely to encounter. In addition, they must have technical and legal expertise. They need not be qualified lawyers, but they must understand rather more than the basic principles of contract law and be capable of understanding the report of judgments, which are frequently cited. Above all, adjudicators need to be skilled in assimilating facts quickly and applying logical analysis in order to reach a decision. There is no place for gut feelings or architects keen to do 'justice' even in the face of contrary evidence.

There are courses for architects wishing to become adjudicators, but care must be taken in choosing the right course. Some are little more than a brief survey of the relevant legislation and a few watchpoints. Even the best and most comprehensive courses cannot produce an adjudicator from an architect overnight. In practice, although adjudicators can be named in the contract or agreed between the parties when a dispute arises, most are appointed by a nominating body to which one of the parties has made application. Therefore, an architect wishing to practise as an adjudicator must apply to such a body and be accepted onto its register. There are currently more than 20 nominating bodies, but most nominations are made by just three or four of them.

Some architects practise as arbitrators. This role requires rather different skills from those exercised by adjudicators. Arbitrators have the luxury of more time in which to consider the issues in dispute, but they are more likely to have to decide complicated procedural questions. Unlike the decision of an adjudicator, the award of an arbitrator is final and binding unless, rarely, appealed to the court. The Chartered Institute of Arbitrators runs training courses for prospective arbitrators. Most arbitrators belong to panels of arbitrators held by the construction professions. With the widespread use of adjudication, arbitration seems to be less popular and adjudication is being used to decide matters for which the process is quite unsuitable. Large claims and allegations of professional negligence ought to be confined to arbitration or litigation.

The role of the expert witness is undergoing change since the implementation of the Woolf Report and the revision of the Civil Procedure Rules. Essentially, anyone can be an expert if they have the required expertise in the appropriate area. In practice, most architects who practise in this field tend to be expert not only in their chosen subject but also in the job of being an expert. There are particular skills involved and experience is important. Both parties to a dispute tend to choose experts (although the appointment by the court of a single expert is becoming more common). The function of an expert, however, is not to press the party's case but to assist the court or the tribunal to find the truth. Experts must never be partisan – a difficult and delicate problem when receiving a fee from just one of the parties. Although there are courses available for budding expert witnesses, nothing can really compare with the experience of being cross-examined in court by counsel. Good experts are difficult to find and most construction lawyers are constantly looking for architects willing and able to produce good reports and give convincing testimony.

References and notes

1. Mirza & Nacey Research (2008) *Architectural Earnings: A Survey of the Earnings and Benefits Received by Architects and Technologists*, Fees Bureau/Mirza & Nacey.
2. *Architect's Employment and Earnings* (2004), RIBA.
3. *Perini Corporation* v. *Commonwealth of Australia* (1969) 12 BLR 82.
4. Principle 1, Guidance Note 1.6, RIBA Code of Professional Practice, effective from 1 January 2005.
5. The Charter was revised in 2008, but this definition was unchanged.

4 Types of Practice

4.1 Sole principal

Many architects carry on practice as sole principals. Precise figures are not available and the numbers fluctuate greatly depending upon the financial climate. When salaried architects become unemployed in large numbers, as has occurred recently, it is difficult to find alternative employment and they sometimes take the opportunity to set up in business as sole traders as a means of earning a living. In 2008, it was estimated that about 14% of all architects practised as sole principals.[1] We would expect that percentage to be substantially increased during 2009 and 2010.

Because a practice is run by a sole principal, of course, does not mean that it is a one-person practice. The sole principal may indeed work entirely alone or may employ several staff of various kinds. The following are factors.

- In times of recession an architect might set up in practice alone as the only way of getting employment. If successful, the architect continues but if not, he or she may look for opportunities in employment again when the recession is over.
- Many young architects look upon sole practice as something to which they aim.
- A really successful sole practitioner cannot remain alone for very long. The workload will become too great and some form of partnership or formal company structure becomes necessary.
- Some architects become sole practitioners by purchasing a practice from a retiring architect.
- Sometimes an architect moves from being a member of staff into partnership as a temporary measure for 2 or 3 years, until the existing sole practitioner retires, and then becomes a sole practitioner.
- An architect will sometimes build up a private practice as a spare-time occupation before taking the plunge and becoming a sole practitioner.

It is probably the most difficult form of practice, but it is potentially very rewarding personally and financially. An architect contemplating this form of practice must have considerable reserves of self-reliance and an iron nerve to face alone all the problems of architectural practice. Most of these problems will have little to do with architecture. They will concern the business. Even though an architect in this situation may have no shortage of friends with whom to talk over important decisions, such as whether expansion should take place or what to do with a difficult client, these friends have nothing riding on the correctness of the decision and their advice has to be weighted accordingly.

4.2 Partnership

Statistics from 1989[2] suggested that nearly 40% of architectural practices were carried on in the form of partnerships. By 2009 the figure had reduced to 22%,[3] presumably as a result of companies opting for limited liability (see sections 4.4 and 4.7 below). Partnership is defined by the Partnership Act 1890 as 'the relationship which subsists between two or more persons carrying on business in common with a view to profit'. It is important to remember that simply sharing accommodation or staff with another on financial terms is not 'carrying on business in common'. If the courts have to decide whether in any particular case a partnership exists, a crucial factor is whether or not the parties share the profits or losses. In general, if they do, it is a partnership.

Partners are jointly and severally liable for the acts of the partnership. Thus, they are liable both as a group and individually and one partner is liable for the act of his or her partner provided only that it was carried out in the course of the partnership business. Normally, in the case of partnership contract debts such as the purchase of IT equipment, they are only jointly liable.

Actions against architects are common. A party seeking damages can pursue all the partners or individual partners in turn or any combination of partners until the damages are recovered in full. This can be disastrous to both the partnership and to the individual partner, because the sums of money involved can be quite beyond the means of a private person and, in the absence of adequate insurance, bankruptcy may be the outcome. In the case of a simple contract debt, the party requiring payment is only entitled to choose one of the options. Invariably, a party seeking recovery of a debt or of damages against a partnership will take action against all the partners together.

A partner is responsible to the full extent of his or her personal wealth for the acts of the partnership; that is, irrespective of a partner's particular partnership share. To take an example: if partner A has a one-third share and partner B has a two-thirds holding and partner B is not available to pay the appropriate share of a debt, partner A will be obliged to pay the whole amount. If the firm is worth less than the amount of the debt, partner A will have to make up the difference. If partner B subsequently becomes available, of course, partner A can sue for the appropriate amount to cover partner B's share. If all partners are available to pay, they will normally contribute according to the proportion of their share holding (see also Chapter 17, section 17.5).

A partnership usually has a written partnership agreement. Although it is not strictly necessary, it can save disputes about trivial things getting out of hand. Written evidence of the agreement is not necessary in order to indicate the existence of a partnership to third parties (who would not know, in any case, that a written agreement existed). It can be seen from the firm's notepaper, bearing the name of the firm and probably the names of the individual partners. As far as third parties are concerned, it is usually sufficient if the architect either states that he or she is a partner (whether or not this is true) or acts as though that was the case.

The advantages of a partnership are as follows.

■ When the business expands beyond a certain point (which will vary depending on the architect concerned), the principal will not have full knowledge of every project nor the ability to give proper supervision. A choice must be made: either to have a very experienced architect at high salary to help with the administration or to have a partner to share the burden, not necessarily on equal terms, but on terms satisfactory to both parties. A partner will have a real interest in the success of the business and an incentive to contribute to the utmost.

■ Economy in expenditure can be effected by the pooling of accommodation, equipment or staff by partners. Whereas one principal might not have enough work to employ three assistants, two jointly might be able to do so. The two partners and staff of three might be accommodated in two rooms, whereas as separate businesses they would need four. Of course, both staff and accommodation can be shared without any partnership existing. Each principal would have his own work, the time of staff being recorded and their salaries allocated accordingly.

■ Two or more partners should be able to generate more ideas and attract more work together than the sum of such ideas and work separately.

■ There may be more capital available for expansion.

■ A partner establishes a goodwill value to a business (more about goodwill later). If an architect is in practice alone, there may be virtually no goodwill value, because if such an architect dies or retires, existing clients are little more likely to continue with a totally new architect who may take over the business than they are to go elsewhere. In both cases they are venturing into completely new territory. A new and younger partner, however, will be able to maintain a continuity of personnel and establish a relationship, even if not primary, with all the firm's clients.

Goodwill is difficult to define. It is the benefit which a practice acquires by virtue of its prestige and the fact that clients return for further commissions. A partnership should not be thought of as stationary. At any time there may be partners leaving or joining and the workload will vary according to the economic climate. All this has a bearing on the goodwill. It used to be the custom for a new partner to have to buy a share in the partnership by bringing in a large capital sum. It was known as 'buying a share of the goodwill'. Fig. 4.1 shows one method of calculation.

If a new partner could not afford to put up the initial capital sum or obtain a suitable bank loan, it was sometimes agreed that payment could be made on an instalment basis – a certain fixed sum every year for a given period. As a result, many partners lived in near poverty for years until they paid off the

Profits		Year 1	£60,000
		Year 2	£95,000
		Year 3	£115,000
Total			£270,000

Average: $\dfrac{270,000}{3}$ = £90,000

Value of goodwill: £90,000 × 2* = £180,000

Existing partners' share: A at 60% = £108,000
                           B at 40% = £72,000

New partner buys, say, 20% share

at cost of $\dfrac{20 \times 180,000}{100}$ = £36,000

A and B might sell 10% each, thus receiving £18,000 each.
If the following year's profits were £100,000, the partners would share as follows:

A at 50% = £50,000
B at 30% = £30,000
C at 20% = £20,000 (new partner)

* The multiplying factor is somewhat arbitrary, but it is not less than 1 and seldom more than 2.

Fig. 4.1 Buying a share of the goodwill.

capital sum required and they only attained a comfortable income late in life. It is now becoming common for goodwill to be given a nil value. More emphasis is placed on attracting a person with the right professional attributes into a partnership. The chances of doing this are obviously increased if the incoming partner is not required to contribute a substantial amount to the partnership coffers. The new partner is given an appropriate share in the partnership and the actual income which the share will generate will clearly bear a relationship to the total fee income over the year.

The new partner, in return, will be expected to leave a proportion of earnings in the practice to act as working capital. It has to be said that existing partners who may have been obliged to purchase shares in the partnership are not always receptive to this approach, because it denies them the chance to sell their own shares to a new partner. Against this must be weighed the consideration that new partners are the lifeblood of any practice and without them income can decrease and existing partners' shares may decrease in value. In essence, the modern approach is a change from looking at capital gains to increases in annual income.

It is obviously advantageous if partners have similar views regarding the general philosophy of a partnership, but there is merit in healthy differences regarding the methods of attaining desired ends. Partners should have the utmost trust and confidence in one another. This suggests that they should know one another quite well before the final step of partnership is taken. It is, therefore, most common for a firm to take its new partners from its own staff, whose capabilities and suitabilities are known and have been judged over a lengthy period.

If a new partner is introduced to facilitate a continuance of the business, age is a factor which must be taken into consideration. 'A' (aged 50) might take a partner aged, say, 35. In 10 or 15 years time, 'A' retires and the new partner continues the business, looking for a successor and so on. Life, and partnerships, never work out quite so neatly, but that is the theory.

It is usual that the rights and duties of each partner are set out in the form of a legal agreement drafted by a legal adviser experienced in that kind of work. Although the agreement (which will be in the form of a deed) can be as long or as short as the partners wish, it is advisable to include any matter which might be anticipated to cause problems. Typical heads of terms (and brief comments) include the following.

- *Name of the firm.* This must not be objectionable or misleading, but it may include the names of former, but now departed, partners.[4]
- *Place of business.* This will often state that it is to be as agreed from time to time, but it can be useful to insert the address of the offices at the time the agreement is signed and also whether the property is owned by the partners in equal shares or in proportion to their partnership shares, whether it is leasehold and any other significant points.
- *Date of commencement.* The date of commencement of the partnership.
- *Value of goodwill.* This will be stated or may be given as 'nil'.
- *Amount of capital provided by each partner.* This is the capital that each partner has contributed to the firm at the date of the agreement in order to provide working capital and each partner has the right to take out that capital either on leaving or before that time. Usually, there are detailed provisions about the withdrawal of capital introduced.
- *Treatment of work in progress.* This can be an important matter in connection with taxation and an accountant's advice is essential.
- *Duties of partners.* This sets out the duties of partners which are fairly standard, but there may be particular duties or exclusions which should be stated here for the avoidance of disputes in the future.
- *Proportions of profits or losses between each partner.* Essentially, the shareholding at the date of the agreement. This, of course, may change during the period of the partnership if one or more partners seeks to increase or reduce their shareholdings.
- *Amount of cash drawings per partner per month.* This provides cash flow for individual partners and it is usually stated as a top limit and the partners agree on the drawings from time to time. Of course, it is open to the partners to agree a change in the top limit, but if there is no agreement to change, it remains as stated in the agreement.
- *Banking arrangements.* The bank or banks used by the partnership, cheque mandates, etc.
- *Partnership accountants.* Not essential to name a firm, but sometimes useful to state a name in case there is no agreement later.

- *Partnership solicitors.* Not essential to name a firm, but sometimes useful to state a name in case there is no agreement later.
- *Termination provisions.* Any special provisions should be set out including the mode and time of payment of any money due, the length of the partnership, etc.
- *Outgoing partners.* Normally, the resignation or departure of a partner will terminate the partnership. If that is not desired, provisions should be set out as well as the mode and time of payment of money due to the outgoing partner.
- *Power of attorney.* Circumstances in which exercised and by whom.
- *Partner insurance.* Against financial liabilities of the other partners after the death of any partner. It can be a heavy burden on a partnership in the case of a sudden death and demands for repayment of capital and all other money due.
- *Professional indemnity insurance and any other professional requirements.* There must be provision for the partnership to obtain and maintain this cover and cover retired partners.
- *Partnership benefits.* This should list all the benefits which the partnership is to provide for the partners, e.g. cars, telephones, travel, health insurance.
- *Arbitration of disputes.* This private system of dispute resolution is better than arguing in open court, to the delight of the partnership competitors and the dismay of its clients.

In fixing the amount of drawings, it must be remembered that the firm is assessed for income tax on the basis of its profits. The cash drawings must allow for this and it is good practice for the partners to set aside an appropriate amount for tax every month as they make drawings. The advice of the firm's accountants should be sought on this and other aspects of the agreement. Unless the agreement specifies a period of notice, a partnership agreement may be terminated by any partner simply by giving notice to that effect. All partnerships are terminated by death and by the taking of a new partner or the retirement of an old partner unless the partnership agreement expressly stipulates to the contrary. This is one of the essential differences between a partnership and forms of corporate body which continue although the persons constituting the membership may change.

Termination of a partnership does not remove liability from any of the partners and it is usual for partnerships to maintain professional indemnity insurance in respect of retired members. Problems can arise if all the partners split up and there is no continuing partnership to carry on insurance premium payments. In these circumstances, some insurers may offer special deals (see Chapter 17, section 17.5).

Many practices use the designation 'associate' to signify that the particular member of staff has attained a status which is higher than other members of staff but short of partnership. Often, it is an indication that the person concerned will eventually become a partner. Although it is usual to list the names of associates on the letterhead, it is good practice to separate the associates from the partners in some distinct form so that there is no doubt in the public mind that an associate is not a partner. It is an important safeguard as far as the associate is concerned who otherwise could be liable as a partner if a court decided that the associate had held him or herself out as such.

Associates are normally appointed by letter, but some firms like to give the arrangement some additional solemnity by having a deed prepared. Associates do not have any share in the partnership profits except they may have a share in a bonus scheme like other members of staff and they often receive extra benefits which may take the form of better than average car, healthcare package and so on.

In the early 1990s, the practice of appointing *salaried partners* appeared to be dying out. Unfortunately, it seems to have been revived. Salaried partners suffer the worst of both worlds. They can be considered to be full partners if there is a question of liability and certainly in the eyes of the public it is likely that such would be the case. On the other hand, they normally receive a very small share of the profits on top of their salary. It is a position to be avoided, because they are often undifferentiated from other partners on the letterhead and, therefore, they are just as likely to be the subject of legal action. Although the partnership agreement may contain an indemnity for all salaried partners from the full partners, the indemnity will be of no avail if there is a large claim which devours the assets of the firm and the individual partners and the professional indemnity insurance does not cover it.

Sometimes, a person is designated 'consultant' on the letterhead. The reality is often that the architect is a retired partner of long standing who is kept on the letterhead to reassure clients that there is a continuity in the partnership. The consultant, more often than not, will be paid a small retainer. A consultant, in these terms, may be called in by the remaining partners occasionally in order to contribute a recollection of an old project or perhaps to deal with some particular small matter which can be kept within precise boundaries.

4.3   Unlimited liability

This kind of company understandably finds little favour with architects' practices; very few firms are set up in this form.[5] The principal advantages are that a director of such a company is free from liability after a period of 12 months has expired from leaving the company and there is no requirement for filing reports with the Companies Registrar. There are, however, some formalities. An unlimited company is one stage removed from a partnership. The members of such a company are liable to contribute in the proportion of their share holdings if the company's assets are not sufficient to pay debts. There may be a maximum of 50 members.

closed

4.4   Limited liability

liquidate

Limited liability is possessed by a company where the liability of the members is limited to the nominal value of the share holding, hence the name. If the company is faced with a debt which is greater than the company's's assets, the company can be wound up and the shareholders have no further liability. The situation may sound attractive to architects as a protection from liability and indeed, that is probably the chief reason for the growth in limited liability companies in architectural practice. In 1989, limited liability companies formed about 7.5% of all practices. In 2009, this figure was 52% with a further 7% operating as limited liability partnerships[6] (see section 4.7 below). Although there was no legal reason why architects should not form limited liability companies, the idea was frowned upon by both the ARCUK and RIBA until 1981. Trading with limited liability is not without its problems, of course, and the Insolvency Act 1986 provides severe penalties for directors who continue to trade whilst insolvent. The court has power to order them to contribute to the company's debts out of personal assets. There are other measures the court may order against culpable directors: for example, that after insolvency liquidation, a former director may not be involved in the formation of a company with a similar name for a period of 5 years.

The principal difference between a limited company and a partnership is that when the shareholders (members) form a company, they are creating a separate legal entity. If the shareholders are also directors, they are employees of the company. Directors are paid a salary by the company and if the year end shows a profit, a dividend may be declared and shareholders share in the dividend according to the amount of their share holding. In the case of architectural practices formed as limited companies, it is likely that the directors will also be the shareholders, holding a similar percentage of the shares as they would have done in the case of a partnership. It is quite possible, however, that some shares may be held by persons not employed by the company or for some directors not to hold shares at all.

The advantages of a limited liability company are as follows.

- Except in exceptional circumstances, the directors are not personally liable for the debts of the company.[7]
- It is more flexible than the partnership, because trusted members of staff can be promoted to director status on a salary without giving them a part of the company.
- Directors can be removed with far less difficulty than is the case with a partner.
- The company does not dissolve when a director leaves or when shares change hands. Therefore, there are no complex legalities involved. The company simply continues as normal.
- Companies attract capital more easily than do partnerships. This is important if expansion is planned. This is because other firms are used to doing business with companies.

■ Companies, but not partnerships, are internationally recognised and there-fore in a better position than partnerships to develop business overseas.

There are disadvantages.

■ A company is governed by the Companies Act 2006 which replaces most of the Companies Acts 1985 and 1989. A company comes into existence only after registration by the Registrar of Companies. From that time, it can act only in accordance with the Acts. If the company carries out trans-actions before registration, they may be treated as the transactions of a partnership.

■ Every company must file accounts with the Registrar where they are open to public inspection. Partnership accounts are private to the partners.

■ A very important restriction is that a company may only act in accordance with the 'objects clause' which is to be found in the Memorandum of Association. This clause sets out the purpose of the company and what its powers are. A company which attempts to do something which is not included in the clause is said to be acting *ultra vires* (i.e. beyond its powers). Such actions can lead to many problems, for the company itself and for those who trade with it. For this reason, the objects clause should always be drafted with great care by an experienced company lawyer.

■ There are certain formalities associated with the running of a company. The Companies Act requires that at least one General Meeting of share-holders must be held every year.

■ The dissolution of a partnership can be a fairly simple, though traumatic, process, but a company must be wound up. This can take a long time.

■ No discretion can be exercised over the apportionment of dividends. They must be divided strictly in accordance with the share holding.

■ In general, a director's tax position is not as good as that of a partner's, because a director pays tax on the PAYE system and there is no opportunity to take advantage of some advantageous 'self-employed' tax concessions. This situation, however, is subject to change depending on government policy.

■ A client may dislike doing business with architects practising as a limited company (even though the client may also be a limited liability company) because it is considered by some to be unprofessional.

Although the shareholders together wield power over the way a company is run and have the power to dismiss a director, they must act within the Companies Acts and the company's objects clause and a single shareholder has no power to bind the others by any of his or her actions.

A company can be tailor-made by a solicitor quite inexpensively. It is even cheaper to buy a company 'off the shelf'. Such companies are ready formed; all the paper work is complete and they generally have a code name. The objects clauses are drafted for various purposes in fairly broad terms and after purchase it is a relatively simple matter to change the name. Some key points in relation to private limited companies are as follows.

- They must have one director (public companies must have two).
- There must be a company secretary who cannot be the same person as a sole director.
- A private company cannot offer shares to the public.
- There is no limit on the number of members, but if the number falls below two for six months, personal liability can be incurred.
- There must be a Memorandum subscribed to by at least two people taking at least one share each.
- The Memorandum must include the following clauses:
  name
  office where registered (e.g. England and Wales or Scotland)
  objects
  liability (whether limited)
  capital.
- The name must have 'Limited' as the last word.
- The name must appear in full on business correspondence.
- The name cannot be registered if there is another company of the same name on the index, if the name is offensive or if it would be a criminal offence.
- Business correspondence must also include the registered number.
- There must be printed Articles of Association.
- The Articles must be signed by the subscribers.
- The company can use another name with which to trade provided that the company name also appears on correspondence.
- A register of directors must be kept and the Registrar must be notified of changes.
- There must be a qualified independent auditor.
- There must be at least one AGM and unless otherwise unanimously agreed by those entitled to attend, 21 clear days notice must be given.

4.5 Public company

A more recent development has been for some architectural practices to carry on business as public companies and, indeed, a few large practices have already taken this route. It is important, of course, that control of the company remains in the hands of architects. That is something which is much more difficult to ensure in the case of a public than a private company. The essential difference between private and public companies is that members of the public can buy and sell the shares of the latter. In theory, it is possible for a publicly quoted company to be completely controlled by people who are not architects. However, since that would fall foul of the ARB ruling which insists that an architectural practice should be controlled by architects, such a move would be self-defeating. It is clearly a valuable asset for a company to be able to describe itself as 'Architects'. Any kind of agreement to restrict the number of shares on sale to the public (e.g. keeping 51% for architect directors) would be frowned upon by the Council of the Stock Exchange.

Members of the public who buy shares receive a share of the profits each year depending on the dividend announced. Therefore, trading as a public company is a useful way of generating finance for expansion. The regulations with regard to public companies are more stringent than is the case with private companies. For example, the nominal value of its allotted share capital must be not less than £50,000. In addition, a public company must put the letters 'PLC' after its name. A public company is normally formed after a period as a private limited company. Floating a company is a specialised operation. It is not essential in order to be a public company, but it is a means of attracting more investors. In order to achieve a successful flotation, the prospective shareholders must be convinced that the company has a good chance of giving a worthwhile return on money invested. Some kind of track record is essential.

4.6   Limited partnership

In this form of partnership, at least one partner must be responsible for all the liabilities of the partnership. In an architectural practice, this partner must be an architect. There can be one or more additional partners who contribute capital to the partnership and whose liability is limited to the amount of capital they contribute, provided that they have no part in the management of the partnership. Such partnerships must be registered under the Limited Partnerships Act 1907.

This is a comparatively little used form of partnership whose chief advantage appears to be the possibility of using funds injected by the limited partners for which they receive appropriate shares in the profit.

4.7   Limited liability partnerships

The Limited Liability Partnership Act 2000 came into force in the UK, except Northern Ireland, on 6 April 2001. Practices in Northern Ireland were able to operate through the medium of a limited liability partnership when the Limited Liability Partnerships Act (Northern Ireland) 2002 came into force on 13 September 2004. Professional firms wish to act and generally organise themselves flexibly and have the tax status of partnerships, but without the burden of joint and several liability. Therefore, the new limited liability partnership (LLP) combines certain crucial structural features of both a company and a partnership, the general intention being that the LLP will have the internal flexibility of a partnership but have external obligations equivalent to those of a limited company. In common with partnerships, the members of an LLP may adopt whatever form of internal organisation they choose. However, they are similar to limited companies in that the members' liability for the debts of the business will be limited to their stakes in it and, therefore, they will be required regularly to publish information about the business and its finances (including the disclosure of the amount of profit attributable to the member with the largest share of the profits). Also, they will be subject to insolvency requirements broadly equivalent in effect to those that apply to companies.

An LLP has a legal personality separate from its members. In this, it is very like a limited company. Like a limited company, it must file returns with the Registrar at Companies House. Partnership law does not apply to LLPs, but substantial regulations have been published which stipulate the extent to which the Companies Acts apply to LLPs.[8]

Other features of LLPs are as follows.

- Any member may cease membership on reasonable notice, but is still regarded as a member by the public unless proper notice has been given to the registrar or the public has notice of the cessation of membership.
- Incorporation documents must state the company name, the registered office, names and addresses of members and specify the designated members (of which there must be at least two).
- Designated members are responsible for administrative duties of the LLP and for filing accounts with the registrar.
- The name of the company must end with LLP or llp.

Seven percent of all architects' practices are now LLPs.

4.8   Co-operative

Although some practices operate as co-operatives, the members must have particular views in common. To operate in this way could be said to be making a social statement as much as acting as a business. Control is on the basis of one member equals one vote. Responsibility and rewards are shared. If it is intended to register under the Industrial and Provident Societies Acts, a co-operative must have a minimum of seven members. If there are fewer than seven members, they must practise as a partnership or a limited or unlimited company. If the co-operative faces large debts to the extent that liquidation is necessary, the liability of individual members is confined to the amount of their share holdings. Generally, the members have shares of only nominal value.

4.9   Group practice

This is a comparatively recent development. The idea is that independent firms of architects associate themselves to mutual benefit, but they do not share profits and neither do they have joint responsibility to their clients. They may share staff and offices, telephones and other overheads, dividing the expenses on an agreed basis. The firms may be situated in different localities; indeed, this is often an advantage in easing the pressure by sharing the load. If one practice is badly affected by recession, another in the group may be able to share out tasks. It is a very worthwhile form of practice provided that all parties are committed to the same ends. There are five common types of group practice.

- *Group association:* a loose association of firms for the purpose of sharing experience and knowledge. Each firm has a clearly separate identity as far as clients are concerned.
- *Shared facilities:* no real association other than sharing accommodation, equipment and, occasionally, staff.
- *Single project group practice:* usually formed for the purpose of carrying out a specific commission, because it is too large for any of the firms to tackle it individually. When the purpose of the association has been accomplished, it automatically comes to an end.
- *Group co-ordinating firm:* another way of carrying out a large project is for one of the firms involved to act as co-ordinator and the other firms to take responsibility for specific parts of the scheme. Obviously, this kind of arrangement can only work for large projects where the parts can easily be identified. The co-ordinating firm normally takes overall responsibility so far as the client is concerned.
- *Group partnership:* a partnership composed of individual firms which continue to practise separately, but which combine on certain large or complex projects on a regular basis.

The distribution of liabilities can be extremely complex in any kind of group practice. It needs very little imagination to see that some forms are more risky than others. Whenever group practice is contemplated, it is essential to take proper legal advice from someone experienced and knowledgeable in the pitfalls to be avoided.

Among matters to be considered are whether a special vehicle should be set up such as a limited liability partnership, a partnership or a limited company; whether there is likely to be a problem in the future if one of the parties wishes to end the arrangement; whether a separate PI insurance policy should be maintained – at least current insurers will have to be informed; whether separate financial provision is required and whether legal formalities such as novation will be needed if existing clients will be affected by the association. Perhaps the most difficult issue is commitment. The loyalties of the participants will firstly be with their respective firms. However, making a new venture work usually depends on all parties being committed 100%. The extent to which these and other matters become crucial will depend on the form of association required.

4.10 Developer/architect/contractor

Subject to the provisions of the codes of conduct (ARB's Standards of Conduct and Practice and, if the architect is a member of the RIBA, Code of Professional

Conduct: see Chapter 2, section 2.6), an architect can practise in any combination of the above. An architect may even act as an estate agent. It is to be welcomed as giving the architect greater flexibility, but an architect choosing to practise simultaneously in two or more of these activities must take great care that his or her professional integrity is preserved. It is important that a client properly understands that, for example, such an architect cannot act as a contractor for a development and at the same time give truly independent advice on that same development as an architect.

References and notes

1. Mirza & Nacey Research (2008) *Architectural Earnings: A Survey of the Earnings and Benefits Received by Architects and Technologists*, Fees Bureau/Mirza & Nacey.
2. *Census of Private Architectural Practices 1988* (1989) RIBA Market Research Unit.
3. Information kindly provided by the RIBA who is the copyright holder.
4. See the Business Names Act 1985, amendments and subsidiary regulations for further information.
5. See section 3(4) of the Companies Act 2006.
6. Information kindly provided by the RIBA who is the copyright holder.
7. *Williams & Another* v. *Natural Life Health Foods* (1998) 2 All ER 577.
8. The Limited Liability Partnership Regulations 2001, SI 2001 No. 1090 and the Limited Liability Partnership (No. 2) Regulations 2002, SI 2002 No. 913.

5 Sources of Information

5.1 Basic library

Every practice needs a basic library. The extent to which an architect must refer to and rely upon technical information cannot be overemphasised. The size and complexity of the library will depend upon the size and needs of the practice.

Although much technical information is now available online, nothing compares with a paper copy when the need arises to study a document at length or incorporate part of the content in drawings or specifications. The paperless office is still a myth. Various kinds of information need to be on hand. First there will be technical books on such matters as design, building construction and contract law. Some of these will be retained from student days, others will be acquired as the practice develops – sometimes new, sometimes second hand. Textbooks, particularly those dealing with the law, have a habit of becoming out of date very quickly and, despite the inevitably high costs, have to be replaced as it is essential that all references are kept up to date. Such books should be kept on a library shelf. Few practices can run to the luxury of a specialist librarian and a system should be devised whereby a record is kept of who has taken a book for reference and when, as it is very easy for books to be mislaid, causing unnecessary frustration to a prospective user who cannot find what is wanted when it is wanted.

The second type of information that needs to be held is technical information on products. Some will be in the form of well-prepared and fully illustrated catalogues, preferably in strong, clearly marked loose-leaf binders. This permits revised sheets to be inserted and the superseded sheets removed and, if not wanted as a record for an old job, destroyed. Other information will be in pamphlet form which can be stored in folders kept in open-ended boxes for ease of retrieval. Again, it is essential that all information is up to date; some practices go so far as to acquire new information every time it is wanted. There is a great temptation to take information which is 2 or 3 months old and assume, often quite wrongly, that it is still current; some material will almost certainly have been withdrawn and new material introduced with concomitant numbering alterations. Office library installation and updating services are available to suit differing sizes and types of practice.

It is good practice to keep copies of all technical information used on a project together with the files on that project. Such contemporary information can be quite crucial in subsequent legal proceedings when the precise circumstances surrounding the choice of product may be forgotten and the relevant technical information may be unobtainable from the original manufacturer. The ability to produce technical information contemporary with the period of the design process may prevent a claim for negligence succeeding.

A third category of information that needs to be available is government and statutory publications. Examples of this type of information include technical circulars from government ministries on such matters as health and education, design criteria and technical requirements. A particular requirement in an architect's office is an up-to-date set of the current Building Regulations and a summary of all British Standards and in many cases the full standard as well.[1]

A question which is asked from time to time is how one should rank the various sources of information in terms of the most reliable/authoritative downwards. This is a very difficult question, because no matter how one sets out a list, there will be some categories which will contain important authorities together with lesser references. What follows is, therefore, a very general grouping.

1. Statutes, statutory instruments, regulations (always the most authoritative)
2. Case law and the decisions of various tribunals (often interprets statute)
3. Government-published or -authorised codes and guidance
4. Books, journals and conference papers (standard of authority varies greatly)
5. Online sources (treat with great care)

5.2 Classification and proprietary systems

5.2.1 Classification

The great increase in technical and trade information in recent years has swamped *ad hoc* systems of classification devised by individuals for their own use. There are three systems in use in the UK.

CI/SfB

This is still the most common system of classification and is used by NBS in its office library systems. It originated in Sweden; the letters SfB stand for *Samarbetskommitten for Byggnadsfragor* (the name of the Swedish committee concerned). Using this system, it is possible to give any book, catalogue, official bulletin or pamphlet used by architects a classification according to its contents. The classifying symbols are easily remembered and frequent use will enable the architect quickly to find the material wanted.

The SfB system classifies information into four main tables:

- Table 0   Built environment
- Table 1   Elements
- Table 2/3   Construction form and materials
- Table 4   Activities and requirements.

Tables 1 and 2/3 include most technical and trade literature while Tables 0 and 4 include most technical references, textbooks, official publications and regulations. Much technical and trade literature has an SfB classification already printed on it and this greatly facilitates the incorporation of such material into the library.[2]

EPIC

Electronic Product Information Co-operation is an internationally recognised classification for construction projects. It originates from a European committee of organisations which provide product information. Although EPIC is probably mainly used in the UK to classify information intended for other countries, information originating in other countries may also be classified according to this system.

Uniclass

This system was developed by the Construction Project Information Committee (CPIC) representing all construction professionals based on principles set out in the International Standards Organisation (ISO) standard which deals with classification of construction information. It is closely related to EPIC, from which it draws some bases. Support was given by the DOE Construction Sponsorship Directorate and the project was led by NBS Services after industry-wide consultation. It is particularly useful where it is desired to arrange files in computer databases.[3]

5.2.2 Proprietary systems

The need to keep a library up to date is all-important and great care has to be taken with incoming information, including allocating an SfB, EPIC or Uniclass reference if one is not provided. It is also necessary to keep the office index up to date, as it is of little use having information stored on a shelf or elsewhere without having the facility to find out, first, whether what is sought is available and second, if it is, where it can be found.

All this can be very time-consuming and there are a number of commercial undertakings which provide an information service for architects' offices, as noted earlier. They obtain the trade and other information, provide files and shelving to keep it in, give a regular updating service to the library and, in some cases, an information advisory service by email, telephone or post. However, remember that these firms have to operate at a profit. Some charge a fee to the firms whose trade literature they circulate, while others charge a fee to the offices receiving the service as well. In each case the trade literature supplied will not be all-embracing, as there will be firms who will rely on advertising their products directly to the profession and the industry. All such firms, however, will include favourite product information if so requested. There are also online services and CD-ROM provisions such as the RIBA Product Selector.

5.3   Information technology

Vast amounts of information are now available through the Internet and the World Wide Web, including Acts of Parliament, Statutory Instruments and recent law reports. The RIBA has its own website (www.riba.net) with links to other useful information centres. Government departments are also well rep-resented and it is possible to download a variety of publications. A major breakthrough in recent years has been the availability of information in readily accessible form on CD-ROM. It is now possible to have whole libraries on a few discs; for example, JCT Contracts Digital Service which provides, at a fee, access and editing facilities to the up-to-date text of all the common JCT con-tracts together with reference to old editions.

5.4   Selected project records and feedback

It will be found very useful to keep a record of all notes and data about a project in a separate file, with a simple history sheet in front to summarise what stage has been reached. The various stages of the work (e.g. sketch plans, applications, approvals) should be listed and the dates on which action was taken inserted against them; references and file numbers should be added as appropriate. This will not only save a considerable amount of hunting through files, but it will also make it that much easier if it becomes necessary to hand the project over to someone else. A specimen project history sheet is shown in Fig. 5.1. Where the office computers are networked, such informa-tion is readily entered as a computer file and thereby immediately available for inspection by any person in the office who is, or may become, involved in the project.

When the project is complete, all the office information (files, drawings, bills of quantities, etc.) becomes history, but for some years at least, important history. Careful decisions will need to be made as to what is destroyed and what is kept (see Chapter 15, section 15.6 for more information on filing material).

Much time and effort are put into every project and as much use as possible should be made of the information which arises, hopefully to save similar efforts next time. For instance, the possibility of standard detailing for another occasion may arise and specification information may be able to be reused,

---

PROJECT HISTORY SHEET
Project .... Project No ....
Address ....
Client ....
Address ....
Tel No .... Fax No .... E-mail ....
Local authority ....
Adjoining owner(s) ....
....
Party wall surveyors ....
Date of instructions ....
Final design approved .... Estimated cost ....
Production drawings commenced .... Completed ....
Application for planning consent ....
    Approval received .... Reference ....
Application for Building Regs approval ....
    Approval received .... Reference ....
Application for approval of means of escape ....
    Approval received .... Reference ....
Quantity surveyors .... Tel No .... E-mail ....
Consultants .... Tel No .... E-mail ....
    .... Tel No .... E-mail ....
    .... Tel No .... E-mail ....
Bills of quantities commenced .... Completed ....
Tenders invited .... Tenders received ....
Successful contractor .... Tel No .... E-mail ....
Address ....
Contract amount .... Date of contract ....
Named sub-contractors and suppliers
....
....
....
....
Agent/foreman .... Tel No .... E-mail ....
Clerk of works .... Tel No .... E-mail ....
Starting date .... Completion date ....
Rectification period commences .... Expires ....
Final account certified .... Amount ....

Fig. 5.1   A specimen project history sheet.

never forgetting the need to check and amend if necessary. The quantity surveyor will usually have made a cost analysis of the tender and will have provided the architect with a copy so that cost information arising from the project can be utilised (after suitable updating) if a similar project is being considered.

Finally, the needs of the lawyers should not be overlooked. If an architect is unfortunate enough to be involved in a project which has ended in arbitration, adjudication or the courts, the information he or she holds may be vital to the client's case. It is an established truism that the side which presents the best records is the side most likely to win, all other things being equal, of course.

5.5   Legal/administrative

5.5.1   Textbooks

Every practice should have a comprehensive set of textbooks dealing with the law relating to architects and construction and also with what might be described as the business side of architectural practice. Architects are not expected to be lawyers nor business tycoons but they are expected to have a fairly detailed understanding of the law as it affects them and to be able to understand and apply basic business techniques. An architect must be able to advise the client on choosing the correct form of contract and understand the principles behind such matters as extensions of time, liquidated damages, variations, termination and the like. It is also conceivable that the client may need some initial advice on easements, boundaries, party walls, rights of light and basic obligations during the progress of the building contract. In some of these areas all that is required of the architect is to know enough to appreciate when it is appropriate to consult, or advise the client to consult, specialised legal, management or other practitioners.

The criticism most often levelled at architects is in this area of business and law. It should be obvious that the person administering the contract should be at least competent in these necessary skills. It should not be something merely left to be picked up as the architect does the job. Although everyone needs practical experience, it is only useful as a way of tempering theoretical knowledge. Without the theory first, there is nothing to temper and the architect simply amasses a motley collection of information, often inaccurate and certainly incomplete. The groundwork should have been laid in the schools of architecture. Schools vary in the time they devote to these topics, but in any event and at best they can only provide a framework which the student or young architect must flesh out by private reading.

There are two kinds of textbook: the simple and the complex. Serious legal textbooks will not only state the law, but also give copious references together with an in-depth discussion of difficult points. This kind of book is fine for the lawyer. It is also useful to have on the shelf as a reference for the architect who takes a keen interest in such things. For most architects, however, an altogether simpler approach is welcomed and, generally, it is all that is necessary. Architects need to know what they should be doing and why they are doing it. The same thing can be said about management textbooks. Every office should have a standard text, but also numerous easy-to-read guides.

Standard forms of building contract loom large in the average architect's working life and architects should be expert in this particular field; after all, they are the professionals whom most forms assume will administer the contract. Guidance and explanatory texts dealing with all the standard forms should be on every practice shelf. It must never be forgotten that architects who cause their clients to suffer loss through ignorance in administering a contract may be liable to professional negligence claims. Thus architects who made several errors when certifying, including deducting liquidated damages in the certificate and deducting them before the contract completion date had been reached, narrowly escaped suffering the consequences of these errors. In passing, the court considered that the architects in question were 'doing their incompetent best'.[4]

Specific topics which should be covered by appropriate textbooks include the following.

- *Law*
  A simple general exposition[5]
  A construction law book[6]
  A good book on contract law[7]
  Some books on specific topics such as planning law,[8] design liability,[9] warranties[10] or accessibility[11]

- *Standard forms of building contract*
  One or two general texts[12]
  Texts dealing with specific contracts, such as SBC, IC,[13] MW[14]

- *Management*
  One or two standard management texts[15]
  Some texts with special relevance to managing a practice, managing contracts, etc.[16]

- *Professional liability*
  One or two texts[17]

5.5.2 Acts of Parliament

Acts of Parliament do not normally make easy or even engrossing reading. Indeed, it sometimes taxes the courts to decide upon the true meaning of the words used. Nevertheless, there are some Acts which a practice must have on its shelves.[18] Care must be taken to keep the Acts regularly updated. Statutory Instruments and Regulations are regularly issued under powers conferred by Acts of Parliament and it may be the Regulations which are most important so far as the busy architect is concerned.[19] It is essential that, in the absence of a librarian, someone in the practice is given the responsibility of making sure that the Acts, Instruments and Regulations are up to date.

5.5.3 Selected law reports

The English legal system depends in large measure on the doctrine of judicial precedent. That means broadly that, in general, a court must follow the decision of previous courts in similar circumstances. To be precise, a court must follow the *ratio decidendi* (the reason for the decision). There may be many other things which a judge will say in the course of giving judgment, but it is only the *ratio* which is binding. The other statements may have persuasive force on another court, perhaps depending on the judge uttering them. The idea behind the doctrine is to impart some degree of certainty to the law. However, there is considerable scope for a court to depart from a previous decision if it is considered that aspects of the earlier case are significantly different from the case being tried. When a court decides not to follow a previous decision, it is said to 'distinguish' the earlier case. The courts may do this to avoid injustice in a particular case.

The general rule is that every court binds a lower court by its decisions. The hierarchy of the courts is shown in simplified fashion in Fig. 5.2. Up until

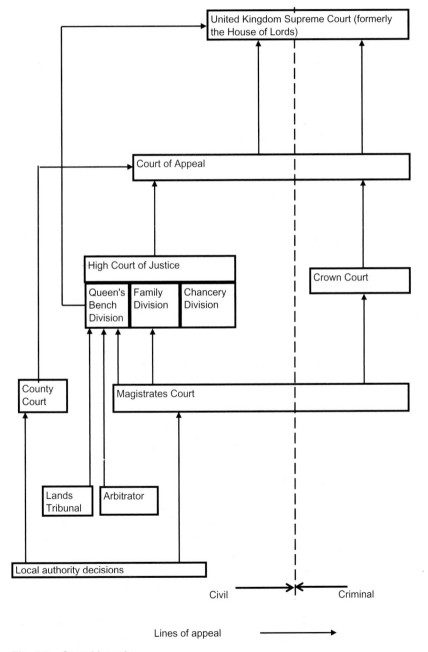

Fig. 5.2   Court hierarchy.

1 October 2009, the House of Lords was the highest court of appeal in the UK. From 1 October 2009 this function was taken over by the United Kingdom Supreme Court. It covers all civil law cases in the UK and all criminal cases in England, Wales and Northern Ireland. The former Law Lords form the first 12 justices of the Supreme Court. A decision of the Supreme Court is binding on all other courts, but it has the right to depart from its own decisions in future cases for very good reasons. It occasionally does so. The Court of Appeal binds itself and all courts below. Most construction cases are dealt with and disposed of, if not appealed, by specialist judges who deal with cases which have a high technical content. Their work is not confined to construction cases, but the construction industry is the major user of their services. This used to be called Official Referees' Business but it is now referred to as the Technology and Construction Court.

In order for this system to work, it is essential that reports of the judgments in decided cases are easily available. Law reports have been available for about 700 years in various forms. It is perhaps a peculiarly English trait that, in spite of the importance, there is no official system of law reporting. Reporting depends on private enterprise. The nearest thing to an official set of reports is The Weekly Law Reports published by the Incorporated Council of Law Reporting since 1965. The are many other series, such the All England Law Reports, Lloyds' Law Reports, Times Law Reports, etc. and some decisions are reported on the Courts website and can be read and downloaded free of charge.[20] There is a multitude of cases available on subscription-only websites. Not all decisions are reported and until comparatively recently, many decisions of importance to the construction industry went unreported.

It is unrealistic to expect architects to read every law report or even to read all the reports relating to construction. However, architects should be aware of legal decisions which might affect them and they should know where to lay their hands on the full report of the judgment. Architects should, of course, be wary of attempting to identify the *ratio* in each case. Sometimes it is obvious, but courts sometimes have grave difficulty in this regard when examining the judgment of higher courts which they are expected to follow. Nevertheless, the reports can provide valuable insights in certain circumstances.

There are now a number of series of reports which are concerned only with construction cases. No one series covers all the cases.

- *Building Law Reports* (BLR): fully indexed series, usually giving full judg-ments, and each case is prefaced by a brief resumé of the key facts and decisions together with a useful commentary on some of the features of the case in question. Published by Informa Maritime & Professional (paperback with annual hardback volume).
- *Construction Law Reports* (Con LR): fully indexed series, usually giving full judgments, and each case is prefaced by a brief resumé of the key facts and decisions. Concentrates, although not exclusively, on the judgments of the Technology and Construction (formerly Official Referees) Courts. Published by LexisNexis (hardback).

- *Construction Law Journal* (Const LJ): fully indexed series, generally giving full judgments, and each case is prefaced by a brief resumé of the key facts and decisions. Each issue also contains articles on some aspect of construction law and contracts and book reviews. Published by Sweet & Maxwell (paperback).
- *Construction Industry Law Letter* (CILL): fully indexed series, giving brief reports on cases of interest together with short commentary. Also contains occasional articles on construction law topics, details of Acts of Parliament, standard contract amendments, etc. Published by Informa Maritime & Professional (paperback with hardback binder).

CILL is probably the most useful for a busy architect, but the practice should back up these 'immediate' quick reports with one or more of the other series in order to be able to refer to the full judgment of a particular case.

References to law reports (there are some references given in the notes to other parts of this book) are given by means of a standardised abbreviation system. The abbreviations referring to the reports noted above are given immediately after the titles in each case, but in addition it is necessary to include further information to enable location of the precise report. Usually that is achieved by giving the volume number and the page number. Therefore, '50 BLR 1' refers to volume 50 of Building Law Reports, page 1. (Cases in later volumes of BLR are cited with the volume date thus '[2000] BLR 764'. CILL has a slightly different system.)

5.5.4 Professional publications

Professional journals offer a quick way of keeping up to date with construction law and standard contract amendments. Many of them offer a regular series of updates on these matters. *Building*, the 'Practice' part of the *RIBA Journal* and in Northern Ireland the *RSUA Practice Bulletin* are all valuable in this respect. Specialist construction law journals entitled *Construction Law Journal* and *Building Law Monthly* are filled with useful articles.

5.6 RIBA information line

This information line was instituted by the RIBA on 1 May 1995, since when it has become extremely popular. It is operated by expert staff of the information unit of the British Architectural Library. The service is available only to RIBA members. A broad range of architecture and architectural practice matters are covered and details of books, articles and seminars can be sent by email, fax or post. The unit can call upon the services of a panel of specialist advisors. The advisors, who are unpaid, are prepared to discuss the member's problem by telephone on a without liability basis. The service is free to members who may then commission the advisor on a consultancy basis if the query warrants it.

References and notes

1. Details of all published construction standards are available from Technical Indexes Ltd or online at www.ihs.com, either online, by post or on DVD. Logicworks Publications and Complete Picture (UK) Ltd produce CD-ROMs on the Building and other regulations which contain much useful information.

2. *CI/SfB Construction Indexing Manual*, 3rd edn (2002) RIBA Publishing.

3. *Uniclass Manual* (1999) is available on CD-ROM together with *Uniclass (Electronic)* and *Uniclass Guidance and Library Conversion Aids* (2000) from RIBA Enterprises who also produce labels and a wallchart.

4. *Lubenham Fidelities & Investment Co* v. *South Pembrokeshire District Council* (1986) 6 Con LR 85.

5. Barker, D. & Padfield, C. (2007) *Law Made Simple*, 12th edn, Elsevier.

6. Furst, S. & Ramsey, V. (2006) *Keating on Construction Contracts*, 8th edn, with supplement, Sweet & Maxwell; Chappell, D., Cowlin, M. & Dunn, M. (2009) *Building Law Encyclopaedia*, Wiley-Blackwell.

7. Furmston, M.P. (2006) *Cheshire, Fifoot and Furmston's Law of Contract*, 15th edn, Oxford University Press.

8. Blackhall, C. (2006) *Planning Law and Practice*, 3rd edn, Cavendish Publishing.

9. Cornes, D.L. (1994) *Design Liability in the Construction Industry*, 4th edn, Blackwell Publishing.

10. Cornes, D. & Winward, R. (2002) *Winward Fearon on Collateral Warranties*, 2nd edn, Blackwell Publishing.

11. Vandenberg, M. (2008) *An Inclusive Environment*, Butterworth-Heinemann, is an excellent book dealing with almost everything one needs to know about accessibility.

12. Chappell, D. (2007) *Understanding JCT Standard Building Contracts*, 8th edn, Taylor & Francis; Furmston, M.P. (2006) *Powell-Smith & Furmston's Building Contract Casebook*, 4th edn, Blackwell Publishing.

13. Chappell, D. (2006) *The JCT Intermediate Building Contracts 2005*, 3rd edn, Blackwell Publishing.

14. Chappell, D. (2007) *JCT Minor Works Building Contracts 2006*, 4th edn, Blackwell Publishing.

15. Drucker, P.F. (1999) *Managing for Results*, Butterworth-Heinman; Drucker, P.F. (2007) *The Effective Executive*, Elsevier; Peter, L. & Hull, R. (1994) *The Peter Principle*, Souvenir Press; Townsend, R. (1985) *Further Up the Organisation*, Coronet; Maister, D. (2003) *Managing the Professional Service Firm*, Free Press.

16. Lupton, S. (ed) (2001) *Architect's Handbook of Practice Management*, 7th edn, RIBA Publishing; 3DReid (2008) *Architect's Job Book*, 8th edn, RIBA Publishing; Chappell, D. (1996) *Contractual Correspondence for Architects and Project Managers*, 3rd edn, Blackwell Publishing.

17. Lavers, A. & Chappell, D. (2000) *A Legal Guide to the Professional Liability of Architects*, 3rd edn, Lavers; Cecil, R. (1991) *Professional Liability*, 3rd edn, Legal Studies & Services.

18. Late Payment of Commercial Debts (Interest) Act 1998; Architects Act 1997; Housing Grants, Construction and Regeneration Act 1996 as amended; Party Wall Act 1996; Arbitration Act 1996; Building Act 1984; Companies Act 2006; Consumer Protection Act 1987; Copyright, Designs and Patents Act 1988 as

amended; Defective Premises Act 1972; Health and safety at Work Act 1974; Insolvency Act 1986; Latent Damage Act 1986; Misrepresentation Act 1967; Occupiers Liability Act 1957, 1984; Partnership Act 1890; Access to Neighbouring Land Act 1992; Sale of Goods Act 1994; Sale of Goods and Services Act 1982; Unfair Contracts Terms Act 1977, Contracts (Rights of Third Parties) Act 1999, Limited Liability Partnership Act 2000.

19. Good examples are the Construction (Design and Management) Regulations 2007, the Scheme for Construction Contracts (England and Wales) Regulations 1998 and the Unfair Terms in Consumer Contracts Regulations 1999.

20. An excellent website for recent law reports, legislation and other related material is the British and Irish Legal Information Institute which has a fully searchable website at www.bailii.org. It covers the UK and Europe and it has links to similar databases in other parts of the world.

Part 2
Running a Project

6 Stage A: Architect's Services

6.1 Enquiries

Marketing is dealt with in Chapter 19. The results of marketing should be enquiries from prospective clients. Enquiries can take many forms. Ideally, they come in the form of a letter, stating requirements and requesting details of fees and conditions of engagement. The reality is almost never like that. Established architects will usually have some clients with whom they do business on a continuing basis. In such cases, the enquiry is likely to be quite informal, during a meeting about some other matter or by telephone. Many new clients make their first approach by telephone; very few call personally at the architect's office in the first instance.

The way in which a client makes an enquiry can often tell the architect a great deal about the kind of client he or she is. It is always wise to respond to any kind of approach from a new client by arranging a meeting. At the meeting, the client can assess the architect and the architect can decide whether it is advisable to work with that client. As in every other field, personalities have a major part to play in the equation. Clients are dealt with in Chapter 1, section 1.4. A client may sometimes be a friend or relative, but more generally is a complete stranger. Some may have built before, others will be building for the first time. By its nature, the production of a building may take a very long time from inception to completion. It is important to start the relationship on a firm foundation or it will not survive.

6.2 Extent of services

There is some confusion regarding the services provided by the architect. On one hand, it is often firmly believed that the architect's fee for a commission will include anything and everything the client may require, provided only that it has some relationship to the project. On the other hand, and equally erroneously, it is believed that the architect will prepare a set of plans, but anything else the client may need will cost extra. There is a grain of truth in each belief, which is why it is often difficult to explain the architect's services satisfactorily.

The question of fees is dealt with below, but it is worth remembering at this point that architects sell their services just like anyone else. If, for example, an architect is asked to prepare a sketch scheme to satisfy the client's requirements; that is what will be done. It is totally unreasonable to expect preparation of working drawings, invitation of tenders and inspection of work in progress at no additional cost. Moreover, the client may not like the sketch scheme produced by the architect, but provided that it satisfies the requirements given by the client, the architect is entitled to the fee. It is not the architect's fault if the client has a dramatic change of mind when presented with the scheme and the client should expect to pay for changes. The same client would not expect to be able to go to a solicitor and request drafting and redrafting of a will without having to pay for each change of mind.

In practice, most architects are prepared to carry out considerable reworking of their schemes until the client is entirely happy. This may be very worthy and helpful, but it is neither strictly necessary nor sensible and in an era of fee competition, it is not always practical to achieve. To overcome this problem, the early stages of the architect's work are often carried out on a time charge basis.

It is unfortunately true that many clients are astonished, if they have never built before, that at the end of the initial stages of the architect's work there is often nothing visible except a set of two or three presentation drawings for which they are expected to pay what may appear to be an exorbitant fee. To take this attitude, of course, is to ignore the vast amount of work which has gone before the preparation of drawings. The prudent architect will usually avoid that situation by involving the client as fully as possible in every stage of the work. Although this approach is in line with best practice, the architect should assess each client, because some want nothing better than that the architect goes away and returns in a few weeks with some proposals. The architect, therefore, is expected to be something of a psychologist alongside all the other skills required.

The relationship between architect and client is often that of agent and principal. The agent exercises contractual powers on behalf of the principal and in doing so the principal is bound by the agent's properly authorised acts. The agency relationship may be created in one of four ways.

- *Expressly,* when the client specifically appoints the architect either in writing or orally. This is the most satisfactory, particularly when done in writing, because there is little scope for misunderstandings or mistakes.
- *By implication,* when it is clear to others that the architect must be acting as agent. Such an instance may occur because the client behaves as if the architect was acting in an agency capacity or simply because the architect is doing the kind of things normally done by an agent.
- *By necessity,* when the architect acts for the client in an emergency and otherwise there would be no agency. There will be very few instances where an agency comes into being in this way so far as architects are concerned. One might just visualise a situation where the architect must give an instruction on the client's behalf in order to save the destruction of property even though the architect may not be empowered to give that particular instruction.

■ *By ratification,* when the architect performs some act which the client subsequently ratifies. Two conditions must be satisfied: (1) the architect must carry out the action on behalf of the principal; (2) the principal must have been capable of carrying out the act at the time it was performed.

The agent's authority is important. It may be actual or apparent (ostensible). An architect's actual authority is defined by the terms of the conditions of engagement. Apparent or ostensible authority is the authority the architect appears to possess so far as parties other than the architect and client are concerned. An architect is liable to the client for acting beyond authority, but provided the architect is behaving in the way in which others expect him or her to act, the client will usually be responsible for such actions to third parties. For example, an architect carrying out functions under a building contract may issue instructions to the contractor. Provided the contract expressly empowers the architect to issue such instructions, the contractor is entitled to carry out the work and be paid. It matters not that the architect may be obliged, under his or her conditions of engagement, to obtain the client's authorisation for such instructions. Of course, in that situation, the architect may expect to be required to reimburse the client for any loss sustained.

The duties of an agent are:

■ *to act:* failure to act if action is called for is actionable at law
■ *to obey instructions:* the instructions must be lawful and reasonable
■ *to exercise skill and care:* the kind of skill and care normally to be expected from a member of that particular profession
■ *not to take any secret bribe or profit:* the principal may recover damages including the amount of such bribe
■ *to declare any conflict of interest*
■ *not to delegate without authority*
■ *to keep proper accounts.*

One of the greatest dangers for an architect is that of exceeding the authority actually given by the client. The possible consequences have already been touched upon. When in doubt, the client's written authority should be obtained. Next best is to confirm instructions to the client. Another danger may arise if the architect fails to disclose that he or she is acting for a client. The architect may become personally liable to the third party in such cases.

Agency may be terminated by the death of the agent or principal, by the performance of the agent's contract, by mutual consent, by breach on the part of either agent or principal, and by bankruptcy of the principal, but not necessarily of the agent.

At one time it used to be thought that the architect was in the position of a quasi-arbitrator or acting in a judicial capacity when carrying out some functions under the building contract. Such things as giving extensions of time or certifying monies due were thought to be in this category. Such notions were dispelled with the case of *Sutcliffe* v. *Thackrah* (1974).[1] The architect has a duty to act fairly in these circumstances, but the duty is owed to the client, not to the contractor: *London Borough of Merton* v. *Stanley Hugh Leach* (1985).[2] If an architect is negligent in the performance of any duty under the contract, the client may issue a claim against the architect direct, or arbitrate under the conditions of engagement as appropriate, in respect of any loss suffered, but the contractor must take action against the client, probably in arbitration, under the building contract.[3] Developments in the law, however, have suggested that there may be circumstances where an architect could be said to assume responsibility to a contractor who can be shown to have relied upon his decisions. The position is complex and still not yet clear.[4]

The architect's services fall into two parts.

1. Services which an architect will undertake as part of the overall design and administration of an entire project from beginning to end.
2. Services which are available from an architect, but not as part of 'normal' entire project services.

A detailed description of these services is included in the RIBA Appointment documents available from the RIBA. They are discussed below.

All architects will be prepared to offer the 'normal' services to their clients, but some of the additional services may call for a degree of expertise in fields which not every architect will be familiar with. In addition, although the architect is still usually the lead consultant and contract administrator, it is no longer a foregone conclusion and some clients appoint a project manager to act as team leader and contractor administrator (an explanation of the two very different roles which can be played by the project manager is given in Chapter 8, section 8.3). In such instances the architect's management services will not be required.

For charging and other purposes, the work is divided into stages. Fig. 6.1 shows them in diagrammatic form. This part of the book is divided into the same stages for convenience and what follows is a brief description of each stage, which will receive more detailed treatment in succeeding chapters. It is not always easy to pinpoint activities within a particular stage, because the whole process is continuous and some activities can be accommodated in

---

Stages
A   Appraisal
B   Design brief
C   Concept
D   Design development
E   Technical design
F   Production information
G   Tender documentation
H   Tender action
J   Mobilisation
K   Construction to practical completion
L   After practical completion

Fig. 6.1   The RIBA Plan of Work (title of stages only).

several stages. For example, application for full planning permission and selection of specialist sub-contractors will take place at a time to suit the circumstances.

6.2.1   Normal services[5]

A   Appraisal

During this initial stage, an important function of the architect is to obtain the client's brief. It can be a laborious process if clients are not, and sometimes if they are, sure of what they want. It is the architect's task to separate what the client wants from what he or she really needs. The architect will need to ask many questions regarding finance available, time schedule and the function required of the building. It is likely that several meetings will be required before the architect is satisfied. If there is any advice the client requires or the architect thinks it proper to give at this point, it will be given. For example, the architect may say at the first meeting that the project is not feasible because of cost, siting or some other reason.

Generally, assuming the scheme is not aborted, the architect will visit the site to get some idea of what is involved. It is at this stage that the architect will be able to provide a rough idea of the cost, time and fees likely to be involved in proceeding with the scheme. If the work the client has in mind is very small, for example an extension to a house, the whole process may take no more than a day or so. In the case of larger projects, a correspondingly longer time will be required. Where extremely large and complex projects are concerned, this stage may be very protracted. On anything other than small projects it represents a considerable body of work, at the end of which the architect might prepare a report, depending upon the size and complexity of the project, for examination by the client. Instead of a report, the architect's conclusions might be presented orally.

This is the stage during which the architect will check thoroughly that the project is feasible, that it can be built for the money the client wishes to spend, that there are no obstacles in the form of planning objections from the local authority or the site conditions, and so on. There will be involvement in discussions with statutory authorities and any consultants appointed and every matter which might affect the client's intention to proceed must be investigated. For example, if the client is proposing a speculative housing development, it might well be prudent to include, for the client's information, details of local schools, shops and bus services near the site. If the site is in a designated conservation or urban redevelopment area, the architect will explain how that will affect the scheme.[6]

At this stage, alternative ways of tackling the design will be suggested and will conclude by a request to the client to make certain decisions. The decision may be simply whether to proceed or it may involve matters thrown up by the investigations. Matters concerning site or building acquisition and the need for a full survey, and of what type, will be considered.

B   Design brief

The design brief will be prepared, possibly by the client but normally by the architect. This brief takes into account all the preparatory work and the client's decisions on any points thrown up by the appraisal. The key procedures must be identified together with the way in which the architect intends to organise the design team to deal with the project. The client can then be given some preliminary thoughts on the need for consultants and specialist sub-contractors. If it has not already been considered, the architect should advise the client about procurement alternatives, making sure that the client fully understands the implications of alternative methods. Few clients will properly understand the meaning of Guaranteed Maximum Price contracts or the restrictions implicit in opting for design and build (see Chapter 8).

C   Concept

This stage is probably better known as 'sketch design'. Taking into account all previous discussions, including the client's decisions at the end of stage A, the architect will develop the brief into a full briefing document for the project intended to indicate the client's requirements in every particular. The architect will then prepare drawings to illustrate the proposed solution to the client's problem. The drawings will not be detailed, but they will be sufficient to show what the architect has in mind in a general way. It should be possible to see the general massing and external appearance of the building, its disposition on site and the arrangement of the interior; there should be a structural analysis and outline proposals for arrangement of services.

To produce these sketches, the architect will have to analyse and consider all the information gleaned during the previous stages. The client should be asked to approve an approximate estimate of cost at this stage. In giving such an estimate, an architect is wise to ensure that it makes proper allowance to reflect the outline nature of the design at this stage by building in an estimating tolerance. This is particularly important, because this is the figure that the client will always remember! Where the project is other than small, the cost estimation should be carried out by a quantity surveyor who should be involved at an early stage by means of a separate appointment to the client. It is not too early for the quantity surveyor to prepare an initial cost plan.

D   Design development

On small jobs, this stage is combined with the previous stage. The architect must take into account any comments the client makes about the concept, complete the full briefing document and work with any consultants who may be appointed to produce a more detailed design for the client's approval. At this stage, the client should have a very clear idea about the appearance of the building, the materials proposed and the layout of the interior. A fresh estimate of cost will be prepared and the dates for commencement and completion will be determined. The architect will require the client's final approval to the scheme, time-scale and cost at this point.

Assuming that the client does approve with little or no amendment, the architect should apply for planning permission. Although an application for outline permission will almost certainly have been made at feasibility stage and thereafter the planning authorities will have been closely consulted, there is unfortunately no guarantee that planning permission will be granted. In the majority of cases, the procedures adopted by the architect avoid a refusal at this stage, but it is not uncommon for the planning authority to require some changes before they will grant permission. Both architect and client will find it frustrating if this happens, in addition it will cause the architect much extra work.

At the end of this stage, the architect should advise the client that any subsequent changes of mind will be costly in terms of time and money. The scheme now should be regarded as fixed.

E   Technical design

As soon as the architect obtains the client's approval to the scheme design, every part of the scheme must be developed in great detail and in relation to the cost plan. This is the first part of what is commonly called 'working drawings'. If consultants are appointed, they will be involved in similar detailed design work. The client will be asked to approve many of the details, particularly as regards standards and quality. The cost of building the project must be kept constantly under review by the quantity surveyor and compared to the cost plan as each detail is finalised. The drawings produced during this stage will be highly technical, dimensioned, noted and coded. On the basis of these drawings, all further negotiations and approvals with statutory bodies will be finalised. The architect should advise the client that if any subsequent changes are required which are other than trivial, the building programme will be disrupted and the client will incur considerable extra cost. The client's idea of 'trivia' may well not accord with the architect's views.

Clients often fail to understand why a change of mind which, on the face of it, appears to reduce the overall cost of the building should result in additional costs. The architect should, therefore, clearly explain that if the client changes something, the architect may have to begin again the process of consultation with statutory bodies (including, on occasions, re-applying for planning and other permissions), consultants and any specialist sub-contractors. Drawings have to be redone, fresh calculations made and new cost estimates prepared. The architect's careful programming of office resources will be upset and there is the very real danger that mistakes will be made. It is the architect's duty to give clear advice in this regard if the client wants any changes. It would be wrong to simply carry out the client's instructions and present a large bill for additional services at the end.

F   Production information

During this usually fairly lengthy, stage, the architect and any consultants should be busy producing all the information which will be required for tendering and, additionally, the information that a contractor will require to proceed subsequently to erect the building. These sub-stages are now labelled F1 and F2 respectively. In addition to the drawings prepared during the last stage, details and schedules will be produced together with a specification of all the materials and items of work required. Applications in connection with the Building Regulations and any other necessary statutory approvals should be finalised during this stage.

G   Tender documentation

If the system of procurement warrants it (see Chapter 8, section 8.3), bills of quantities should be prepared by the quantity surveyor from information supplied by the architect and other consultants. The architect must be ready to supply any additional information which the quantity surveyor requires. Unless the project is such that the contrary is suggested, the architect should know the building in detail at this stage. The documents must be assembled in a suitable form to allow the prospective contractors to tender. All relevant information should be included so that the contractors can include for every aspect of the work.

It is usual for the architect or quantity surveyor at this stage to prepare a final cost estimate to ensure as far as possible that the client will not receive an unpleasant surprise when tenders are returned.

The CDM co-ordinator will be notifying the Health and Safety Executive and the architect must pass on copies of the final production information.

H   Tender action

Prior to this stage, the architect should have advised the client on the most appropriate way of obtaining a price for the work. It may be by means of negotiation or tendering. During this stage, everything needing to be done before prices are obtained should be organised and, if tendering is decided upon, tendering information should be sent out to all the contractors on a list which the client has previously approved. A prudent architect will have requested references from every contractor on the list and at the same time ascertained by discrete enquiry some idea of their financial stability. This is essential.[7] In some cases, a formal pre-qualification process will be carried out in order to produce a shortlist of the most appropriate contractors. In the case of public sector tendering, the relevant EU procurement legislation must be satisfied.

In due course, the architect, together with the quantity surveyor, will assess all tenders received and advise the client accordingly. If the lowest tender is too high to suit the client's pocket, the architect may be involved in revising the project. Unless it is the architect's fault that the project is too expensive, an additional fee is appropriate for this work.

J Mobilisation

During this stage, the architect should give advice to the client with regard to contractual matters, insurances and the like and should be ready to answer any questions. Discussions will have taken place concerning the appropriate form of contract, including any necessary amendments, before tender stage and the contract documents prepared for signature. All the information to enable construction to commence on the appointed date must be assembled and it is usual for a number of meetings to be held with consultants, specialist sub-contractors, the contractor and possibly representatives from statutory authorities.

K Construction to practical completion

During the course of work on site, the architect will carry out his or her duties under the contract and make regular visits to site to inspect the general progress and quality of workmanship and materials. It may be necessary to supply further production information from time to time or as set out in an information release schedule. The client should be kept up to date on the progress of the work and supplied with financial reports at regular intervals, depending upon the client's requirements and the size and complexity of the project. The client should be given any additional advice required concerning the project.

L After practical completion

When work is completed, the architect must ensure that all defects are made good and that loose ends are tied up and generally make sure that the financial aspects are settled accurately, with the help of other consultants as appropriate. The client should be supplied with some general notes on maintenance together with a set of drawings showing the building and the main lines of drainage and the services installations which will be required for the Health and Safety file.

6.2.2 Other services

Sites

The architect can advise on site suitability and negotiate on the client's behalf. He or she can prepare survey drawings and undertake site investigations, in collaboration with the appropriate consultant.

Buildings

The architect can produce survey drawings of buildings and prepare schedules of conditions. Depending upon the skills within the office, it may be possible to carry out structural surveys and investigate defects and failures. The preparation of specifications in connections with repairs can be undertaken and the inspection of work in progress carried out. Advice may also be offered on many other building problems, such as accessibility audit, energy conservation, fire protection, change of use and economic costs in use. For completed buildings, architects can provide as-built drawings, maintenance and operational manuals.

Development

The architect should be an expert in the production of special plans for many purposes in connection with building development. Elaborate models and perspectives are available from some offices; other specialist services which may be available include montages, detailed plans and specifications for roads and sewers, demolition and environmental studies and conveyancing plans.

Town planning appeals and advice

Some architects specialise in town planning matters and have considerable experience in the field. Although some will concentrate on planning advice, there are many architects who develop the expertise alongside architectural practice. They can be invaluable where difficult planning questions have to be resolved and where complicated negotiations with planning authorities are involved.

Design

The architect should be able to offer a wide variety of services under this general head. Among them are interior design, the design and selection of furnishings and decoration, exhibition design, shop-fitting and advice on the commissioning or selection of works of art. The architect may be able to offer specialist services in landscape design, acoustic investigations, development and testing of systems of building, including testing of prototypes or models.

Financial

Depending on the disciplines within the architect's office and the existence of appropriate professional indemnity insurance, it may be possible to offer complete cost planning of building projects, advice on cash flow requirements, life cycle cost analyses, value management and engineering, valuation of buildings, preparation of schedules of rates or quantities, estimates and negotiations in connection with fire damage and grant negotiations. Otherwise these matters are best left to a quantity surveyor with the relevant expertise.

Negotiations

It is common for architects to offer services in connection with planning appeals and special negotiations, building regulation relaxations, submissions to bodies such as English Heritage and submissions to landlords, etc.

Legal

The architect should be able to offer a substantial knowledge of the law as it relates to construction and provide services in connection with easements, party wall negotiations and rights. With appropriate experience and training, it should be possible to give expert evidence in proceedings and advise during conferences with solicitors and counsel. Although in theory all architects can act as adjudicators or arbitrators in appropriate cases, in practice only those architects who have had proper training and experience should do so (see Chapter 3, section 3.10). Some architects offer a service representing clients in adjudication proceedings.

Contractor's claims

Dealing with claims under the building contract is becoming more specialised. Most architects' fee structures recognise that determining applications for loss and/or expense and making a fair and reasonable estimate of an extension of the contract period is something which does not automatically arise under every contract. When claims do arise, they demand particular skill in resolution, particularly where large sums of money are involved and rough calculations and errors are not easily tolerated. Every architect involved in the administration of building contracts should be able to offer a reasonable degree of skill in this area.

Management

Management services include entire project management of building works, provision of constant site inspection, co-ordination of separate trade contracts, co-ordination and supervision of direct labour contracts and services to either party in connection with design-and-build contracts. 'As-built' drawings can be prepared, together with detailed maintenance manuals and maintenance programmes.

Historic buildings

Some architects can offer services in connection with historic buildings and conservation areas, embracing research, inspections, detailed reports, specifications and applications for planning approvals.

Consultants

If architects have appropriately qualified personnel within their practices and have the requisite professional indemnity cover, they will be able to offer services normally provided by the appropriate consultant. They can offer these services either on projects for which they are the project architects or project managers or on projects for which another architect has been engaged (with the agreement of that architect). An architect may also be engaged as an independent consultant on a regular basis if required.

CDM co-ordinator

Many, although not all, architects have undertaken training to enable them to offer services as CDM co-ordinator in connection with buildings under the Construction (Design and Management) Regulations 2007. The RIBA has produced special terms of engagement for the purpose. It is not uncommon for an architect to combine both architectural and CDM co-ordinator services on the same project.

Summary

The services which the architect may offer as part of the normal or additional services cover every facet of construction work and the care and maintenance of buildings in use. It should be noted that, although all architects will be willing to offer some of the services outlined above, architects, like other professionals, tend to develop their own specialisms. There will be serious legal implications for architects who hold themselves out as qualified to offer a competent service in something which they are not equipped to do. In addition, of course, it must not be forgotten that architects should not offer services for which they do not have appropriate professional indemnity cover (see Chapter 17, section 17.5).

6.3   Fee negotiation or tendering

At one time, architects used to have a mandatory fee scale. The RIBA then published recommended fee scales. That has also vanished, and the RIBA then published indicative percentage fee scales for architects' services in the form of percentage fee graphs for new works and works to existing buildings, and a classification of building types based on the ones which used to form part of the RIBA Architect's Appointment (the 'Blue Book'). Fee scales and graphs were subsequently published in the form of statistical records of fees actually charged by a cross-section of architects for various types of work. Percentage fee scales are no longer published, but concise written advice is available about the way in which practices calculate fees and how they structure payment options.[8] Architects are now encouraged to charge on a time charge, resource-based or value-added basis – whether they will persuade clients to pay is another matter. Negotiations can take place with a prospective client to arrive at a mutually agreeable figure. There is a point, however, below which the architect cannot give a satisfactory standard of service. To negotiate a fee below that point is commercial suicide, to say nothing of being unprofessional. In practice, it seems that architects commonly do some initial work for less than the scale fee and sometimes for nothing at all if it appears likely that a reasonable commission may result.

The numbers of architects prepared to do so-called 'speculative work' in this way shows no signs of decreasing and some unscrupulous clients use, as an excuse for not paying, the suggestion that they thought the architect was working speculatively. Although everyone in business must face commercial reality, architects do the profession no favours by working for very low fees or for nothing at all.

The fees negotiated will depend upon many factors, of which the following are the most significant.

- The amount of work the architect has in progress.
- The size of the office related to turnover and hence the overhead costs.
- Whether the project is 'one off' or simply the first of many similar jobs which the architect can expect to receive from the same client.
- Whether the project is particularly interesting to a particular architect, perhaps because the architects wishes to gain experience in that building type.

Most architects use the published fee scales or at least employ them as a basis. A small, one-person office may charge less, but offer fewer resources than a larger firm which may charge more to cover its larger overheads. The smaller firm may argue that it is giving a more personalised service. It is now possible for a client to obtain competitive quotations from a number of architects for the same project. However, to avoid a breach of the Code of Conduct, it is necessary to ensure that the terms are absolutely clear and on the same basis for each of the architects involved in giving a quotation.

The basis of fees is usually:

- a percentage of the construction cost of building; or
- a time charge; or
- a lump sum.

6.3.1 Percentage charges

Architects will normally charge a percentage of the actual construction cost if they are providing the normal full architectural service. The RIBA used to publish (but no longer does) indicative percentage fee scales which divided buildings into classes and provided graphs showing indicative percentages for each class over a range of construction costs. Class 1 buildings were the simplest, class 5 were the most complex. The recommendations were detailed. Among points worthy of note are the following.[9]

- Consultants' work is included in the total cost even if carried out under a separate contract.
- Specialist sub-contractors' design fees are excluded.
- If the architect carries out work on parts of the building which are eventually omitted, the total construction cost will be estimated for fee purposes.
- Built-in furniture and equipment are included in the total cost.
- If clients carry out any work direct or supply materials at their own cost, the architect should estimate the value and include it in the total construction cost for fee purposes.
- Where there is a substantial element of repetition, the fees may be reduced.

The RIBA now publishes *A Client's Guide to Engaging an Architect*[10] which has a chart showing typical building types divided into 'low', 'mid-range' and 'high' according to the amount of resources which an architect has to devote and a graph showing a range of average fees on a percentage basis based on the survey of architects' fees carried out by the Fees Bureau.[11]

It is normal for fees to be paid in instalments based upon the estimated final cost. The final fee account will be adjusted to take account of the actual final cost of the building. Payment should be agreed as being made at the end of each stage or, better, monthly. It is essential that the basis of charging is settled before the architect undertakes any work.

During the construction stage, the architect will usually charge based on the amount of monthly certificates. This is sensible. Occasionally, the architect will base the fee instalment on the final cost estimates. Since such estimates are often pessimistic, in the sense of forecasting a large expenditure, the architect may receive a severe shock at final account stage when it becomes clear that the final construction cost is significantly lower than the forecast – a nice surprise for the client perhaps, less pleasing for the architect who may be faced with repaying fees.

6.3.2 Time charges

Time charges are based on an hourly rate. The RIBA Appointment documents 1999 (April 2004 update) and the 2010 versions do not set out recommendations.

The RIBA's *A Client's Guide to Engaging an Architect* is helpful about the percentage fee rates, but it gives no guidance about the appropriate hourly rate for any given circumstance or professional. Perhaps more helpful is the annual survey of architects' fees which breaks down hourly rates by region, by office size and by status of architect.[12] Of course, these are actual fees paid and not merely aspirations.

The actual amount charged per hour varies from practice to practice and from one part of the country to another. Charges are usually higher in the London area than in the regions and larger practices usually charge more than small practices. In the latter case, the large practice will probably argue that the increased cost arises from higher overheads needed to maintain a better standard of service.

It is very difficult to arrive at a figure for an hourly rate, because the rates from practice to practice are not generally known. Thus, an architect fixing an hourly rate for his or her technical staff may wonder where to start. A commonly used guide used to be the $1 \times 1 \times 1$ formula where the rate was made up of equal parts of salary, overheads and profit. In practice, the architect worked out the amount paid to a staff member per hour, then multiplied by three to find the hourly rate to be charged to the client. It was a very rough guide and current evidence suggests that the profit element is now very much below a third of the total. Architects should go through the exercise, perhaps using 0.3 for the profit (i.e. $1 \times 1 \times 0.3$), to see if they are charging anything like this figure. Another approach is to calculate the rate based on the cost plus 50% for overheads and a small percentage (up to 5%) for profit. It is our experience that most architects and surveyors, particularly outside London, charge very low hourly rates when compared with other professions.

Work for which an hourly rate would be appropriate could include:

- constant site inspection
- partial services
- additional services
- any instance where the client has agreed with the architect that a time charge should be made
- additional work beyond the architect's control such as:
    — revisions to documents due to changes in the law
    — changes in client's instructions
    — delay or disruption in building operations caused by others.
- dealing with contractor's claims for extension of time and loss and/or expense.

Many clients are wary of paying on an hourly basis. They tend to liken it to a blank cheque. It is, however, perfectly possible for an architect to state an hourly rate and to give a rough estimate of the length of time needed. Another variant is the hourly rate plus ceiling figure beyond which the architect must not go without further authorisation. Rendering monthly accounts in such instances assists both architect and client to keep control of the situation. In certain instances, there is no option but to state an hourly rate. It need not be more expensive than a lump sum (see below) because the architect is certain to make a reasonable profit from an hourly rate, whereas he must add something for contingencies when arriving at a lump sum.

6.3.3 Lump sum charges

There is nothing to prevent the architect from quoting a lump sum fee to cover all the work expected to be carried out. Indeed, clients often require that approach. However, this should only be done if:

- the extent of the work required is absolutely clear, and
- the time-scale of the service is known.

It would be unusual, for example, if an architect were to quote a lump sum fee for carrying out negotiations with a local authority in regard to development work. On the other hand, a small project requiring full services over a comparatively short time-scale is the sort of job architects can cost in their offices and for which they can give a firm quotation.

There are two kinds of lump sum fee. The first is simply a lump sum. The second is a lump sum which is tied to something, often the construction cost. It is calculated by reference to a percentage and the result is a lump sum which is subject to change if the construction cost changes from the budget by more than a stated amount. Most lump sum quotations appear to fall into the first category (but see section 6.5.1).

There is a danger for clients if they require lump sum quotations and the architect has a duty to explain the implications fully. Clients must know precisely what they want, they must not cause delay nor change their minds. If architects are involved in additional work clearly not included in the original sum, clients can be required to pay additional fees. Where architects are requested to quote on a lump sum basis, they must take care to specify precisely the services which are included, particularly whether or not they are inclusive of VAT, expenses, etc.

An architect may not take part in a Dutch auction so as to effectively undercut another architect's fee quotation. That would infringe the RIBA Code of Professional Conduct.

6.3.4   Other fees

It is perfectly possible for architect and client to decide upon an entirely different system of calculating fees. One such system is payment on results. This is often, less bluntly, referred to as a 'value-added' fee. Essentially, the architect is paid according to the money generated for the client. This is often in terms of increasing the value of a plot of land, perhaps via a clever planning application or a unique approach to developing a site. Sometimes it is agreed that the architect is paid fees based on a percentage of any such increase. There is no limit on the ways in which fees can be calculated to suit special circumstances.

6.3.5   Project teams

The practice of project team fee negotiations is very popular among many clients. These clients commission buildings which, by their nature, require a considerable input from consultants in several disciplines. Traditionally, such clients would be left to negotiate terms and fees with each consultant individually as recommended by the architect, and clients fear that this is an expensive process. Moreover, experience has shown that different consultants do not always fit together harmoniously. Indeed, many disputes arise out of conflicts between the approaches of differing disciplines. The idea of project team fee negotiations is that an integrated approach is presented to the client consisting of all the consultants under the co-ordination of a lead consultant (who may not be an architect). Fees and the individual responsibilities are expressly set out, including specific professional indemnity responsibilities.

Where the lead consultant effectively sub-contracts to all the other consultants, as is usual when this system is adopted, there can be considerable risk attached, financial and otherwise. The lead consultant will be liable to the client for all the services carried out by all consultants. The effect of this is that if there are any defects in the services, the client's redress is directly against the lead consultant. It is then a matter for the lead consultant to seek redress from the sub-consultant or sub-consultants concerned. If the method of dispute resolution is adjudication or arbitration, there may be difficulties because, unless all parties agree, it will not be possible to resolve a dispute between client and lead consultant at the same time as a related dispute between lead consultant and sub-consultant. Separate adjudications or arbitrations may result in differing decisions. In order to assist the lead consultant to pass on the liability to sub-consultants, the sub-consultancy agreements must be carefully worded to step down liabilities. Put simply, each sub-consultant must be liable to the lead consultant for services for which the lead consultant may be liable to the client.

Further problems may arise if the lead consultant has difficulty getting paid by the client. The lead consultant's invoice will contain fees charged by the sub-consultants. Although it is usual for the payment period for sub-consultant invoices to be longer than the lead consultant's invoice, that is little help if the client simply refuses to pay. The sub-consultant's redress is directly against the lead consultant who must, in turn, seek payment from the client. The lead consultant cannot, even if the sub-consultants agreed, insert a pay when paid clause in the sub-consultancy agreement, because such a clause is unlawful under section 113 of the Housing Grants, Construction and Regeneration Act 1996. In practice, this can lead to serious problems and the lead consultant becomes reliant on the goodwill and patience of the sub-consultants. Moreover, taking action to recover fees from the client is entirely at the lead consultant's cost. These are all cogent reasons why architects acting as lead consultants should ensure that the team is structured so that each member is responsible under a separate contract directly to the client and also responsible for rendering and recovering their own fees.

6.3.6 Work to existing buildings

If the work the client wants done involves an existing building, a larger fee is chargeable. This is because the architect will be involved in much more work due to the constraints of the original structure, planning, services, etc. If, in addition, the building is of architectural or historic interest, if it is a 'listed building' or in a conservation area, the client may also be paying for the architect's special skills in dealing with buildings of that type. Even if the building is a new construction to be joined onto an existing building, the client will be charged a higher fee for that portion of the work where new and old connect. It is impossible to give other than such rather general indications, because each old building has its own special identity which requires individual consideration. For example, a very ancient town wall of considerable length might attract a lower percentage fee than a complicated Victorian building. It is very risky, from the architect's point of view, to agree to take on this kind of work for a lump sum.

6.3.7 Termination

Whether the architect can recover fees, and how much, in the event of termination will depend on whether formal conditions of engagement have been entered into and the circumstances of the termination. SFA/99 provides that either architect or client can determine on reasonable notice. It also provides that the architect is then entitled to fees for all work completed up to the time of termination. The exact method of calculating the fees will depend upon the basis originally agreed. The architect is also entitled to charge all expenses arising from termination if due to the client's termination (provided that it was not a result of the architect's material breach) or breach of contract. An architect in the middle of producing working drawings, specifications and schedules for the contractor cannot be expected to move staff onto other work immediately.

If there is no formal agreement between the architect and the client, there will be no provision for termination and no provision for subsequent recovery of fees. In this situation the parties will find themselves locked into litigation unless they suddenly display a streak of reasonableness which, had it been present in the first place, may have resulted in an agreement on clear terms (see section 6.4 below). Anecdotal evidence suggests that many architects do find themselves in awkward situations as a result of a failure to enter into a proper formal agreement with clients. Architects not only are the authors of their own misfortunes in this situation, they are also in breach of both the RIBA and ARB codes of professional conduct.

Ignoring what may be in the terms of engagement, it is worth remembering that an architect's engagement is a contract and that it may be brought to an end in the same way as any other contract (see Chapter 13, section 13.1) unless the contract expressly stipulates otherwise. The RIBA Appointment documents 2010 include provisions which expressly change the consequences of such termination (see section 6.5).

6.3.8 Expenses

There is no automatic right to expenses. A client is entitled to assume that expenses are included in any fee quoted unless they are specifically stated to be extra. It is also advisable to state precisely what the architect considers to be reimbursable expenses. Expenses and disbursements are often confused and 'disbursements' is often wrongly used to mean expenses. The terms must be clearly differentiated. Disbursements are sums which are expended on behalf of a client to other parties and they are usually recovered as a net amount. Statutory fees and direct payments to consultants fall into this category. Common expenses items include:

- postage, telephone, fax, email and other means of communication or delivery
- hotel and travelling expenses (mileage rates should be stated in the agreement)
- charges for travelling time if the time spent on travelling is exceptional (this should also be agreed in advance)
- printing, reproduction and purchase of all drawings, documents, photographs and models, etc. which the architect must or the client requests him or her to produce in order to carry out the work
- payment for specialist advice which the client has authorised, for example legal advice
- special hire charges for equipment if authorised.

6.4   Terms of appointment

6.4.1   The basic contract

The relationship between an architect and his or her client is contractual. Depending upon circumstances, there may also be a tortious liability. Principally, however, the relationship will depend upon the terms of the agreement made between the parties.

There are two types of contract:

- a simple contract (under hand)
- a specialty contract (a deed).

There are important differences. In the case of a simple contract, there must be consideration present (each party must contribute something to the bargain) or the contract will not be valid. In addition, an action for breach of that contract can be defended by reference to the Limitation Act 1980 if brought by one party against the other more than 6 years after the date of the breach. A specialty contract does not require consideration to make it valid and the limitation period is 12 years from the date of the breach. There are other differences, but the two noted above are the most important so far as architects are concerned. Effectively, the result is that an architect who enters into an agreement as a deed with the client doubles the length of exposure to actions under the contract or for breach of its terms.

A contract is a binding agreement between two or more persons which creates mutual rights and duties and which is enforceable at law. There must be an intention to create legal relations. In the case of agreements between business people, such an intention is implied. In the case of friends or relatives, the intention normally has to be demonstrated. For a valid contract there must be:

- an offer by one party
- unqualified acceptance by the other party
- consideration (except in the case of a specialty contract)
- capacity to contract. Certain persons, e.g. drunkards, the insane and minors, have very limited capacity to contract
- intention to create a legal relationship
- genuine consent, i.e. there must be no duress
- a legal objective
- an objective which is possible.

Although it is traditional to analyse a contract in terms of an offer and an acceptance, in practice the situation may not be so clear cut. Although it may be easy to establish that the parties are in agreement about all the essential terms of the contract, the agreement may not fall simply into an offer and an acceptance, but rather a complex series of meetings, discussions and correspondence which taken together show agreement.

A simple contract can be entered into in writing or orally. The problem with an oral contract, of course, is uncertainty about its terms. Even if there are witnesses, they may later disagree about what they heard. Many architects are engaged purely on the basis of an oral agreement and, indeed, some clients may appear offended if asked to put the commission in writing, as though it was some reflection upon their honour. In truth, the purpose of recording the terms in writing is to protect both parties, not only against sharp practice but more commonly against imperfect memory or plain misunderstanding. At the very least, the architect should confirm in writing the terms of the appointment at the earliest opportunity.

It used to be the case that a specialty contract had to be made under seal.[13] This was usually a round piece of red paper on which a seal was embossed or it could be a rubber stamp or, indeed, anything so long as the parties clearly intended the document to be sealed.[14] However, the Law of Property (Miscellaneous Provisions) Act 1989, in the case of individuals, and the Companies Act 1989, in the case of companies, removed the necessity to use a seal. Indeed, the use of a seal alone will not create a deed.

In the case of a company all that is required is for the document to state on its face that it is a deed and for it to be signed by two directors or one director and the company secretary. In the case of an individual, the document must state on its face that it is a deed and it should be signed by the person making the deed in the presence of a witness who must attest the signature. Alternatively but rarely, an individual may authorise another to sign on his or her behalf in which case there must be two witnesses who must attest the signature. The stamping of such documents is not generally required unless part of a conveyance.

An important principle used to be privity of contract. That was the rule that only parties to a contract could bind or be bound by that contract. However, it was thought that such a rule could result in unfairness in certain circumstances and the Contracts (Rights of Third Parties) Act 1999 was passed to allow persons who are not parties to a contract to enforce rights under the contract. A fuller explanation of these principles is to be found in section 6.5. It is to be noted that most contracts now exclude the effects of the Act as a matter of course, thus restoring privity of contract to all intents and purposes. All the RIBA terms of appointment and most building contracts contain such exclusions.

6.4.2   The effect of the Construction Act

All terms of engagement entered into by architects after 1 May 1998 are subject to the Housing Grants, Construction and Regeneration Act 1996 (commonly referred to as the Construction Act. In Northern Ireland, legislation to the same effect is the Construction Contracts (Northern Ireland) Order 1997). Part II of the Act deals with construction contracts and every architect should have a copy. Part II is only a few pages long. Included in the definition of such contracts is an agreement 'to do architectural, design, or surveying work, or … to provide advice on building, engineering, interior or exterior decoration or on the laying out of landscape in relation to construction operations'.

'Construction operations' are defined in some detail. Broadly, they are the construction, alteration, repair, etc. of buildings, structures, roadworks, docks and harbours, power lines, sewers and the like. They also include installation of fittings such as heating, electrical or air conditioning, external or internal cleaning carried out as part of construction and site clearance, tunnelling, foundations and other preparatory work and painting or decorating. Excluded are such things as drilling for natural gas, mineral extraction, manufacture of certain components, construction or demolition of plant where the primary activity is nuclear processing, effluent treatment or chemicals, construction of artistic works, sign writing and other peripheral installations. More importantly, it does not bite where one of the parties intends to take up residence in the subject of the construction operations.

The provisions of the Act apply only to 'agreements in writing' and there are detailed provisions as to what that entails. Apart from the obvious, it also covers situations where there is no signature, where the parties agree orally by reference to terms which are in writing and where agreement is alleged in arbitration by one party and not denied by the other.

The Act requires that all construction contracts must include certain provisions.

- *Adjudication.* Either party must have the right to refer disputes to adjudication with the object of obtaining a decision within 28 days of referral. A party may give notice of intention to refer at any time and the referral must take place within 7 days. The 28-day deadline may be extended by up to 14 days if the referring party wishes or indefinitely if both parties agree. The adjudicator may take the initiative in ascertaining the facts and the law. In other words, the adjudicator does not have to wait until one party raises a point, but can ask for evidence. The adjudicator's decision is binding until the dispute is decided by litigation, arbitration or by agreement. The parties may agree to accept the adjudicator's decision as final. The adjudicator is not to be liable for acts or omissions unless there has been bad faith.

- *Stage payments.* A party is entitled to stage payments unless the duration of the project is less than 45 days. The parties are free to agree the intervals between payments and the amounts of such payments.
- *Date for payment.* Every contract must contain the means of working out the amount due and the date on which it is due and must provide a final date for payment.
- *Set-off.* Payment may not be withheld, nor money set off unless notice has been given particularising the amount to be withheld and the grounds. The notice must be given no later than the agreed period before final payment.
- *Suspension of performance of obligations,* If the amount properly due has not been paid by the final date for payment and no effective notice withholding payment has been given, a party has the right, after giving 7 days written notice, to suspend performance of obligations under the contract until payment has been made.
- *Pay when paid.* Except in cases of insolvency, a clause making payment dependent upon receipt of money from a third party is void. This is intended to outlaw the so-called 'pay when paid' clause but it may not be sufficient to do so. It does not take effect if the third party is insolvent.

To the extent that a construction contract does not include these provisions, the Scheme for Construction Contracts (England and Wales) 1998 comes into effect just as if the clauses contained in the Scheme were written into the contract. Most standard form construction contracts and all the RIBA terms of engagement comply with the Act and, therefore, the Scheme is not relevant where such terms are used. Where architects contract on the basis of an exchange of correspondence or on terms drawn up by the client's legal advisors, it is likely that some, if not all, of the Scheme will be effective. The industry and professional response to the Act has been generally very positive.

At the time of writing, a review of the Act has taken place. The Local Democracy, Economic Development and Construction Act 2009[15] has received Royal Assent. Part 8 of this Act amends the Housing Grants, Construction and Regeneration Act 1996. No date for commencement of Part 8 of the 2009 Act has been set although it is thought that it may be late in 2010. The new Act will apply only to contracts entered into after the commencement date. Part 8 effectively removes the requirement for construction contracts covered by the 1996 Act to be in writing, amendments are made to the adjudication provisions and substantial changes to the way payments due are determined. The notice provisions relating to payments due and withholding of payments are completely revised and certain other minor changes have been made.

6.5   Standard forms of agreement

Some bodies insist that the architect contracts on the basis of their own particular terms and conditions. In such cases, the architect should take the greatest possible care, including, if necessary, obtaining expert advice. Wherever possible, the architect is well advised to contract on the basis of standard terms. The best known terms are the RIBA Forms of Agreement for the Appointment of an Architect. Although it is possible to incorporate these terms by stating in a letter to a client that they are so incorporated, such a practice can lead to confusion because some versions of the terms are intended to be applied on the basis of a Memorandum of Agreement and schedules which provide for the inclusion or omission of certain matters as appropriate. Simply to write a letter to the client stating that 'the RIBA terms apply' seems to be actively encouraging confusion. Another difficulty which can arise is that the document is drafted with a traditional contractual arrangement in mind. If some other arrangement, such as employment by a contractor or in connection with a management contract or as a project manager, is intended, some amendment of the terms will be necessary.

The Architect's Appointment[16] was introduced by the RIBA in 1982. It was the successor to the Conditions of Engagement and followed the report of the Monopolies and Mergers Commission on architects' and surveyors' services and remuneration. There was also a small works edition. In 1992, the RIBA introduced SFA/92. Significantly, this allowed for changes to the services when something other than the traditional architect's role was required. Therefore, it had supplements for use with historic buildings and for community architecture work. There was also a special edition for use with design and build where the architect was employed by the employer or by the contractor. A version designed for use with projects for which IFC 84 might be used was issued in 1995 (CE/95) and then a version for use for small works (SW/96). These documents had a mixed reception, many architects continuing to use the Architect's Appointment. The impetus for a new set of terms of engagement was a general dissatisfaction with the existing forms, the Latham Report,[17] calling for a suite of interlocking contracts and the Construction Act which necessitated certain revisions to the existing forms in any event. The forms were revised in 1999 and updated in April 2004. The forms are as follows.

- *Standard Form of Agreement for the Appointment of an Architect (SFA/99).* For general use for the appointment of an architect.
- *Conditions of Engagement for the Appointment of an Architect (CE/99).* For use in straightforward situations where it is considered preferable to the more formal agreement (SFA/99) or the Small Works form (SW/99).
- *Employer's Requirements Amendment DB1/99 for use on a Design-and-Build Contract.* For use with SFA/99 or CE/99 if the architect is acting for the employer under a design-and-build contract.

- *Contractor's Proposals Amendment DB2/99 for use where the Client is a Contractor.* For use with SFA/99 or CE/99 if the architect is acting for the contractor under a design-and-build contract.
- *Small Works (SW/99).* For use where the professional services are relatively straightforward, construction works are of no more than about £150,000, where MW is used on the basis of a simple contract (i.e. not a deed) and the applicable law is the law of England and Wales or Northern Ireland.
- *Sub-Consultant Form of Appointment (SC/99).* For use where an architect appoints a sub-consultant to perform part of the architect's services.
- *Project Manager for a Construction Project: Form of Appointment (PM/99).* For use where the architect is appointed as project manager.

In August 2007, the RIBA revised all the forms of agreement and made them available online. The new forms were not greeted with unanimous approval and the forms were revised again in 2010 and published in the following versions.

- *The Standard Agreement 2010 (S-10-A).* For use on a wide range of projects using most procurement methods, for business or commercial purposes or a large-scale or large-value residence, where detailed terms are necessary.
- *The Concise Agreement 2010 (C-10-A).* For use for business or commercial projects, using intermediate or minor building contracts and where concise terms are appropriate.
- *The Domestic Project Agreement 2010 (D-10-A).* For use for domestic projects, using intermediate or minor building contracts and concise terms are appropriate.
- *The Sub-Consultant Agreement 2010 (SC-10).* For use where one consultant appoints another to perform part of the services.

SFA/99 is in common use among architects and many architects continued to use this form despite the publication of the 2007 agreements, because of perceived shortcomings in the new forms. That situation is likely to change with the introduction of the 2010 suite of agreements. In view of its continued use, the SFA/99 will be considered in detail below, followed by a consideration of the Standard Agreement 2010 (S-10-A).

6.5.1 Standard Form of Agreement for the Appointment of an Architect (SFA/99)

SFA/99 is in the following parts.

Memorandum of agreement

It is important that *article 1* is amended if appropriate to include any other letter or document on which the agreement is based.

Space is left for the insertion of a named representative of the client. This is important where the client is a corporate body.

Article 7 gives the opportunity for the parties to agree a time limit for the bringing of legal actions. From the architect's point of view, the shorter the period the better and although legislation sets out specific periods (6 or 12 years for simple contracts or deeds respectively), a lesser (or longer period) inserted here will be upheld in the courts.[18]

Article 8 allows a limit of liability to be inserted and a provision similar to this one has been held to satisfy the requirements of reasonableness in the Unfair Contract Terms Act 1977.[19] This provision assumes that the limit of liability is the same as the level of professional indemnity insurance cover. Although it is obvious that it should not exceed the professional indemnity insurance level of cover, there is no reason why it should not be less. Indemnity insurance is fixed at a figure to cover any project which the architect might undertake. It could be many times greater than a reasonable limit of liability in any particular instance.

Although the parties have the right to adjudication, they are also given the option of choosing either arbitration or litigation. Previously, arbitration was the designated method of dispute resolution. Arbitration offers distinct advantages over litigation. The arbitrator can be an architect agreed upon by the parties, the proceedings are private and they are usually considerably faster than legal proceedings. Arbitration also has an element of finality which is absent from litigation. It is rare for an appeal from an arbitrator's award to be entertained by the courts. The reforms in legal procedure (the Woolf reforms) were aimed at streamlining the legal process. Although they appear to have had some success, there is still room for improvement.

Schedule 1

This is for the insertion of a description of the project. It is really the client's brief and any change may result in varied services and fees. Therefore, it is essential that it is completed.

Schedule 2

This is for the architect to set out the services to be provided. There are two options. The services can be set out in detail by the architect or the square box can be ticked and reference made to an attached services supplement. The headnote advises that architects who are setting out their services in detail should identify any services which are additional to normal services. However, 'normal' services are not defined and as clients' views may be substantially different from architects' views on the subject, we suggest that where the architect opts to set out full details of the services, the full intended services, including what the architect believes is 'normal', should be written in.

The supplement, pages A–D, is fairly straightforward, but there are pitfalls for the unwary and care is required in ticking and crossing out. Although reference is simply made throughout to ticking services required, it is prudent to firmly cross out those services which are not being offered.

Page A

The top half of this page contains boxes to be ticked if the architect is to perform the particular tasks during work stages and the work stages are to be inserted. Thus, if the architect was to be designer for work stages A–F and lead consultant for work stages A–L, the second and fourth boxes would be ticked and the appropriate work stages inserted opposite. For clarity, it is preferable to write 'A, B, C, D, E and F' rather than 'A to F'. Page B identifies such things as 'design leader'. The first box is to be ticked only if other services have been identified on page D. However, it should be noted that if other services are identified and included in the 'Services', the fee will be deemed to cover them.

There is reference to 'Work Stages' in the lower half of the page, but it would have assisted clarity to have referred to 'RIBA Work Stages'. That would have provided a means of amplifying the necessarily brief descriptions. A client may also argue that the words 'The purpose of each Work Stage is to achieve the outputs described …' impose on the architect a fitness for purpose liability. It is suggested that this phrase should be deleted.

Page B

This page is headed 'Architect's Management Services'. The idea is that if the architect has ticked design leader, lead consultant or lead consultant and contract administrator, he or she will carry out the services listed under those heads on page B. It has to be said that the services descriptions could be clearer and architects intending to use this agreement regularly might benefit from rewriting these services.

Page C

This page is headed 'Architect's Design Services'. The services on this page form part of the architect's services if identified on page A (presumably identified by work stage letter: A, B, C, etc). Therefore, where work stages are identified on page A, the architect should go through the relevant work stage on this page and firmly delete any services not to be undertaken.

Page D

Page D is a list of 'Other Services' which are to be ticked if included in the fee. If not ticked, they are not included in the fee, but the client may instruct the architect to carry out some of these services during the progress of the project. At the bottom of the page, some other services, headed 'Special Services', are to be instructed as necessary during the commission. Presumably, the purpose of listing them is to make clear that they are not included in the fee.

It should be noted that, if DB1/99 or DB2/99 is to be used, there is a new services supplement to be inserted.

Schedule 3

Here the fees and expenses payable by the client are to be set out. Many architects inadequately complete this schedule and it is extremely important to complete it thoroughly and in its entirety, listing the applicable clauses. Failure to properly complete this schedule can result in fees being paid late or not at all. For example, we know of an architect who, under 'Instalments', entered the percentage division of total fee according to work stages. The result was that this architect was not entitled to be paid any of the fee for a particular work stage until that work stage was entirely completed. The irony is that if the section had been left blank, the note says that fees and expenses would be payable in accordance with clause 5.10, i.e. every month.

Schedule 4

This is the place to set down the names and addresses of other persons appointed or to be appointed by the client in connection with the works and parts of the project to be designed by others.

Conditions of engagement

These consist of a set of defined terms and the clauses themselves. It is worth looking at the conditions of engagement in greater detail.

The definitions speak for themselves and they will be referred to as necessary in what follows, but it should be noted that the definition of 'Brief' inconsistently (compared to the services supplement) refers to 'RIBA' work stages. The 'CDM Regulations' are, of course, the 2007 version and not the 1994 version and 'Planning Supervisor' is no longer required, being replaced by the CDM Co-ordinator in the 2007 version of the Regulations.

Before moving on to the conditions, it is worth looking at the definition of construction cost on which the calculation of percentage fees will depend. 'Construction cost' is defined in three options, the first being 'the latest professionally prepared estimate …'. Therefore, unless the architect has, unusually, taken responsibility for preparing cost estimates, the quantity surveyor's last estimate is to be used. However, caution should be exercised, because quantity surveyors' estimates of out-turn costs during the construction stage will include allowances for all potential costs in order that the client is not asked to pay more than he expects at final account stage. This may result in the architect having to repay fees which have been charged on the basis of an inflated account. The second option is 'the lowest acceptable tender'. Architects must be careful with this definition. The lowest acceptable tender is not the same as the lowest tender. It has been known for an architect to try to charge a final fee on the basis of the lowest of the tenders received, after the professional relationship with the client has broken down on receipt of tenders judged by the client to be too high. This approach is doomed to failure.

The third option is the final cost of constructing the project. A list of what that final cost includes is listed in the definition. The definition states that the final cost 'includes' the items on the list, therefore, the items are not necessarily everything in the final cost. If that were the case, one would expect to see the word 'comprising' rather than 'including'. This particular option has been the subject of dispute from time to time. Therefore, we set out the included items below with our comments.

- *Any contingency or design reserve cost allowance.* This appears to refer to any contingency sum even though not expended. The logic of including such sums in the definition is questionable. They will not be included in the final certificate.
- *The cost as if new of any equipment and/or materials provided or to be provided by the Client to a contractor for installation during construction of the project.* This is to be included, because the percentage fee assumes that the construction cost is the cost of all work and materials. If the client was minded to engage in a contract in which the contractor carried out the work but the client provided all goods and materials, the architect's fee would not properly represent the services performed unless it was specifically increased to take the lower construction cost into account. It is easier in theory for the client to notify the architect of the cost as new of everything supplied. We say 'in theory', because it is sadly too common for clients to decline to provide the information, thus obliging the architect to base fees on an estimate. These costs will not be included in the final certificate but, where appropriate, they will have to be added to the certified sum to represent the 'ascertained final Construction Cost' referred to in clause 5.2.
- *Any direct works carried out by or on behalf of the Client.* This is to be included for exactly the same reason as the previous item. This item refers to work whereas the previous item referred to goods and materials.
- *Provision for contractor's profit and overheads.* In traditional building contracts, profit and overheads will be included in the total contract sum in various ways. However, the client may enter into a contract which does not expressly provide for these costs notwithstanding that they are an indisputable part of the construction cost and must be included.

The definition then sets out items which are to be excluded.

- *Value-added tax.* This is logical.
- *Fees.* This clearly refers to any fees which are paid out for any purpose whatsoever. Therefore, it covers statutory fees and fees paid to other consultants.
- *Any loss and/or expense payments paid to a contractor nor should it be adjusted for liquidated damages deducted by the Client.* This is an awkwardly drafted item. The second part should be in the first set of included items. This item means that sums which the architect certifies as being payable to the contractor in respect of loss and/or expense must not be included as part of the construction cost. A cogent argument, if one was required, in favour of the architect being able to recover additional fees for

dealing with loss and/or expense applications. However, any sums deducted by the client from sums due to the contractor in respect of liquidated damages must not be excluded from the construction cost. In other words, the construction cost is the cost as if no liquidated damages had been deducted.

- *The costs of resolution of any dispute.* Costs in relation to dispute resolution have a straightforward meaning. They refer to the amounts expended by the parties on legal representation, expert witnesses and the like. It may also refer to the costs of an arbitrator or adjudicator. It is not at all clear why anyone should imagine that there is a danger that they might form part of the construction cost. In any event, this item removes all doubt.
- *The Client's legal and in-house expenses.* This must refer to expenses other than those incurred in connection with dispute resolution which are dealt with in the previous item.

The meat of the contract begins at *clauses 1.4 and 1.5* which set out the requirements for notice and that, when calculating periods of time within which actions must be performed, public holidays are excluded. That means, of course, that ordinary weekends are included. All notices must be in writing. It should be noted that the deemed date of receipt of a communication is 'subject to proof to the contrary'. In practice, this means that although the clause deems that a special delivery or recorded delivery letter is deemed received on the second day after posting, it is open to either party to prove that it was received either later or earlier. The deeming provision takes effect only if there is no other proof.

Clause 1.6 places a duty on both the architect and the client to advise each other if they become aware that there is a need to vary the services, timetable, fees or, indeed, any part of the agreement or if there is incompatibility in or between the client's requirements, instructions, cost, timetable or approved design. Anything else likely to affect progress, quality or cost and any information or decisions from the client must be notified as soon as they become aware. An obligation that the client and the architect must work together in a spirit of mutual trust and co-operation is laudable, but quite out of place in a legal contract. How a party obtains redress if the other is in breach of this obligation is difficult to envisage.

Clause 1.7 requires both client and architect to comply with the CDM Regulations and notes that the Regulations prevail over SFA/99 if there is any conflict. This, of course, would be the position in any event.

By *clause 2.1* the architect is to exercise reasonable skill and care in conformity with the normal standards of the architect's profession. This term simply states the general law. In *Bolam* v.. *Friern Hospital Management Committee* (1957)[20] the judge defined the standard required of a professional person thus:

'But where you get a situation which involves the use of some special skill or competence, then the test whether there has been negligence or not is not the test of the man on top of the Clapham omnibus, because he has not got this special skill. A man need not posses the highest expert skill at the risk of being found negligent. It is well established law that it is sufficient if he exercised the ordinary skill of an ordinary competent man exercising that particular art.'

Clause 2.2 is very important. It sets out the architect's authority to act on behalf of the client. It gives the architect power of agency in respect of the matters set out or implied in the Architect's Appointment, but it must be read with *clause 2.3* which stipulates that the architect must keep the client informed of progress and anything which might affect timing, quality or cost. Although the express requirement for the architect to seek authority to proceed is now gone, it is implied that such authority must be sought if the architect finds it necessary to report anything. It is good practice for progress reports to be sent to the client at such intervals as seem appropriate to the type and size of project. Unless the client is familiar with the construction industry, the reports should be couched in straightforward terms so that the implications can be grasped immediately. The architect as agent has been discussed in section 6.2.

Clause 2.4 contains valuable protection for the architect. The architect quite specifically does not warrant that the services will be completed in accordance with the timetable, that planning or other permissions will be granted, that the performance, work or products of others will be satisfactory or that any other body will be solvent even if the architect recommended the body. Given the unwise propensity of architects to recommend products and contractors to their clients, this last part is a very useful safeguard. The importance of this clause cannot be overestimated. In its absence there is a real danger that architects will be held liable for matters which are essentially the responsibility of the contractor and others or that architects will be thought responsible for matters over which they can have no control.

Clause 2.6 requires the architect to co-operate with any of the persons listed in schedule 4. Such co-operation will take the form of supplying drawings and information as necessary and commenting on their work. In addition, and significantly, the architect is made responsible for integrating into the architectural design any relevant information provided by the consultants.

Clause 2.7 serves to qualify the architect's actual authority in that substantial changes from the approved design must not be made without the client's agreement unless it is a matter of urgency, in which case the architect must notify the client without delay.

It should be noted that the contractor is only concerned with whether the architect acts within the powers given by the building contract. If the contract empowers the architect to instruct the contractor to carry out extra work, it matters not that the architect has not obtained the client's permission. The contractor is entitled to do the work and be paid by the employer. In such a situation, however, the employer might well have a valid claim against the architect for exceeding his or her actual authority as set out in these conditions.

Clauses 3.1 to 3.6 are procedural in character. *Clause 3.2* provides that the client will supply necessary information, decisions and approvals when requested. Such a provision must be implied or the architect would be unable to function properly. An important safeguard states that the architect is entitled to rely on such information. Where the client directly appoints consultants, information provided to the architect by the consultant will fall into this category, because it is provided by the client's consultant. Therefore, if any information provided by or on behalf of the client is inaccurate, but the architect has no reason to believe that it is inaccurate, the client will be responsible for the consequences.

Clauses 3.3 to 3.6 provide that the client must give decisions and approvals as necessary for the timely performance of the services when so requested. The architect must also be notified of the relative priorities of brief, cost and time. The client must nominate a responsible representative in article 5. This is a sensible procedure which would probably be adopted in any event. The representative may well be a project manager acting in this capacity rather than actually managing the project. Obviously the client must have authority to issue instructions to the architect. Perhaps surprisingly, the client is required to instruct when applications for statutory and other consents are to be made. The way in which the clause is structured is unfortunate. In practice, the architect would advise when such application was required and the client would make a decision about the advice. That might well be an instruction, but the client is reacting rather than taking the lead. The client's responsibility for paying statutory charges, fees and disbursements is usefully set out.

Part of *clause 1.6* and *clauses 3.8 to 3.11* deal with consultants. The case of *Moresk* v. *Hicks* (1966)[21] decided that architects have no implied authority to delegate design responsibility and unless they obtain the client's agreement, they will be held liable to the client if a delegated design proves to be defective. The architect is to advise the client about the appointment of consultants (other than those already named in schedule 4) to design, carry out parts of the works or to give specialist advice. It is for the client to appoint and pay each consultant and to confirm to the architect the services which they are to perform. However, either architect or client may propose the appointment of consultants at any time for the other's agreement.

A very important provision states that the client will hold each consultant, and not the architect, responsible for the competence, inspection and performance of the work carried out by them. That is a very good reason, quite apart from the question of professional indemnity cover (see Chapter 17, section 17.5), why the architect should not undertake to carry out what would normally be consultants' work by direct engagement of consultants. The efficacy of this clause, which in effect limits the architect's liability, has been accepted by the court in *Investors in Industry Commercial Properties Ltd* v.. *South Bedfordshire District Council* (1986)[22] where a similar clause in the previous RIBA Conditions of Engagement was considered. The client must require that consultants co-operate with the architect both by providing drawings and other information in good time and by their willingness to consider and comment on the architect's work to enable any necessary changes to be made.

If this term was not expressly included, it would have to be implied to enable the carrying out of the architect's duties.

Many problems have been caused by the architect's obligation to inspect the works. Nowhere does it state that the architect must 'supervise' the works although the courts, and architects themselves, regularly refer to the architect's duty to design and supervise. Supervision implies constant inspection and direction and has been held to be a more onerous duty than inspection.[23] In building contracts, this duty lies with the contractor.

Clause 3.10 does not even refer to site inspection.[24] Visits to site, but oddly not inspections, are covered in the services. This clause simply states that if site inspectors, presumably a reference to clerks of works, are to be appointed, the client must do it.

In the case of *Kensington & Chelsea & Westminster Area Health Authority v. Wettern Composites* (1984),[25] it was held that the damages awarded against the architect should be reduced by 20% to take account of the negligence of the clerk of works. Being employed by the client, it was held that the client was vicariously liable for the clerk of works' actions. It is clearly in the architect's interest that the clerk of works is employed directly by the client. It is not expected that the architect should make frequent or constant inspections. If such a degree of inspection by the architect is agreed to be necessary, a part-time or full-time resident architect may be appointed or otherwise a full-time clerk of works will be employed and the architect should advise the client about this.

Clause 3.12 is especially useful to bring home to a client the true situation in respect of the building contract although it only states the general law. In practice, a client will always blame the architect if anything goes wrong with a project. This clause makes clear that, where the client has entered into a building contract, the contractor, not the architect, must be held responsible for the contractor's methods and for the proper execution of the works.

Clause 3.13 states that the client must obtain legal advice and provide 'such information and evidence as required for the resolution of any dispute between the Client and any other parties providing services in connection with the Project'. It is not entirely clear what this clause means. It is tempting to assume that it merely refers to a situation where the client has a dispute with the contractor, but it probably has wider implications in regard to consultants and clerks of works. The architect is also a party providing services.

Clause 4.1 prohibits either party from assigning the whole or any part of the agreement without the other's written consent. This is simply stating the position under the general law whereby a party may usually assign a right but not a duty without consent. Applied to architectural practice, it simply means that the architect must perform his or her part of the contract, say to make application for planning permission, and the client must do its part, i.e. to pay the architect's fees, and neither party can assign these duties to another person. *Clause 4.2* forbids sub-letting by the architect without consent, but the consent is not to be unreasonably withheld. Many architectural practices sub-contract work to other architects on a regular basis. This can be very useful for practices with a fluctuating workload. The architects to whom work is sub-let establish in time a very close working relationship with the practice and if the workload grows on a permanent basis, they are often taken on as part of the permanent staff.

It is important to understand the difference between assignment and delegation. If an architect delegates any duties (which as noted earlier may not be done without permission), he or she still retains responsibility for the proper carrying out of such duties. If, however, some of those duties are allowed to be assigned, the architect is no longer responsible for them. The responsibility passes to the person to whom they have been assigned. Where an assignment of both rights and duties is intended, it is usual to prepare a three-way contract, called a 'novation', between the parties. What the novation agreement does is to bring the original contract to an end and replace it with a contract under exactly the same terms except that the identity of one of the parties is changed. Some people find it easier to think of this as replacing one party by another, although that is not strictly correct.

Clauses 5.1 to *5.17* deal with payment of fees and expenses. Fees are to be:

- a percentage of the construction cost; or
- a lump sum; or
- a time charge; or
- another agreed method.

The principle of percentage fees is well understood, but less understood is the way in which such fees are to be calculated at various stages in the project. In practice, it sometimes leads to disputes.

Clause 5.2 sets out how fees are to be charged. What constitutes the construction cost is set out in the definitions as discussed above but it will not be properly ascertained until the end of the contract when the final certificate is issued. Before that, interim fees are to be calculated using the 'current' construction cost, which is nowhere defined, but presumably refers to the construction cost as ascertainable at the time of the fee calculation. The final fee is to be calculated on something referred to as the ascertained final construction cost. This awkward phrase sits strangely with the three definitions of construction cost, one of which refers to the 'final cost'. Translated, the 'ascertained final construction cost' therefore means the final final cost of construction which someone has properly calculated. Taking the definition of construction cost into account, this cannot mean the amount certified in the final certificate under the building contract, but often rather more than that.

Where a lump sum is to be the basis of fees, there are options, two of which, to varying degrees, alleviate the risk for the architect. It can be:

- calculated by using the percentage stated in the schedule of fees applied to the approved construction cost at the end of stage D; or
- calculated, stage by stage, by using the same percentage, but applying it to the approved construction cost at the end of each stage and arriving at a lump sum for the next stage; or
- a fixed lump sum as generally understood.

Time charges needs little explanation. Travelling time to and from the architect's offices is chargeable. Lump sum (but not lump sums calculated stage by stage) and time charges are reviewable every 12 months in accordance with the Retail Price Index. The 12 months is calculated from the 'effective date' which is either the date on which the architect commenced performance of the services or the date which has been inserted in the memorandum of agreement. Where lump sums are concerned, the 12 months is from the date the lump sum was calculated.

There is extensive provision for additional fees in *clause 5.6*. This should not be difficult but, in practice, architects vary tremendously in what they are prepared to do for the fee. In most cases, architects are prepared to do rather more than should be expected of them. The important criterion is that the extra work or expense caused to the architect must be for reasons beyond his or her control. Payment is to be on a time basis or, if it is appropriate (more suitable) to do so, by adjusting the basic fee. That is a perfectly adequate clause, but it was clearly considered to be necessary to give some examples and although the reasons are stated not to be limited to the examples, the danger is that clients will not be prepared to look beyond them. Some of the examples are that the client varies any item of work, or where performance of the services is delayed, disrupted or prolonged by others. As soon as the architect becomes aware that this clause is going to apply, the client must be informed. In most cases, the architect will be aware before the event or, in the case of external disruptive elements, immediately they occur. Failure to promptly notify the client may result in difficulty in recovering fees. The clause somewhat unnecessarily states that it does not apply if the extra work is caused by a breach on the part of the architect.

Clause 5.6.2 states that if, after the agreement is executed, the architect agrees to enter into a warranty, the architect will be entitled to extra costs including taking legal advice, additional professional indemnity insurance and, importantly, the reasonable cost of assuming the additional liability. Architects should not underestimate the additional liability undertaken with each warranty.

Clause 5.7 states that if the architect does not complete the services, payment is to be in accordance with schedule 3 for complete services or stages; otherwise the fee is to be proportioned based on the architect's estimate of the percentage complete.

The architect is only entitled to recover expenses which are specified in schedule 3 unless the client has given prior authority for the expenditure. Expenses can amount to a substantial sum and architects can easily be caught out by this provision. Disbursements are to be reimbursed in the usual way. The architect must keep records of all expenses and disbursements and also of time spent, if that is to be the basis of charging. The client has the right to see the records.

Clause 5.10 is an important clause dealing with payment and it makes clear that payment is due on the issue of accounts which must be at not less than monthly intervals. The final day for payment of each account is specified in order to conform to the requirements of the Housing Grants, Construction and Regeneration Act 1996. It is stated to be 30 days after the due date. Each fee account is to include all additional fees and expenses and the method of calculation of the account. If the basis of monthly calculations is very clearly set out in schedule 3, it may be sufficient if the calculations in the accounts are referenced to schedule 3.

Clause 5.11 provides that the client may not set off against payments to the architect. Needless to say, this is one of the clauses to which most clients object. It is seen by many architects as a valuable safeguard because, at least in principle, it requires the client to pay even disputed amounts and then to seek to recover the disputed sums by negotiation or via the dispute resolution procedures in the agreement. Against this view, there are three important arguments.

- If the architect tried to claim fees, the court would favour trying the claim and any counterclaim together to dispose of the claims together rather than separately at greater cost. This argument overlooks the fact that, unless the claim is under the current limit of £5000, the method of dispute resolution is either adjudication (where the adjudicator has no jurisdiction to hear counterclaims other than as defences) or arbitration and not litigation through the courts. In arbitration, the dispute may well encompass whether or not the client is entitled to set off despite the provision.
- The clause may conflict with the provisions of the Unfair Contract Terms Act 1977 which generally provides that any clauses seeking to restrict or exclude the liability of the party putting it forward (in this case, the architect) must be reasonable. It may be questioned whether an all-embracing exclusion of set-off clauses could be seen as reasonable.
- The clause is in clear conflict with the provisions of the Housing Grants, Construction and Regeneration Act 1996, section 111 of which appears to allow set-off subject to the service of an effective notice. This provision is included in SFA/99 by clause 5.12 which sits badly with clause 2.11.

The client is to give notices under *clause 5.12* within 5 days of the date the account is issued, stating the amount to be paid and how it is calculated and not later than 5 days before the final date for payment if the client intends to withhold money from any payment. An important part of the clause states that if these notices are not given, the amount that the client is due to pay is the amount stated in the architect's account. There is no further opportunity for the client to query the amount due, even if it seems there is a good reason, until after payment has been made. The philosophy is clear: the client can query the amount in the account while holding onto the money if the required notices are given. If the notices are not given, the amounts in the account must be paid and the client may then query it while the architect holds the money. It has already been remarked above that the no set-off clause (5.11) sits very uneasily with this provision.

Clause 5.13 provides that interest is payable on amounts unpaid after 30 days in accordance with legislation which is incorrectly quoted. The legislation in question is the Late Payment of Commercial Debts (Interest) Act 1998 and, as the name suggests, it applies only to debts between commercial parties. Architects intending to use this agreement should amend the clause accordingly. If the Act does not apply, presumably in the case of a domestic consumer, interest is still indicated at 8% above Bank of England base rate which is the current rate under the Act. However, the Bank of England Base Rate in the Act is the rate in force during the 6 months between 31 December and 30 June. Where the Act does not apply, the rate is stated as the rate current at the date of issue of the account. *Clause 5.14* makes clear that the interest also applies to money awarded in adjudication, arbitration or legal proceedings.

Clause 5.16 provides that where the client determines or suspends the architect's performance, the architect is entitled to all fees due at that date. If the client suspends or determines otherwise than for the architect's breach or the architect suspends or determines due to the client's breach, the architect is to be paid all loss and damage directly incurred. This could be substantial and should roughly equate to what the architect could claim for repudiation at common law. The architect ought to be able to claim money to the extent that he or she is out of pocket due to the determination. Such things as the profit which would have been made if the project had proceeded and cost of shedding staff could be claimable. The clause expressly refers to a claim for a copyright licence fee and the amount of such fee should be stated in schedule 3.

The copyright position is regulated by the Copyright, Designs and Patents Act 1988 as amended by various subsidiary Regulations. There is also case law which has a bearing on the situation. There is no copyright in ideas or concepts, but only in the way in which they are expressed. Section 1 of the Act states that copyright is a property right in, among other things, original literary, dramatic, musical or artistic works. Section 4 makes clear that 'artistic work' includes 'a work of architecture being a building or a model for a building' and that 'building' includes any fixed structure and part of a building or fixed structure. 'Artistic work' also means 'a graphic work, photograph, sculpture or collage, irrespective of artistic quality'.

In general, copyright remains with the originator or creator of an artistic work for his or her lifetime and for 70 years after the end of the year in which the creator died. Work produced by an employee is the copyright of the employer. Section 2 of the Act makes clear that no one may reproduce or copy any work without the consent of the originator. Assignment of copyright from the creator of the work to another may only be accomplished in writing. Such assignment can never be inferred (section 90). It is not usual to transfer copyright, but rather to grant a licence to use the copyright material for a particular purpose or for a particular period of time. It is not necessary to register ownership of copyright in any way, but in published works it is usual to indicate a claim to copyright thus: © John Smith (1991).

The Act introduces the concept of 'moral rights' (sections 77(4) to (5)). An architect has the right to be identified as the originator of the building 'in the case of a work of architecture in the form of a building or a model for a building, a sculpture or a work of artistic craftsmanship, copies of a graphic work representing it, or of a photograph of it, are issued to the public'. Section 77(5) states that 'The author of a work of architecture in the form of a building also has the right to be identified on the building as constructed or, where more than one building is constructed to the design, on the first to be constructed'. The author may object to derogatory treatment of the work, principally by asking for identification to be removed from the building. There are also rules about the issuing of copies to the public of pictures of the derogatory treatment. The creator must assert the right to be identified before an infringement can take place. Solicitors acting for clients will often attempt to insert a clause removing this right. Such attempts to remove a statutory right should be resisted.

Architects have copyright in their designs and a client usually has a licence, which may be express or implied, to reproduce the design as a building. In the absence of any agreement, the client must have paid a sufficient fee before a licence will be implied: *Stovin-Bradford* v. *Volpoint Properties Ltd* (1971).[26] In any event, even if sufficient fee has not been paid for a licence to reproduce in the form of a building to be implied, the client will be entitled to possess the drawings: *Gibbon* v. *Pease* (1905).[27]

The architect's normal remedy for infringement of copyright is to take out an injunction to prevent the carrying out of the work. This will not normally be granted if building work has already commenced on site: *Hunter* v. *Fitzroy Robinson and Partners* (1978).[28] The alternative remedy is for the architect to sue for damages. Large amounts of damages will not usually be recovered unless it can be shown that the infringement of copyright was flagrant or a substantial benefit accrued to the infringer.[29] Section 107 of the Copyright, Designs and Patents Act 1988 makes certain instances of infringement a criminal offence with penalties of fines and imprisonment. That particular provision is unlikely to have much application to the architect.

Clauses 6.1 and 6.2 do not attempt to amend the position under the general law. They simply clarify the architect's position. Copyright in all the architect's drawings and documents and in any building produced from such documents is the property of the architect and the architect asserts the right to be identified as the author of the project. The client, however, is to have a licence to copy the architect's drawings and other documents or software and to allow the other consultants to do the same, but only for the purpose of constructing the building on the site to which the design relates and related maintenance, operation, promotion, leasing or sale.

There are four provisos.

■   The architect is not to be liable if the designs are changed or used for any purpose other than the purpose for which they were intended. It is probably useful to spell out this point although that would be the legal position in any event.

■   If the client wishes to use the designs after the architect has completed the last service but before the building has reached practical completion, the client must seek the architect's confirmation of the degree of completion of the documents and the client must pay the architect a reasonable licence fee (unless one is set out in schedule 3). This is probably somewhat stricter than the position under the general law.

■ A valuable right is given to the architect to refuse to allow the client to use the documents, etc. if the client has not paid any monies properly due. The architect must first give 7 days notice. The client may resume the use once the outstanding sums are paid.

■ The client is to 'obtain or ensure' that a third party must get any necessary licence and pay fees arising for access to software used to prepare the drawings and documents. It is not immediately obvious what purpose is served by this proviso. The wording leaves a great deal to be desired.

The architect may publish photographs, but not any other information about the project, without consent. *Clause 6.4* is a confidentiality clause which indicates specific exceptions. This is essentially a restatement of the general law.

Clause 7.1 states that the client may not start any action against the architect in contract or in tort after the period stated in the Memorandum of Agreement has expired. The period is to be calculated from the date of completion of the last service or from the date of practical completion of the project, whichever is earlier. This is the opportunity for the architect to reduce the period of time for which he or she will be liable.

Clause 7.2 is an attempt to limit the architect's liability to the lesser sum of either the amount stated in the Memorandum of Agreement or the amount resulting from the operation of clause 7.3. The SFA/92 clause restricting liability to no more than a specified sum was upheld.[30] *Clause 7.3* is a 'net contribution clause'. In the absence of this clause, the client may take legal action against an architect for 100% of damages suffered even though he or she may be less than 100% liable. The architect would then be left to seek a contribution from all others who might be liable. This clause seeks to prevent that by providing for the way in which any lesser liability is to be assessed. It is said to be the extent to which it is 'just and equitable' having regard to the architect's liability for the damage in question. The architect's liability is to be compared to the responsibilities of others concerned and assuming that the others have provided contractual undertakings to the client which are as stringent as the architect's undertakings. It also assumes that there are no exclusions of liability or joint insurance provisions and the other parties are deemed to have paid their share of the damages. This clause, or something similar, is now fairly standard in professionals' terms of engagement and it is a valuable protection. Recently, in connection with the ACE terms of engagement, it was held that the Unfair Contract Terms Act 1997 did not apply to this clause.[31]

Clause 7.4.1 obliges the architect to maintain professional indemnity insurance for the amount and during the period stated in the Memorandum of Agreement. There is the usual proviso that the insurance is available at commercially reasonable rates to the architect. It is the rates available to the architect which are important. The fact that insurance is available at commercially reasonable rates to architects in general is not relevant if the rates available to the architect under this agreement are higher for some reason. Some bespoke terms drafted by clients' solicitors attempt to restrict the availability by referencing it to architects with a good claims record. That, of course, is of no assistance to an architect who has a bad claims record. The bottom line for the architect is whether he or she can pay the premium. The architect must produce insurance documents on reasonable request and inform the client if such insurance ceases to be available.

Clause 7.4.2 requires the architect to notify the client if the insurance becomes unavailable in whole or in part or if it becomes unavailable at commercially reasonable rates. In this eventuality, the architect and the client are supposed to discuss how best to protect themselves in the absence of insurance. It may be that the client is able to take out insurance which will deal with the problem, or at least part of it.

Clause 7.5 deals with the provision of a warranty by the architect. The clause refers to 'an agreement with a third party' (see section 6.6 below). Before the architect is obliged to provide a warranty, the client must have:

- notified the architect prior to signing the agreement that a warranty with third parties will be required
- attached to the agreement the terms of such warranties
- attached details of other parties who will sign similar warranties
- paid all amounts due to the architect.

If these criteria are satisfied, the architect must provide the signed warranty within a reasonable time of it being requested by the client.

Clause 7.6 has become a fairly standard clause in most contracts. It is designed to avoid the effects of the Contracts (Rights of Third Parties) Act 1999 (see section 6.6 below).

Clauses 8.1 to *8.8* deal with the position if the contract is suspended or terminated. Without such a provision, neither party would be entitled to terminate or suspend unless they could establish grounds at common law, e.g. repudiation. It is worth noting that usually there is no right to terminate at common law because the client fails to pay unless such failure is evidence of an intention not to pay at all.[32] That is simply a breach of contract for which the remedy is damages. The client is entitled to suspend any or all the architect's services by giving 7 days notice. To comply with the Housing Grants, Construction and Regeneration Act 1996, the architect may also suspend performance on 7 days notice if the client fails to pay. The notice must state the grounds for suspension. The architect must resume performance when the money is paid in full. Insofar as the contractual provision falls short or is more onerous than the Act, the Act applies. The Act also provides that a suspending party is entitled to have the period of suspension ignored when the total period for performance of obligations is calculated. In effect, the architect will be entitled to an extension of time. SFA/99 extends that principle to cover suspension by the client. The architect may also suspend on 7 days notice if the client fails to comply with the CDM Regulations. Any suspension by either architect or client which lasts longer than 6 months entitles the architect to request instructions. If no instructions are given within the next 30 days, the architect can treat performance of his or her obligations as determined.

Clause 8.5 provides that either party may determine performance of any or all of the architect's obligations by the giving of reasonable written notice to the other. The notice must state the grounds for determination and the services affected. It would have been better if a definite period of notice had been specified. Reference to 'reasonable notice' leaves the door open for one party to argue that whatever notice has been given by the other is unreasonable. Reasonable notice requires the determining party to take all circumstances into account. For example, if the architect is giving notice, the period should allow time for the client to engage another architect to continue the work without delays. This may be a fairly short period in the early stages of the project, but it is likely to be much longer when the project is on site and the presence of an architect who is familiar with the production information is crucial.

If it is the client giving notice, regard should be paid to the number of staff and other resources engaged on the project and the ease with which the architect can transfer or terminate such resources. Any loss suffered by the architect will be part of the damages referred to under clause 5.16. Architects should be wary of 'reasonable notice' and always try to err on the side of longer notice than necessary, otherwise the client may be able to allege repudiation by the architect and claim damages.

It is not immediately obvious why the notice should state the grounds for determination, because no particular required grounds are set out in the agreement. Neither, it seems, must the grounds be such as would entitle a party to treat the agreement as repudiated under the general law. Presumably the requirement will be satisfied by the flimsiest of reasons such as that the necessary relationship of trust and confidence has broken down. An alternative provision for determination allows the deed to be done immediately on notice by either party if either becomes insolvent or the architect cannot continue with the commission due to death or incapacity. After determination for any reason and if the client requests, the architect must give the client copies of the drawings and other documents, etc. which the client has a licence to use, but subject to the copyright restrictions in clause 6.2 and payment of the architect's reasonable charges for copying.

There is a provision preserving the parties' 'accrued rights and remedies'. The purpose of this provision is to safeguard each party's rights to take action and it makes clear that the parties are not constrained by the remedies in the contract.

Dispute resolution is dealt with under *clauses 9.1 to 9.6*. It is a complex set of clauses, including four possible methods of resolving disputes. It is essential that the parties do not make a mistake in deciding upon the appropriate method or there may be financial consequences. The methods are as follows.

- *Negotiation or mediation.* These are optional and the parties may attempt to settle their differences by negotiation or by means of the RIBA or RIAS Mediation Services. Discussion, which is essentially what this option involves, is always available to the parties whether or not expressly so stated and the only purpose in including this method in the conditions is simply to draw the parties' attention to an alternative to confrontation.

- *Adjudication.* Where the Housing Grants, Construction and Reconciliation Act 1996 applies, either party may opt to have any dispute or differences arising under the agreement settled by an adjudicator. The procedure is to be as set out in the Model Adjudication Procedures published by the Construction Industry Council current at the date of the adjudication. At the time of writing, the fourth edition of the Model Procedures applies. An important part of the clause refers to the deletion of clause 28 of the Model Procedures and the substitution of a clause which permits the adjudicator to order one of the parties to pay the legal costs of the other. This is important, because statutory adjudication under the Act does not allow for the recovery of costs. However, it should be noted that the reference to clause 28 is an error and the clause to be deleted should be clause 29. The adjudicator is either named in the memorandum of agreement or is to be nominated by the nominator in the memorandum. If neither adjudicator nor nominator is inserted, the nominator will be the President of the RIBA.

- *Arbitration.* Where the parties have opted for arbitration as the principal method of dispute resolution, they may agree a person or, failing agreement, a person may be appointed at the application of either party by the appointor named in the memorandum of agreement. If no one is named, the default provision is for the President of the Royal Institute of British Architects to appoint. This is an agreement to arbitrate which falls under the Arbitration Act 1996. There is a proviso that, if the law of the agreement is stated to be the law of England and Wales, either party may choose to pursue a remedy through the courts if they are seeking to recover a sum of money not exceeding £5000 or whatever other sum is set out by legislation in accordance with section 91 of the Arbitration Act 1996. In addition, if the claimant in an arbitration is an architect under an unamended SFA/99, the arbitrator does not have the power to award security for costs.[33]

- *Litigation.* If, in the articles of agreement, the parties have opted for litigation instead of arbitration, any dispute can be dealt with in the courts. The parties must give careful thought to the possibility of litigation although most architects might prefer an architect arbitrator appointed by the President of the RIBA rather than a judge to deal with disputes about the appointment.

Very importantly, under *clause 5.14*, the client must indemnify the architect for all the architect's costs in any proceedings together with a reasonable sum for the architect's time if the architect gets a judgment or award for fees and expenses or if the client fails in any claim against the architect. This has the effect of reimbursing an architect who is successful in arbitration or litigation for virtually the whole amount of costs. Without such a provision, a successful litigant can usually expect to recover anything between 65% to 85% of costs, dependent upon circumstances.

6.5.2   The Standard Agreement 2010

At time of writing, we only have the final draft of this document and it is possible that minor changes will be made before publication. This form is a tremendous improvement on the 2007 Standard Form of Agreement and architects should not be concerned about using this form instead of the familiar SFA/99. The components of the Agreement are the Conditions of Appointment, the Schedule of Project Data, Services, Fees and Expenses and any appendices. The Agreement can be put in place by means of a memorandum of agreement, which is probably to be preferred for projects where this Agreement is to be employed, or by using a letter of appointment.

Filling in the Schedule of Project Data and other documents will be a slow process when first undertaken and one might have wished for something more streamlined, but when completed properly, architects should be confident that they have the benefit of a sensible contract. The Conditions of Appointment fairly closely follows the arrangement in the SFA/99 Conditions. We comment below on some changes.

The definitions section now includes welcome definitions of 'collaborate' and 'confidential information' which sometimes give rise to difficulties. The problem is that most people believe they know what such words mean, but in practice, people disagree over the detail. The definition of 'construction cost' has been sharpened but, in the draft, the professional estimate was subject to the approval of the client which of course could be withheld. It is good to see that the obligation on architect and client to work together in a spirit of mutual trust and co-operation seems to have been removed. The way in which parties work together cannot be dictated successfully in a contract.

Clause 2.7 permits the architect to publish photographs of the project and allows reasonable access for 2 years after completion for that purpose. *Clause 2.8* requires the architect to seek the consent of the client if publication of other information is desired. Importantly, such consent must not be unreasonably withheld or delayed. These provisions are in SFA/99, but the new drafting is to be preferred.

Clause 5.8.2 prevents the downward adjustment of the architect's fee if there are deflationary trends on the construction cost. The reference to termination in *clauses 5.17* and *8.2* is to termination of the Agreement, whereas in *clause 8.1* the reference is to termination of performance or of obligations. The latter is correct. The House of Lords has criticised the use of expressions conveying the idea that a contract is at an end, or dead or displaced, because what is meant is no more than that a party is excused from further performance.[34] This part of the Agreement is under review and may well be amended before publication.

An interesting change occurs in *clause 9.2.2*. The whole dispute resolution provisions have been simplified by reference to information to be inserted in the Project Data. The adjudicator is given the power to allocate costs between the parties, but only if the referring party confirms the provision in writing to the other party and to the adjudicator after serving the notice of adjudication. It is likely that the architect will be the referring party in most instances – usually to recover unpaid fees – and the architect can choose whether or not the adjudicator is to decide the question of costs. The usual position in adjudication is that the parties pay their own costs, whatever the outcome, and the adjudicator decides which party must pay the adjudicator's fees and expenses.

6.5.3 Other standard forms of appointment

- *The Association of Consultant Architects Standard Form of Agreement for the Appointment of an Architect (ACA SFA/08)* is a set of standard terms of appointment produced by the ACA. It is described as a development of the SFA series of appointments. It is intended for use where the architect is to provide services for a wide range of projects.
- *The Appointment of a Consultant Architect for Small Works, Works of Simple Content and Specialist Services ACA98 (2004 revision)* is also produced by the ACA. It is intended for use for small projects of about £250,000 or if the work is simple in nature.
- *The CIC Consultants' Contracts Package* is a set of documents produced by the Construction Industry Council for the use of consultants involved in major projects.

6.6   Duty of care agreements (collateral warranties)

Strictly speaking, a collateral warranty[35] is a contract which runs alongside another contract and is subsidiary to it. Such documents have proliferated in recent years and it is common for contractors, nominated and domestic sub-contractors and suppliers and all the consultants to be required to execute collateral warranties in favour of the building owner, the funder providing the money for the project and/or any number of prospective tenants. It used to be the view that such an agreement was not very important because it merely stated in contractual terms the duties which everyone knew the architect owed to a third party in tort. That view is no longer tenable.

Before looking at some of the provisions commonly encountered in forms of warranty, or duty of care agreements (as they are often called when used in relation to consultants), it should be understood why they are so important to the building owner. There used to be a fundamental contract principle that only the parties to a contract have any rights or duties under that contract. The principle was called 'privity of contract'. For example, in a contract between a client A and an architect B, each has rights and duties to the other. B has a duty to design a building for A, but B used to have no duty to any third party, C, to design that building. That was the case even if the contract stated that B had such a duty.

However, since the coming into force of the Contracts (Rights of Third Parties) Act 1999, persons who are not parties to a contract may be able to obtain a benefit from the contract if it appears that the contract is intended to give them such a benefit.

To put it at its most basic: if A and B now include a term in their contract that they will each pay £100 to C, the term will be effective in that if they fail to honour it, C will be able to enforce it, even though C is not a party to the contract. Even if the contract simply refers to a class of people as beneficiaries, they are entitled to claim using whatever machinery (e.g. arbitration) is available in the contract. However, parties to a contract may exclude third party rights by inserting a provision to that effect in the contract. Some of the newer and redrafted contracts (such as the JCT Standard Building Contract SBC) are experimenting with the use of clauses giving an express benefit to specific third parties in order to avoid what has become a snowstorm of collateral warranties around every construction contract. It remains to be seen how effective that will be in practice. Currently, there is no indication that collateral warranties are decreasing in number; rather the reverse.

But if, as usual, third party rights are excluded, only the client can take action against the architect for breach of the conditions of engagement. For example, if an architect designs a house for the client, the house is sold on to a third party and a design defect then becomes apparent, the third party cannot take action against the architect under the conditions of engagement between the architect and client. At one time it was thought that the third party would have been able to overcome this kind of problem by suing in the tort of negligence if there was no contractual relationship. A plaintiff suing in negligence must show that:

- the defendant had a duty of care to the plaintiff; and
- the defendant was in breach of that duty; and
- as a result of the breach the plaintiff suffered damage of a kind which is recoverable.

So, in the first place, the plaintiff would try to show that the defendant architect owed a duty of care. The courts appeared willing to find such a duty in many instances but the House of Lords case of *Murphy* v. *Brentwood District Council* (1990)[36] made it very difficult for a third party to successfully sue in tort for a defective building.

In broad terms, the decision in *Murphy* means that if an architect negligently designs a building, recovery in the tort of negligence will only be possible if the defective design causes injury or death to a person or if it causes damage to property other than the building which is the subject of the defective design. Even then, the recovery will be limited to compensating for the injury or damage to other persons or property and will not cover rectification of the original design defect. The concept is much the same as product liability and the Lords saw no reason for making any distinction.

The result is that a third party can no longer rely on suing an architect in negligence except in very circumscribed situations, such as if the action can be brought under the reliance principle set out in *Hedley Byrne* v. *Heller*[37] as interpreted in *Caparo Industries plc* v. *Dickman*.[38] Essentially, the principle is that where the parties are in a relationship of sufficient proximity and the architect makes a negligent misstatement, the architect will be liable to the other party if the architect knew the other party would rely on the statement and if the other party did so rely and suffered a loss as a consequence. A negligent misstatement given to one party and relied upon by another who suffers loss will not give rise to liability to the other party, because the statement was not given to the other party and the architect was unaware that it would rely on it. What constitutes a negligent misstatement has been interpreted fairly broadly by the courts and it is probable that an architect's drawing falls into this category.[39]

Contracts are concerned with achieving specific results and contain many terms relating to quality. Tort is concerned with remedying wrongs. The courts now emphasise the difference. To take a simple example: if an architect specifies the wrong external cladding which soon deteriorates, that is a breach of contract for which the law lays down remedies as between the architect and the client. If the cladding is so inadequate that it falls off the building and injures a passer-by, that may be negligence for which the passer-by has a remedy against the architect in tort. The situation has been muddied by a number of legal cases which have enabled the original party to a contract to bring an action against the other party for breach of contract even though the original party has since sold on the building to a purchaser and received full value for it.[40] However, the situations where that can occur are likely to be limited, because it appears that if the original party (but no longer the owner of the property) is to be able to take action, among other things the other party must be shown to have known at the time of entering into the contract that the building was to be sold on or tenanted.

The purpose of a duty of care agreement is to create a contractual relationship between the architect and third parties who otherwise would be unlikely to have any remedy if design defects became apparent after completion. At the time of writing, there is a form of warranty (CoWa/F) in favour of funders and (CoWa/P&T)[41] in favour of purchasers or tenants. There are also a great many other forms of warranty in circulation, some of which have been especially drafted by solicitors with greater or lesser experience of the architectural profession and the construction industry generally. The following are points which architects should bear in mind when called upon to sign any warranty or duty of care agreement.

6.6.1   General

The basic problem is that, by virtue of the agreement, the architect acquires liabilities towards a party who has paid no fee for the privilege. If the architect does not take care, greater duties may be undertaken towards the third party than those which the architect already owes to the client under the conditions of appointment. If it can possibly be avoided, an architect should not enter into a duty of care agreement. Some architects take the view that they should not resist requests to execute duty of care agreements because, as professionals, they should be prepared to take responsibility for their actions. This is a most laudable sentiment, but architects should consider whether they wish to accept a greater burden of liability than the general law would impose. That is the situation where a duty of care agreement is executed as in any other freely negotiated contractual situation. If architects do execute such agreements, there seems to be no good reason why they should not charge an appropriate, rather than a nominal, fee for the warranty. The opportunity afforded to a third party to take legal action should be worth a substantial sum. However, in this as in most other matters, commercial pressures may force the architect into executing such agreements without charge.

Considerable pressure may be put upon architects to enter into onerous warranties and to agree to the incorporation of clauses which impose unacceptable degrees of liability. When architects are being pressured to accept such clauses, various arguments may be put forward by the client's solicitors.

- *The clause is standard.* There are no standard clauses in warranties. A warranty, like any other contract, is a bargain between two parties. Any clauses may be accepted or rejected. While it is true that certain clauses crop up again and again in warranties, frequency of occurrence does not make a bad clause good. The client's solicitor would have no compunction in striking out any clause in a contract, standard or otherwise. When reference is made to a clause being standard, the solicitor means that it is one which is often used. That does not mean to say that architects must accept it.
- *All the other consultants have signed similar warranties.* Architects who order their businesses on the basis of what others do (or are said to have done) are heading for disaster. Even if true, the reason may be because other consultants have not understood the dangers in certain clauses.
- *The client is not prepared to change its position on this clause.* In that case, it looks as though the client will not get a warranty. Clients often lose sight of the fact that it takes two to make any contract. In agreeing the terms of warranties, it is essential for architect to decide what they will not under any circumstances accept and what they prefer not to accept but which are not showstoppers. In practice, architects often accept clauses simply because they are frightened of losing a lucrative commission. That is perfectly understandable, but it must be remembered that a lucrative commission may turn into the reverse after a successful claim from the beneficiary of a warranty.

6.6.2 Execution

The essential differences between a deed and a simple contract have been explained in section 6.4.1 above. Architects will usually be asked to enter into a collateral warranty in the form of a deed, because it extends the potential liability period to 12 years and no consideration is necessary. If the original conditions of engagement are under hand, an architect could be in the position of having a longer period of liability to the third party than to the original client. In duty of care agreements executed as simple contracts, there will always be a term stipulating that the architect receives a small sum, usually about £10, in order to make a valid contract. This is because the agreement is always very one-sided and, without the nominal sum, it is very unlikely that any other consideration on the part of the third party would be present. Indeed, apparently from an abundance of caution, many warranties executed as deeds also refer to a nominal payment in consideration.

6.6.3 Skill and care

There is usually a term by which the architect warrants reasonable skill and care in the performance of his or her duties. This is the normal professional standard of care and as such it is not inherently objectionable. Some warranties, however, take the position further and ask the architect to warrant 'due' or 'all proper' skill care and 'diligence' and continue to refer to architects having the experience of architects commonly performing these services. Because it is not at all certain what greater liability such terms may impose, architects should be wary about entering into agreements on that basis and should stick to tried and tested definitions of their professional obligations. There should also be a proviso that the architect will under no circumstances have a greater liability to the third party than the architect already owes to the client.

An architect should never warrant fitness for purpose. That is clearly a very much higher standard of care. It is common for this higher standard to be included in bespoke warranties, but in a disguised form. It is rare that a clause will actually require an architect to warrant in so many words that the building will be fit for its purpose. For example, a warranty in connection with an office building may include a clause which requires the architect to take care that the building, when complete, is suitable in every respect for its function as an office building. It may seem innocuous and, indeed, it may seem only reasonable that an architect designing an office building should give such a warranty, but it should be rejected.

6.6.4 Liability

There must be a net contribution clause in every warranty to safeguard the architect's position in the event of multi-party liability. The effect of such a clause is considered in section 6.5.1 in relation to SFA/99 clause 7.3.

In general, architects should avoid all clauses requiring them to 'ensure' anything. That is equivalent to a guarantee. Often such a requirement can be changed to the use of 'reasonable endeavours' – an obligation somewhat less onerous than 'best endeavours'.[42] However, 'all reasonable endeavours' amounts to the same as 'best endeavours'. Architects should also avoid any clause which attempts to make them liable if they put the beneficiary of the warranty in breach of another contract. Such clauses are extremely common. Such an obligation can only be undertaken, if at all, if the architect has had the opportunity to consider the terms of the other contract before executing the appointment.

6.6.5 Materials

Architects are often asked to warrant that they will ensure that certain materials will not be used in the construction of the building. An architect cannot warrant any such thing. The best that can be done is to warrant that the architect will not specify certain precisely defined materials. Vague references, such as 'any materials generally known to be deleterious', are to be avoided. At least one manufacturer has mounted a successful legal challenge against the black-listing of its products and there is scope for further challenges in the future.[43] The golden rule is that architects should not warrant anything without very clearly knowing what it is they are warranting. That seems obvious, but experience shows that many architects are content to execute warranties without understanding the terms.

6.6.6 Copyright

Copyright has been considered earlier in section 6.5.1 when considering clause 6. There is no sensible reason why a professional should surrender his or her copyright. It is enough to grant a licence for certain specific uses such as repair and maintenance. If an architect does agree to assign copyright in the designs, it seems that the architect would not be precluded from reproducing particular details in another design provided a major part of the original design was not reproduced. Architects should beware the granting of an *irrevocable* licence to use their designs, because it means exactly what it says and the licence could not be withdrawn in the future even if the client fails to pay. Any licence granted should be 'non-exclusive'.

Architects should always make sure that warranties include a clause in which moral rights are asserted under the Copyright, Designs and Patents Act 1988. Frequently, bespoke warranties attempt to remove moral rights. This should always be resisted.

6.6.7 Assignment

This is a provision which allows the party to whom the architect gives the warranty to assign the benefits of the warranty to other parties. It is this clause which gives the agreement much of its value. The biggest problem with the right to assign is that the architect has no control over the identity of the future warrantee. The worst clauses allow assignment, without consent, to unlimited numbers of people for an indefinite period of time. If the architect agrees to an assignment clause, it should allow assignment once only within a limited period of time, say 2 or 3 years after practical completion, subject to the architect's consent.

6.6.8 Professional indemnity

The party taking the benefit of the warranty will principally be interested in the architect's professional indemnity insurance. Many architects enter into duty of care agreements with terms so onerous that the insurance would be repudiated by the insurers if ever a claim was made. Every agreement must be put to the insurers before it is signed, or the indemnity insurance will be at risk, but architects should be aware that their interests and those of their professional indemnity insurers do not always coincide. A term by which the architect agrees to maintain indemnity insurance cover at a particular level for a specific number of years is very common, but virtually useless for practical purposes. The most an architect can do is to agree to use best endeavours to keep such a policy in force provided cover remains available at commercially viable rates for the architect.

An interesting question concerns the damages which a client could recover from the architect for breach of such a condition. If the breach was not discovered, as seems likely, until the occurrence of an event which warranted calling upon the architect's indemnity insurance, there would be no such insurance to meet the claim and, therefore, presumably no money to pay damages caused by the breach. Those damages would, in any event, be what the client would have lost. The client would have lost the chance to call upon the architect's insurance.

6.6.9 Funders

Where the third party is providing financial backing for the development, it will require some kind of control over the situation if things go wrong between architect and client. It is usual for a term (called 'step in rights') to be inserted, which provides that if the architect wishes to terminate the appointment, the architect must give a specified number of days notice to the funder. If the funder then gives notice to the architect, the architect loses the right to terminate or accept repudiation and must, thereafter, accept the funder's instructions in respect of the development.

This type of clause poses two basic difficulties: first, the original client may object if it is not a party to the warranty; second, the architect loses the right to terminate. If architects agree to the inclusion of this type of term, they should ensure that the original client is a party to the warranty for the purpose of acknowledging that the architect is not in breach of the appointment by accepting instructions from the funder. They should also ensure that the funder can only take over the appointment by novation subject to payment of all outstanding fees and leaving the architect free to pursue termination thereafter if the original reason for the termination has not been removed. This last point is important, because many warranties with step in clauses remove the architect's ability to terminate after the funder takes over even if the original reason for termination has not been addressed. The problem lies partly in the fact that there seems to be a general assumption that the reason for termination will be failure to pay. That may indeed be the case in many instances but there can be other reasons for termination and they should not be ignored.

References and notes

1. (1974) 1 All ER 319.
2. (1985) 32 BLR 51.
3. *Pacific Associates* v. *Baxter* (1988) 6 Con LR 90.
4. See *Michael Sallis and Co Ltd* v. *ECA Calil* (1987) 4 Const LJ 125; *Pacific Associates* v. *Baxter* (1988) 6 Con LR 90; *Henderson* v. *Merritt Syndicates* (1994) 69 BLR 26; *Conway* v. *Crow Kelsey* (1994) 39 Con LR 1.
5. See Green, R. (2001) *Architect's Guide to Running a Job*, 6th edn, Architectural Press Ltd.
6. Chappell, D. (1996) *Report Writing for Architects and Project Managers*, 3rd edn, Blackwell Science.
7. See *Partridge* v. *Morris* (1995) CILL 1095 and *Valerie Pratt* v. *George Hill* (1987) 38 BLR 25.
8. Guidance on the various ways in which fees may be calculated is in *A Client's Guide to Engaging an Architect* (2009, November revision) RIBA Publishing and *Good Practice Guide: Fee Management* (2009) RIBA Publishing.
9. It should be noted that the RIBA 2009 forms of agreement do not reflect this position.
10. Published by RIBA Publishing, November 2009.
11. Mirza and Nacey Research, *Architects' Fees*. The reports are published on an annual basis. The current one is Mirza & Nacey Research (2008) *Architectural Earnings: A Survey of the Earnings and Benefits Received by Architects and Technologists*, Fees Bureau/Mirza & Nacey.
12. Mirza & Nacey Research (2008) *Architectural Earnings: A Survey of the Earnings and Benefits Received by Architects and Technologists*, Fees Bureau/Mirza & Nacey.
13. In Northern Ireland, the need for a seal in relation to companies was removed by the Companies (No. 2) Order (Northern Ireland) 1990. In the case of individuals in Northern Ireland the requirement for a seal was removed by the Law Reform (Miscellaneous Provisions) (Northern Ireland) Order 2005.
14. See *Whittal Builder* v. *Chester-Le-Street District Council* (the 1985 case) (1996) 12 Const LJ 356.
15. Local Democracy, Economic Development and Construction Act 2009.
16. Described in the 7th edition of this book.
17. Latham, M. (1994) *Constructing the Team*, HMSO.
18. *Oxford Architects Partnership* v. *Cheltenham Ladies College* [2007] BLR 293.
19. *Moores* v. *Yakeley Associates Ltd* (1998) 62 Con LR 76.
20. (1957) 2 All ER 118.
21. *Moresk Cleaners Ltd* v. *Thomas Henwood Hicks* (1966) 4 BLR 50.

22. (1986) 5 Con LR 1.

23. *Consarc Design Ltd* v. *Hutch Investments Ltd* (2002) 84 Con LR 36.

24. See the excellent book on this topic: Jamieson, N. (2009) *Good Practice Guide: Inspecting Works*, RIBA Publishing.

25. (1984) 1 Con LR 114.

26. (1971) 3 ALL ER 570.

27. (1905) 1 KB 810.

28. (1978) 10 BLR 84.

29. For example, see *Charles Church Development plc* v. *Cronin* [1990] 17 FSR and *Potton Ltd* v. *Yorkclose Ltd* (1989) The Times 4 April.

30. *Moores* v. *Yakeley Associates Ltd* (1998) 62 Con LR 76.

31. *Langstane Housing Association Ltd* v. *Riverside Construction (Aberdeen) Ltd and Others* [2009] ScotCS CSOH.

32. *C J Elvin Building Services Ltd* v. *Peter Noble & Alexa Noble* (2003) CILL 1997 and *D R Bradley (Cable Jointing) Ltd* v. *Jefco Mechanical Services Ltd* (1998) 6-CLD-07-1 are slightly conflicting cases on this point.

33. Section 38(3) of the Arbitration Act 1996 and clause 9.5.3 of the SFA/99 Conditions.

34. *Photo Production Ltd* v. *Securicor Transport Ltd* [1980] 1 All ER 556.

35. Winward F. (2002) *Collateral Warranties*, 2nd edn, Blackwell Publishing.

36. (1990) 50 BLR 1.

37. [1964] AC 465, and see section 6.2 earlier.

38. [1990] 1 All ER 568.

39. *Henderson* v. *Merritt Syndicates Ltd* [1994] 3 All ER 506.

40. *St Martins Property Corporation Ltd and St Martins Property Investments Ltd* v. *Sir Robert McAlpine & Sons Ltd and Linden Gardens Trust Ltd* v. *Lenesta Sludge Disposals Ltd, McLaughlin & Harvey plc and Ashwell Construction Company Ltd* (1992) 57 BLR 57; *Darlington* v. *Wiltshire* (1994) 69 BLR 1.

41. Published by the British Property Federation.

42. *Philips Petroleum Co UK Ltd* v. *Enron Europe Ltd* (1997) CLC 329.

43. *Kirkforthar Bricks* v. *West Lothian Council* (1995) unreported. See also 'Blacklists', *RIBA Journal Practice*, issue 150, January 1998, pp. 83–4.

7 Stage A: Appraisal

This stage is defined by the RIBA as:

> 'Identification of client's needs and objectives, business case and possible constraints on development.
>
> Preparation of feasibility studies and assessment of options to enable the client to decide whether to proceed.'

7.1 Feasibility studies

Once the architect has found out what the client wishes to build, where and when, the next stage is to decide whether it is feasible to build. If not, the project will abort at that stage. Feasibility, however, may depend upon any one of a number of factors or a combination of several factors. The decision to proceed or to stop lies with the client, of course, but it is the architect's function to present the appropriate information to the client in a structured way so that it is made as easy as possible for the client to come to a decision. Clearly, the client's decision may be influenced by matters which are not known to the architect so it is always wise for the architect to investigate more rather than less widely. Because it is difficult at this stage to decide just what data might be relevant, the architect should always include rather than exclude information.

There are some very small projects for which a formal feasibility study may be inappropriate. It should be remembered, however, that it is not the size of the project which determines whether a feasibility study should be done, but associated factors such as complexity, situation, type of development, and so on. It is a sensible procedure for the architect always to approach a feasibility study as though the client requires a formal report to be prepared. In some cases, particularly in the case of a large company or any organisation whose officers have to satisfy others besides themselves, a feasibility report will be mandatory.

Whether the architect is to produce a report or simply to investigate and report orally to the client, it is vital to have a checklist in order to prevent the inadvertent omission of an important item. The following checklist and brief notes are not intended to be exhaustive, and some of the items will apply only to certain developments, but it is a suggested starting point which architects can mould to suit individual requirements.

Terms of reference

It is always sensible to bear in mind the terms of reference or, put another way, what it is that the architect is being asked to do. It is important to include a list of the assumptions being made so that the client is clear about what is known for certain, what is estimated and what is merely assumed for the moment. Typical areas for assumption are that a proper measured survey has not been carried out, in the case of an existing building a structural analysis may not have been done and the structural stability of the building may be assumed. If there is any reason to doubt the structural stability, short of a detailed structural survey and calculation, no assumption should be made and the architect should obtain authority to have the structure properly investigated. Other assumptions which may have to be made concern boundaries and the ground condition.

Consultants

Consultants who might be involved in the study include:

- quantity surveyor
- structural engineer
- geotechnical engineer
- mechanical and electrical services engineer
- acoustics engineer
- landscape architect
- drainage engineer.

Authorities

Statutory and other authorities and suppliers who may be involved are:

- Planning
- Highways
- Drainage
- Housing
- Education
- Police
- Transport
- Fire
- Coal Authority
- Electricity
- Water
- Gas
- Telephone services supplier
- Broadband supplier
- Cable television supplier
- Commission for Architecture and the Built Environment
- Forestry Commission

- English Heritage
- National Trust.

Site location

This should be considered in relation to the distance from the nearest centre of population and the general topography. Neighbouring watercourses, trees and use of adjoining land and any possible nuisance should be examined and recorded.

Access

The means of getting to the site is always important and in some cases it can be crucial to the success or otherwise of the project. Bus, train and air services can be vital to a building which hopes to prosper as a conference centre. Road routes are also important and the proximity of ports.

Shops

The type of project will determine the importance of nearby shops on its viability. Housing must be reasonably near to shops and accommodation for older persons is more attractive if it has a few small shops nearby such as newsagents, chemists and general stores. Mobile shops are still very important in some areas and the distance of the project from, and ease of access to, the nearest large shopping centre should be recorded.

Health

The following are important.

- Doctors' surgeries
- Dental surgeries
- Opticians
- Chiropodists
- Complementary therapies such as acupuncturists, osteopaths, chiropractors, homeopaths, herbalists, etc.
- Clinic
- Health centre
- General hospital facilities
- Proposed future provision

Social and recreational

It is worthwhile making a complete list of this type of provision in the area for certain kinds of proposed development. Although much information can be obtained online or through local libraries, the only accurate way to compile such a list is for the architect to walk over every part of the surrounding area.

Education

A wide range of educational provision is possible and in the case of residential development, it is essential that appropriate provision is available. Any projected educational developments in the area must also be noted. It should not be forgotten that for some people, the proximity of schools will not be thought advantageous.

Employment

The names and locations of principal employers in an area may be a crucial factor in the viability of housing developments.

Rights

The following rights should be recorded if existing or if thought to exist.

- Light
- Way
- Support
- Party walls
- Easements
- Covenants (restrictive or otherwise)

Planning points

- Whether there is any agreement in principle
- Whether there is any earlier permission concerning the same site
- What are the usual standard conditions inserted in planning permissions in that area?
- Specific requirements in regard to storey heights and number, densities, access provision, permitted materials, parking provision
- Any other planning permissions for nearby sites
- Building lines
- Improvement lines
- Road proposals

Licensing

If required.

Drainage

General provision and problems.

Architectural/historical

Matters such as whether the building, if an existing building is being examined, is listed and if so what grade or whether the site is in a conservation area should be considered. Even if there is no statutory protection for the building, the architect will want to record whether there are any interesting and attractive features. The reaction of local amenity societies should also be considered. Although not decisive, opposition from such a quarter can cause serious delays to the process of obtaining appropriate statutory approvals.

Geological factors

Fault lines, unusual ground conditions, old quarries, tunnels and mining subsidence are all problem areas.

Statutory undertakings and services

What services, if any, are readily available to the site or can be connected without undue problems. Any easements or diversions required. Other points regarding street lighting, high-voltage cables overhead or underground, and sub-stations.

Policy

Whether there is any local or central government policy which affects the scheme.

Grants

If any are available.

Structural analysis

Comments on existing structures, if any, in relation to the proposals.

Access

Number of entries to site and width, if metalled surface or special difficulties.

Design possibilities

Options available in broad terms with regard to disposition of various elements set against the site factors, structural options, aesthetics, historical and urban factors.

Estimate of cost

In broad terms, stating the basis of the estimate (i.e. 'current prices'), whether VAT is included and so on. Some clients insist upon a fairly sophisticated life cycle analysis and a facilities management cost programme which the architect would usually request the quantity surveyor to carry out. In fact, there is little to be gained from such an exercise at this stage, when very little is known about the building.

Programme

Possible design team programme and future building programme in the form of key start and finish dates.

Conclusions

Advice to the client, with short reasons.

Approvals/decisions

A list of the approvals and decisions required from the client and a time schedule for receipt if the programme indicated earlier is to be implemented. This is a valuable method of getting the client to respond.

Additional material

Whatever is useful to assist the client in understanding the issues and reaching a decision such as charts, graphs, maps, drawings and photographs.

7.2   Sequential framework and Plan of Work

For every activity there is a need for a sequential framework so that the correct operations can be carried out at the right time and, probably most important, in the right order. The things which an architect has to do throughout the process of design and construction of a building are so numerous, complex and interactive that, without such a framework, chaos would soon result. Architects have long produced such frameworks for themselves. Sometimes they were not much more than lists. In 1964, the RIBA Plan of Work was first published in the RIBA *Architect's Handbook of Practice Management*.[1] The intention was to provide a model procedure for the design team. It was never the intention that the Plan of Work would be slavishly followed under all circumstances. Indeed, certain assumptions were made.

■ A building cost of about £300,000 and a full team of designers. It is now considered relevant to most building projects.

- The architect is responsible for leading the building team. That is not now necessarily the case.
- The earliest possible appointment. What the architect does may vary according to the time of his appointment.
- The degree of complexity was such as to involve the stages set out in Fig. 6.1, the objective of each stage being to commence the next.
- In each stage the cycle of work is:
  — stating objective and assimilation of relevant facts
  — assessment of required resources and setting up of appropriate organisation; planning the work and setting timetables
  — carrying out work
  — making proposals and recommendations
  — obtaining client decisions
  — setting out objectives for the next stage.

The Plan of Work was revised in 1999 as part of the revision of the Appointment documents, SFA/99, etc. It was revised again in 2007 as part of the revision of Appointment documents S-Con-07-A. Although the revisions are largely cosmetic, they take account of some perceived changes in architectural practice, other professions, the JCT development of multidisciplinary documents and BS7000 Part 4: The Guide to Managing Design in Construction. The Plan is an ideal tool provided it is remembered that it is only the basic outline. There are many instances when two or more stages may be combined. The stages may often interweave and it is rare, certainly up to stage H, that there is any definite point at which it can be said that the project is moving from one stage to another.

The Plan, in its complete form, indicates the principal tasks for the major participants at the stage when they are usually carried out and shows the architect's tasks in two sections: design function and management function. The architect should not slavishly follow this time schedule, but must carefully assess each project in the light of the Plan and adjust the Plan to suit. A very full fleshing out of the Plan of Work is represented by the RIBA *Architect's Job Book*.[2] The use of the Plan of Work will not eliminate mistakes, but it will very much reduce their incidence by ensuring that crucial steps are taken in logical order, paving the way for the architect to co-ordinate the members of the design team (see also Chapter 6, section 6.2.1 for a description of each stage).

7.3   Site and building acquisition

In most instances clients already have a site when they approach an architect for the first time. Giving advice on site or building acquisition is one of the additional services which the architect can offer. Clearly, the choice of site should follow the architect's assessment of the client's brief (see section 7.5). If a new building is being considered, the shape of the site, the contours and the location can have a marked influence on the finished building. There are some buildings, such as factories, which require virtually flat sites, others which need sites in sunny locations, by a railway or central road network, in an urban centre and so on. A key factor is the size of the site and whether it is acceptable to erect a high-rise building. There are several factors which can influence this kind of decision. Among them are the attitude of the Planning Authority, market value of floor area at different storey heights above ground level and, particularly in the case of dwellings, social considerations.

It is even less likely that an architect will be asked to advise on the acquisition of a suitable building although it does sometimes happen if the client is seeking a suitable building to convert to a specific purpose. In such a case, the architect has to start from the brief and assess the ease with which any particular building can be converted to its new purpose and the degree to which it is capable of fulfilling the client's brief when so converted. It can be a difficult and complicated task. The key factors to be considered are as follows.

■ *Structure.* In most instances a survey will be required.[3] In addition, it will be necessary to consider the constructional implications of the following.
— Columns
— Internal heights
— Changes in floor level
— Access between floor levels
— Unusual roof shapes
— Towers, spires, etc.
— Basements and underground features
— Windows and doors
— Special architectural features, e.g. finials, drip moulds, etc.
— Decay
■ *Heating and insulation*
— Need to change to comply with current legislation
— Compatibility of electricity, gas, solid fuel, solar heating, organic heating, etc.
— Compatibility of systems such as radiators, warm air, pressured air, underfloor heating, ceiling panel, etc.
— Insulating qualities (heat and sound) of existing fabric
— Ease of upgrading the insulation
— Any obvious restrictions on materials
■ *Materials*
— Durability
— Appearance
— Appropriateness
— Consider floor, walls and ceiling and roof
— Heat-retaining qualities
— Susceptibility to condensation
■ *Ventilation*
— Natural
— Artificial

- *Lighting*
  - — Natural
  - — Artificial
- *Acoustics*
  - — Materials
  - — Room shape and volume and texture
- *Design considerations*
  - — Possibility of division vertically and/or horizontally
  - — Possibility of creating large unobstructed spaces
  - — Means of escape in the event of fire
  - — Pedestrian and vehicular access
  - — Disabled access
  - — General shape as existing compared to the required or ideal shape
- *Environmental requirements*
  - — Internally: problems in heating, lighting, humidity, ventilation, damp penetration
  - — Externally: effect of alterations on external appearance and the relationship to other buildings and spaces
- *Possible adaptation techniques*
  - — Complete gutting
  - — Partial gutting
  - — Virtually complete retention of existing structure
- *Likely costs*

In practice, the architect will not separate the above into separate categories. Indeed, it can be seen that some factors fall into or have relevance in several categories. Part of the architect's skill in assessing whether an existing building is appropriate for a particular use is to keep all these factors in mind and weigh one against another in arriving at a considered view. There are certain other legal considerations which are addressed later in this chapter.

7.4 Surveys

Whether the architect advises on the acquisition of land or buildings or whether the client presents a *fait accompli*, a survey will be required before the architect can proceed with design work. 'Survey' is an imprecise term referring to an activity which may range from taking a detailed set of measurements, including levels, and translating them into careful drawings, to an inspection of varying degrees of thoroughness resulting in a written report. It is, therefore, very important for the architect to establish from the outset the kind of survey which will be required.

For example, if the client is simply considering purchase and development of existing property, an inspection and written report is appropriate together with a rough sketch containing a few key dimensions. However, if the architect is presented with a site and instructed to produce a feasibility study, a very general idea of the dimensions, levels and other features is required sufficient to determine whether the project can be fitted onto the site and a wholly different set of information must be considered (see section 7.1). In practice, however, the most common kind of survey in which the architect will be interested is the measured survey.

The next thing the architect must decide is whether to advise the client to engage a surveyor (land surveyor or building surveyor as appropriate) to carry out the work. If the site is relatively small and uncomplicated or the existing building and its proposed alterations are simple in character, the architect can probably do the survey work without difficulty. For anything other than the simplest sites or buildings, a survey produced by an independent surveying firm is indicated. The main reason is that surveying is becoming very sophisticated and the equipment tends to be highly expensive. It makes no economic sense for the architect to have that kind of equipment and be trained in its use unless it will be operated on a regular basis. Moreover, in the case of complex surveys, the architect cannot hope to compete in speed and accuracy with the surveyor who is doing the job full time. However, in the case of an existing building, the architect may wish to augment the survey with further detailed sketches and photographs, particularly if it is an historic building.

7.4.1   Preliminary enquiries

Before tackling the survey or instructing the surveyor to do the work, the architect should make certain enquiries. Some of these enquiries will produce information which is vital to the survey or which assists the architect at the feasibility stage. It is suggested that the following should always be consulted.

- *Local Planning Authority:* they have a wealth of information and they will advise on such things as the structure plan, local plans, unitary development plans, conservation areas, listed buildings and trees with preservation orders. In addition, of course, they will have a view on the acceptability of the proposed development.
- *Building Control Office:* old deposited drawings may be very revealing, but often the Building Control Officer may be the best source of information.
- *Local history department of the public library:* the curator will normally have a great deal of information in the form of old maps and plans of the area or of the building. Such things as ancient quarries, river courses and even tunnels may be discovered in this way.
- *Local inhabitants:* they can give helpful information, but this should always be supported in some other way if possible. Pointers to the possibilities of easements may be obtained (see Chapter 9, section 9.6.7), but watch out for petty rivalries which may fog the memory. It has been known for an old person to positively remember that the site in question used to harbour an old mineshaft only for it to be discovered much further down the road.
- *The mineral valuer:* useful in respect of the nature of the subsoil and the possibility of faults, filled ground, etc.

- *Coal Authority:* for a fee they will provide a short report about the past and projected mine workings which may affect the site. For a larger fee, they will supply more detailed information which may require an expert to interpret.
- *Deeds Registry or County Office:* tend to be the repository of legal information and deed plans, but it is amazing what can be discovered in the conveyancing history of a piece of land.
- *Client's solicitor:* with the client's permission, of course, for advice on any matters affecting the land such as covenants or easements.

7.4.2   Site investigation

This term has come to mean the investigation of the ground under the site. Some of the information discovered when conducting the preliminary enquiries will give valuable hints regarding the kind of site investigation which should be carried out. If the building is other than relatively small and light, a specialist consultant engineer should be engaged by the client to advise on and oversee the investigation. Such a consultant should be nominated by the architect. There are firms which specialise in ground investigations, but it is essential that they are given a proper brief so that they can form conclusions regarding the scope of the investigation. Even where the proposed building is very light and the ground has no known problems, the architect will have some trial pits dug in order to confirm that all is well. It is usual to set out the positions of the pits with regard to the actual siting of the building.

If a specialist firm is employed, the type of investigation proposed will depend on the proposed building and the kind of ground conditions expected. The usual method is to sink boreholes and measure the samples, taking various tests for acidity, sulphate content, strengths under varying conditions and so on. If the height of the building suggests that piles will be required, the boreholes may well be sunk to great depths. The firm will prepare a report which will repay careful study. If in doubt, the architect should never hesitate to request the firm or specialist to produce a further report to explain the first. The interpretation of soil investigation reports is something for an engineer to advise upon.

A major problem is deciding where to take the boreholes so as to reveal the true nature of the ground. Again, this is a task for an expert engineer, but it is common for the boreholes to be set out in a random formation, particularly when checking to find shallow mine workings, such as pillar and stall workings which are sometimes flooded. Setting out boreholes regularly in such situations may lead to each borehole being sunk down the centre of a pillar and giving an entirely false picture.

7.4.3   General considerations

Other considerations which should be carefully studied are the aspect, orientation, shelter, overshadowing from adjacent buildings, existence of services such as sewers, water, electricity and gas, means of access to the public highway and communications. In rural districts the suitability of the site for sewage disposal plant or the sinking of a well may also have to be considered. Topographical and other features of the site must be recorded, including such things as levels, dimensions, benchmarks, positions and types of trees, existing buildings on and near the site and their character, overhead cables and poles, rivers, lakes, springs, rocky outcrops, fissures and the type of vegetation.

The architect must never make the mistake of thinking that a first-class survey is a substitute for visiting the site. Not even a superb set of photographs taken from every angle or a video of the site will suffice. Often an architect will spot a potential problem or get a feeling for the kind of building required during the first site visit. It may be because of a particular view or a grouping of existing buildings or something as intangible as the atmosphere. It is our opinion that site visits are essential.

Even if a surveyor has been engaged to carry out the survey, the architect should make a point of walking all over the site or, in the case of a building, walking throughout the building and actually entering every room, stopping and looking all around, including ceiling and floors. Only by doing this will the architect thoroughly know the site or building and satisfy the duty of care owed to the client.

7.4.4 Surveys of existing buildings

Unless it is absolutely out of the question, the architect should always carry out an existing building survey.[4] Not only will the architect know precisely what is required in the form of illustrative drawing so far as difficult details are concerned, he or she will learn about the way the building is constructed by the very process of carrying out the survey and plotting the results.

If a simple extension is to be made to an existing building, as opposed to the alteration of the building itself, it will be sufficient to survey only the part of the building immediately adjoining the proposed extension. Some suitable point on the existing building probably will be chosen as a temporary benchmark which may or may not be related to ordnance levels. The exact positions of all plinths, string courses, openings and other features on the elevations which have to be taken into consideration should be noted. The precise level of every floor should be established, carefully checking that the floors are themselves level and, if not, the taking of several levels along the edge of each floor at the point of extension. The thickness and construction of any walls to be cut through should be determined also. In old buildings, it is not unusual to find dummy columns and pilasters, and even the wall thickness itself may consist of battened out voids covered in thick plaster or stucco. The levels of the external ground must be established.

The first thing the architect will do after arriving at the building is to take a general walk around and observe the surroundings, the condition of boundary walls and fences and any outbuildings. After looking at the outer elevations and looking into each room internally, the architect will be able to form an opinion regarding the overall condition and place the building in one of the following categories.

- In good repair
- Neglected, but basically sound structurally
- In poor condition structurally, perhaps in a dangerous state

In some instances, the architect will find a very serious problem during the initial walkabout. In such circumstances, there is no alternative but to telephone the client immediately for further instructions. Clearly, there is little point in continuing to survey a building which is only fit for demolition. Whatever the client's instructions may be, the architect should always confirm them in writing.

During the survey, it may be necessary to obtain the client's authority to employ a builder to assist the investigations by taking up floor boards or exposing part of the foundations. This kind of investigation cannot be carried out if the client does not own the property unless the actual owner has given express permission. The architect is always wise to get such permission in writing through the client.

Investigations should encompass the various services – whether they exist and if they do, what their condition is. Gas, water, electricity, drainage, hot water, cable TV, etc. may all require substantial overhaul or renewal. The condition of the roof, eaves, flashings, rainwater pipes and gutters, damp-proof course and any other features which prevent moisture from penetrating into the building deserve particular attention, as all the money spent on improving or redecorating the property may be wasted if some fault in these areas is overlooked. It would not be overstating the point to say that damp is at the root of most building defects.

Although it may be that the eventual scheme for the building will only affect certain parts, it is usually best to make an accurate measured survey of the whole, including all internal heights, so that sections can be drawn through any part without much difficulty. The only exception to this general rule is if the architect knows clearly in advance just which parts of the building are to be affected. Some architects advocate the making of a rough survey in the first instance, to be followed by a thorough survey only when the new design has been approved by the client. Down that road lies disaster. The architect may find that he or she is faced with trying to make a scheme work which the later detailed survey shows cannot work, possibly because of an impossible change in levels or of headroom.

The golden rule is never to make assumptions. Inevitably, if the architect has done the survey, he or she will discover, when plotting, that certain dimensions have been forgotten. There is no alternative but to return to the building and check them. This can be difficult if the building is some distance from the office. In those circumstances, the prudent architect will take equipment along to enable the building to be roughly plotted out on site as a check.

Each room or space on the survey drawing must be given a number so that they can be identified easily by giving them the same number on the alteration drawings. Describing the rooms simply as 'N-E bedroom' or 'small rear office' simply leads to confusion. It is good practice to provide the contractor with a set of drawings of the building as existing so that comparison of existing and proposed can be made readily. The following is a brief checklist covering the major areas to be considered when carrying out a survey.

Building site

Development

- Permitted development and restrictions under the structure and local plans
- Zoning, density, floor space index, etc. as applicable
- Improvement lines
- Proposed adjacent development

History of the site

- Rights of public and adjoining owners
- Boundaries or party walls or fences

Nature of ground and subsoil

- Trial holes or other evidence of nature of subsoil
- Precautions against subsidence, seasonal variations in subsoil and water table
- Safe bearing capacity of subsoil
- Report from mineral valuer and geologist
- Susceptibility to flooding

Condition of site

- Levels and gradients
- Benchmarks
- Shelter from or exposure to surrounding ground
- Direction of prevailing wind
- Aspect and orientation
- Dimensions and area of site
- Existing trees and features
- Existing buildings on the site and on adjoining land
- Overhead cables and poles

Services

- Position, size and depth of public sewers
- If no sewer, suitability and possible siting of septic tank and overflow outlet

- Utility services available, such as gas, water, electricity, etc. with names and addresses of supply undertakings
- Position and pressure of water main
- Electricity supply, voltage, capacity of any existing cables
- Position and size of gas main
- Telephone service
- Possibility of sinking well

Communications

- Means of access
- Nature and proximity of public highway
- Rights of way across site

Existing buildings (in addition to the foregoing, so far as applicable)

Drawings

- Plans, elevations, sections, details as necessary, drawn to scale

Construction

- Type and method of construction of foundations, walls, floors and roof
- Wall and floor thicknesses
- Hidden construction features
- Special finishes

Condition of structure

- Signs of rot, beetle or other infestation, etc., in timber
- Decay or spalling in concrete
- Excessive rusting or distress in steel members
- Looseness of plaster surfaces
- Deterioration of UPVC
- Damp penetration through roofs, flashings and gutters
- Condensation
- Damp-proof course to walls
- Settlement cracks
- Windows and doors, etc.

Condition of services

- Gas, water, electricity, drains, central heating, hot water, TV cable, aerial or dish, vacuum, computer, specialised gases or other links
- Possibility of extending the services

History of the building

- Age
- Purposes of previous occupation
- Quality of previous maintenance work

7.5   The brief

One of the architect's most important functions is the taking of an accurate brief from the client. Yet many architects are very careless in this respect. The brief is the client's instructions to the architect. It may be intensely detailed and complex and, since the architect's task is to satisfy the brief, it is essential that it is as clear as possible. Of course, it may not be possible to produce a very clear brief. Indeed, the very essence of some briefs is their vagueness and the freedom of the architect to produce a solution within very broad parameters. This is probably because, in those instances, the client does not know what he or she wants.

That raises another important point. The architect's function is really to produce not what the client wants but what the client needs. That is the function of every professional person. The process of setting down what the client needs may take a long time. Once accomplished, the design process may be swift. In some cases, such as the brief for a new hospital, the pace of development may be so quick that there is never any hope of the architect producing anything more than a loose brief designed, hopefully, to accommodate as many changes as possible so that the design will never be finally fixed until the contractor has left site.

The traditional method of taking a brief would result in a schedule of accommodation required. That system has long since been defunct in favour of a user requirement study or some development of that principle. The idea is that the architect analyses the client's needs in terms of activities and identifies, in respect of each activity, a number of key criteria including direction of movement, areas, volumes, requirements for finishes, orientation and aspect, interaction with other activities and to what extent, numbers of persons involved, special requirements ancillary to the activity, social and psychological needs.

A great deal of work may be necessary to produce a brief of this nature in terms of research or operational study or both. In many cases, it will not be justified if the proposed building is a common building type. Even if that is the case, the architect should always be wary that the brief which the client has come to know and love over the years may be flawed or may have become flawed with the passing of time and the introduction of new processes, etc.

The result of any briefing exercise will be something in writing or, in some instances, in graphical form. Wherever possible, the architect should try to schedule information in logical form and to confine other written material to note form. There will be much information in the form of hard facts, but there will also be much in less tangible form. It is often useful to separate the two. The brief should always be confirmed to the client before the next stage is commenced.

7.6 Reporting

Architects are expected to report to their clients at various stages throughout the design and construction period. Stage B is probably the earliest stage at which a client can expect a formal report and, of course, such a report will not always be in writing. Indeed, for a very small project and an unsophisticated client, a written report is probably quite inappropriate.

It is often difficult to decide when to report and when a report is unnecessary, but it is usual to make a report of some kind whenever an architect wants some kind of decision from the client. The purpose of the report in such an instance is to acquaint the client with the appropriate information on which to base a decision. There will be other instances when the architect requires no decision, but it is simply good client relations to report on progress. A client, like anyone else, always likes to know that he or she is not forgotten.

The following list indicates typical reports the architect may produce while running a project, not all of which will be applicable on every project.

- Feasibility
- Outline proposals
- Scheme design
- Progress reports
- Extension of time
- Loss and/or expense
- Special reports, i.e. before termination, after insurance risk damage, etc.

The architect will also be responsible for passing on and, if appropriate, commenting upon reports received from other consultants – for instance, cost reports from the quantity surveyor, reports on structural condition from the structural engineer, etc. Sometimes such reports are submitted direct by the consultant concerned and the client may particularly require cost reports to be submitted directly. However, from an organisational point of view, it is better that they pass through the hands of the architect so that the employer deals with one person and a possible clash of professional interests is avoided. Some brief comments on report writing are covered in Chapter 15, section 15.5.

References

1. Lupton, S. (ed) (2001) *Architect's Handbook of Practice Management*, 7th edn, RIBA Publishing.

2. 3DReid (2008) *Architect's Job Book*, 8th edn, RIBA Publishing.
3. Glover, P. (2008) *Building Surveys*, Butterworth-Heinemann; Hoxley, M. (2002) *Construction Companion to Building Surveys*, RIBA Publishing.
4. Hollis, M. (2005) *Surveying Buildings*, 5th edn, RICS Books.

8 Stage B: Design Brief

This stage is defined by the RIBA as:

'Development of initial statement of requirements into the Design Brief by or on behalf of the client confirming key requirements and constraints. Identification of procurement method, procedures, organisational structure and range of consultants and others to be engaged for the project.'

8.1 Consultants

A consultant is someone who gives expert advice or assistance. Common types of consultants in connection with construction work are:

- quantity surveyor/cost manager
- structural engineer
- electrical services engineer
- mechanical services engineer
- planner
- interior designer
- landscape architect.

A consultant, of course, can be anyone the client or the architect considers necessary to assist in the development of the project. The architect may be a consultant on the same basis as other consultants in those instances when another construction professional has been chosen to be the lead consultant or where a project manager has been engaged to administer the contract. In many cases, however, the architect is the lead consultant because of the particular breadth and scope of training he or she has undergone and we will assume that to be the case in this instance (see section 8.2 which deals with project managers).

If the project is small, the architect may feel capable of carrying out the whole of the design work. The professional indemnity insurance, however, must always cover all the kinds of work the architect undertakes to carry out. On larger projects, the architect should nominate consultants to deal with those areas of work which are outside the architect's competence. Consultants are employed either directly by the client or by the architect. It is better for the architect if the former is the case, because there is then a direct contractual link established between consultant and client which is clearly useful in the case of problems with liability and fees (see Chapter 6, section 6.4). Where the architect appoints the consultant, any action in respect of the consultant's negligence will be taken by the client against the architect. In order to recover the whole or a contribution to any damages, the architect will join the consultant as third party. Therefore, care must be taken that the consultant has appropriate professional indemnity insurance and provides the architect with an indemnity in respect of the work carried out.

It is good practice, indeed almost essential, that consultants be appointed as soon as their need is identified. In practice, this will be shortly after the architect has clarified the brief with the client. It is sometimes difficult to convince a client that consultants are necessary. The client is conscious of the additional fees. It is part of the architect's duty to advise the client when consultants are required. To delay the appointment of consultants may result in the redesign of large parts of the project at a late stage.

Most architects are aware of the need for early appointment of the quantity surveyor, structural engineer and building services engineers, but the value of early appointment of the landscape architect is sometimes overlooked. Often, the landscape architect's appointment in the design team occurs after feasibility studies and sketch design when it suddenly becomes apparent that their services are required to gain planning consent. This is unfortunate, because the landscape architect offers the greatest value to a project at the beginning of the design process. The synergy of the architect and landscape architect from the beginning of the project will ultimately be more cost effective for the client as the design will be appropriate from the outset.

However consultants are appointed, they must be made aware of the extent of the services required from them. Ideally, this information should be imparted at the time of appointment, carefully recorded and made the basis of the contract of engagement in each case. It is also crucial that an early design team meeting is arranged at which all consultants, and the client, are present so that any problems in the interface of responsibilities can be ironed out. All consultants must report to the architect unless another construction professional has the co-ordinating role.

The traditional standard forms of contract do not generally make any reference to consultants other than the quantity surveyor. An exception is the JCT Management Contract 2005, but there the reference is confined to the Articles and they are not mentioned in the conditions. The ACA Project Partnering Contract (PPC 2000) makes a feature of being a multi-party contract. All consultants should report to the architect if acting as lead consultant. Obviously, it is essential that all consultants inspect their own work on site, but no contract gives them power to give instructions. A consultant who wishes to issue an instruction should first submit it to the architect who may incorporate it into an architect's instruction. Indeed, strictly they can only enter the site if the architect makes them authorised representatives for the sole purpose of inspecting their own portions of the works. Before issuing the certificate of practical completion for the works, the architect should obtain an appropriate certificate from each consultant in respect of the practical completion of each specialist section of work.

8.2 Project managers

Although at one time architects were considered to be the obvious choice as the professionals most suited to lead the building team, that is no longer necessarily the case as the concept of project management has become established. A project manager, however, may or may not be the same person as the lead consultant or the contract administrator. All these terms contain a mixture of the woolly and the legally specific. A definition of a project manager approved by the RIBA is:

> 'The Project Manager is a construction professional who can be given *executive authority and responsibility* to assist the client to identify the project objectives and subsequently supply the technical expertise to assess, procure, monitor and control the external resources required to achieve those objectives, defined in terms of time, cost, quality and function.'[1]

That definition is worth careful study. Clearly, the kind of person capable of carrying out that role will be formidable. The reference to 'control the external resources' opens up a whole new dimension and one wonders how feasible it is to have one person in this position. It could never be said of architects in traditional scenarios that they controlled external resources. To control is to dominate and to regulate. It could never be said that architects controlled contractors.

So far as the courts are concerned, project manager is not a specific discipline.

> 'There is no chartered or professional institution of project managers nor a recognisable profession of project managers. In so far as it may be appropriate to accept expert evidence, the nature of the evidence that might be acceptable will depend on what the project manager has agreed to do.'[2]

Essentially, the court was saying that the duties of a project manager would depend on the construction professional who carried out that role and what the role was in a particular case. Project management considered in the vacuum, unfortunately all too common, is the subject of many books and articles. The concept of project management is not particularly linked to construction; there is no good reason why it should be so linked. It is well expressed by the following definition:

> 'Project management is a collection of loosely connected techniques, some of which are useful in bringing projects to a successful conclusion. Clearly, the project manager manages. He must think about motivation, team building, career growth, financial control, and all the other things that concern managers. In addition he has to head off into the unknown. His path is not clear, his path has not been trod before, but his objective will be clear.
>
> Something that is special about project management, something that separates project management from plain old management, is the need and the emphasis on planning. Simply because the project management team is following no known path, they must think ahead all the time. They are

continually faced with decisions about the route ahead and must plan for events that are long distant in the future. Hence here is a formula that neatly paints a picture:

$$\frac{\text{management} + \text{planning}}{\text{project management.}^3}$$

Project managers may be divided broadly into two categories.

- Project managers (type 1) who act as the technical arm of the employer.
- Project managers (type 2) who carry out the contract administration role in regard to building contracts.

The contractual relationships are quite different. If this difference is not appreciated, very serious consequences may result.

Project manager type 1

This type of project manager acts as the client's representative. Generally, they act as agent for the client with the power to do, in relation to the project, everything the client could do. They will interview and appoint consultants and carry out the briefing exercise, having first been briefed by the client. The advantage is that there is a skilled professional looking after the client's interests and being paid to watch the other professionals. The project manager has no powers under the building contract. Indeed, most building contracts do not even acknowledge the project manager's existence as distinct from the architect or contract administrator. Thus, the project manager has no power to verify or sign any certificates nor to recommend payment. Indeed, any interference by the project manager in the running of the contract can be interpreted as interference by the employer, with significant adverse consequences.

There is provision under clause 3.3 of the SBC for an employer's representative, who might well be the project manager, to be appointed to carry out the employer's functions. Unless the standard form contracts are amended, project manager type 1 has no more right than the employer to enter site, nor to attend site meetings and certainly not to give instructions to the contractor. Most project managers in this position tend to be notable for strong views forcibly expressed. A contractor should not take instructions from a project manager in this position. The project manager has no status on site during the progress of the works. Attempts by the project manager to organise, run or chair site meetings should be firmly resisted.

This is probably the usual position occupied by the person termed project manager. It should be noted that it does not replace the traditional architect's role and there is still a need for a lead consultant, whoever that might be.

Project manager type 2

This type of project manager performs all the functions of a contract administrator in regard to the building contract and, indeed, must be named as contract administrator in the contract. This person alone may issue instructions and certificates. In such circumstances, it is essential that the appointment documents of the other construction professionals reflect the situation. For example, the project manager is responsible for co-ordinating their roles and must have the authority to do so. The project manager in this situation wields a great deal of power. If the project manager's function is to manage the project, this type of project manager is closest to that role. However, it is comparatively rare to find a project manager in this position. Because this is the role traditionally taken by architects, an architect trained in project management techniques makes a good type 2 project manager.

General

Whatever the role, and it is possible to find a project manager working solely for a contractor or for a large consortium, the project manager is supposed to have certain skills. Dependent upon the role, the required skills may vary or they may be applied in different ways. Shorn of excessive jargon, they are as follows.

- Management
- Construction law
- Contract law
- Value management
- Value engineering
- Procurement and contract options
- Project planning and programming
- Briefing
- Cost control
- Risk management
- Contract administration
- Dispute resolution

There are various courses on which a budding project manager may enrol. Before choosing a course, the prospective project manager may care to reflect on the fact that project management is not a universal skill. Project management of a building project, with its many disparate elements, is quite different from, say, project management of a new product through a factory. The two tasks may use some similar skills, but they are not comparable.

8.3 Procurement paths and implications for the professional

The procurement system should be the most appropriate in the light of the criteria signalled to the architect by the client during and after the briefing stage. In choosing a procurement path, the key criteria are the client's priorities in respect of:

- *time:* economy and certainty
- *cost:* economy and certainty
- *control:* apportionment of risk
- *quality:* in design and construction
- *size/value:* small/medium/large
- *complexity:* complex/simple.

There are as many different procurement systems as there are pebbles on the beach, but some of them are different only in detail. The principal systems may be expressed as follows:

- traditional
- project management
- design and build
- design and manage
- management contracting
- construction management.

These systems are different from each other in significant ways. Other systems of procurement are touted from time to time, but they tend to be based on one or other of these six processes.

8.3.1 Traditional

Very broadly, this is where the client commissions an architect to take a brief, produce designs and construction information, invite tenders, administer the project during the construction period and settle the final account. If the building is other than small and straightforward, the architect will advise the client to appoint other consultants to deal with particular items, such as quantities and cost estimating services generally, structural calculations and building services design. The contractor, who has no design responsibility, will normally be selected by competitive tender or there may be good grounds for negotiating a tender.

It should be noted that the JCT 2005 suite of traditional contracts provides options for the contractor to carry out and to be responsible for design of specific parts of the building (the Contractor's Designed Portion) and this option is available in SBC, ICD and MWD, but that is a sophistication.

The essentials of traditional procurement are that the architect is the independent advisor to the client responsible for the design. The contractor is only responsible for executing the work in accordance with the drawings and specifications produced by the architect and other professionals. Figure 8.1 shows the relationships of the parties in diagrammatic terms.

8.3.2 Project management

Although this is a somewhat imprecise term, it has much in common with the traditional system (see section 8.2 for a description of the role). However, here

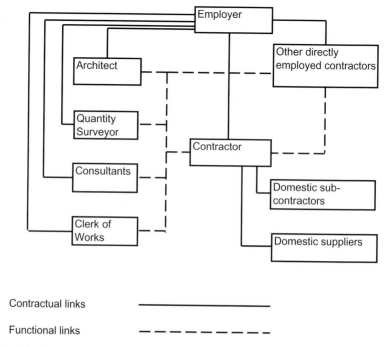

Contractual links   ——————————

Functional links   – – – – – – – – –

Fig. 8.1   Traditional contract.

the architect is not the leader of the team but rather the project manager takes the lead. The project manager, of course, can be an architect and most architects would say that an architect is the obvious choice for the post in view of his or her particular training. Essentially, the project management system places most emphasis on planning and management. Therefore, a person, whether architect, engineer or surveyor, with the relevant project management skills is required. The project manager is likely to appear in one of two principal roles: either simply as the technical agent of the employer for the purposes of the project or as the professional with the authority to manage the project, including organising and co-ordinating all consultants. In either case, the project manager acts as a link between the client and the design team. Depending upon the particular kind of project management chosen, the contract administrator may be the project manager or the architect. Figures 8.2 and 8.3 show the relationship of the parties in diagrammatic terms.

8.3.3   Design and build

This is a system which has grown in popularity and which appears in various guises. Many so-called new procurement systems have design and build at their heart. It places responsibility for both design and construction in the hands of the contractor. There are variations in the name and there are subtle differences in meaning. *Design and build*, for example, refers to the basic system where a contractor carries out the two functions. *Design and construct* includes

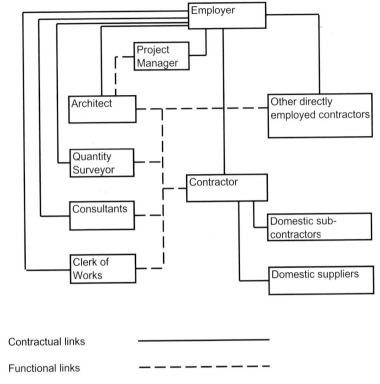

Contractual links

Functional links

Fig. 8.2   Project management type 1.

design and build and other types of construction such as purely engineering works. *Develop and construct* often describes a situation where a contractor takes a partially completed design and develops it into a fully detailed design. *Package deal* can be used to refer to either of these. In theory, the term suggests that the contractor is responsible for providing everything in one package and it is particularly apt when referring to an industrialised building. *Turnkey* contracting is a system in which the contractor really is responsible for everything, including furniture and pictures on the walls if required. The idea is that the employer simply turns the key and begins using the building – hence the name.

Many architects are unduly concerned about design and build, as though every such contract is one less for an architect to design. Nothing could be further from the truth. Unless the building is very simple, the contractor will seek an architect to carry out the design, including all the preliminary briefing and feasibility work, where necessary, and also the preparation of constructional drawings. From the client's point of view, an independent advisor is required to look after the client's interests before, during and after construction. There is no doubt that the architect's role is different from the traditional one, but that should not be a problem. It does not necessarily mean, because an architect has a contractor for a client, that he or she will be unable to

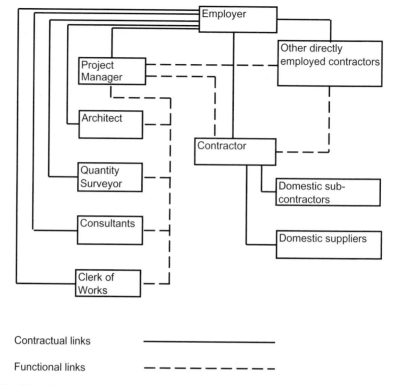

Fig. 8.3 Project management type 2.

produce good architecture. It is very much in the contractor's interest that the employer is happy with the finished building.

The employer may approach a design-and-build contractor as soon as the intention to build starts to form. The contractor then takes charge of the project until completion. The architectural function will either be carried out in the contractor's own architects' department or, more commonly, by subletting the work to a firm of architects in private practice. An architect in such an instance will owe a duty to the contractor, which will depend on the conditions of engagement agreed for the work. Generally, the duty will probably be to carry out the architectural functions in obtaining and satisfying the brief and perhaps to carry out quality control duties on behalf of the contractor during the construction period. An architect in those circumstances will have no duty to the employer other than the common law duty to ensure that the design will not result in injury or death to the employer or those who will use the building and damage to property other than the building itself.[4]

Alternatively, the employer may engage a full design team to complete the design of the building and a great many production drawings in some detail before seeking tenders from contractors to complete the design and construct the building.

Most commonly, however, the employer will engage an architect to prepare an outline scheme together with a performance specification on which contractors will be invited to tender. The architect will organise tendering and will act as the employer's agent under the contract. The contractor will engage an architect to do the detailed design development work and to produce the production information to satisfy the performance specification.

A system which is increasing in popularity involves what is known as a 'consultant switch'. In this system, an architect or even a full design team is engaged by the employer to prepare all the initial material. This contract comes to an end at about tender stage and tenders are invited on the basis that the successful contractor will take the design team on board as the contractor's consultants to complete the work. When a contractor is appointed, it is obliged to enter into a contract with the architect to carry out the relevant services for the contractor during the construction period. There must be a term in the original contract with the employer which obliges the architect to enter into the contract with the contractor and there must be a copy of the architect/ contractor contract attached to the original contract with the employer to signify that the parties agree the wording. When tenders are invited, the contractor must agree to the switch and to the terms of the contract with the architect. The two contracts may be, and often are, entirely different. There is no need for a three-way agreement. The architect and employer still retain liability to each other for the performance of the original contract and none of this liability is assumed by the contractor. The architect must remember who the client is at any particular moment, because the contractor will require somewhat different service than that which was given to the employer. After the switch, the employer must either do without independent advice or engage another architect for that purpose.

This system is often wrongly referred to as 'novation'. Novation is similar in general effect, but with some important differences. It is a legal procedure by which a contract between the architect and the employer is replaced by another contract on identical terms between architect and contractor. Because, as noted above, the contract between architect and employer and architect and contractor will require different terms, novation agreements commonly incorporate a schedule of changes. The agreement must be made between all three parties. In novation, a contractor who effectively replaces the employer assumes all the responsibilities of the employer to the architect as though the contractor had been a party to the contract instead of the employer from the beginning. The architect assumes liabilities to the contractor and releases the employer from liability. The architect is released from liability to the employer. To be effective, the original contract between employer and architect must contain a clause agreeing to the novation and the three-party novation agreement must be attached to the contract to signify that both parties are agreed on the wording. When tenders are invited, the contractor must agree to the novation and to the terms of the novation. It is sometimes seen as a means of assembling all the design responsibility in one place more effectively than can be achieved by other means. Whether that is so is open to question.

Most so-called 'novation agreements' are not strictly so. Most such agreements simply replace the employer with the contractor, releasing the employer from any liability to the architect and vice versa. The contractor is inserted into the contract as though the contractor had been the employer from the beginning. Novation agreements drafted by the contractor's solicitors will invariably contain what has come to be called a 'Blyth and Blyth clause'. This follows a case in which a contractor unsuccessfully attempted to recover damages from a firm of engineers who, it was alleged, had acted negligently during the time they were engaged by the employer.[5] The contractor failed, because it was unable to show that the employer, in whose place the contractor now stood, had incurred any loss as a result of the alleged negligence although the contractor certainly had done so.

Although both consultant switch and novation are popular, it is difficult to see how the architect or any of the design team in such instances do not find themselves in a conflict situation. Doubtless, the only thing which prevents such situations becoming serious professional issues is the fact that both employer and contractor agree to the arrangement in full knowledge of the implications.

The very worst thing that an architect could do would be to try and act for both employer and contractor. There is a clear conflict of interest. Although it may be thought that no architect would be so ill-advised as to attempt to act for both parties at the same time, the reality is that many clients have their own solicitors draft architect's terms of engagement which, surprisingly often, provide that the architect must report back to the employer on progress and other things while working for the contractor. Clearly, that is completely untenable and one may imagine the reaction of those same solicitors if it was suggested that they should act for one party while reporting back to another.

A particular point which architects should watch if they are asked to carry out work for contractors in a design-and-build scenario is the extent of the design obligation. An architect's normal obligation, like that of any other professional man, is to use reasonable skill and care. In contrast, the normal design-and-build liability, unless expressly amended, is to produce an end result which is fit for its purpose if that purpose is made known. The contractor may well attempt to engage an architect on 'fit for purpose' terms. Quite apart from the fact that such liability is very onerous and admits of no 'state of the art' defence, the architect's insurers are almost certain to refuse cover (see Chapter 17, section 17.5). The JCT DB contract, like its predecessors, restricts the contractor's design obligation to the normal duty of an architect – to take reasonable skill and care.

Figure 8.4 shows the relationship of the parties in diagrammatic terms.

8.3.4   Design and manage

This is comparatively rare in this country. Single-point responsibility rests with a professional who may be architect, engineer or surveyor. Besides being responsible for the design of the project, the professional also manages the project in the sense of managing the other professionals and also the construction process in the form of, probably, a number of sub-contractors and sup-

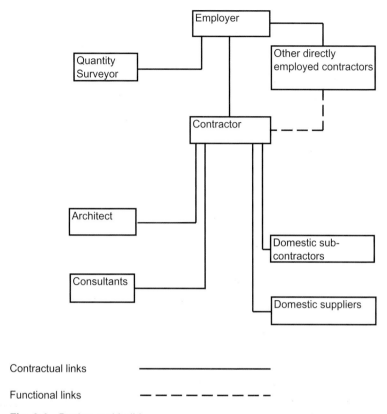

Contractual links ————————————

Functional links – – – – – – – –

Fig. 8.4 Design and build.

pliers. The few architects who become involved in this type of procurement have a background, or employ others with a background, in contracting. In this situation, the architect must be careful to explain to the employer that if the employer requires independent professional advice, another architect must be appointed. This type of procurement is ideal where relatively small projects require very detailed control over every aspect of the design detailing.

Figure 8.5 shows the relationship of the parties in diagrammatic terms.

8.3.5 Management contracting

This system seems to be waning in popularity as design and build increases its stake in the construction market – or perhaps design and build is gaining in popularity as management contracting is decreasing.

The contractor is selected at an early stage. It is not normally responsible for carrying out any of the construction work. The contractor simply has a management function for which a fee is paid. The construction work is divided into a number of packages with the contractor's advice and tenders for these individual packages are invited as appropriate to suit the programme. The works contractors are in contract with the management contractor and the

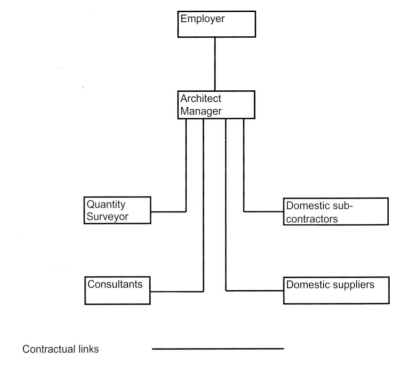

Contractual links   ————————

Fig. 8.5   Design and manage.

employer pays only the works contracts costs without the addition of any contractor's overheads or profit. In this respect the system has something in common with prime-cost contracting.

This type of contract has much in common with earlier forms of traditional contract in which all the work was sub-let to nominated sub-contractors. Management contracting is commonly said to allow the employer considerable freedom for change of mind while preserving price and end date. Such a contention is clearly contradictory and management contracts in practice appear notable for escalating costs and shifting end dates. The employer takes more risk under a management contract than would be the case under a traditional procurement system, but this is the price paid for greater control over the work. Although it is often said that the contractor is one of the design team under this procurement system, the reality is different. The fact that all the works contractors are in contract with the management contractor means that defective work or materials are the responsibility of the management contractor.

This is the system most often referred to as 'fast track', the idea being that work begins on site as soon as sufficient information has been produced to enable the first works contractors to start. The architect and other consultants are then involved in a constant race against time to produce the remainder of the drawings in time for the succeeding works packages. The architect must also be sufficiently organised to ensure that subsequent drawings do not necessitate the reconstruction of work already executed.

A few years ago, architects who failed to have all the drawings ready before a project began on site were heavily criticised by quantity surveyors, contractors and employers alike. From that point of view, management contracting could be said to have made a virtue out of necessity. Architects should not be misled, however, by the apparent glamour of fast-track contracting. The architect's liability is exactly the same. The system imposes a tough discipline on all sides. The employer must be precise in its stated requirements and prepared to hold fast to decisions. The preparation of information must be scheduled and on target, and the management of the contract must be tight. Any disputes which may arise can usually be traced to a failure to adhere to these principles.

It is, of course, quite difficult to perform under conditions of stress such as occur during fast-track building. It can be compared to driving a car: the faster the car is driven, the better the road and the mechanics have to be, and the further the driver has to see ahead. The driver is called upon to exercise more, not less, skill. The fast driver who has an accident is told that he or she should not have been driving so fast. The architect who makes a mistake purely as a result of fast building techniques must be told to get out of the fast lane.

Figure 8.6 shows the relationship of the parties in diagrammatic form.

8.3.6   Construction management

Once again, this system calls upon the contractor to act simply in a management capacity for which a fee is paid. The design team is often appointed directly by the employer, but in some instances the contractor may appoint. In such cases, the system has some of the flavour of project management. The key difference between this system and management contracting is that the individual works contractors (they are usually termed 'trade contractors' under this system) are in contract with the employer.

This overcomes a number of problems encountered under the management contracting system; notably, it allows the contractor, as construction manager, to become one of the team alongside architects, engineers, quantity surveyors, etc. and the trade contractors are liable for their breaches directly to the employer without the problems of an intervening contractor in the contractual chain. Although details vary, the construction manager is usually responsible for managing not only the trade contractors, but also the other consultants. Some very large projects have been carried out using this system which calls upon the same kind of skills from the design team as required under the management contract.

Figure 8.7 shows the relationship of the parties in diagrammatic form.

There are other ways of separating procurement systems such as by method of price determination, i.e. measurement or cost reimbursement contracts which must in any event be taken into account, and by reference to the method of contractor selection, i.e. competitive tender or negotiation.

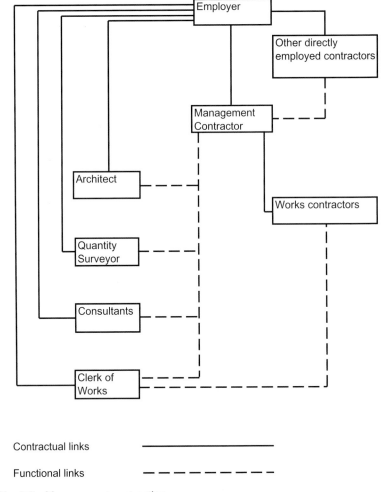

Contractual links

Functional links

Fig. 8.6 Management contracting.

8.4 Guaranteed maximum price

It has become common for contracts to be carried out on the basis of a guaranteed maximum price (GMP) as an add-on to virtually any of the basic procurement systems. Despite the title, the price under such contracts is neither guaranteed nor maximum. The term is misleading and encourages employers to believe that the price is the maximum amount to be paid no matter what the circumstances arising during construction. Employers may be under the impression that the contractor is giving an unconditional guarantee that under no circumstances will the price be exceeded. GMP contracts aim to achieve a degree of certainty about the maximum final cost of the project for the employer – no more and no less. The intention under a GMP contract is to place all the risk with the contractor except for employer changes or varia-

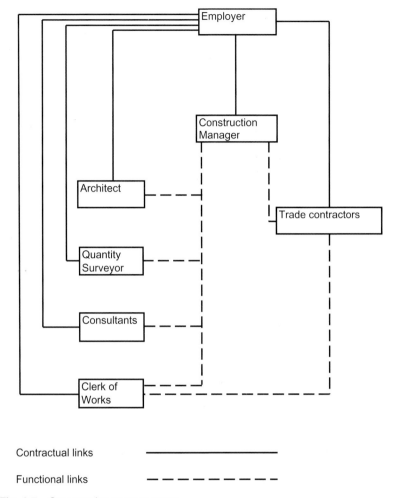

Contractual links ——————————

Functional links — — — — — — — —

Fig. 8.7 Construction management.

tions or employer's acts of prevention which result in loss and/or expense. Almost invariably, such contracts are based upon a design-and-build model. The contractor is expected to carry the risks associated with matters such as ground condition, services, weather and changes in legislation. There is no true GMP standard form of contract and most are specially drafted.

This kind of contract often has a target cost figure and the guaranteed maximum price is fixed above that. Any variations which increase the cost cause the target cost to be raised and the GMP to be raised by the same amount so that there is always a 'buffer zone' between the two. GMP contracts can be an effective method of keeping costs within a specified limit, but the disadvantages have to be accepted. The reality is that the contracts are usually on a design-and-build basis, which places a great deal of responsibility on the contractor in any event. This type of contract is often used in conjunction with terms dealing with sharing savings and some kinds of losses in certain circumstances.

8.5   PFI contracts

The Private Finance Initiative was introduced in 1992. It is not a procurement system, because any of the systems set out in section 8.3 can be used with PFI. It has become clear, however, that procurement routes based on some form of design and build, certainly contractor led, are the standard. The idea was that the private sector should be involved in providing and operating various assets which might otherwise never have been started. The system envisaged the eventual return of the project to the public sector. The idea had much to commend it and many PFI projects have been commenced. Private finance invested in the public sector introduces a high level of technical, managerial and financial skills and experience. By this means a construction company might actually be in the position of creating its own workload.

It is usual for a special purpose vehicle (SPV) to be set up for the express purpose of obtaining finance and carrying out the project. More often than not, it is a joint venture (JV) company between the finance providers and the building contractor. In order to ensure that the SPV secures a satisfactory return on investment, the agreements with central or local government are normally for periods of as much as 30 years. While apparently ensuring the time to make a substantial profit, the long time period places a high level of risk on the SPV which will have entered into several undertakings about the services to be provided. The system is not yet proven. There has been criticism of the system and there are misgivings among some construction companies who have indicated that they have had to bear most of the losses. A closely related system is public-private partnership (PPP).

Some types of development which the government has said would be suitable for PFI schemes include hospitals, prisons, public sector offices, types of housing, roads and railways. There are many complications and, of course, a whole new set of jargon is being created. Nevertheless, architects must have a thorough grasp of the implications.[6]

8.6   Partnering

Partnering has been defined as:

'A management approach used by two or more organisations to achieve specific business objectives by maximising the effectiveness of each participant's resources. The approach is based on mutual objectives, an agreed method of problem resolution and an active search for continuous measurable improvements.'[7]

Or, more succinctly as: 'a structured approach to facilitate team working'.[8]

It is important to know the difference between 'partnering' and 'partnership'. Partnership has been described in Chapter 4, section 4.2. When parties enter into partnership, they intend to, and do, enter into a very specific legal relationship. This is not what is intended by parties who enter into a partnering arrangement. Very often, the parties will prepare a 'charter' which will set out their joint aspirations. It is rare for the charter to define a legal relationship although it may sometimes overlap into that territory. There is still a necessity for a legally binding contract.

Basically, there are two approaches to partnering. The first requires the parties to enter into a legally binding contract which includes partnering principles such as trust as part of the contract. A problem with that is that many partnering concepts depend upon the good sense and goodwill of the participants for their implementation. The chance of making them enforceable at law may be slim. There are some contracts specifically intended to include partnering principles. PPC 2000 and Constructing Excellence are examples. Even the traditional JCT contracts SBC, DB, IC, ICD, MW and MWD were revised in 2009 (revision 2) to include supplemental provisions to deal with collaborative working, cost savings, value improvements and prompt notification of disputes.

The second approach involves the parties entering into a standard form of legally binding contract while at the same time setting out the partnering objectives in a separate non-binding charter. This has the great advantage of separating the agreement which can be enforced at law from the other agreement, which is simply an expression of how all parties want to work.

Partnering was one of the recommendations in the Latham Report.[9] Ideally, it should be a means to enable employers and contractors or contractors and sub-contractors or professionals and clients to work together with the object of reducing costs for mutual benefit. It should also have the effect of reducing conflict between the parties. It is not a procurement system, rather it is a commercial system. If all the people interested in getting a finished building on site were working in the same direction instead of constantly fighting, there would be benefits all around.

Some basic principles have been established. Not all of them are common to all partnering arrangements.

- Interests of all the participating parties must be identified.
- Potential conflict areas must be identified and eliminated if possible or, if not possible, they should be reduced.
- A system of incentives and rewards must be established which enables all parties to share in the rewards.
- Quality and production targets must be set for each project and improved upon in succeeding projects. Systems of measurement against those targets must be devised.
- Systems must be put in place to encourage the parties to work ever more closely together.
- Each party must be open with the other – the so-called 'open book policy'. The employer must have access to the contractor's costs.

Any kind of building contract can be used to procure the project, but very often some kind of cost plus or target cost arrangement, with some form of incentive arrangement, is used. Some contracts are framed so that the contractor is always sure of getting the costs of the project, even if there is no profit. Theoretically, in such cases, the contractor cannot actually make a loss, although the employer certainly can do so.

One of the problems is that partnering can suffer from the same affliction that bedevilled such concepts as 'fast track' and 'management contracting'. Many people are unsure what constitutes partnering. They have heard that it is 'a good thing' but they are not sure why that is the case. Just as every self-respecting large contractor used to bill themselves as 'managing', so no project seems to be worth considering unless 'partnering' is mentioned in there somewhere. Partnering is more about setting in place a particular ethos than anything else. Concepts of good faith, trust and fair play are important. No two partnering arrangements need be, and probably are not, the same.

The chances of successful partnering are very much increased when there is the prospect of a continuous string of projects, because the carrot of further work and turnover is always there even if the current project is a bit of a disappointment. The chances are lowest if just one project is involved or when tackling the last of a series of projects. Cynics may point out that partnering is merely serial contracting with attractive packaging. There is nothing wrong with that, of course.

'Serial contracting' works like this. On the basis of the successful tender for the first contract, further contracts are negotiated. To operate properly, the projects should be similar in construction and type so that negotiation for future contracts on the basis of original contracts is feasible. It is usual for the employer to make some sort of limited commitment to the contractor for the whole series. However, it is not something which can be legally enforced since it is always subject to the successful outcome of negotiations. The advantage is that one set of tendering takes place and the contractor can use the experience gained on the first contract to improve efficiency on the second, and so on. The maximum benefit is gained for the employer if the basic terms for the whole series can be established when calling for the initial tender. An intended programme for all the contracts in the series should be set down at the outset in order to allow the contractor to calculate the potential benefits to the full. The system should produce savings for both parties.

The results of the first partnering arrangements are making themselves known. Anecdotal evidence suggests problems arising from either employers or contractors using the cover of partnering to disguise business as usual. There are also success stories. The procedures will not be capable of serious analysis until they have been in place for a number of years or over a number of projects. Doubtless, by that time it will have been replaced by a new approach.

References

1. *Project Management – A Role for the Architect* (1995) RIBA Practice Committee, paragraph 3.2.

2. *Pride Valley Foods Ltd* v. *Hall and Partners (Contract Management) Ltd* (2000) 16 Const LJ 424.
3. Reiss, G. (2007) *Project Management Demystified*, 3rd edn, Taylor & Francis. This is an excellent book.
4. *Murphy* v. *Brentwood District Council* (1900) 50 BLR 1.
5. *Blyth and Blyth Ltd* v. *Carillion Construction Ltd* (2002) 79 Con LR 142.
6. Arrowsmith, S. (1999) *Public Private Partnerships and PFI*, Sweet & Maxwell; Geddes, M. (2005) *Making Public Private Partnerships Work*, Gower; Akintoye, A. and Beck, M. (2008) *Policy, Finance and Management for Public Private Partnerships*, Wiley-Blackwell.
7. *Trusting the Team* (1995) Centre for Strategic Studies in Construction, University of Reading, and the Reading Construction Forum.
8. CIB (1997) *Partnering in the Team: A Report by Working Group 12 of the CIB*.
9. Latham, M. (1994) *Constructing the Team*, HMSO.

9 Stages C and D: Concept and Design Development

9.1 Design data

The RIBA Plan of Work describes stage C as:

'Implementation of Design Brief and preparation of additional data.

Preparation of Concept Design including outline proposals for structural and building services systems, outline specifications and preliminary cost plan.

Review of procurement route.'

During these stages the architect will be involved in developing the brief, carrying out user requirement studies, gathering appropriate information, trying out solutions in consultation with other members of the team and preparing an outline proposal. It has already been seen (see Chapter 7, section 7.5) that the architect must prepare a brief on the basis of client needs rather than client wants, if the two do not coincide. If the brief is considered as a problem, the architect can only start to find the answer when all the necessary data have been assembled.

Much of the data will be collected as part of the feasibility study (see Chapter 7, section 7.1). Other factual material will concern relevant Acts of Parliament, Statutory Instruments and Regulations and the recommendations of appropriate bodies (e.g. Sports Council). In addition to this material, the architect will be concerned with user requirement studies. Some of this work may have been carried out while preparing the brief, but it is usual for more detailed studies to take place after the feasibility stage has been completed.

User requirement studies, put simply, attempt to encapsulate in easy reference form all the criteria which the user requires of the building. All buildings have more than one user, and there is the problem. Each user may have slightly, or even widely, differing requirements. Sometimes, different classes of person use the same building but they have almost opposing requirements. An example of a building where this is the case is a courthouse, where not only are the requirements of judges, prisoners and public quite different, but also the circulation routes must not cross. When one takes into account the needs of police, court officials, solicitors and others involved in the cases for trial, not to mention the complex administration requirements, a courthouse of any size becomes a very complex building. There are other buildings with equally complex user requirements.

Some part of the user requirement study will be factual, other parts will be more subjective and need to take into consideration such things as suitable environmental, social and psychological factors. During this stage, the architect will try to visit some good examples of the building type under consideration. Much other design data will be standard for most projects (see Chapter 5, section 5.4).

The point to appreciate is that all relevant design data must be available before the architect can seriously attempt to formulate even outline proposals. There is a need to emphasise this point because the temptation to launch into the design stage of an interesting project before all information is to hand can be hard to resist. The quantity surveyor will be providing advice about cost planning at this preliminary point.

9.2   Concept design and development

This is not the place to discuss architectural design. It is beyond the scope of this book. Most clients are not at all interested in design theory, they are only interested in results. If the results are bad, the theory is irrelevant.

As a basic principle, the architect should always keep the client informed of the progress of the design work. This is especially the case if the architect wants to attempt something rather different from the norm. In such a case, the client's agreement should be obtained first. In most cases, a client is interested only in such fundamentals as whether the building will successfully keep out the rain and the cold, how well it works and how much it will cost to build and to run. An architect who can keep a client happy on those points will have little to worry about. We are not aware that any architect has been the subject of legal proceedings purely because the client disliked the proportions of the front elevation or the overall massing of the building.

As a general rule, the architect should only present one proposal to the client. There are exceptions to this, as to every other rule, but they will be rare. The client looks to the architect and other members of the design team to produce a solution to the problems contained in the brief. Above all, a client expects advice. The team may well come to the conclusion that any one of a dozen different schemes could be developed into an acceptable project, but it is their function to recommend the one they consider to be the best. Unless the client has expressly asked for alternative proposals, one proposal shows that the architect is carrying out the job of eliminating options. Most options should be eliminated by a consideration of the brief, and the rest at feasibility stage. To present proposals which show major differences at this stage suggests that the architect has not carried out earlier tasks adequately.

During this stage, the architect will perform certain management functions. Co-ordination of the design team is an ongoing process throughout the design and construction stages of any medium to large project. As part of this process, the architect will be concerned with putting in place the procedures which will ensure that the team works as a team and not as a group of individuals, although it must be admitted that the ideal is easier to envisage than to achieve. A key factor will be the lines of, and frequency of, communication. As a general rule, all communications should be to the architect whose job it is to see that the appropriate information is properly distributed. Although it is vital that the structural engineer has all the information needed to enable a proper contribution to be made to the project, the architect must take care that individual team members are not swamped with information 'just in case' it might prove useful. This is where the managerial qualities of the architect should come to the fore.

It is useful to have a meeting for the team at the beginning of this stage to establish the following (adapted from the RIBA Plan of Work).

- The objectives (often overlooked; see Chapter 14, section 14.1).
- Available information regarding the brief, basic design data (see section 9.1 above), cost limits, timetable set by client or other restraints.
- Matters to be dealt with as priorities.
- Design team procedures, including roles and communications.
- The very important topics of procurement systems and contractual arrangements, tendering, type of bills, specification, schedules, and work methods.
- Any particular drawing techniques or systems (such as computer-aided design). It may indeed be a little late in the day to decide this point and it is something which the architect should consider at the briefing stage. The reason is that some consultants may not be willing to work within any given system of drawing. They may in fact have a fully operational computer drawing system which is incompatible with the architect's own system or they may have no system at all.
- System of carrying out cost checks during design.
- List of actions to be taken.
- Programming and progress techniques for the design team and for the project in construction.

At some point in stage C the architect will apply for outline planning approval. At the end of stage D, full planning permission should be sought (see section 9.4 below).

The RIBA Plan of Work describes stage D as:

'Development of concept design to include structural and building services systems, updated outline specification and cost plan.
  Completion of Project Brief.
  Application for detailed planning permission.'

The team should have a very clear idea of the brief during this part of the work. Indeed, the brief should be finalised and there should be no question of changing it once this stage is complete and the client should be so informed, otherwise much wasted time and money will be involved. What was thought of in terms of concepts during the last stage now have to be developed, with the advice of appropriate consultants, into a design which is quite detailed, i.e. the staircase must be capable of being made to work without altering its dimensions, and space allocations for columns, beams and services ducts must be adequate. Structural and services systems must be agreed. It is during this stage of work that every member of the team has to make a determined effort to work together. It really is no use the architect saying that all the other members must fit their designs into his or her master design and neither should any other consultants stick out for their own particular preferences. Unless the final design is a true combination of all the team working single-mindedly to solve the client's problems, the end result will be lacking in valid-ity. A modern building is so complex that single-handed design is not feasible.

At the end of this stage, the architect should be able to present the client with design drawings which show how the building will work and look and, if up-to-date computer techniques are employed, how the users will experience living and working in and around the building as part of the overall environ-ment. The effect of the building on that environment is an important part of current design and the architect will be reporting on the environmental impact of alternative materials and techniques.

The management function is much the same as in stage C, except that the procedures set up then should be fully operational and the architect is simply in the position of setting fresh objectives and timescales and ensuring that every member co-operates properly and at the right time. In addition, the architect will be ironing out any problems with relevant authorities, the most important of which will be:

- Water
- Electricity
- Gas
- Highways
- Drainage
- Fire
- telephone/communications
- Environmental Health
- Cleansing.

Many of these authorities require layout plans before they can comment sen-sibly and it is essential that the architect has agreements before this stage is completed or the whole scheme can be put at risk. Even something like refuse collection may pose severe problems if not tackled early with the support, rather than the opposition, of the local cleansing department. The need to divert the course of a substantial length of main drainage can jeopardise the entire project.

It is useful for the architect to submit a written report with the presentation drawings in which the major strengths can be emphasised and any weaknesses made clear. The architect should ask the client for agreement to proceed to tender stage through the technical design, production information and bills of quantity stages.

9.3   Cost estimates and planning

The quantity surveyor is the expert on costs. There is a world of difference between producing an estimate of the probable cost of a building from a set of drawings and producing a similar estimate from a brief and, as the design develops, putting together a cost plan which enables the architect to work within known cost limits in respect of each element. The cost plan will be developed and refined as the design crystallises. An experienced architect may make a reasonable attempt at the former, but only a skilled and experienced quantity surveyor will be able to carry out the latter with sufficient accuracy to be useful.

The client will have stated what can be afforded, but the architect may have to use some strategy in getting the true figure. On the basis that all building work costs more than expected or planned, the client will often present the design team with a reduced figure. When this happens, the team set their sights accordingly and when construction is nearing its end the client sometimes indulges in an orgy of expenditure and uses up his hidden balance in pointless extras when it would have been put to better use in perhaps increasing the overall floor area or heights, or other fundamental provision. Be that as it may, the team can do nothing other than to work to the budget given by the client. To do otherwise would amount to negligence and, at the very least, the professionals would lose their fees.

Although the client may state that the maximum expenditure is, say, £10,000,000, that information is of little help to the architect except in very general terms. It can be translated into rough areas or volumes on the basis of different constructional systems and finishes, e.g. expensive or basic. What the quantity surveyor can do is to produce a cost plan for the designers which allocates a sum of money to each element. For example, the cost of walls may be expressed as £x per square metre, similarly for floors, roofs and so on. Allocations for furniture can be made on a room-by-room basis. More importantly, the quantity surveyor can give the architect an idea of what those sums of money represent in terms of construction and finishes by giving a range of examples in each case. In order to be able to do this, the quantity surveyor has to be able to call upon a file or database of cost information and trends built up over a considerable period.

The cost plan can be presented in different ways so that, for example, if a housing estate is being considered, a price per dwelling may be expressed together with a figure for district heating, another for roads and footpaths, landscaping and so on. Over the years, professional journals have featured buildings whose costs have been presented in this way.

Irrespective of the level of detail within the cost plan, the overall accuracy of the costs is ultimately dependent on the design detail available and the extent of outstanding risks with potential cost implications at the time of estimating.

9.4   Town planning applications and approvals

9.4.1   Administration of planning control

Town planning functions in the UK operates on two main tiers: a central government tier under the mantle of a Secretary of State or Minister, responsible to Parliament or the national assembly, and a local government tier under elected councillors in the shape of local planning authorities. Across most parts of the UK, more emphasis has been placed on regional planning, generally under regional planning bodies comprising elected members from constituent authorities and other stakeholders.

This section gives an overview of the key elements of the planning function in the UK. Apart from some initial summary of the positions in Scotland, Wales and Northern Ireland, to try to cover all parts of the UK in detail would be overcomplicated, although the planning system is broadly similar throughout.[1]

Where there are complex planning issues involved, the use of a planning consultant is advised.

National planning

In England, town and country planning currently comes within the remit of the Secretary of State (SoS) for Communities and Local Government (DCLG), whose responsibilities include planning, the regions, housing, local government, building regulations and sustainable communities, and who is supported by a number of ministers.

National Planning Policy Statements and new National Planning Statements for major infrastructure projects are prepared by the SoS. The Departments of Transport, the Environment, Farming and Rural Affairs, and of Culture, Media and Sport under their respective Secretaries of State hold responsibilities for some other planning functions.

The Scottish Parliament is responsible for making laws affecting that country and Scottish ministers prepare a National Planning Framework (NPF). The main planning law in Scotland is the Town and Country Planning Act (Scotland) 1997. The Planning, etc. (Scotland) Act 2006 amended the 1997 Act, and is now in force with regard to development planning and development management (including appeals, local reviews and enforcement). In the Scottish Executive, the Directorate of the Built Environment has several key roles to play within the Scottish government. It maintains and develops the law on planning, provides policy and advice on key policy subjects, approves structure plans, and makes decisions on some major planning applications and appeals.

The NPF sits at the top of the policy hierarchy and is the long-term strategy for the development of Scotland until 2025. It is supported by the consolidated Scottish Planning Policy (SPP) documents that have now replaced Planning Advice Notes (PAN).

Much primary legislation passed by the UK Parliament applies to both England and Wales but devolved government in Wales gives specific planning policy powers to the Welsh Assembly. The Minister for the Environment, Sustainability and Housing has overall day-to-day powers on planning matters.

The context for planning policy in Wales is contained within two main documents: Planning Policy Wales gives guidance on the preparation and content of development plans and advice on development control decisions and appeals; and Minerals Planning Policy Wales contains guidance for the extraction of all minerals and other substances in, on or under land. Changes or updates to planning policy are issued in Ministerial Interim Planning Policy Statements (MIPPS). Planning Policy Wales and Minerals Planning Policy are supplemented by a series of topic-based Technical Advice Notes (TANs) and Minerals Technical Advice Notes (MTANs).

In Northern Ireland, the Planning Service is an Executive Agency within the Department of the Environment following the restoration of devolution in 2007. The Agency's work includes providing operational planning policy, development plans and planning decisions across the province for the time being, although some planning powers are being transferred to local councils in 2011 under major local government reform.

Regional planning

At a regional level in England, regional planning bodies (RPB)[2] have prepared regional planning guidance in the form of a spatial strategy to submit for approval by the SoS after an Examination in Public. Regional Spatial Strategy (RSS) (soon to combine planning and economic policies and be called Regional Strategy), once adopted, sets the strategic framework for other lower levels of development plans throughout the region. The RPB will also scrutinise those other development plans as they come forward in their region and are consulted about major strategic development applications. Their powers are currently being transferred to regional development agencies in England.

In Scotland, the NPF deals with most strategic issues but the four largest city regions, Edinburgh, Glasgow, Aberdeen and Dundee, have strategic development plans that address land use issues across local authority boundaries and strategic infrastructure.

In Wales there is no tier of regional government. Local planning authorities work together through four regional forums two in the south, one in the centre and one in the north, to ensure that strategic issues are considered across a number of parts of the country. There are also national forums on various subjects such as rural issues.

Local planning

The administration of the planning system on a day-to-day basis still rests largely with local planning authorities (LPAs) which take a number of different forms.[3]

In the English shire counties, there is generally a two-tier system with the planning function split between the county councils for minerals, waste and transportation issues and the district councils for the rest. Some larger district councils and a few counties may, however, be unitary authorities, responsible for all their functions. These are slowly increasing in number. In metropolitan areas too, a single tier of cities, metropolitan districts or boroughs, known as unitary authorities, administers the planning system. A planning board generally carries out the planning function in national parks.

Local planning authorities are responsible for preparing development plans and processing planning applications for development as well as other planning-related work. Decisions are normally made by planning committees composed of elected members or by planning officers under delegated powers. In recent years some other agencies, such as development corporations and joint planning boards, had the same powers as local planning authorities, but these have largely been disbanded.

In Scotland, planning powers at local level rest with 32 unitary councils, some of which are cities or shires. These presently prepare development plans, both Structure Plans and Local Plans, for their area, but these are soon to be replaced by a single tier of Local Development Plan for most local authority areas, apart from the four main city regions where the two-tier system will remain. Decisions on most planning applications are generally made by the unitary councils.

In Wales, local government is single tier, although some are called counties and some cities. There are 22 local unitary authorities in Wales and they work together with the Assembly government in a statutory Partnership Council that also includes members from community councils, national park authorities, fire authorities and police authorities. Together, they develop and implement policy that promotes a joined-up approach to local government. Together with national park authorities, they each prepare local development plans under the Community Strategy, and determine planning applications.

In Northern Ireland, there will soon be 11 local government local councils, but they do not currently carry out the same range of functions as those in the rest of the United Kingdom apart from building control and local economic development. The role of LPA is presently taken by the Planning Service for the province but a full range of services, including responsibility for planning, is due to be transferred to local councils in 2011.

9.4.2   Legislation in England

Town planning legislation in England derives principally from the Town and Country Planning Act 1990 (the 1990 Act). Under this are a number of subsidiary Acts, and the 1990 Act itself has been amended twice.

Revisions to the 1990 Act were made firstly by the Planning and Compensation Act 1991 (the 1991 Act). This introduced new provisions in those four Acts about what was controlled and made some important new changes to planning law, including changes in relation to development plans, the definition of development, appeals, enforcement and other matters. Further major revisions to planning legislation were proposed by government in the late 1990s and after a lengthy period of consultation they were incorporated in the Planning and Compulsory Purchase Act 2004 (the 2004 Act). The 2004 Act focuses on major changes to the development plan system described below, with some significant changes in relation to development control. The subsidiary legislation is contained in:

- The Planning (Listed Buildings and Conservation Areas) Act 1990[4]
- The Planning (Hazardous Substances) Act 1990
- The Planning (Consequential Provisions) Act 1990.

Mainly in response to delays in dealing with nationally significant infrastructure projects (NSIPs), such as energy generation, airports and docks, the government is introducing National Planning Statements. The Planning Act 2008 (the 2008 Act) also includes extensive provision for dealing with those major applications via a new streamlined system of process under an Infrastructure Planning Commission, which will determine the approval of major proposals.

These seven Acts together, along with a number of rules, regulations and orders, comprise the Town and Country Planning 'Code' which controls development and use of all land and buildings in England and Wales. Some of the more significant statutory instruments made by the First Secretary of State's predecessors in recent years remain.

- The Town and Country Planning (Use Classes) Order (1987, with later amendment) (UCO) which provides that certain changes of use are not material (i.e. important) and, therefore, are not development.
- The Town and Country Planning (General Permitted Development) Order (1995), with later amendments) (GPDO) which provides that certain minor developments will be deemed to be permitted, often subject to extensive qualifications and restrictions. Development specified in the Order is commonly referred to as 'permitted development'.
- The Town and Country Planning (General Development Procedure) Order 1995, with later amendment) (GDPO) which specifies the procedures to be adopted in the making and processing of all types of applications.

Government also lays down policies for the guidance of local planning authorities in the exercise of their day-to-day control duties, and also directs how certain matters are to be dealt with. Policies are normally developed through a consultation process to clarify, update and simplify control of uses and development and in response to changes in procedure, as well as draft guidance documents on various topics.

Policy guidance

Planning policy has been issued over a number of years as guidance notes (PPGs). These cover a wide range of topics including housing, economic development, green belts, the historic environment and noise. They are now all being gradually replaced by Planning Policy Statements (PPSs), which have sustainability as the underlying theme.[1] PANs in Scotland (being replaced by Scottish Planning Policy (SPP)) and TANs in Wales perform a similar function.

National Planning Statements are soon to be introduced to cover England and Wales or any major cross-country proposals. These are intended to set broad planning policy in respect of major nationally significant infrastructure projects such as energy generation, airports, docks and strategic rail and road development.

Planning Policy Statement 1 deals with 'Creating Sustainable Communities' and sets out the government's main vision for planning and the key policies and principles which should underpin the planning system. Other PPSs included 'Housing' (PPS3), 'Sustainable Development in Rural Areas' (PPS7), 'Renewable Energy' (PPS22), and 'Planning and Pollution Control' (PPS23). A full list of these can be found on the CLG website.[1] The policy contained in PPGs and PPSs constitutes a material consideration for the decision maker on planning applications (local planning authorities, and the SoS), which must be taken into account by RPBs and LPAs in their development plan policies, and in the determination of planning applications both by the LPA and in appeals. Consultation drafts on proposed PPSs, as well as a variety of ministerial statements and White Papers, will carry limited weight too, as an indication of future policy.

Legislative and procedural matters are contained within government circulars and directions. Included in the latter are rules governing circumstances where applications have been made for major proposals or significant departures from the development plan. These proposals have to be notified to the SoS who has powers to 'call in' the application to be determined by him or her, usually after a public inquiry.

9.4.3   Development plans in England

The UK planning system is plan led, and therefore development plans play a vital part in the system for the control of development.[3] They constitute the main framework for allocating new major land uses, and against which applications for planning permission are determined and decisions are made about whether or not to issue enforcement notices against unauthorised development. The development plan system helps ensure that there is a rational and consistent basis for making these decisions. It also influences the scale, location and timing of development or redevelopment of land, having regard to the extent and availability of the necessary infrastructure. The 2004 Act in England has reaffirmed that general principle in section 38(6), as follows:

'If regard is to be had to the development plan for the purposes of determination to be made under the planning Acts the determination must be made in accordance with the plan unless material considerations indicate otherwise.'

The starting point for the LPA in considering any planning application is therefore the development plan, and any provision in it relating to the specific site or area, or type of proposed development. The 2004 Act has radically altered the form of development plans for the future. The Unitary Development Plan or Local Plan remains temporarily, pending a new Local Development Framework being introduced over the next few years (see below). Work on preparing core strategies for those has already begun. Minerals and Waste Plans will continue to be prepared by county councils to contain policies on those matters.

Supplementary Planning Documents

In order to give further guidance in interpreting and implementing policy, the LPA will produce a series of Supplementary Planning Documents (SPD) (previously known as Supplementary Planning Guidance (SPG)) on a range of issues that are of local importance. These guidance documents should have been subject to consultation and formal adoption and, as they carry much weight, are material considerations in determining planning applications.

Supplementary Planning Documents will form part of the Local Development Framework (LDF) and must be founded on the broader policies set out in the LPA's development plan. They will usually include design codes and guidance, conservation area guidance, town, village and parish plans, development briefs for particular sites, vehicle parking standards and guidance on affordable housing provision. Early preparation of any application should involve searching the LPA's website both for relevant policies in the Development Plan and for any relevant SPDs.

9.4.4   New-style development plans in England

The new style of development plans, introduced in the 2004 Act, is grounded in an approach for more community involvement as well as contributing towards the achievement of sustainable development. Plans will have to be kept under constant review, and their implementation monitored. Most LPAs have produced a Statement of Community Involvement setting out how they will consult with the community about all planning matters, including emerging policies and applications.

The Regional Spatial Strategy (RSS), once adopted, will set out key matters such as the number of new homes, shopping centres, employment land and business parks, etc. required to meet the future needs of the region as a whole, and where in very broad terms they should be located. For some issues, notably housing and employment, there may be sub-regional plans covering only part of a region, if there is a need to address those in greater focus.

At the LPA level, councils must prepare a Local Development Scheme (LDS), which will set out what Local Development Documents (LDDs) they will be preparing. Gradually these make up a Local Development Framework (LDFs) which will replace all Unitary Development Plans and District Local Plans.

An LDF is a portfolio of LDDs all of which will have to be subject to a sustainability appraisal and must generally comply with the RSS.

9.4.5 Development control

With a few minor exceptions, the development of land in the UK may only be undertaken with written permission of two bodies: the LPA or the SoS (or an appointed Planning Inspector, on behalf of the SoS, on appeal).

Defining development

At the core of the planning system of controlling development is the definition of 'development'. In England, 'development' is defined in the 1990 Act as the carrying out of building, engineering, mining and other operations in, on, over or under land or the making of any material change in the use of any buildings or other land.

If any works or change of use come within that definition then it will amount to 'development' requiring planning permission. In most cases where a person intends to carry out an act of development they must, therefore, obtain planning permission by applying to the LPA. If they carry out development without planning permission, they are liable to the process of enforcement.

Permitted development

Certain minor works, operations or changes of use, which otherwise fall under the definition of 'development', are granted deemed planning permission by legislation. The GPDO sets out, in separate subject areas, a list of types of development that (subject to complying with criteria set out for each) are granted automatic planning permission by the state. These sorts of development are known as 'permitted development' or 'PD rights'. Examples include:

- enlargements or alterations to dwellings, e.g. garages and extensions
- the erection of walls and fences in any location
- building and other operations on agricultural land
- some changes of use to retail or commercial premises
- temporary buildings and uses
- certain industrial development
- some developments carried out by local authorities or statutory undertakers
- certain types of demolition.

In some cases of agricultural development, telecommunications or demolition, prior notification has to be given in writing to the LPA, which in turn may require a formal submission or indicate that it does not wish to intervene.

Almost all permitted developments are subject to sometimes complex qualifications and restrictions, e.g. the amount a dwelling can be extended before planning permission will be required, whether the site is in a conservation area or whether the property is a listed building, etc. Permitted development rights can be removed by conditions put on a planning permission by the authority or by a formal direction under Article 4 of the GPDO. Article 4 directions are mostly, although not exclusively, used in conservation areas and normally they must have the approval of the Secretary of State.

Confirming whether the proposed development is in any area of special control, such as a conservation area, or is a listed building is an important initial exercise to determine what additional consents may be required, and whether there are any special design requirements.

Use classes

The UCO sets out a range of retail, commercial, residential and institutional uses in four basic classes. It provides that a change from a use in one use class to another use in the same use class may not be material and involve the need for planning permission.

The UCO does not cover every possible use of land. Each case has to be assessed for the primary and any secondary or subsidiary use on a site, to determine whether it clearly falls within one of the classes in the UCO. If a particular use does not fall clearly within a category in the UCO, it may be considered to be *sui generis* – outside the scope of the Order. In that case planning permission is needed to change to any other use. It does not always mean that any change of use to or from a use so classified is a material one. The land use may also be mixed, perhaps with complicated primary and ancillary uses, such that an alteration in the respective relationship of uses may also require formal planning permission.

Although changing from a use in one use class to a use in a different use class generally will require permission, the question must still be asked if there is a 'material' (important) change. Furthermore, the GPDO specifically grants planning permission for certain changes of use, for example, from a use in class A3 (restaurant or café) to a use in class A1 (general shop use), but not vice versa.

9.4.6   Making a planning application

The architect should always consult the planning authority or, with the consent of the client, engage a planning consultant at an early stage (see Chapter 7, section 7.1).

Pre-application consultation with the LPA is positively encouraged by government and can help to identify the major issues or any problems related to the site or area, or provide advice about the type of supporting information that may be required with a particular type of proposal. Such discussions may also identify the possible need to carry out consultation with the local community, and help to minimise the likelihood of the application being rejected. In some areas, LPAs may have a Development Panel of experts that can be set up to meet developers and their advisors and discuss early proposals. However, it will not usually be possible to gain any certainty as to whether a application is likely to be approved, although LPAs now have powers to charge for such an approach. Reference to any pre-application consultation will need to be made at the time of any application.

Because of the complexity of dealing some of the planning conditions that are likely to be imposed on any planning permission, it is often sensible to include a significant amount of detail in any full application. This could include a full detailed landscaping scheme, highway design detail, etc. It may also be prudent to submit a draft planning obligation, if one is likely to be required at some stage.

Types of application

A national planning application form is now in use and is available online via the Planning Portal and increasingly it should be possible to submit applications, supporting statements and drawings online to a local planning authority.[5]

There are two main types of application: full (or detailed) application and outline application. For extensions to dwellings, householder applications are somewhat simpler full applications in terms of the information to be provided, but with a shorter form. Most proposals will be sufficiently advanced to be able to apply for full permission. Such an application must provide all the details of a proposed development including design, external appearance, access, parking, landscaping as appropriate and so on.

In certain cases, a developer may wish to establish at an early stage the likelihood of a proposal being approved by the LPA, without submitting a full application with all the detailed drawings required. Seeking outline planning permission can establish that certain aspects of the development, such as the scale, access or layout, are acceptable. While any details not provided at this stage can be reserved for subsequent approval (a 'reserved matters' application), it is increasingly likely that applications will have to include a reasonable amount of detail to show the siting, scale and basic design of the proposed development, as well as the access, so that a simple site plan is no longer enough.

Planning application fee

A fee will need to be submitted with nearly all types of application (apart from applications for Listed Building Consent, which are free). The fee scale is set nationally under Regulations and relates to the scale and nature of the application. Normally the client is responsible for paying the planning fee, as it is their application. If an application is withdrawn or refused, it may be possible to submit a revised application within 12 months as a 'free go'.

Ownership and the application site

It is important to clarify with the client who is to be the applicant for planning permission as this may have legal implications. Certainty is also required as to the extent (if any) to which the client owns the site or part of it, as well as the access to it from the public highway, and the extent of any other ownership interest in the site.

Most applications must include a completed Certificate of Ownership and declaration in respect of any tenant of an agricultural holding. Planning applications can be submitted where none or only part of the land is in the ownership of the applicant, provided that the proper formal notice has been served on any person (other than the developer) who has an ownership interest in the land. The application site, including any land involved in servicing the proposed development, should be edged red on an OS location plan. It must make clear to the LPA what is the precise area of land in which all aspects of the development are proposed to take place, including all areas affected by construction, and service. It is normally necessary to include within the application site an access to a public highway. In some cases the applicant may own more land around the site, in such circumstances this needs to be shown with a blue border on the site plan.

Supporting documents – validation criteria

Because of variance between LPAs in the past on the documentation and supporting statements needed to accompany an application, national validation criteria have been established setting basic requirements, such as numbers and types of forms and plans, as well as the planning fee, etc.

A Design and Access Statement is required for all applications apart from most household applications. Detailed advice on preparing this is available from the LPA[6] or CABE[4] and should include illustrations to show how the design of the project has evolved and how it relates to the context of the site. In an application with some significance, use of coloured drawings, perspectives and models can help to inform the decision maker about the proposed development, and will often minimise the extent of written explanation. Additional supporting information, known as local validation criteria, is set by each LPA although generally take the same form and depend on the scale and nature of the proposals.

Householder and the simpler full applications should be accompanied at least by a full letter to explain the background to the proposal, as well as listing all the documents and plans, etc. being submitted.

For more important applications, a full supporting Planning Statement should be prepared, often using a planning consultant,[7] to set out the context of the proposals, including an analysis of the planning policies relevant to the proposal, summarising the conclusions of any other specialist supporting reports, emphasising the supporting grounds and reasons why planning permission should be granted. For more complex cases, the application may also need to include all or some of the following full reports as set out in the local validation criteria.

- Transport assessment
- Travel plan
- Tree survey and arboriculture impact assessment
- Affordable housing statement
- Retail impact assessment
- Biodiversity statement
- Flood risk assessment
- Economic impact assessment

Plans and drawings

The basic plans are an accurate location plan, usually at 1:1250, and a site block plan at 1:500. Floor plan drawings, existing and proposed, with detailed site plans will also be needed with full elevations of all sides of the building. Additional drawings will be set out in the national validation criteria, and it may be useful to include street elevations showing adjoining buildings with further illustrative material including coloured perspectives.

Environmental assessment

Environmental assessment is a formal procedure that ensures that the environmental implications of decisions are taken into account before the decisions are made. It is likely to be required to accompany most major applications. Detailed guidance is given in the still useful *Environmental Impact Assessment: A Guide to Procedures* (DETR, 2000), although the CLG website will provide up-to-date advice.[2]

The process involves an analysis of the likely effects on the environment, recording those effects in a report, undertaking a public consultation exercise on the report, taking into account the comments and the report when making the final decision and informing the public about that decision afterwards. If a development proposal requires such an assessment, the summary, in the form of an environmental statement, with supporting technical appendices, must accompany the planning application. An environmental assessment may need to be undertaken for individual projects such as a dam, motorway, airport, large extension to an existing town or factory ('Environmental Impact Assessment') or for plans, programmes and policies ('Strategic Environmental Assessment').

Before and after submission

Local publicity

Engaging the community around a proposal in the early stages is commended by both government and LPAs, and the national planning form requires reference to that. It may be appropriate for some schemes to arrange a session(s) for community involvement by way of a drop-in exhibition and feedback forms so that local issues of concern can be recorded which may also influence the final design before it is submitted as an application. A statement on that exercise should be included with any major application.

Publicity for planning applications is required by the 1990 Act, but is largely the responsibility of the LPA, not the architect/applicant (except in Scotland). The type of publicity required usually involves a combination of newspaper, neighbour notification and site notice. Sometimes the LPA or elected councillors for the area affected by the proposal may also undertake direct consultation (e.g. a public meeting) with local residents.

The type of publicity will depend on the type and size of development, e.g. major or minor, those that involve a departure from the development plan and those that require an environmental statement or affect a public right of way. Applications in conservation areas or those which will affect the setting of a listed building require a notice in a local paper and a site notice.

Consultation

Where there are particular issues in relation to development of a site, it is usually sensible to discuss preliminary plans of a proposal with particular interest bodies prior to submission of an application. Apart from neighbours, the planning authority is under a duty to consult certain other interested parties before they make a decision on certain types of application, and early consultation may help to identify issues and to address them before plans become too advanced.

These bodies fall into two broad categories. First, statutory consultees who must be consulted subject to the criteria in the Town and Country Planning (General Development Procedure) Order 1995. For example, the Highway Authority must be consulted for developments that will affect access or highway conditions. Other statutory consultees include, in England, the Environment Agency, Natural England, Sport England, and English Heritage. A duty is imposed on statutory consultees to respond on consultations within a set time period. The LPA must take into account the views of a statutory consultee in determining an application, and may take into account views from others. A statutory consultee can require the SoS to call in an application if it believes that the LPA is ignoring its views.

Second, there is wide range of non-statutory consultees whose views may be sought by the LPA. These include local interest groups, nature conservation bodies, the police and fire services, and environmental health, etc.

Processing the application

Once submitted, each application will be checked administratively for compliance with the national and local validation criteria, and if it complies, it will be formally entered in the Register of Applications, and an acknowledgement will be formally sent to the applicant/agent setting out when a decision can be expected under normal circumstances, a receipt for the planning fee, details as to who is dealing with the application, and various rights of appeal.

Publicity and consultation will then commence with copies of the application documents being circulated and letters, etc. sent out. It will usually take 3–4 weeks before any responses are received and an initial consideration given by the Case Officer to the proposal, who may by then have visited the site and area around to look at the proposals and identify any issues of concerns.

There will then be a period of internal consultation to consider whether the application should be determined by a committee of elected members or by officers, how the application should be dealt with, any other issues that have arisen or that need to be investigated, and to analyse the responses to any publicity and consultation.

The Case Officer should then prepare a report on the application, identifying any planning history, relevant policies, the responses to consultation and publicity, and the main issues that have been identified in relation to the proposal. The report should then go on to assess those main issues in turn and to draw a conclusion on each. Those should then be summarised and weighed in the balance, particularly regarding any conflict with adopted policies or guidance. The Case Officer's report should then conclude with a recommendation as to the decision he/she considers should be taken on the application, or if the matter should be deferred for other information, etc. A Case Officer's report is normally directed at the Head of Planning or another senior officer, who may or may not agree with the Case Officer's conclusion. At the end of the process it is normally the Head of Planning whose final recommendation takes precedence.

Negotiation and amendment

Applicants or agents should seek to find out periodically how their application is progressing so that any clarification or additional information can be supplied before the application is determined. It may also be possible to see whether the application is likely to be approved or refused, and to keep the client informed as to progress. Negotiation with the Case Officer may be appropriate or possible to try to rectify any matter of concern, but any significant amendment of the application may mean that the application cannot be progressed as it would be too different from the proposals as submitted. In the latter case it may be appropriate to withdraw the application and resubmit the revised scheme.

If the application is likely to be refused, the applicant/agent may have the option of withdrawing it before a decision is made, but unless there are any legal reasons for the client to do that, it may be wiser to let the application go through to decision so that clear reasons for refusal can be addressed in a re-application.

Material considerations

In determining any planning application, apart from the Development Plan, the decision maker must take into account all other material considerations relevant to the site and proposal.

A material consideration can be pretty much anything relating to planning matters, depending on the particular circumstances of the case. For example, it could be something in a PPS, SPD, the conservation status of a site/area or local road capacity. The potential effects on property values, land ownership and legal covenants are not relevant to planning and are not normally material considerations.

The decision-making process

The LPA must come to a decision within 8 weeks (13 weeks for major proposals) of the application date, unless (theoretically) agreement is reached to extend this period. Most LPAs do not seek an extension of time, and it is for the applicant or agent to monitor progress.

If there is no such agreement and the authority fails to determine the application within that time period, the applicant has a legal right to appeal against 'non-determination', but that appeal to the SoS must be made within 6 months of the expiry of the statutory primary decision period. If discussions were continuing and a decision is within 'sight', it may be quicker to allow the decision to be made rather than subject the application to the appeal process, for once an appeal is lodged the decision is taken out of the hands of the LPA.

Final decisions on applications by the LPA are made by either a committee of elected councillors or the Head of Planning, or a nominated officer in his or her department, perhaps in consultation with the chairman of the relevant committee.

The criteria for such delegated decisions are usually set out in a Delegation Agreement between the committee of elected members and officers. This is designed to allow the Council's Planning Committee or Sub-Committee to concentrate on more significant/contentious proposals. Delegated decisions are usually made where proposals are not contentious, have not attracted significant objection and accord with policy and guidance. Applications may be refused if they clearly conflict with policy and there are no very special reasons advanced to depart from that policy. Sometimes elected councillors may request that an application should be referred to committee for open scrutiny.

The decision

The LPA may eventually either grant permission subject to conditions or refuse it, giving reasons for the conditions or refusal. Any planning permission is granted subject to the works being carried out in accordance with the approved plans, either as originally submitted or as amended before the grant of planning permission. Both outline and full permissions are normally valid for 3 years and must be implemented before then. The need to discharge any conditions, and for any variation of plans or conditions, are considered below.

A LPA can decline to determine an application in certain circumstances. These powers were increased under the 2004 Act and now cover such instances as where a similar application is submitted within 2 years of a previous refused application that has also been dismissed on appeal. A planning authority cannot approve an application for certain types of development which are not substantially in accordance with the Development Plan without going through a special procedure of advertising and notifying the SoS, who will then decide whether or not to call in the application for decision.

Planning conditions

In approving an application, the LPA may impose such conditions in the Decision Notice as it considers necessary to control the development. Although somewhat dated, DOE Circular 11/95[2] sets out most model conditions, although LPAs should tailor all conditions to the particular proposal concerned.

Certain standard conditions will appear on every permission, such as a time limit on commencement (usually 3 years) or the procedure and timing for submitting the reserved matters under outline permission. Those will appear together, usually with a series of special conditions to suit particular sites. Some of these conditions will apply for the lifetime of the development, for example, hours of opening or delivery, whilst others (called either 'pre-commencement' or 'conditions precedent') require the submission of further details to the LPA or works to be carried out before development can commence on site. Examples of the latter might include the submission of drainage details, details of external facing materials or that works to improve the highway access directly to the site are carried out in advance of the development itself.

Planning conditions must comply with five tests – they must be relevant to planning, and to the development concerned, necessary, reasonable and enforceable. Permission is usually given for the land; it is rarely personal to the applicant. Therefore, when the land is sold, the permission is transferred also.

If development is commenced without compliance with the terms of all the pre-commencement conditions, or works required by those conditions have not been executed, the planning permission itself will be at risk of being invalidated and the whole development will be considered unauthorised. It is the responsibility of the developer, applicant or agent to ensure that a development proceeds in accordance with the approved details and in compliance with any conditions on the planning permission. However, where a developer commences operations in breach of such a pre-commencement condition, then, provided the details are submitted for approval *before the consent expires* and those details are approved, this can save the consent from lapsing. The permission is likely to be wholly invalidated if the time limit for commencement has expired.

Many permissions for major development may include a 'Grampian condition'. This is a planning condition attached to a Decision Notice that prohibits the start of a development until certain specified off-site works have been completed on land not controlled by the applicant – for example, until a nearby road junction has been improved or sewage works upgraded. Often this will be linked to a planning obligation as it is likely to be the developer who is to pay for that work.

A national application form is available to use for the discharge of conditions, and there is a fee payable for each application. It is normal practice to seek to discharge as many conditions as possible in one application to reduce the fee cost.

After the decision

It is for the client to decide whether to appeal in the case of a refusal or to proceed to implement an approval. Appeals are dealt with below. The reasons for refusal may relate to 'technical' matters that are possibly resolvable in a fresh application, or policy issues that may not be easily overcome, unless further special circumstances can be argued.

If a decision to implement an approval is made straight away, it is necessary to secure approval for all pre-commencement conditions before any work begins. If the decision to start is to be delayed, pre-commencement conditions should still also be discharged well before the time limit of the permission. If necessary, the applicant can then make a meaningful start before the expiry date.

If work is not likely to start in time, it will be necessary to seek an extension of the time limit permission, which may not be granted as such extensions are normally 'outlawed'.

Commencement

Preserving a planning permission, particularly if there is a possibility that it may not be granted again once the time limit expires, can be very important. A planning permission must be implemented within 3 years from the date it was granted, unless expressly stated otherwise. It is implemented by the carrying out of a 'material operation' which can include:

- any work of construction in the course of the erection or demolition of a building
- the digging of a trench to contain foundations, or part of the foundations of a building
- the laying of any underground main or pipe to the foundations, or part of the foundations, of a building or to any such trench as is mentioned in point 2 above
- any operation relating to the laying out or constructing of a road or part of a road.

Such a material operation should be undertaken once all the pre-commencement conditions (see above) have been discharged, and should be significant and noticeable in terms of physical works. It should be notified to the LPA, and arrangements should be made for it to be independently verified – if possible by the LPA or Building Control Officer.

Previously there was some doubt as to whether such work could be carried out simply to keep an approval alive, with no intention to actually carry out the development, but recent case law has held that the intention of the person carrying out the work is irrelevant provided the work has been done in accordance with the planning permission.

Some preparatory works may be needed to the site before development proper commences, such as demolition or service diversions. These should be agreed with the LPA, who may also wish to approve a construction method statement, by way of a condition.

Variation of plans and conditions

All development should be built fully in accordance with the approved plans and any conditions attached to the permission. There may be serious consequences for the developer if not. Applications may be made to retain unauthorised development, or to vary or delete a planning condition, other than (at present) the time-limit condition to start the development. Failure to start on time risks the life of the planning permission.

If any variation in plan is required by the developer, or found necessary because of, say, ground conditions, early discussion should be held with the LPA to see whether the variation would be acceptable and if so how it should be dealt with. In the past LPAs may have allowed some flexibility to grant approval to very minor amendments by way of 'rider' plans after planning permission had been granted, but now any deviation, however minor, from the approved plans will require a fresh application.

9.4.7   Other permissions

Listed building and scheduled monument consent

A building of special architectural or historic interest may be listed for its exterior, interior or any feature, and will be graded a 1, 2* or 2, dependent on its quality and importance.[8] Additionally, scheduled monuments, registered battlefields, protected wreck sites and registered parks and gardens are afforded protection. A full site analysis with information from the LPA/English Heritage should identify any historic constraints.

English Heritage (EH) is the government's statutory advisor on the historic environment. Officially known as the Historic Buildings and Monuments Commission for England, EH is an executive non-departmental public body sponsored by the Department for Culture, Media and Sport (DCMS). Amongst a wide range of work, EH maintains and compiles the schedules of listed buildings and ancient monuments, and can recommend the DCMS to list individual buildings.

Religious bodies, which have approved systems of control, including the Church of England, the Church in Wales and the Roman Catholic Church, benefit from exemption from listed building control ('ecclesiastical exemption'). All other religious bodies not benefiting from exemption are subject to normal listed building and conservation controls.[9]

It is an offence to demolish, alter or extend a listed building unless the LPA or SoS has granted a written listed building consent. If work is carried out without such consent, it may be possible (but not without some convincing) to make out a defence on the grounds that the works were urgently necessary for safety, health or to preserve the building, but the LPA must be notified in writing as soon as possible. The LPA or DCMS/EH can give temporary protection to an unlisted building which is in danger of demolition or alteration, by the service of a Building Preservation Notice by the authority. Its effect is immediate and it lasts for 6 months during which time the DCMS/EH can decide whether or not to list it.

Conservation areas

The LPA has power to declare certain areas to be of special architectural or historic interest as conservation areas, any proposal pertaining to which must be assessed by the LPA as to how it would affect the area's character or appearance.[8] The controls in a conservation area include generally the need for consent for demolition of all but the most minor buildings and for the felling of trees. Additionally, the LPA may have removed PD rights for alterations and extensions to properties by way of an Article 4 Direction. Checking fully with the LPA should identify those constraints. The controls on development are not as extensive as for listed buildings, but more restrictive tolerances may be applied in certain instances.[10]

Conservation area consent is the mechanism for obtaining consent to demolish an unlisted building in a conservation area. It will not normally be granted in respect of demolition of a large building unless it is accompanied by an application for planning permission for its replacement, and may be subject to a requirement that a contract has been let to construct the new building before the older building is demolished.

Trees

As part of any application, a full detailed site survey should be prepared, including detailed information on the location of trees on a site. In some cases it may be necessary to undertake a full survey and assessment of every tree, and to prepare a tree impact assessment so that any development, so far is possible, is restricted to those parts of the site where the least important trees are located.

Most significant applications should include information on site layout plans of those trees and other landscape features that are to be retained, and where new landscaping and tree planting are proposed. Details of this are usually prepared by a landscape architect engaged by the client.

Every LPA has the duty to ensure that adequate provision is made for the preservation and planting of trees when planning permission is granted.[11] It may also make tree preservation orders for trees, groups of trees and woodlands which contribute to the amenity of the area. Notice must be given to the owners and occupiers of the land and neighbouring land owners who may be affected by it, who are entitled to object.

It is an offence to cut down, lop, top or wilfully damage such trees without the consent of the LPA, unless it can be demonstrated that they are dangerous, dying, dead or the work is executed in compliance with another Act of Parliament. Even in such cases, the prior consent of the authority should be sought. Trees in conservation areas are automatically protected and prior notification must be given to the LPA if such trees are to be felled or pruned, after 6 weeks of which works can be carried out if the LPA has not imposed a formal tree preservation order on the tree(s). The authority is entitled to insist on the replacement of a felled tree by another of appropriate size and species.

A provisional tree preservation order is made in the first instance which, except in cases of urgency, is valid for 6 months, to allow for the resolution of objections and any changes to be made to the order. The order becomes permanent upon confirmation by the LPA.

Certificates of Lawfulness

In some cases existing development or operations or a use may have been carried out some time ago, or is proposed in the future, and it may be necessary to establish that those are lawful and exempt from any action by the LPA.

Sections 191 and 192 of the 1990 Act allow anyone to apply to the LPA to determine whether any of the following matters are lawful and, if so, to be granted a Certificate of Lawfulness to that effect. The matters are:

- an existing or proposed operational development on land
- an existing or proposed use of land
- any other matter constituting a failure to comply with any condition or limitation subject to which planning permission was granted
- carrying out development that would be in accordance with an existing planning permission.

The burden of proof is on the applicant, who must accurately describe the existing development or use, or the proposal in sufficient detail to enable the authority to make its decision. The local authority must grant a certificate if the case is proven on the balance of probability. This certificate replaces the former Certificate of Established Use.

Advertisements

Local planning authorities are responsible for the day-to-day operation of the advertisement control system and for deciding whether a particular advertisement should be permitted or not. The control relates to a wide range of advertisements and signs including posters, notices, placards, fascia and projecting signs, directional signs, flag adverts, captive balloon adverts, etc. The rules which govern advertisements[12] effectively divide them into three main groups, each subject to very detailed criteria.

- Advertisements which are deliberately excluded from any control.
- Advertisements for which the rules give a deemed consent so that the LPA's consent is not needed, provided the advertisement meets certain criteria.
- Advertisements for which the LPA's 'express consent' is always needed.

Applications must be made using the appropriate forms accompanied by a fee, suitable drawings and site plan.

In deciding an application, the local authority may consider only two issues: amenity and public safety. Consent when granted is normally for 5 years (although a shorter period can be stipulated). However, unless a condition is imposed that requires removal of the advertisement after the consent expires, the sign can continue to be displayed without making further application. In the case of refusal or imposition of a condition with which the applicant is dissatisfied, there are rights of appeal to the Secretary of State.

9.4.8 Planning obligations

Planning obligations are also known as planning agreements, S106 agreements (from section 106 of the 1990 Act (as amended by the Planning and Compensation Act 1991)) or planning gain.

Legislation provides that developers may enter into a 'planning obligation' which may restrict the use of land, require specified operations to be carried out or require sums of money to be paid to the local authority. By doing so, the local authority may be prepared to grant planning permission, but a planning obligation should not be a reason to grant permission for a proposal that should otherwise be refused. Nor should an agreement be used when planning the use of conditions would be more appropriate. The obligation may be done either by a legally prepared agreement with the LPA or by the developer giving a unilateral undertaking. Common examples are the carrying out of off-site highway or drainage works specifically to allow the particular development to be built, or in relation to agricultural workers' dwellings which tie the existing land and property to the agricultural holding.

In more recent years, the agreements have been used frequently to secure funding and provision of affordable housing and public open space, particularly in connection with larger residential developments.

Community Infrastructure Levy

The 2008 Act includes powers to introduce a new form of tax, a Community Infrastructure Levy (CIL), to be paid by a developer dependent on the size and nature of the proposed development and to support local infrastructure provision. The definition proposed for what constitutes infrastructure will be wide enough to enable local authorities to decide what infrastructure is appropriate for their local areas. Affordable housing will continue to be provided through the existing system of negotiated planning obligations (i.e. the section 106 route).

Local planning authorities which prepare Development Plans will be the charging authorities and they will have the freedom to work together to pool contributions for CIL. Public sector bodies, like the regional development agencies, could provide funding for infrastructure reimbursed from a CIL income stream on a forward funding basis. Before CIL can be charged there must be an up-to-date Development Plan for the area that has set out the likely cost of the required infrastructure. Authorities will be expected to prepare a new type of document, a draft charging schedule within the LDF, though not formally part of the Development Plan. The schedules will be subject to rigorous consultation, including a public inquiry.

A national-level description of the unit of development that may be charged (i.e. 'per dwelling or per habitable room' for residential), as well as exemptions, are likely to be set by government but CIL will not be charged on householder applications. The amount of CIL to be paid will be calculated when planning permission is granted, and may be payable within 28 days of commencement of the scheme although payment by installment is also being considered. Where development is phased (i.e. an outline planning permission followed by reserved matters), each phase could pay CIL separately.

Use of the CIL regime will be discretionary and it will sit alongside the current S106 arrangements, and there may be restrictions on the use of planning obligations once CIL is introduced later in 2010.

9.4.9 Appeals

An applicant may appeal against refusal of planning permission, conditions attached to the permission and various other matters, including lack of decision in the statutory time period. Technically the appeal is being made to the Secretary of State, but in reality appeals are dealt with by the Planning Inspectorate (PINS) which is an executive agency based in Bristol.[13] PINS will administer the process, and it has a large panel of qualified inspectors available to determine cases. An inspector will be appointed to consider the case and make a decision. The SoS retains powers to 'call in' or 'recover' cases to decide personally, although those are usually after an inquiry has been held in front of an inspector who prepares a report on the evidence and arguments made with his/her recommendation.

The appeal must be made using the appropriate form within a stipulated period from the date on which the refusal was received or, in the case of non-determination, within the period from the date on which the determination should have been made. An appeal must normally be submitted with all the related documentation within 6 months of the LPA decision or, in the case of non-determination, the expiry of the 8(13)-week primary period for the LPA to have made its decision. An appeal may be dealt with in one of three ways.

- *Written representation*: this is the most common type of appeal and it is used in about 85% of planning appeals. It has the benefit of speed and relative cheapness.
- *Local (public) inquiry*: these will deal with the most complex or major applications and they usually involve legal representation and the cross-examination of witnesses. They take much longer to arrange and are the most expensive procedure.
- *Informal hearing*: a simple procedure with some characteristics of written representations and public local inquiry. Here the inspector will lead a round table discussion about the matters at issue, usually without lawyers present.

Normally each side must bear its own costs in appeals, but where one side or the other has shown unreasonable behaviour or acted improperly, after hearing the arguments, application with reasons can be made to the inspector for an award of costs against the offending party. Under new procedures introduced in 2009, some significant changes have been made, which include the following.

- Although the LPA or appellant may request an informal hearing or local inquiry, the SoS (PINS) will determine the method by which an appeal is to be dealt with, normally favouring written representations unless there are particular reasons otherwise.
- A new process of appeal for householder applications means that in those cases, the appeal must be made within 12 weeks of the decision, and it will rely on the information submitted to the LPA as the application – no provision remains for making any further representations.
- The award of costs may also be made in written representation cases, as well as previously in the case of local inquiries and hearings.

The LPA can provide details of the appeals procedure and helpful guidance is provided by the Planning Inspectorate.[13]

9.4.10 Remedies

Completion Notice

Under section 94 of the 1990 Act, a local authority may serve a Completion Notice on a developer where it is of the opinion that, although construction has commenced, it will not be completed within a reasonable period. The Notice must then specify a reasonable time, which must not be less than 12 months, to complete the development. Failure to comply will result in the planning permission being invalidated.

Enforcement

The local authority is empowered under the provisions of the 1990 Act, as amended by Part I of the Planning and Compensation Act 1991, to take action to enforce against unauthorised development. The weapons at their disposal are as follows.

1.   Enforcement Notice

The authority has discretionary power to serve this Notice where there has been a breach of planning control, such as development undertaken without permission or in contravention of the condition imposed by the authority. The Notice must require the building owner or occupier to do whatever is necessary to remedy the breach. A reasonable time limit must be imposed.

An appeal on specified grounds must be lodged with the Secretary of State within 28 days. While the SoS is deciding the appeal, the Notice is of no effect. It is not unknown for a building owner to appeal for that very reason. The LPA has other enforcing powers, however.

2.   Stop Notice and/or Injunction

The authority may seek to ensure that construction ceases or to prevent a material change of use as a matter of urgency by serving a Stop Notice or Injunction. A Stop Notice may only be served after an Enforcement Notice, and only if it seems that the building owner is intent on pressing ahead with work during the appeal procedure, and the continuation of the development or use is causing particularly significant harm to an area.

There is no appeal against a Stop Notice. If the appeal against the Enforcement Notice is successful, the Stop Notice is automatically void. Failure to observe a Stop Notice results in very heavy penalties and further daily penalties for continuing failure.

In some instances, a building owner may be able to obtain compensation after a successful appeal against an Enforcement Notice which was followed by a Stop Notice. For this reason alone, planning authorities are reluctant to serve Stop Notices.

3.   Planning Contravention Notice

This is a procedure introduced under the Planning and Compensation Act 1991 whereby a LPA can obtain information about activities being carried out on a site where a breach of planning control is suspected. The owner, occupier or any other recipient is required to reply within 21 days.

4.   Breach of Conditions Notice

The LPA has the power to serve a notice requiring compliance with a condition in a planning permission. There is no appeal against such a notice and failure to comply within 28 days is a summary offence.

9.5 Other approvals

A development may be subject to a great many approvals other than planning and building control (see 9.2 above). The following are building types which require special approvals of various kinds.

- Licensed premises and restaurants
- Music and dance halls
- Cinemas
- Petrol stations
- Nursing homes
- Abattoirs

In addition, approval may be required from landlords or funders of development.

9.6 Property

9.6.1 Boundaries

Boundaries are the demarcation lines between separate properties. They can be the source of many problems when the properties either side of the line are in different ownerships, as is usually the case.

When investigating the feasibility of building, the architect should make it an early task to establish or verify the apparent boundaries of a site. The only safe way to do this is for the architect to request verification from the client's solicitor. Since deed plans and the deeds themselves are often unclear on the matter, the solicitor will often be loath to put forward a definitive view, but it is certainly not the architect's duty to decide on boundaries and the architect who does so risks an action for negligence at some stage. On occasion, boundaries are so vague that all the adjoining owners have to agree the boundaries afresh. Certain presumptions may be made from inspection of such things as fences, ditches and hedges.

Very great care must be taken when dealing with old properties which adjoin. Ownership of a cellar may extend under the ground floor of the other property and the buildings themselves may actually interlock, i.e. first floor projects over neighbouring ground floor and under second floor. Such cases, however, would more usually fall under a consideration of party walls (see 9.6.2 below).

If a building is constructed so as to infringe a neighbouring boundary, the building owner will have committed trespass against the neighbour. The matter can only be rectified by the removal of the building or the purchase of the portion of neighbouring land on which it stands, probably at an inflated price. Common infringements occur in the projection of footings or eaves across the boundary. Where a neighbour permits an eaves to project onto his or her land, the building owner is said to have a 'right of eavesdrop'.

9.6.2   Party walls

There are three types of party wall. The most common type is where the wall is divided vertically and reciprocal easements are in force over the whole wall. The second type is where the wall is divided vertically into two strips, one strip belonging to each owner. In the final type, the wall belongs completely to one owner and the adjoining owner has the right to have it maintained as a dividing wall.

There are special procedures for party walls under the Party Wall Act 1996 which came into force on 1 July 1997. It applies only to England and Wales at present. What follows in this section is not a substitute for reading the Act itself, which affects all architects. If anything is to be done to a party wall, as defined by the Act, notice is to be given in certain forms.

A party wall is defined as a wall standing on land of different owners not taking account of projecting foundations, which is part of a building, or that part of a wall which separates buildings belonging to different owners. A 'party structure' is a party wall, floor or other structure separating parts approached by separate entrances, while a 'party fence wall' is a wall standing on land of different owners not taking account of projecting foundations, which is not part of a building, but separates adjoining lands.

If the two adjoining owners do not agree (and it is often unwise to agree in advance), each party must appoint a surveyor to whom certain powers are given by the Act to determine the difference and to decide, subject to the provisions of the Act, what contribution each party is to make to the cost of the work. Both building and adjoining owners have statutory rights which they can exercise under the Act and those rights can never be ignored or set aside. Care must be taken to adhere to the periods of notice laid down. When acting for the building owner and in view of the time required for notice, counter-notice and negotiation, the architect must take early steps to set the machinery in motion.

There are three basic situations covered by the Act:

- building a new party wall
- work to existing party walls
- adjacent excavations and constructions.

Building a new party wall

Where adjoining land is not built on line of junction or only built as a boundary wall (i.e. not a party fence wall or the external wall of a building), there are two situations. If the wall is intended to straddle the boundary, 1 month's notice of the wish to start work must be given. The notice must indicate desire to build and describe the intended wall. If notice of consent is received, the wall must be built half and half, or as agreed, the cost borne by each in proportion to use. Alternatively, if the wall is wholly on the applicant's own land, 1 month's notice of a wish to start work must be given. The notice must indicate a desire to build and describe the intended wall as before, but the building owner has the right to project foundations, if necessary, under adjacent land any time within 12 months from expiry of the notice. However, the work must be at the building owner's own expense and the adjoining owner or occupier must be compensated for damage caused by building the wall or the foundations. This also applies where the adjoining owner refuses consent to a party or party fence wall.

Work to existing walls

A building owner has certain rights in respect of existing walls. The scope is very broad and the following is a brief summary. The building owner has the right:

- to underpin, thicken or raise, but if not due to defect or lack of repair, must make good all damage to adjoining premises, internal furnishings and decorations. Furthermore, if a party structure or external wall is concerned, any adjoining owner's flues and chimneys which rest on or form part of the party structure or external wall must be carried up as may be agreed or settled by the disputes process
- to repair or demolish and rebuild a party structure or party fence wall if the work is necessary as a result of defects or lack of repair
- to demolish a partition which does not conform with statutory requirements and build a party wall which does conform
- to demolish structures over public ways or passages belonging to other persons and rebuild so as to make them conform to statutory requirements
- to demolish a party structure and rebuild so as to make it of sufficient strength or height for any intended building of the building owner or to rebuild to lesser thickness or height, provided it is still sufficient for any adjoining owner. All damage to adjoining premises, internal furnishings and decorations must be made good and if a party structure or external wall, any adjoining owner's flues and chimneys which rest on or form part of the party structure must be carried up as may be agreed or settled by the disputes process
- to cut into a party structure or away from a party wall, party fence, external or boundary wall any foundation, chimney breast or other projection over the building owner's land or take away or demolish overhanging parts of wall or building of adjoining owner to the extent necessary to enable a vertical wall to be erected or raised against the wall or building of an adjoining owner. All damage to adjoining premises, internal furnishings and decorations must be made good
- to cut into an adjoining owner's wall to carry out weatherproofing of a new wall erected against it, but must make good all damage to the wall
- to carry out other necessary works incidental to the connection of a party structure with the premises adjoining
- to raise a party fence wall or to raise it for use as a party wall or to demolish it and rebuild it as a party fence or party wall

- to reduce or to demolish and rebuild a party wall or party fence wall either to not less than 2 metres if not used by adjoining owner other than as a boundary wall or to a height currently enclosed by the building of an adjoining owner, but must reconstruct or replace any existing parapet or construct one if needed
- to expose a party wall or structure, but adequate weathering must be provided.

A building owner may exercise these rights with the written consent of the adjoining owner. If adjoining land is built on at the line of a junction as a party wall or party fence wall or the external wall of a building, before exercising any right under the Act the building owner must give a 2 months 'party structure notice' of the date when work will start. The notice must state the name and address of the building owner, particulars of the proposed work, whether special foundations are intended and include plans, sections and details, including the loads to be carried. The notice ceases to have effect if the work is not begun within 12 months of the date the notice is served or if it is not continued with due diligence. There is provision for the adjoining owner to serve a counter-notice. If no consent is received within 14 days of the date of service of party structure or counter-notices, dissent is deemed and a dispute is deemed to have arisen.

Adjacent excavations and constructions

There are two situations:

- where a building owner proposes to excavate and erect a structure, any part of which is within 3 metres horizontally from any part of a structure of an adjoining owner and which extends to a lower level than the level of the bottom of the foundations of the adjoining structure
- where a building owner proposes to excavate and erect a structure any part of which is within 6 metres horizontally from any part of the structure belonging to an adjoining owner and which extends to a lower level than a point measured at 45 degrees from the point of intersection of the external face of the adjoining structure and the bottom of the foundation.

The owners of such structures are deemed to be adjoining owners for the purposes of this section even though the property is not touching the boundary.

The building owner must give 1 month's notice of the date when work will start. The notice must set out the proposals and whether underpinning or other strengthening or protection is proposed. Plans and section must show the site and the depth of any excavation proposed and, if the erection of a building is proposed, its site. The notice ceases to have effect if work is not begun within 12 months of the date the notice is served or if the work is not continued with due diligence. The building owner may at own expense strengthen the foundations of the adjoining structure or may be required to do so by the adjoining owner. If there is no consent within 14 days of the date of service of notice, dissent is deemed and a dispute is deemed to have arisen.

There are various other provisions in relation to matters such as disputes and access which should be carefully studied.

9.6.3 Neighbouring land

A difficult problem can arise when it is necessary to enter upon a neighbour's land in order to carry out work. Neighbours could be held to ransom where the work was essential to deal with weather ingress or structural problems. The Access to Neighbouring Land Act 1992 was intended to deal with such matters. It came into force on 31 January 1993. Like the Party Wall Act, it only extends to England and Wales. The Act deals with 'basic preservation works'. The term is broad and it includes, but is not necessarily restricted to, such things as maintenance or repair of a building, clearance or repair of a drain or cable, treatment or cutting back of any growing thing and the filling in or clearance of a ditch.

An application must be made to the court, which must be satisfied that the work is reasonably necessary for preservation and that it cannot be carried out without substantial difficulty without entry on the adjoining land. The court cannot make an order if the adjoining owner would suffer interference with use or enjoyment of the land or would suffer hardship. Of course, the court may include whatever terms and conditions it deems appropriate to protect the adjoining owner's property or privacy. These terms may include the payment of money to the adjoining owner by the person desiring to carry out the work.

9.6.4 Trespass

This is a category of the law of tort. Trespass to land is of most concern to the architect. The general rule is that if a person enters upon, remains upon or allows anything to come into contact with another's land, that person is committing trespass. Trespass can occur under land, on the surface or to a reasonable height over the land. Contrary to popular misconception, there is no necessity to prove damage in order to sue for trespass. There is a requirement for damage before action in the case of nuisance, however, with which trespass is often confused. If a person demolishes a wall by pushing it onto adjoining property, that is trespass; if the wall simply collapses with old age and falls onto adjoining property, that is nuisance. Building a foundation across a boundary is trespass, allowing tree roots to grow across is nuisance. Trespass is a direct invasion of another's land.

The usual legal remedies for trespass are to take action for damages, if any, and/or an injunction to prevent further or continuing trespass. A form of self-help is for the person in possession of the land to forcibly evict the trespasser who refuses to leave, but this option should be a last resort and exercised with great care.

A contractor carrying out work on a site is said to have a licence to be on the site for the purpose of carrying out the building. There may be an express licence, but it is more usual that the licence will be implied. A contractor who stays on the land after the work is complete or after determination of employment will be a trespasser. Trespassers, particularly children, can be a real problem on construction sites and those in possession of the site have an especially strict duty to ensure that children do not suffer injury.[14]

An occupier owes a duty to trespassers by virtue of statute[15] if:

> 'he is aware of the danger or has reasonable grounds to believe that it exists; … he knows or has reasonable grounds to believe that the other is in (or may come into) the vicinity of danger; … the risk is one against which in all the circumstances of the case, he may reasonably be expected to offer the other protection'.

The duty is to take such care as is reasonable in all the circumstances of the case to see that the entrant to the property does not suffer injury on the premises by reason of the danger concerned. This duty may be discharged by giving warning of the danger on an appropriately worded notice.

9.6.5 Nuisance

Nuisance has been mentioned briefly under trespass. It is another category of the law of tort. There are three types of nuisance.

- Public nuisance
- Private nuisance
- Statutory nuisance

Public nuisance

An act or omission without lawful justification which causes damage, injury or inconvenience to the public at large. It is a crime as well as a tort. It must affect a reasonable-sized group of people or the nuisance cannot be categorised as public. An example is the obstruction of a highway. A private person has no remedy for public nuisance unless that person suffers from that nuisance over and above the damage suffered by the public at large.

Private nuisance

An unlawful interference with the use or enjoyment of land. The usual examples are smell, smoke, dirt, noise, vibrations and tree roots. If a person wishes to sue for nuisance, damage must be proved. Remedies available are damages or an injunction. It is only in wholly exceptional circumstances that the suffering party may take direct action to abate the nuisance. In some instances, building work can be held to be nuisance.[16] It is now rare for actions to be brought in this respect, however, because building operations are generally of quite short duration, it is usually reasonable use of property to permit or cause building work to be carried out from time to time and there are statutory powers for the local authority to regulate building work to prevent excessive noise, dust, etc.[17] It is not sufficient to show reasonable fear of danger or damage; the fear must be well founded.[18] Nuisance is a complex subject and should any problem arise, the architect should advise the client to seek legal advice.

Statutory nuisance

Anything which is declared by statute to be a nuisance.[19] The local authority may serve an abatement notice to require the perpetrator to bring the nuisance to an end.

9.6.6   Rights of light

Sometimes called 'ancient lights'. This is a negative easement (see section 9.6.7 below) which entitles an owner to prevent his neighbour building so as to obstruct the flow of light through particular windows. The right is not acquired in respect of the whole building, unless it is entirely glazed, but only in respect of the window openings. For this reason, when considering the redevelopment of a property which has rights of light to certain windows, it is essential that a careful measured survey is carried out so that any new windows will be replaced exactly in the same positions as the original windows. The right is usually acquired under the Prescription Act 1832 which requires the right to be enjoyed for 20 years without interruption and without written consent.

The existence of a building with rights of light on adjoining land can put severe constraints on the development potential of a site. In order for an act to be considered as an interruption, it must continue for at least a year. At one time, it was necessary to erect a screen to block the light to prevent the right being acquired. Since the Rights of Light Act 1959, the owner of land over which a right of light might be acquired may register as a land charge a notice identifying the properties and specifying the size and position of a notional screen. Parties likely to be affected must be given prior notice and the notice itself is in force for a year, during which time an affected party may seek to have it varied or cancelled. In order to prevent the right being acquired, it is necessary to re-register at least every 19 years.

If a party considers that another is infringing his or her right of light, the injured party must show that the light which remains is not sufficient for the comfortable use and enjoyment according to the ordinary notions of mankind.[20] Any action would be brought in nuisance (see 9.6.5 above) and a practical test, which is often adopted, is whether the light can flow into the window without interruption at an angle of 45 degrees from the horizontal measured at the window cill. The nature and use of the building will determine the amount of light entitlement. Thus a greenhouse will need more light than a private house.[21]

9.6.7   Easements

A right held by one party to use the land belonging to another or to restrict the use of such land by another. Common examples are rights of way and rights of drainage or for services. These are known as positive easements as compared to easements such as rights of light or right of support, which are negative easements. An easement relates to land, not people. The land which enjoys the right is called the dominant tenement; the land on or against which the easement is exercised is called the servient tenement. It is essential that the two pieces of land have different owners.

There is often confusion with regard to right of support although the position is very clear. All land enjoys right of support from adjoining land. In the present state of the law, no successful action would be possible against a person excavating near a neighbour's boundary unless the excavation caused actual physical damage to the adjacent land. A neighbour could not successfully bring an action for the cost of building a retaining wall to prevent possible future slippage. That is simply economic loss and it is not recoverable in tort. There is no natural right of support for buildings (however, see section 9.6.2 above relating to the Party Wall Act).

If, however, the removal of support from land causes the collapse of that land and the building standing on it, the building owner would have the right to bring an action. The right of support when applied to a building is usually acquired by prescription, but it can also be acquired expressly. A fairly common situation is where a property has been in existence for some years when the adjoining owner builds next to, and taking support from, the original property. There may be an express agreement entered into before building or to regularise the position, or the owner of the original property may take no action for 20 years.

A *profit a prendre* is a right to remove something from another's land, for example turf. Easements and profits may be created by Act of Parliament, express grant, usually by deed, express reservation, when land is sold, or prescription (see section 9.6.6 above).

9.7   Contract selection and implications

If the architect is carrying out his or her normal duties in contract administration, it is the architect's duty to advise the client about the most suitable form of contract to use for the particular project. This is recognised by most standard forms of appointment and noted in the list of services. Even if not expressly stated, it seems likely that such a duty would be implied. No two projects are exactly the same and, therefore, very careful thought must be given to the appropriate form. Architects do not have a good reputation in this field. In the rush of practice, it is all too easy to advise the client to use a contract form with which the architect is familiar. There are a considerable number of standard forms to suit varying situations and procurement routes.

The forms to be used for building works are summarised in Fig. 9.1 together with available supplements. Ideally, the architect should have a thorough knowledge of each contract so as to be able to properly advise the client. It has been suggested that an architect who advises the use of the wrong form of contract, which results in the client suffering loss, would be negligent.[22] We can see no good reason in principle to doubt that view although assembling the necessary proof might be a different matter. In any event, it is certain that an inappropriate choice of contract will make it very much more likely that problems will occur and that when they do, the contractor will have a justifiable claim for additional money. There are various publications which can assist the architect.[23]

Sometimes, a client will insist that the company solicitor draws up a suitable contract. The task of drawing up a suitable form of contract would be daunting to say the least, even if the solicitor is well experienced in construction matters. In most cases, the result will be disastrous. It is always worth the architect explaining to the client the basic advantages of using a standard form, as follows.

- It is comprehensive, covering most common construction situations.
- It is drawn up and updated at regular intervals to take account of the most recent legal decisions.
- It is known to the contractor and widely accepted in the industry. The contractor will be aware of the advantages and shortcomings and thus there will be no necessity for the employment of specialist professionals to advise on the pitfalls. Therefore there will be no inflation of the tender figure from this cause.
- Many of the standard forms have a range of related documents.
- Some of the standard forms and all the ones current in the JCT range a re negotiated documents and will not normally be caught by the *contra proferentem* rule. That is the rule of interpretation of a contract which states that where there is an ambiguity in a document which other means of interpretation have failed to resolve, the court may choose the meaning least favourable to the party seeking to rely on it. Such contracts will not be caught by the Unfair Contract Terms Act 1977 either, because they are not the employer's 'written standard terms of business' under the Act.

The choice of contract should be the end of a sequence of activity on the part of the architect and the client. The contract should fit the procurement system (see Chapter 8, section 8.3).[24]

Once a decision has been made in regard to the procurement system, the number of possible standard forms will be reduced. There will be some procurement systems which have no standard form. A current example is design and manage which is commonly dealt with by the use of purpose-written forms or design-and-build forms with amendments. Fig. 9.2 shows a flowchart method of getting a rough idea of the appropriate form of contract.

Joint Contracts Tribunal (JCT 05) Series with Revision 2 (2009)

Standard Building Contract (SBC)
  With Quantities (SBC/Q)
  With Approximate Quantities (SBC/AQ)
  Without Quantities (SBC/XQ)

Intermediate Building Contract (IC)
  Incorporating Designed Portion Supplement (ICD)

Minor Works Building Contract (MW)
  Incorporating Designed Portion Supplement (MWD)

Design and Build Contract (DB)

Prime Cost Building Contract (PCC)

Management Building Contract (MC)

Construction Management Appointment (CM/A)

Construction Management Trade Contract (CM/TC)

Major Project Construction Contract (MP)

Measured Term Contract (MTC)

Framework Agreement (FA)

Constructing Excellence Contract (CE)

Constructing Excellence Project Team Agreement (CE/P)

Repair and Maintenance Contract (RM)

Pre-Construction Services Agreement (PCSA)

Home Owner Contracts (HO)

Provision for sections is incorporated into relevant contracts and there are other supplements available.
There are adaptation schedules available for use with SBC, IC, ICD MW, MWD and DB in Northern Ireland.
Scottish contracts are available to amend the SBC, MW and DB.

Association of Consultant Architects

Form of Building Agreement 1998 (ACA 3) 1999 revision

Standard Form of Contract for Project Partnering (PPC 2000)

Institution of Civil Engineers

Conditions of Contract (ICE 7)

Engineering and Construction Contract (ECC)

Engineering and Construction Short Contract (ECSC)

Term Services Contract (TSC)

Most of these contracts are supported by matching sub-contracts.

Fig. 9.1   Standard forms of building contract.

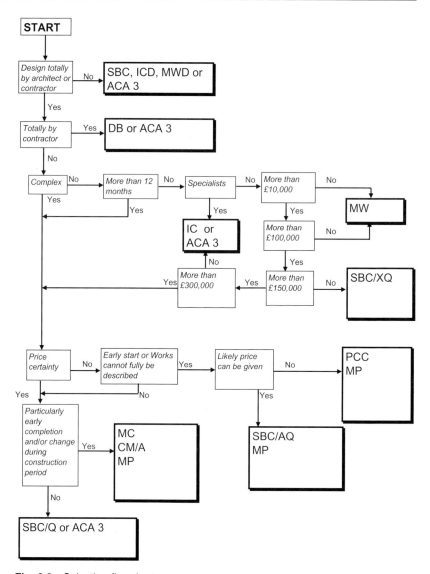

Fig. 9.2 Selection flowchart.

It is not unusual to find that after a contract has been chosen as being most suitable, it still leaves a great deal to be desired in detail. It is possible to amend the standard forms, but five points should be noted.

- Any amendments must be kept to a minimum, because amendments often cause problems during the course or at the end of a contract period.
- Amendments invariably lead to concomitant amendments being required elsewhere in the contract and it is easy to overlook them. For instance, changes to the content of clause 4.16 'Gross Valuation' of the Standard Building Contract (SBC) would have severe repercussions throughout the contract. Failure to pick up all the implications can have dire results.

- Amendments should be drafted by someone with specialist construction contract expertise.
- Since many standard forms contain a clause giving the printed form priority over other documents, amendments should be made on the printed form itself or the priority clause should be struck out. If the amendment is simply made in the specification or the bills of quantities, it will be ineffective.[25]
- The *contra proferentem* rule may apply to amendments.

References and notes

1. More information about the planning system in each country of the UK can be obtained from the various government websites – England (www.communities. gov.uk), Scotland (www.scotland.gov.uk), Wales (www.wales.gov.uk) and Northern Ireland (www.northernireland.gov.uk).
2. See the CLG website: www.communities.gov.uk.
3. Regional planning information is available from www.englandsrdas.com or www. berr.gov.uk.
4. CABE (2006) Design and Access Statements. www.cabe.org.uk.
5. Information about local government and local councils is available from www. direct.gov.uk where there is also a link to individual LPAs from which detailed local planning guidance on plans, policies and making applications can be obtained.
6. Much more information and documents on this and other planning matters, including making applications online, are available from the Planning Portal at www.planningportal.gov.uk.
7. A list of planning consultants is available from the Royal Town Planning Institute at www.rtpiconsultants.com.
8. Planning (Listed Buildings and Conservation Areas) Act 1990. This Act consolidates all listed building and conservation area legislation and covers such things as listing, getting listed building consent, appeals and enforcement.
9. Ecclesiastical Exemption (Listed Buildings and Conservation Areas) Order 1994.
10. The Town and Country Planning (General Permitted Development) Order 1995, Schedule 1 (termed article 1(5) land).
11. The Town and Country Planning Act 1990, sections 197–214, cover the requirement for local authorities to consider the protection and planting of trees and the making of tree preservation orders.
12. The Town and Country Planning (Control of Advertisement) Regulations 2007.
13. See the Planning Inspectorate website for appeal information: www. planninginspectorate.gov.uk.
14. *Pannett* v. *McGuinness & Co* (1972) 2 QB 599.
15. Occupiers' Liability Act 1984, section 1(3).
16. *Andreae* v. *Selfridge & Co Ltd* (1938) Ch 1.
17. Control of Pollution Act 1974.
18. *Birmingham Development Co Ltd* v. *Tyler* (2008) 122 Con LR 207.
19. Public Health Act sections 91 and 92.

20. *Colls* v. *Home & Colonial Stores* (1904) AC 185.

21. *Allen* v. *Greenwood* [1979] 1 All ER 819.

22. Powell J, Stewart R, Jackson R. (2008) *Jackson & Powell on Professional Liability*, 6th edn and second supplement, Sweet & Maxwell.

23. JCT Practice Note 5, series 2, Deciding on the appropriate form of JCT Main Contract (2001) (deals only with JCT 98 series forms).

24. These factors, together with systems of contract choice. are explained in Chappell, D. (1991) *Which Form of Building Contract*, Longmans.

25. *M J Gleeson (Contractors) Ltd* v. *London Borough of Hillingdon* (1970) 215 EGD 495.

10 Stages E and F: Technical Design and Production Information

10.1 Technical design

This stage of the architect's work is essentially a completion of the design stage. The architect must collaborate with, and co-ordinate the work of, the design team. This is easy to say and less easy to do.

During this period, the architect must ensure, as far as possible, that all conflicts between consultants' work are ironed out. If any specialist sub-contractor design work is involved in the project, this must also be co-ordinated, together with final details from statutory and other authorities. Construction safety must be taken into account during this stage.

As a general rule, the use of sub-contractors in a design capacity is not advisable, because it can cause complications. The principal problem is that, unless the sub-contract work is part of the contractor's designed portion work under SBC, ICD or MWD, the contractor will have no design responsibility to the client for the work, even though the sub-contractor may have a design responsibility to the contractor. For example, if after practical completion a defect becomes apparent and it can be shown that the defect is due to a design error, the employer will have no obvious cause of action against the contractor. In practice, no doubt the contractor would pass the client's concerns to the sub-contractor and press for rectification. But if the sub-contractor became insolvent or simply refused to act, the employer could be without an adequate remedy except perhaps against the architect.

In any event, the client must authorise such design delegation (Chapter 6, section 6.4). It has to be acknowledged that there are some instances in which the use of specialist sub-contractors in a design capacity cannot be avoided due to the nature of the specialism. In such instances, the use of a form of collateral warranty between sub-contractor and employer is required to protect the client.

Ideally, at the end of stage E all the major decisions about structure, services, materials and construction techniques must have been made. Careful cost checks will be made by the quantity surveyor, if the project is large enough to support one; otherwise the architect must carry out this exercise.

If the project is sufficiently large to support a design team, they will be carrying out specific functions during this period, culminating in a meeting of the full team under the chairmanship of the team leader. This may be a project manager especially appointed by the client, but this will usually be as the employer's technical representative (Chapter 8, section 8.2). The separate functions of members of the design team will depend on the type of project, but as a general guide, they may be expected to be carrying out the following tasks.

Quantity surveyor/cost manager

- Reviewing the cost plan in the light of the client's comments and decisions on the scheme design. The review highlights potential additional cost and risk areas and indicates scope for maximising value.
- Carrying out cost studies and cost checks as the design team finally shapes the details. There must be a constant flow of information between the architect and the consultants, the architect and the quantity surveyor, and the quantity surveyor and the architect (Fig. 10.1 shows the principle).

Civil and structural engineers

- Collaborating in the cost plan review and cost checking procedures.
- Finalising all details in respect of dimensions, levels, loadings, concrete mixes, etc.
- Developing the specifications in detail.

Mechanical and electrical engineers

- Collaborating in the cost plan review and cost checking procedures.
- Refining the design of all services to be incorporated in the building.
- Developing the specifications in detail.

Strenuous efforts must be made to obtain the client's decision on any outstanding items. If the client makes any change in the size, location, shape or cost of the scheme after this stage, there will be a cost penalty for the redoing of work already carried out. Ideally, there should be no changes at all in the design after this point but in practice, it is impossible to eliminate all changes. Particularly in the case of projects such as hospitals, the brief will be constantly evolving and the client just has to accept that there is a price to pay for changes. The difficulties may sometimes be eased by the choice of a particular procurement path and/or contract form, but it can never be removed entirely. When faced with a constantly changing brief, some clients have been known to opt for design and build as a way of washing their hands of the problem. Such an approach is misguided. Design-and-build procurement is not appropriate unless the brief is fixed. To use design and build where the work is being constantly varied is a very expensive and ineffective way to proceed.

Stage E (technical design) of the RIBA Plan of Work usually merges imperceptibly into stage F (production information) and both stages amount to what would once have been termed 'working drawings'. To be precise, technical design is probably composed of roughly equal parts completion of design and

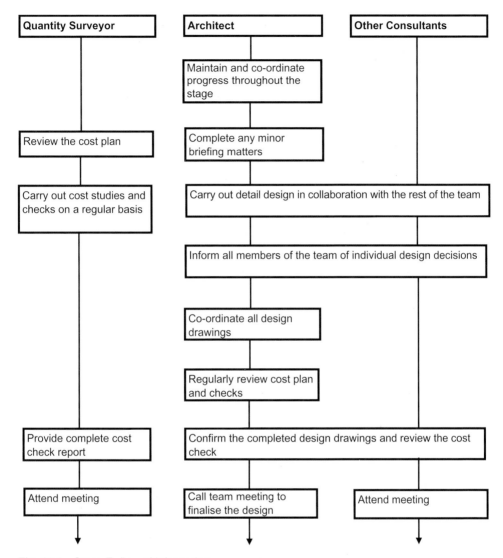

Quantity Surveyor	Architect	Other Consultants
	Maintain and co-ordinate progress throughout the stage	
Review the cost plan	Complete any minor briefing matters	
Carry out cost studies and checks on a regular basis	Carry out detail design in collaboration with the rest of the team	
	Inform all members of the team of individual design decisions	
	Co-ordinate all design drawings	
	Regularly review cost plan and checks	
Provide complete cost check report	Confirm the completed design drawings and review the cost check	
Attend meeting	Call team meeting to finalise the design	Attend meeting

Fig. 10.1   Stage E: flow of information.

commencement of working drawings. It does not matter. Indeed, it is perfectly proper that the process of design should not be divorced from the crucially important construction process.

The architect will continue the important twofold function of designer and manager throughout this and the next stage. It is likely that, insofar as the architect can ever be said to have reached a finite end to this stage, he or she will have a large collection of detailed design studies in a very final condition and covering every part of the project. This is the raw material from which the production information will take shape. There are several systems of setting out production information (section 10.3), but in every case, the architect cannot simply start by drawing a foundation and working up or start with the roof and work down.

It is essential that the architect thoroughly understands the nature of each part of the building and it is during this stage, more than any other, that the building takes shape as a whole. It cannot be overstressed that all parts must progress together so that the architect is aware, when considering the ducting details, what effect they have on the foundation designs, lift wells, room plans and so on. This is in fact the most important stage in the architect's work on a project.

10.2   Building Regulations 2000 (as amended)

10.2.1   General

The Building Regulations in England and Wales are made by the Secretary of State under the Building Act 1984. Their purpose is to secure the health, safety, welfare and convenience of people in or about buildings and of others who may be affected by buildings or matters connected with buildings and to further the conservation of fuel and power and prevent waste, undue consumption, misuse or contamination of water. The purpose for which Building Regulations may be made has been extended to include furthering the protection or enhancement of the environment, facilitating sustainable development, and furthering the prevention or detection of crime. These changes were introduced by the Sustainable and Secure Buildings Act 2004. The Building Act does not extend to Scotland or to Northern Ireland.

Most cases of building or alteration to buildings must be notified to the local building control authority except where the services of an approved inspector are employed. The following building types, at present subject to certain conditions, are exempted, by virtue of Schedule 2, from the Regulations.

- Buildings subject to the Explosives Acts 1875 and 1923.
- Buildings (other than dwellings, offices and canteens) on a site with a licence under the Nuclear Installations Act 1965.
- Buildings subject to the Ancient Monuments and Archaeological Areas Acts 1979.
- Buildings into which people cannot or do not normally go, subject to siting.
- Detached buildings containing fixed plant or machinery to which people only go intermittently to inspect or maintain the plant or machinery subject to siting.
- Greenhouses (unless used for retailing, packing or exhibiting).
- Any building used for agriculture, including fish farming, sited one and a half times its height from any point of a building containing sleeping accommodation and having no point more than 30 metres from an exit which may be used in the case of fire (unless the main purpose of the building is retailing, packing or exhibiting).

- Building intended to remain where erected for not more than 28 days.
- Any building on a site used in connection with the sale of buildings or building plots, provided there is no sleeping accommodation.
- Any building used by people in connection with the erection, extension, alteration or repair of buildings and containing no sleeping accommodation.
- Small detached single-storey buildings not exceeding 30 square metres floor area containing no sleeping accommodation and either sited more than 1 metre from the boundary of its curtilage or constructed substantially of non-combustible material.
- Nuclear, chemical or conventional weapon shelters not exceeding 30 square metres and which do not affect the foundations of adjoining or adjacent buildings, i.e. sited at a distance of the depth of excavation plus 1 metre.
- Any conservatory, porch, covered way or carport at least open on two sides. The extension which has a floor area not exceeding 30 square metres subject to glazing requirements of Approved Document N.

The Regulations are expressed fairly simply in functional terms, but there is a set of Approved Documents which indicate ways in which compliance with the Building Regulations may be achieved. However, it is possible to show compliance with the Regulations by reference to other standards or by calculation.

There are Approved Documents relating to the following requirements of the Building Regulations:

- AD A Structure
- AD B Fire safety – Volume 1 Dwellinghouses
- AD B Fire safety – Volume 2 Buildings other than dwellinghouses
- AD C Site preparation and resistance to contaminants and moisture
- AD D Toxic substances
- AD E Resistance to passage of sound
- AD F Ventilation
- AD G Hygiene
- AD H Drainage and waste disposal
- AD J Combustion appliances and fuel storage systems
- AD K Protection from falling, collision and impact
- AD L1A Conservation of fuel and power – new dwellings
- AD L1B Conservation of fuel and power – existing dwellings
- AD L2A Conservation of fuel and power – new buildings other than dwellings
- AD L2B Conservation of fuel and power – existing buildings other than dwellings
- AD M Access to and use of buildings
- AD N Glazing – safety in relation to impact, opening and cleaning
- AD P Electrical safety
- AD to support Regulation 7 – materials and workmanship.

Copies of the Approved Documents can be freely downloaded from www.planningportal.gov.uk/england/professionals/en/1115314110382.html.

The building control function can be exercised by local authorities or by approved inspectors. The latter system operates under the Building (Approved Inspectors, etc.) Regulations 2000. Control is operated through three procedures.

10.2.2   Notification

It is an offence to commence building operations without first depositing plans or a Building Notice giving at least 2 clear days' notice to the local authority. Note, however, that it is not necessary to await approval before commencing work.

It is not necessary to give notification for classes of work given in Schedule 2A where the work is undertaken by a competent person who is a member of an approved self-certification scheme. There are schemes covering:

■ installation of gas appliances
■ installation of oil appliances
■ installation of solid fuel appliances
■ installation of heating and hot water systems in dwellings
■ installation of heating, hot water, mechanical ventilation and air conditioning systems in buildings other than dwellings
■ electrical installations.

The principles of self-certification are based on giving people who are competent in their field the ability to self-certify that their work complies with the Building Regulations without the need to submit a Building Notice and thus incurring local authority inspections or fees. The notice procedures are as follows.

Deposit of full plans

This is the traditional system. A full set of plans must be deposited with the local authority in duplicate together with completed forms, which may vary in layout from authority to authority but which all contain requests for the same basic information. Where Part B Fire Safety imposes a requirement, two further copies must be deposited demonstrating compliance except in regard to dwelling houses. It is now possible to request, at the time the plans are deposited, that the local authority issue a completion certificate in accordance with the regulations. The Building (Local Authority Charges) Regulations 1998 gives the local authority power to determine the scale of plan or inspection charges as may be necessary to discharge its duties under the appropriate regulations. Charges can relate to the passing and rejection of plans, site inspections, building notices, reversion, regularisation and determinations. Charges are now payable when appeals are made to the Secretary of State. Current charges are available from the building control department of the local authority.

The drawings, each of which must be signed by the applicant or appointed agent, are generally expected to consist of the following.

- A block plan, not less than 1/1250 scale, showing the size and position of the building in relation to adjoining buildings, boundaries, position of all buildings within the curtilage, width of adjoining streets, lines of drainage, size, depth and gradient of drains and means of access, position and level of drain outfall and sewer connection.
- Sufficient plans and sections to suitable scales (usually not less than 1/100) showing full details of the intended construction of the project including site and floor levels, number of storeys, foundations, construction of floors, walls and roof, windows, doors, barriers to moisture, fire safety, means of escape, insulation, ventilation and access for all users of the building.

The local authority must give written notice of approval or rejection of the application within 5 weeks of the date of deposit of plans provided the requisite fee has been paid and a reasonable estimate of the cost of the work has been submitted. The period may be extended in writing to a total of not more than 2 months by agreement of both parties. Approval may, with the agreement of both parties, be given subject to conditions. The conditions can only relate to the deposit of further information or the modification of the details submitted.

If the authority fails to give written notice, it is in breach of its duty and the plan charge must be refunded. There is no deemed approval and indeed, even if there were such deemed approval it would be of little value if there was any disconformity, in the face of the applicant's obligation to construct in accordance with the Building Regulations.

Once plans have been deposited for approval and a question arises as to whether the plans of the proposed work conform with the Building Regulations then the question can be referred to the Secretary of State for determination (in Wales, the question is referred to the National Assembly of Wales).

Building Notice

There is no approval of plans by the authority where this procedure is adopted and work can be commenced subject to the submission of notices (see above). A Building Notice is now valid for 3 years if work is not started and it cannot be given for a building which is or will be subject to the Regulatory Reform (Fire Safety) Order 2005.

This applies to both new and existing buildings, including alterations or extensions. Effectively a Building Notice cannot be used in relation to buildings other than dwellings. Additionally, a Building Notice cannot be used in the case of a building fronting onto a private street nor in the case of work over or within 3 metres of an existing drain or sewer shown on the Sewerage Undertaker's sewer records. The local authority will be able to provide details of these records. There is no prescribed form for the notice, but it must contain certain basic information: the name and address of the person intending to carry out the work, notice that it is given under Regulation 11(1)(a) of the Building Regulations and a description including the use of the building to which the application relates. In addition, appropriate drawings and the prescribed charge must be deposited.

The drawing, to a scale of not less than 1/1250, will usually show the size and position of the building, its relationship to adjoining buildings, boundaries, position of all buildings within the curtilage, width of adjoining streets, numbers of storeys, building use, means of drainage, building over sewers. Details of insulation and hot water storage systems must be given in a detailed statement.

The authority may request the submission of whatever additional drawings or information it requires to enable it to carry out its duties. Where unauthorised work has been undertaken on or after 11 November 1985, the owner has to apply to the local authority for a Regularisation Certificate which is subject to a non-refundable charge at the time of submission.[1]

Initial Notice

This procedure is used if private certification is to be employed, using an approved inspector (see section 10.2.1 above). The notice must be in the prescribed form and must contain a description of the work, whether it is 'minor work' under the Building (Approved Inspectors, etc.) Regulations 2000, an undertaking to consult the fire authority, a statement of awareness of statutory obligations and a declaration that an approved insurance scheme is in operation (Fig. 10.2 is an example of such a notice). The notice must be signed by the inspector and by the applicant. It must be accompanied by an appropriate drawing, which must be a site plan to not less than 1/1250 scale showing location of the site, boundaries, connections to sewers and any proposed work over a sewer.

The local authority has 5 working days from the date of receipt of the notice to accept or reject it. If the notice is not rejected within this period, the authority is presumed to have accepted without conditions. The authority may impose various conditions when accepting the notice.

A local authority may reject an Initial Notice on the following grounds only.

- The notice is not in the prescribed form.
- The work is not within the area of the authority on which the notice has been served.
- The person signing as approved inspector is not an approved inspector.
- Insufficient information about description, use of building, location or drainage.
- An Initial Notice is not accompanied by notice of the inspector's approval.
- There is no evidence of insurance cover.
- There is no undertaking to consult the fire authority (if applicable).
- The inspector has a professional or financial interest in the work (unless 'minor work' involved).

The Building Act 1984, section 47, and the Building (Approved Inspectors, etc) Regulations 2000

INITIAL NOTICE

To: The Kirdale Metropolitan District Council, Department of Planning (Building Control Section), Old Town Hall, Kirdale, KD1 2FT

1.   This notice relates to the erection of a home for older persons, corner of Low Road and High Street, Kirdale, KD2 4EV

2.   The approved inspector for the work is:
      Seymore Thanniew RIBA
      Canny Buildings
      Kirdale, KD5 6PC
      Tel: 0111 234567

3.   The person intending to carry out the work is:
      Hope Furthurbest
      Penury House
      Neely Spent
      Kirdale, KD2 7EV
      Tel: 0111 345678

4.   The following documents relating to the work are enclosed with this notice:
      A copy of the approved inspector's notice of approval.
      A scheme of insurance approved by the Secretary of State, issued on behalf of Yorisk Insurers plc. relative to the work described.
      A plan to 1:1250 scale indicating site location, boundaries, drainage, connection and location of existing sewers.

5.   The work is not minor work.

6.   I, Seymore Thanniew, declare:
      a)   that I have no professional or financial interest in the work; and
      b)   that I will consult the fire authority before giving a plans certificate in accordance with section 50 of the Act or a final certificate in accordance with section 51 of the Act in respect of any of the work; and
      c)   that I am aware of the obligations laid upon me by Part II of the Act and by the 2000 Regulations.

Signed   Signed

Approved Inspector   Person intending to carry out the work
18 June 2009   18 June 2009

Fig. 10.2   Example of an Initial Notice.

- The drainage proposals are unsatisfactory.
- The authority is not satisfied that it may consent to building over a public sewer (if applicable).
- Local legislation will not be complied with.
- There is an overlap with a still effective Initial Notice.

Upon acceptance, supervision of the work becomes the responsibility of the inspector and the authority's powers to enforce the Building Regulations are suspended until either the Initial Notice is cancelled by the inspector or it ceases to have effect on the lapse of certain defined periods.

10.2.3 Commencement, completion, etc.

Where full plans have been deposited in the traditional way, building works must be commenced within 3 years of the date of deposit of plans with the local authority. Once work has started, neither the Regulations nor the Act itself stipulate the speed at which the work must progress, probably because it would not be feasible to so specify. It is possible for the work to be carried out over a very protracted period without the applicant incurring any penalty.

If the local authority is to supervise the work by means of its own inspectors, the Regulations require the applicant or the contractor to give the following notices in writing. The authority may, and often does, inspect on the basis of a telephone call, where it is permitted by the Regulations, but it is preferable from every point of view if the proper written notices are served and that:

- at least 2 days have elapsed before commencement of work on site
- at least 1 day has elapsed before any excavation is covered
- at least 1 day has elapsed before any foundation is covered
- at least 1 day has elapsed before any damp-proof course is covered
- at least 1 day has elapsed before any site concrete is covered
- at least 1 day has elapsed before any drainage or sewer is covered
- not more than 5 days have elapsed after the covering of any drain or sewer
- not more than 5 days have elapsed after completion
- at least 5 days have elapsed before occupation (if the building is occupied before completion).

'Day' means any period of 24 hours but excludes any Saturday, Sunday, Christmas Day, Good Friday, bank or public holiday.

The person carrying out the work must also provide the local authority with:

- in the case of a new dwelling, a calculated energy rating for the property
- in the case where Part E (Resistance to passage of sound) applies, the results of appropriate sound testing unless approved constructional details have been used.

Local authorities must now issue completion certificates in the following cases:

- when requested at the time of full plans submission
- where due notification has been received that the building will be put to a designed use under the Regulatory Reform (Fire Safety) Order 2005
- when notices have been received for completion or part occupation before completion.

A completion certificate will only be issued after compliance with the relevant requirements of Schedule 1 and compliance with:

- Regulation 16B – Provision of fire safety information; see Section 10.2.6
- Regulation 17C – Target CO_2 emission rates and predicted CO_2 emission rates for new buildings
- Regulation 17E – Provision of energy performance certificate; see section 10.2.7
- Regulation 17K – Water efficiency for new dwellings.

Where an approved inspector is involved, the inspector must issue a final certificate when work is complete (it should be noted that this is not the same as the final certificate under the provisions of JCT or other building contracts). The local authority is deemed to have accepted the certificate if it does not reject it within 10 days of receipt.

10.2.4 Dispensations and relaxations

The local authority has the power to dispense with or relax a regulation. This is a power delegated from the Secretary of State. The authority must be satisfied that the requirement would be unreasonable in a particular instance. Unless it concerns internal work only, a relaxation application normally must be advertised in a local newspaper by the authority at least 21 days before a decision is to be made. If the authority refuses the relaxation or, because of failure to respond within 2 months, it is deemed refused, the applicant has the right to appeal to the Secretary of State. The applicant must appeal within 1 month of refusal, setting out the grounds for appeal and all relevant information.

10.2.5 Contraventions

The local authority may require the removal or amendment of work which is carried out in contravention of the Regulations. This is normally done by service of a notice on the building owner. Failure to comply with such notice within 28 days entitles the authority to take action itself to correct the contravention and charge such costs to the owners. Such notice may not be served after the expiry of 12 months from the date of completion of the work. Appeal from such notice is to a magistrates court. An alternative is for the building owner to obtain a written report from a suitably qualified person in regard to the subject of the notice. The time for compliance with the notice is then extended to 70 days. On receipt of the report, the authority may withdraw the notice and may pay the building owner appropriate expenses.

10.2.6 Fire precautions

Fire has proved to be a major hazard in buildings for centuries. The Building Regulations 2000, Schedule 1, Part B, Fire Safety, contains five requirements.

- B1 Means of escape from all buildings, including dwelling houses
- B2 Internal fire spread (linings)
- B3 Internal fire spread (structure)
- B4 External fire spread
- B5 Access and facilities for the fire service

In large and complex schemes, the only viable and acceptable standard would be achieved by the fire engineering approach coupled with consultations with the building control authority and the fire authority at every stage in any project.

The Fire Safety Order reforms the law relating to fire safety in non-domestic premises. Specifically, it replaces the Fire Precautions (Workplace) Regulations 1997 and the Fire Precautions Act 1971. It imposes a general duty to take such fire precautions as may be reasonably required to ensure that premises are safe for the occupants and those in the immediate vicinity. By virtue of the Order, the responsible person is required to carry out a fire risk assessment of their premises. This must be a suitable and sufficient assessment of the risks to which relevant persons are exposed for the purpose of identifying the general fire precautions they need to take to comply with the requirements under the Order.

Although these requirements are applicable to premises whilst in operation, it would be useful for the designers of a building to carry out a preliminary fire risk assessment as part of the design process. If a preliminary risk assessment is produced, it can be used as part of the Building Regulations submission and can assist the fire safety enforcing authority in providing advice at an early stage as to what, if any, additional provisions may be necessary when the building is first occupied.

The Order applies to all non-domestic premises, which includes the common parts of blocks of flats and HMOs.

This is an important piece of legislation which is closely linked to the Building Act 1984. Architects should be familiar with its provisions so as to be able to advise clients broadly concerning its application in particular instances.

10.2.7 Energy Performance Certificate

The way in which a building is constructed, insulated, heated and ventilated and the type of fuel used all contribute to its energy consumption and carbon emissions.

When a building is built, an Energy Performance Certificate (EPC) is required under the Building Regulations. The certificate provides energy efficiency A–G ratings and recommendations for improvement.

The EPC is one measure introduced to help improve the energy efficiency of our buildings. Other changes include requiring larger public buildings to display certificates showing the energy efficiency of the building and requiring inspections for air conditioning systems.

Energy Performance Certificates must be produced by accredited energy assessors. They are produced using standard methods and assumptions about energy usage so that the energy efficiency of one building can easily be compared with another building of the same type. This allows prospective buyers, tenants, owners, occupiers and purchasers to see information on the energy efficiency and carbon emissions from their building so they can consider energy efficiency and fuel costs as part of their investment.

An EPC is always accompanied by a recommendation report that lists cost-effective and other measures (such as low and zero carbon generating systems) to improve the energy rating. Each recommendation is assessed against the potential impact over three payback periods in addition to other measures based on an understanding of the building and indicates whether the impact is high, medium or low.

10.2.8   Further legislation

The construction of buildings, their subsequent alteration or adaptation for other use is becoming more complex and may be subject to other Acts and regulations which may be outside the remit of the Building Regulations. The following list is an *aide mémoire* for other legislation connected with buildings and structures, but it is not intended to be fully comprehensive. Scotland and Northern Ireland are not always included. Most local authority staff are happy to confirm whether a particular Act or regulation is applicable to a scheme.

- *Health & Safety at Work Act 1974.*
- *Building Regulations and Amendment of Building (Scotland) Act 1959.*
- *Highways Act 1980.* Means of access to premises from highways, bridges in England and Wales, certain footpaths in buildings by agreement, footbridges over highways linking buildings, doors not to open onto highway, power to prescribe building lines, control of builders' skips, dangerous land adjoining highway.
- *Safety of Sports Grounds Act 1975.* Not applicable to Northern Ireland. An Act to make provision for safety at designated sports stadia and other sports grounds where accommodation is in excess of 10,000 spectators.
- *Fire Safety and Safety of Places of Sport Act 1987.* Provisions in respect of stands at sports grounds, indoor sports premises, amending statutory provisions, regulating entertainment licences and charges for fire certificates. The Act does not extend to Northern Ireland and there are certain sections which apply to England and Wales only and to Scotland only.
- *Building Act 1984.* The most commonly encountered sections deal with dangerous and defective premises, demolition of buildings, means of escape from certain high buildings and the raising of chimneys if over-reached by building work.
- *London Building Acts 1930 to 1982.* Most of the content of the London Building Acts has been repealed but certain sections have been retained. These sections deal primarily with fire safety measures in large buildings.
- *Local Acts of Parliament.* There are still over 30 local Acts of Parliament in existence enforced by the local authorities. Many of the Acts deal with fire

safety matters in large or tall buildings. The local authority will be able to provide details of the legislation that applies specifically to its area.

■ *Constructional Products Regulations 1991.* The Regulations require products to have such characteristics that works in which they are incorporated, if properly built, satisfy any essential requirements which apply to the works. Products which bear the CE marking will be presumed to satisfy this requirement.

■ *Disability Discrimination Act 1995 amended by the Disability Discrimination Act 2005.* Buildings should be designed for access and use by everyone and designed to create a barrier-free environment. From 2004, service providers have had to take reasonable steps to remove, alter or provide reasonable means of avoiding physical features that make it impossible or unreasonably difficult for disabled people to use a service.

■ *Party Wall Act 1996.* See the fuller description in Chapter 9, section 9.6.2.

■ *Workplace (Health, Safety and Welfare) Regulations 1992.* Implement provisions of the EU Workplace Directive, general duty imposed on employers to comply with the regulations, ventilation, lighting, adequacy of room dimensions, washing facilities, etc.

10.3   Production information

10.3.1   General

This is stage F of the RIBA Plan of Work. It has already been remarked that this stage merges imperceptibly with stage E. However, this stage does mark the firming of all detailed construction decisions and the completion of all information in readiness for the quantity surveyor to produce bills of quantities if that is part of the chosen procurement route.

During this period, the architect prepares drawings, specifications and schedules. These are the instructions to the contractor to tell him what is to be built and the quality required. Although some architects leave the detailed specification to the quantity surveyors, this is thoroughly bad practice because the architect is ultimately responsible for the specification and from every point of view it is best if the architect prepares it.

It is also the time for agreeing details of the contract with the client and for obtaining quotations from those who are to be named or listed sub-contractors. The architect must be in a position to inform the quantity surveyor of the nature and amounts of all provisional sums which are to go into the bills of quantities. Stage F is now divided into F1 and F2. Broadly, F1 is the preparation of sufficient information for tenders to be invited whereas F2 is the further information which will be required to amplify the contract drawings and to enable the contractor to carry out and complete the works by the date for completion in the contract. If the architect provides an information release schedule, it is the information on that schedule which is produced in stage F2.

10.3.2 Drawings

There are several different ways of producing the kind of drawings which make up the bulk of the production information. The design presentation drawings usually form the starting point for the preparation of working drawings. It has already been observed that by this stage the design drawings will be very detailed. Computers are now standard practice for the production of drawings (see Chapter 15, section 15.9). Although at one time a slow and laborious task, with the right equipment and architects who are practised in its operation, drawings can be produced quite quickly. Few architectural practices still use traditional methods and the need to be able to send drawings quickly as email attachments has made the production of drawings by computer essential. Having said that, many architects still believe that the initial sketch planning is best done with pencil and paper.

Under most standard forms of building contract, the responsibility for supplying the contractor with correct information lies with the architect. It is not the contractor's responsibility to look for errors and inconsistencies.[2] Mistakes will always occur, but in view of the cost of rectifying a mistake on a drawing which no one has spotted until too late, it is of the utmost importance that the drawing system should be simple and capable of highlighting errors. Of course, there is no such foolproof system, but some methods are probably better than others.

Traditionally, architects worked on all aspects of the building at once, having half-finished drawings showing plans at each level, elevations, sections and rough sketch drawings of all the major details to a large scale. These 'typical details' were often drawn on the same sheet as a plan or section which included the detail to a much smaller scale. The drawings were all brought to completion together and generally formed a well-integrated set. Such sets of drawings were characterised by very many more lines than strictly necessary to tell the story and an apparent desire on the part of the architect to leave no square millimetre of paper unused. Notes littered the drawing and they were often repetitive in nature.

This kind of drawing system is quite satisfactory, although expensive, if the building is relatively small and uncomplicated by special services. It is likely to be accurate because it is produced as a set and it has the advantage of having all the large-scale details on the same sheet as the small-scale information to which it relates. Moreover, the bricklayer can see what the carpenter has to do and the steel erector can readily appreciate the reason for any fine tolerances which have been specified. In fact, each part of the building can be understood in relation to every other part.

The problems with this kind of drawing system stem from the advantages. Although the system is fine for small buildings, it is very difficult to build a medium-to-large building from such drawings. One problem is the change in number of drawings from perhaps an optimum of two or three to perhaps 50 or more for a building only marginally larger and more complex than a large detached family house. The other problem is the unstructured way in which the information is presented. If details are drawn on the same sheet as small-scale drawings, finding such a detail will be difficult if there is more than one drawing showing the small-scale item, but the large detail is only on one drawing. There is a rule, whose name escapes the authors at present, which states that whichever drawing the site agent picks up, the detail will be on another. The sheer complexity of such drawings, when multiplied for a large building, makes errors almost certain (see Chapter 11, section 11.2 Co-ordinated project information).

A drawing system which attempted to overcome the defects in what can be termed the traditional method was the elemental drawing. The idea of this was that each element of the building was given a special drawing or set of draw-ings. Each item of information was given just once, in the appropriate place and to an appropriate scale. Among other things, the alteration of a drawing was made easier than where a traditional drawing was involved. Thus there was a complete set of reinforced concrete drawings showing every detail of the concrete, including dimensions, but nothing else. Similar sets are provided for brickwork and blockwork, plastering, joinery, plumbing, etc. Further drawings in outline were provided to show the way in which the elements fit together. This was an excellent system provided that it could be guaranteed that there were no errors on the drawings and that the drawings were comprehensive. Therefore, an enormous drawback to this system was that the inevitable errors which are present in any set of drawings had much less chance of being dis-covered, because the site operative could not easily see how the various seg-ments interfaced.

Although flawed, this system was developed into a four-stage and more practical drawing method:

- location drawings
- assembly drawings
- component drawings
- details/schedules.

Location drawings

These drawings are produced to a small scale, typically 1:100, but sometimes, for very large buildings, 1:200 is used. The purpose of the drawings is reflected in the content. They are intended to show the location of the building and other elements on the site, so as to enable the site agent to set them out prop-erly, and to show the position of all other major elements in the building itself. Thus there is a site plan, plans at each level, elevations and sections through every difficult portion of the building. Such plans and sections are not intended to show how the building should fit together; they principally serve as an index or menu from which the site agent can get a reference number for the required drawing. Some additional information may be included, such as finished floor and foundation levels and setting out and other dimensions, but the golden rule is that every line must be on the paper for a definite purpose.

Very often, these drawings are produced on a standard grid basis to simplify location of walls, doors and windows.

Assembly drawings

These are the drawings which show how the components of the building fit together. They are the successors to the traditional 'half inch sections' although they may not be sections and the scales can be any standard scale from 1:50 to 1:10. These drawings tend to contain the information which is not to be found elsewhere.

Component drawings

Component drawings show how the parts of the building are to be manufactured. Such items as fitted joinery, windows, doors, stairs, screens, concrete products and standard panels would be shown on these drawings. Generally, there is a separate drawing for each component. Components are often drawn full size or to some other appropriate large scale.

Details/schedules

The final category of drawings includes large-scale details of specific items of construction not shown sufficiently clearly elsewhere. Special details of damp-proof courses, weatherings, eaves, junctions and external hard landscaping may be included. This category also includes schedules. Schedules are a very good way of presenting information for categories of building element. They also impose a good discipline on architects, who learn a lot about their buildings in particular and construction in general by producing schedules. The architect who schedules everything possible accurately will make a friend of the quantity surveyor. Common schedules include the following.

- Ironmongery
- Sanitary fittings
- Precast concrete
- Doors
- Windows
- Floor, wall and ceiling finishes
- Lighting
- Glazing
- Tiling
- Colour
- Inspection chambers and manholes
- Lintels

Some less obvious subjects for schedules, but which are well worth doing, include the following.

- Architraves
- Skirtings
- Casings
- Plumbing pipe runs
- Rainwater pipes and gulleys
- External paving

References and notes

1. A number of excellent books have been published to assist the architect or building designer to meet the ever-increasing legal responsibility applied to buildings. *Knights Building Regulations 2000: With Approved Documents* (2001), Butterworths Law, is perhaps the most extensive and detailed general guide but it is not a substitute for legal advice or for the wording of the various Acts and Regulations. Billington, M.J., Bright, K.T., Waters, J.R. (2007) *The Building Regulations*, 13th edn, Wiley-Blackwell, is also a detailed source of information.
2. *London Borough of Merton* v. *Stanley Hugh Leach Ltd* (1985) 32 BLR 51.

11 Stages G and H: Tender Documentation and Tender Action

11.1 Introduction

The alternative procurement paths have been described in Chapter 8. All of them require tender documentation to be prepared in some form to enable the tendering contractors to submit a tender for the Works. Whilst the composition of such documentation will vary, it is essential that it is in a form adequate for the tenderer to fully understand the scope of the Works and the requirements of the tender submission, and that it be fully co-ordinated.

On major projects, where the traditional procurement approach is adopted, it is commonplace for bills of quantities to be prepared. In the absence of bills of quantities the tender documentation will comprise specification and drawings, with the tenderers having to prepare their own quantities in order to price the Works.

11.2 Co-ordinated project information

One of the prime causes of disruption of building operations on site has been highlighted as the inadequacy of drawn information, together with a lack of compatibility in project information generally, i.e. the drawings, specifications and bills of quantities not being consistent.

In order to improve the situation, the Co-ordinating Committee for Project Information (CCPI) was set up by the major bodies in the construction industry and after consultation with all interested parties, it produced a publication entitled *Common Arrangement of Work Sections for Building Works* (CAWS). It also produced Codes of Project Specification, Writing and Production Drawings, and worked with the producers of the Standard Method of Measurement for Building Works (SMM7).

The purpose of CAWS, as set out in its introduction, is to define an efficient and generally acceptable identical arrangement for specification and bills of quantities. The main advantages are:

- easier distribution of information, particularly in the dissemination of information to sub-contractors. One of the prime objects in structuring the sections was to ensure that the requirements of sub-contractors should not only be recognised but be kept together in relatively small tight packages
- more effective reading together of documents. Use of CAWS coding allows the specification to be directly linked to the bill of quantities descriptions,

cutting down the descriptions in the latter whilst still giving all the information contained within the former

■ greater consistency achieved by implementation of the above. The site agent and clerk of works should be confident that when they compare the drawings with the bill of quantities, they will no longer ask the question 'Which is correct?'.

CAWS is a system based on the concept of work sections. To avoid boundary problems between similar or related work sections, CAWS gives, for each section, a list of what is included and what is excluded, stating the appropriate sections where the excluded item can be found.

CAWS has a hierarchical arrangement in three levels. For instance:

■ Level 1   R   Disposal systems
■ Level 2   R1   Drainage
■ Level 3   R10   Rainwater pipes/gutters.

CAWS includes some 300 work sections encountered in the construction industry. They vary widely in their scope and nature, reflecting the extensive range of products and materials that now exist for use by contractors, sub-contractors and specialists. Although very much dependent on size and complexity, no single project will need more than a fraction of this number, perhaps as a very general average 25–30%. Only level 1 and level 3 are normally used in specifications and bills of quantities. Level 2 indicates the structure, and helps with the management of the notation. New work sections can be inserted quite simply without the need for extensive renumbering.

11.3   Bills of quantities

11.3.1   General

The work of the quantity surveyor/cost manager is described in Chapter 1 and whilst the role was traditionally to measure and value, as will have been seen, today it covers a much wider range of activities. The comments in this chapter are restricted to the preparation of bills of quantities, a key part of the measuring and valuation function.

Whilst bills of quantities are not always required, measurement of quantities in some form, either on behalf of the client or by the contractor, will be necessary and therefore it is important to understand the process involved and the need to provide adequate and timely design information.

11.3.2   Preparation of quantities

The quantity surveyor's work in preparing quantities is the last stage prior to issue of the tender documentation. Consequently, there is a tendency for the cumulative result of delays during the earlier stages of a scheme to have its effect on the time allocated for this process. With drawings completed and everything apparently cut and dried, it is sometimes difficult for clients to understand further delay.

Surveyors can and will work at high pressure when necessary, but they cannot do so for everybody and all the time. They are, after all, preparing a contract document, which will define the contract work precisely. Accuracy in the bill depends on a systematic checking of each stage, and a very careful reading through of the final draft. Excessive pressure can only result in work being done hurriedly or in part omitted, resulting in the potential for subsequent disruption and additional expense to the client. Therefore no attempt should be made to reduce the period for taking off the quantities to compensate for earlier delays.

It is a great help in shortening the time required for preparation of a bill if the quantity surveyor is fully involved throughout the design stages and is able to plan ahead and ensure the necessary resources are available. They should be kept informed of the programme and advised of any slippages as they arise. When drawings are approaching the final stages, they should be given a definite date which, once given, will be adhered to. They will then be able to plan their work so that the job can be done in the minimum of time. Moreover, if surveyors are expecting drawings, they can do the work in, say, 6 weeks; the same period may not be sufficient if the drawings turn up a fortnight late or if they come slowly in batches.

In order that the architect may appreciate the requirements of the quantity surveyor in terms of drawings and other particulars, it is necessary to give some idea of how they set about their work.

The building is divided into sections structurally, and each section is individually measured one section at a time. A list of sections in a typical building might be as follows.

(a)	Substructure	(1)	Substructures
(b)	Superstructure	(2)	Frame
		(3)	Upper floors
		(4)	Roof
		(5)	Stairs
		(6)	External walls
		(7)	Windows and external doors
		(8)	Internal walls and partitions
		(9)	Internal doors
(c)	Finishes	(10)	Wall finishes
		(11)	Floor finishes
		(12)	Ceiling finishes
(d)	Services	(13)	Sanitary appliances
		(14)	Disposal installations
		(15)	Water installations
		(16)	Heating installations
		(17)	Electrical installations
		(18)	Gas installations
		(19)	Lift installations
		(20)	Communications installations
		(21)	Builder's work in connection with services
(e)	External works	(22)	Site works
		(23)	Drainage

This list is obviously elastic, and a particular building might introduce additional sections, e.g. kitchen equipment, laboratory installations. The list is in a logical order, more or less following the construction of the building. The surveyors going through these sections envisage the erection of the building carried through in their mind's eye and must see every detail (even the fullest of drawings cannot show everything); they must decide for themselves what that detail is, for they cannot measure without something definite in mind.

Obviously it will be of great assistance to the surveyors if all the drawings are made available at one time but if certain drawings are delayed, the surveyors will not necessarily be held up. However, careful consideration must be given to the sequence of issuing drawings; surveyors may be able to do without joinery fittings or drains and not upset their measurement programme but if they are sent foundation drawings and are told by the architect 'You will have to wait for the depths', the drawings are of little use.

When complete drawings are not going to be available, the surveyors should be consulted as to priorities.

11.3.3 Standard methods of measurement

Standard methods of measurement have been introduced over the years to ensure that all bills of quantities are prepared on the basis of a set of rules accepted and agreed by the industry.

The most common in use at present is the Standard Method of Measurement of Building Works agreed between the RICS and the Construction Confederation. This is currently in its seventh edition (SMM7), revised in 1998, and is a set of rules structured in CAWS, which provides a uniform basis of measuring. Under the JCT forms of contract, bills of quantities are deemed to have been measured using SMM7 unless specifically stated to the contrary. SMM7 is accompanied by a Measurement Code for use as a non-mandatory explanatory document.

The RICS is in the process of publishing New Rules of Measurement (NRM) with the aim of providing a more consistent approach to the measurement of buildings throughout all stages of the project, i.e. estimating through to whole-life costing. The rules of measurement for procurement, when published, will provide an alternative set of rules to SMM7.

For engineering works, the ICE publishes a Civil Engineering Standard Method of Measurement which, like its counterpart in the building field, provides a uniform basis for measuring. This method of measurement does not have the same contractual significance as SMM7 in that it is not mandatory under the ICE form of contract.

Deviation from a standard method of measurement is to be avoided unless there are very good reasons for doing so. If deviations are chosen it is essential that they are made clear to tendering contractors and in the contract itself, otherwise disputes are certain to arise.

11.3.4 Provisional sums

Provisional sums are included for work for which there is insufficient information available for proper measurement and/or pricing. For various reasons, it is not always possible to define finally, at design stage, everything necessary for the completion of the building. For instance, it may be necessary for the architect to select certain articles such as sanitary appliances, ironmongery and the like in consultation with the client, and the details of these may well not have been considered at the early stage when tenders are being sought. (Under previous editions of the JCT standard contract this was dealt with by the use of 'nominated suppliers'.) Provisional sums may also be included to cover possible expenditure on items which may be required but for which there is no information available at tender stage.

Under SMM 7, provisional sums may be for either 'undefined' or 'defined' work, i.e. work which can be described fairly fully but not measured, perhaps because the extent is not known or some other finite detail inhibits full description. In respect of the latter, the contractors are expected to have taken into account all their own costs and when the actual sum expended is ascertained for the final account, no other adjustment to prices or time is made. On the other hand, if the Works are 'undefined' then other prices, such as items of plant, may have to be adjusted when the work is valued for the final account and the contractor may be entitled to an extension of time and loss/or expense.

In most if not all construction projects, there are bound to be unknown matters arising such as changing ground conditions, new by-law requirements or problems emerging when an old building is opened up. In order to ensure that funds are available to pay for these unexpected extras, it is usual to include specific risk allowances or alternatively a sum of money known as a *contingency sum*. These are to be used if required or if not omitted in whole or part as the case may be. It should be emphasised that these sums, which of course are undefined provisional sums, are there for the very purpose described and not to be spent because the architect has had a change of mind or has forgotten to include part of the client's brief.

Sub-contractors

Under the SBC, the contractor can sub-contract parts of the Works (with consent). However, it may be desirable to select a shortlist of specific specialist firms to carry out certain works and not leave the choice solely to the main contractor: for instance, curtain walling, mechanical and electrical services and lift installations. The SBC provides for a list of such companies to be included from which the contractor makes a selection. (Under previous editions of the standard form, this was addressed by the use of PC sums and the appointment of 'nominated sub-contractors'.)

Figured dimensions

Figured dimensions on drawings may be divided into three categories.

1.   Overall dimensions of the building.
2.   Subdivision of the last for setting out, showing spacing of structural open-
     ings for frames, windows and doors.
3.   Internal dimensions of rooms.

Quantity surveyors will require (1) and (3). They use (1) to calculate the girths
of the walls, and a whole series of items are dependent on these girths:
trench excavation, concrete foundations, brickwork, damp-proof courses,
facings, copings, etc. They must have (3) to record the measurements of ceiling
and floor finishes and to establish the girths of the rooms for wall plaster,
skirtings, etc.

Architects should ensure, therefore, that they give overall dimensions of all
sides of the building and that the exact dimensions of every room in either
direction can be seen at a glance. Where there is a range of rooms of similar
dimensions, obviously the figuring need not be repeated for each, but otherwise the two dimensions should be clearly given on the plan. The dimensions
of piers, recesses, cupboards, etc. should be clearly marked. The figuring of
heights on sections is important and it must be made clear as to whether they
are floor-to-floor or floor-to-ceiling heights.

Category (2) of the figured dimensions is not of interest to quantity surveyors but, of course, is absolutely necessary on drawings from which the building
is to be constructed.

Contractors also require the overall dimensions (except where setting out is
for a steel frame) as they will be setting out the corners of the building before
they have to think about the position of the window or door openings, etc. In
the same way, the inside sizes of rooms will assist them in setting out the
internal walls and partitions.

All figured dimensions on plans will normally be of the shell of the building,
i.e. between wall faces before plastering. It should be made quite clear whether
heights are to finished level or surface of the structure: the allowance to be
made for thickness of finishes should be definitely given so that the agent has
precise dimensions to follow. Architects must, however, remember that where
there is any requirement of a minimum height for rooms, that such minimum
will be between finished surfaces, and they must make due allowance.

It may be found convenient to mark floor levels on each floor in relation to
a specific datum, particularly where they vary on a floor. It should be made
clear by a note on the drawing whether these are finished or slab levels (usually
the former).

11.3.5   Specification notes

Drawings need to be supplemented by descriptive information. This may be
either a full specification such as would be used if there were no quantities, or
in the form of notes expressing the architect's requirements (see also section
11.4 below). Where the Government Form of Contract (GC/Works/1) is used,
the specification is a contract document, and is usually supplied to the quantity

surveyor in full. In the JCT 'with quantities' forms, the specification is not a contract document.

Following the introduction of co-ordinated project information (CPI) referred to above, the specification now plays a key role in tender documentation and whilst not itself a contract document, the relevant parts need to be incorporated in some way. The fuller the information given to quantity surveyors, the more the bill will represent the architect's requirements and the less trouble there will be in answering questions raised by the quantity surveyors. The surveyors, as already explained, have to envisage the whole building; they must decide every detail that is not shown on the drawings or included in the information. This must then be ascertained from the architect.

Specification notes are sometimes found written all over the drawings. If they are at all extensive, they hinder easy reading of the drawings, particularly if the same note is repeated in several places. For instance, a note '255 mm cavity wall' is sufficient if the bricks are known to be 102.5 mm thick. Detail as to bond, ties, etc. is not necessary for the drawing but is, of course, essential for the specification.

11.3.6   Corrections to drawings

The very detailed analysis made by surveyors can be of great assistance to architects in that it will bring to their attention any errors or inconsistencies in the drawings or specification. However, this should not be relied upon. Even if not definite errors, points raised by the surveyors may sometimes involve alteration.

The contract drawings must correspond with the bill of quantities and they must also be identical to the tender drawings, so if, as sometimes happens, alterations are discovered to be necessary after the bills have been prepared, and the surveyor is told to leave the alteration to be adjusted as a variation, it is most important that the drawings to be signed with the contract should not show the alteration. When it comes to signing the contract, if prints of the original drawing cannot be made or if the architect, not realising the discrepancy exists, supplies the revised prints, inconsistency is caused between drawings and the contract bills of quantities and the client may incur additional expense.

If, during the preparation of the bill of quantities, the architect proposes to alter the drawings, her or she should immediately advise the quantity surveyor. Even a line altered or erased may involve substantial alterations to the dimensions. Such changes as reducing the length of a building by 250 mm or the pitch of a roof by 5° involve complications not apparent at first sight.

Alterations made during the measurement process are not only a waste of valuable time but mean that, when it comes to adjusting variations, it is necessary for the quantity surveyor to hunt in two or three places to find what is in the contract. The adjustment is therefore complicated. If revised prints are to be sent to the quantity surveyors to correct drawings already issued, it is useful if the architect circles the revision using a coloured pen. This ensures time is not spent searching for the alteration and avoids the risk that minor alterations will not be noticed.

11.4 Specifications

11.4.1 General

In the context of tender and contract documentation the specification has always played a key role. With the introduction of CPI, as described above, the specification has become more important than ever. The CCPI in its publications makes it clear that the specification is the key document from which all other information, either for drawings or bills of quantities, will flow.

The writing and use of specifications is a subject in its own right and as such warrants separate study.[1] Comments in this book are restricted to explaining the purpose of a specification and the changes that have come about in recent years in the way that they are drafted.

11.4.2 The purpose of a specification

The specification has three important purposes, in each case in conjunction with the drawings.

- To be read by the contractor's estimator as the only information available on which to prepare a competitive tender.
- To be read by the quantity surveyor to enable a bill of quantities to be prepared as a basis for such competitive tenders.
- To be read by the contractor's agent and the clerk of works during the progress of the contract as the architect's instructions for carrying out the Works.

11.4.3 The specification as a basis for tenders

In small contracts, usually those under about £100,000 in value, or for packages of work where the Works are procured on a package-by-package basis, contractors prepare their tenders from drawings and specifications only. Estimators take their own measurements of the work from the drawings and build up their estimates, relying on the specification for a full description of quality, materials and workmanship. Besides this, drawings and specifications, when read together, must indicate everything required to be included in the estimate. If anything is omitted, something that is required is not mentioned or shown, or very obviously necessary or implied, such work will not be part of the contract. If it is required, the contractor will be entitled to additional payment.

The writer of a specification for this purpose will, therefore, realise the importance of the work necessary. Instructions must be crystal clear and complete in detail. The specification will be one of the contract documents and it is not to be hurriedly thrown together. It must have all the precision of an agreement (in fact, it will be part of such an agreement), conveying to the contractor exactly what is wanted and protecting the client from claims for extra payment that would arise from vagueness and uncertainty.

11.4.4 The specification for the quantity surveyor

For contracts where it has been agreed that bills of quantities are to be supplied to the contractor on behalf of the client in order to obtain competitive tenders, the measuring work, which in the previous case would be done by all the tenderers, is in these circumstances done for them by the quantity surveyor who puts the facts before them, but each tenderer is left with the estimating, this being largely a matter of individual judgement.

In order that the quantity surveyor may prepare the bill, instructions must be given by the architect. While such instructions need not be as complete as those required by the contractors when taking their own measurements, they must be sufficient to ensure that all cost-significant matters are fully described. In this case the architect's full specification is not usually a contract document, although bearing in mind the dictum of CPI, it may very well form an adjunct to the bill for cross-referencing purposes. It can, however, be less formal and convey the information in the form of notes either separately or on the drawings. For certain standard clauses, reference may, with care, be made to similar clauses in other contracts.

The specification preambles will be in CAWS order to facilitate easy reading with the measured items. These specification preambles must convey the specific information so that when read in conjunction with the measured items (the bills), they 'fully describe and accurately represent the quantity and quality of the work' as required by the SMM.

11.4.5 The specification for site agent and clerk of works

When erection of the building starts, the work will be supervised on behalf of the contractor by the agent. On large projects a clerk of works will be employed as an inspector on behalf of the client, since frequent or even constant inspection will be necessary and the architect is not expected to be continuously on the site. Both site agent and clerk of works require instructions and they take these, subject to any variations ordered by the architect, from the contract documents, i.e. drawings and specifications or drawings and bill of quantities. Where quantities have been prepared, the quantity surveyor will have incorporated the specification in the descriptions or in the bill preambles.

There is, however, certain information required by the site agent and clerk of works which will have been excluded from the bill. The locations of items, for instance, will not usually be mentioned in the bill because they do not normally affect price; however, the site agent must have this information when it comes to erecting the building. Spacing of joists, colour schedules and fittings location are other matters which, while not included in a bill of quantities, need to be available to the site staff.

11.4.6 Drafting specifications

For many years it was common practice for specifications to be hand-written, albeit often using previous documentation suitably amended. Over the intervening years the practice of writing specifications fell into decline. Regrettably, on many occasions specifications became a matter of a few sheets of hastily drafted notes; more often it was a case of 'It's all on the drawings'.

Today, owing to advances in computer technology, slowly at first but with gathering momentum, standard specifications have become commonplace. Now architects and surveyors can enjoy the benefits of having the facility to use mark-up copies of a standard specification to be adapted for each specific project.

11.4.7 National Building Specification

The National Building Specification (NBS) is not a standard specification; rather, it is a large library of specification clauses all of which are optional; many are direct alternatives, and often require the insertion of additional information. The NBS thus facilitates the production of specification text specific to each project, including all relevant matters and excluding text that does not apply.

The NBS is available only as a subscription service, and in this way it is kept up to date by issue of new material several times a year via disk and hard copy for insertion into loose-leaf ring-binders. The NBS is prepared in CAWS (section 11.2), matching SMM, and complies fully with the recommendations of the CPI Code of Procedure for Project Specifications. There are three versions of the NBS: the Standard Version, an abridged Intermediate Version and a Minor Works Version.

11.5 Schedules of work

A schedule of work is a list of items of work required to be done and should not be confused with a specification. It is mainly used in works of alteration to spell out the items that are only covered in the specification in general terms. Schedules of work as an adjunct to the specification have to be used with care.

A specification, like a bill of quantities, incorporates contract particulars, employer's requirements, contractor's liabilities as well as a full specification of the materials and workmanship. A specification, however, should never contain quantities. To quote quantities in a specification is inviting trouble: the contractors will say 'We've priced the quantities we were given' whereas they should have priced everything that they considered necessary from their own measurements to arrive at a lump sum price. Where the specification option is used in some standard forms of contract, the inclusion of quantities can lead to those items gaining priority over the drawings.

In the same way problems can arise when the description of the work is set out in schedule form following the materials and workmanship clauses. Old-fashioned specifications used to end up with words such as 'Carry out all the work shown on the drawings'. Today there is a tendency for clients to require the lump sum to be broken down into component parts, with schedules of work indicating specific packages – alterations, sub-structure, brickwork, roofing, etc. – and a £ sign against each of the packages.

Whilst this can be of some assistance in checking interim valuation applications, in giving the client a breakdown of the price and in some ways costing variations, the same problem exists: 'We only priced what was written down', whereas the intention was that everything necessary should have been priced. It is therefore important that the same care be taken in drafting schedules of work as is taken in drafting the specification itself. It must be very clear to the estimator exactly what is wanted and nothing must be missed.

11.6   Activity schedules

An alternative basis on which to obtain tender prices is by way of priced activity schedules (e.g. as provided for in the Engineering and Construction Contract, and SBC). Such a schedule is either prepared by each tenderer or alternatively is provided as part of the tender documentation in order to aid ready comparison of tenders submitted. An activity schedule is a list of activities, normally relating to programmed activities, that the contractor needs to carry out in order to complete the Works. Activity schedules are considered by some to be more suited to method driven projects, e.g. those of a civil engineering nature, but they have become more widely used on building projects.

11.7   Tendering

11.7.1   Procedure in preparing a tender

The preparation of a contractor's estimate may be divided into two parts: the ascertaining of facts and the application of judgement. The facts are the nature and quality of the materials and the workmanship required, which must be set out in a form suitable for pricing. A bill of quantities provides these. Where no bill of quantities is supplied, the tenderers must, with the guidance of the specification, prepare their own quantities from the drawings.

The key factor in the preparation of a tender when quantities are supplied is the tenderers' judgement on prices. They should not follow rule-of-thumb or price books (although some inexperienced firms have been known to do so) because every contractor's office has to take different circumstances into account.

Tenderers will in all probability have the actual cost of the main components of a building from their own records of other projects, and these costs will help them as a basis for pricing new work. They may have particularly good workmen in certain trades or may be in a position to procure certain materials at advantageous prices. They must consider the particular location of the project in question, its distance from the office, its accessibility, etc., and adjust their costs accordingly. An isolated site involving transport and travelling time for workmen can make a big difference to the real cost of an hour's work. There will be many items for which tenderers must obtain quotations in order to build up suitable rates.

They may well adjust their tender according to their need for new work. If they are short of work, they may be satisfied with a low level of profit and sometimes with no profit at all, although this can cause problems on all sides as the work progresses and the contractor is faced with unexpected costs. If they are busy, they may not want the work unless they can get it at an enhanced profit.

It is important to remember that in submitting competitive tenders, a mistake may involve serious financial loss. Contractors do not enjoy the luxury of subsequently correcting their mistakes, as do architects, engineers and quantity surveyors. It is therefore most important that contractors should have all possible information available and every facility to acquire as full a knowledge as possible of the proposed work.

11.7.2 Documents for tendering

Where a bill of quantities is supplied, it will be accompanied by a copy of the general 1:100 or 1:50 scale drawings together with any component details required. The supply of this type of drawn information gives tenderers a better idea of the nature of the project and their probable commitments than does a hurried look in the architect's office. Where no quantities are supplied, each tenderer must, of course, be given a complete set of all the drawings from which to prepare their estimate.

In the case of works of alteration, a set of drawings issued to each tenderer is almost indispensable. If, however, for some special reason each is not issued with a set, one should be made available on the premises to be altered; the difficulties of an estimator going round a building pricing spot items without a drawing must be appreciated. Where there are substantial alterations to be priced, a set of drawings to be inspected at the architect's office is of no use.

In works of alteration, where rooms are divided or two or more are to be made into one, rooms should be given serial numbers on the drawings according to the existing plan. The specification and the bill of quantities should be similarly referenced. The numbers then have a clear meaning to the estimator walking around the building before any alterations have been made. If identification of new rooms is required in a similar way, a series of letters can be used (or vice versa).

Where there are no quantities, a full specification will be supplied to each firm tendering, but not when quantities are provided: everything affecting a price should be in the bill of quantities.

11.7.3 Selection of contractors

The selection of contractors to tender for each project should be made having full regard to its size and nature. It should be the aim to have contractors of similar standing tendering in order to make tenders properly comparable. A small house will warrant a different list from that for a civic centre and contractors who may be suitable for a civic centre contract may not necessarily be suitable for a steel-framed factory. Whereas many contractors could tackle a dozen houses in a housing scheme, the number in the locality who could undertake a contract for 200 houses is certainly more limited.

Consideration needs to be given to the nature of the work, together with the prospective contractor's financial capacity, experience of work of a similar nature, and reputation. JCT Practice Note 6 – Main Contract Tendering[2] provides guidance as to good practice in the selection of contractors and awarding contracts, this being the successor to the Code of Tendering Procedure published by the National Joint Consultative Committee (NJCC).

Public sector construction contracts within the European Union over approximately €5.15m (approximately £3.5m) must be invited and awarded in accordance with the procedures laid down in EU Directives. These provide for a 'restricted tendering procedure' which permits the selection of technically and financially competent contractors following advertisement in the official journal of the European Union circulated throughout member states.

Certain public authorities, by their standing orders, are required to advertise their contracts publicly even when below the EU threshold. This can result in a mixed list, and many of the better firms, as long as they have plenty to do, will refrain from tendering in such circumstances. They have to compete with inexperienced firms, who may cut the price merely to get a start in the contracting business. As they are often unknown, tendering in this manner is the only way in which to make a start. The lowest price in those circumstances is not necessarily the best or even the most economical in the end. If the authority could be persuaded to advertise that it will select a list from the applicants, there would probably be an actual saving in public money instead of an apparent saving which turns out to be illusory.

Where open invitations are issued, it is not uncommon for the client to require the successful contractor to provide a guarantee bond, and this may be obligatory to comply with the standing orders of some public authorities. The guarantor undertakes to meet any deficiency due to the failure of the contractor to carry out the contract, up to an agreed specified limit, commonly 10% of the contract sum. The details of the bond are a matter for the client's solicitor and are usually outside the province of the architect.

11.7.4   Time for tendering

With the object of ensuring that contractors have every opportunity of preparing a proper tender which they can safely stand by, the time allowed for tendering should be as long as possible. An excessively short period results in rushed work and inability to get estimates in proper time, and in consequence increases the risk of errors.

When a bill arrives in a contractor's office for pricing, the usual procedure is for the estimator to go through it and mark up those parts for which quotations are required, either for the supply of materials or the sub-letting of work. The marked portions will then be copied with any adaptations necessary and these portions will be used for competitive enquiries. The bill will then be put aside because it cannot be priced until all replies have been received, as to do so piecemeal is a waste of time. When the replies are received, they are sorted and examined and the most suitable used, with the necessary additions for profit and fixing if appropriate.

Prequalification and the process of establishing the list of appropriate contractors interested in tendering should be carried out in good time. Any firm that cannot tackle the project in the time will then be able to say so and last-minute requests for extensions of time will be avoided. Adequate warning should also be given as to when documents will be sent out and the date for delivery of the tenders. Four weeks should be regarded as the minimum time for tender.

It is obvious that when contractors are tendering on a specification and drawings only basis, they will need longer to tender than when a bill of quantities is supplied for a similar building, as they will have to prepare their own quantities.

11.7.5   Sending out documents

The architect or the quantity surveyor will send to each firm tendering a copy of the specification and tender form and a complete set of drawings or, if a bill of quantities is used, that too with a selection of drawings (see below) under a covering letter which should state:

- invitation to tender, if not already sent
- list of enclosures
- date and place for delivery of tenders
- whether the site is open for inspection and if so, what arrangements should be made to visit it
- request for acknowledgement.

Figure 11.1 illustrates a typical letter.

Tenders will usually be delivered to the architect or the quantity surveyor, unless particularly requested to be delivered direct to the client. In the case of public authorities, both the sending out of documents and receipt of tenders will be handled by a representative of the authority. A recommended form of tender is illustrated in Fig. 11.2. A suitable envelope should accompany the documents for delivery of the tender, ready addressed and marked 'TENDER FOR …' on the face. These envelopes will on receipt be recognised as containing tenders and will be left unopened until the time stated for delivery has passed and a check has been made that all have been delivered. If this procedure is not scrupulously observed, the client may be liable for a tenderer's abortive expenditure.[3]

Where there is a bill of quantities, much the same procedure is followed, although the documents are usually (but not in the case of a public authority)

Dear Sir
[insert heading]

We refer to your letter of the [insert date] in which you expressed willingness to submit a tender for the above project. We now have pleasure in enclosing the following:

1. Two copies of the bills of quantities.
2. Two copies of each of drawings numbers [insert numbers] giving a general indication of the scope and character of the Works. These will become the contract drawings.
3. Two copies of the form of tender.
4. An addressed envelope for the return of the tender and instructions relating thereto.

Please note the following:

(a) Drawings may be inspected at [insert place].
(b) The site may be inspected by arrangement with [insert person and telephone number].
(c) Examination and correction of priced bills will be in accordance with alternative 1/2 [delete as appropriate] in the JCT Practice Note 6 – Main Contract Tendering.

The completed form of tender is to be sealed in the endorsed envelope provided and must arrive at [insert place] not later than [insert time] on [insert date].

Please acknowledge safe receipt of this letter together with the enclosures noted and confirm that you will submit a tender in accordance with these instructions.

Yours faithfully

Fig. 11.1 Letter to contractor: invitation to tender (assumes bills of quantities used).

sent out by the quantity surveyor on completion of the printed bills, so saving a little time. There will be a selection of small-scale drawings with perhaps typical details and special drawings required by the SMM to accompany tenders, indicating broadly the scope and quality of the work, and the covering letter will state where the remaining drawings can be inspected if required (usually the office of the architect or surveyor).

If the bill is to be delivered with the tenders, as is often the case, the documents must include a separate envelope of suitable size and strength to hold the bill, addressed in the same way as the envelope for the tender. The tenderers should be notified in the covering letter to put their name on the outside of the bill envelope so that only the bill accompanying the lowest tender is opened. The remaining bills should be returned unopened.

11.7.6 Opening of tenders

Before opening the tenders, it is important to ensure that they have all been delivered, and care is necessary if any tender is delivered late. Most contractors will find out quite easily the identities of the other tenderers. After the time fixed for delivery, there may be enquiries from one contractor to another as

---

Tender for [describe works]
at [insert location]

To [insert name and address of client]

We, having read the conditions of contract, articles of agreement, appendix and specification/schedules of work/bills of quantities [delete as appropriate] delivered to us and having examined the drawings referred to therein, do hereby offer to execute and complete the Works described in accordance with the terms therein for the sum of_____

_____ (words) £_____

We agree that

(a) The employer is not bound to accept the lowest or any tender.
(b) Persons tendering do so at their own cost.
(c) If errors in pricing or errors in arithmetic are discovered in the priced specification/schedules of work/bills of quantities [delete as appropriate] before acceptance of this offer, such errors will be dealt with in accordance with alternative1/2 [delete as appropriate] in the JCT Practice Note 6 – Main Contract Tendering.
(d) Unless and until a formal agreement is prepared and executed, this tender together with your written acceptance thereof shall constitute a binding contract between us.

We confirm that this is a bona-fide competitive tender and we have not fixed or adjusted the amount by reference to any other person, body or organisation or divulged the amount of this tender.

This tender remains open for acceptance for [insert days] from the date of this tender

Dated this .... Day of .... 20 ....

Signed ....

in the capacity of ....

duly authorised to sign tenders for and on behalf of:

Name ....

Address ....

Fig. 11.2   Form of tender.

to figures and one must accordingly be sure that no late tenderer has taken advantage of this.

If tenders are delivered to the architect's office, they will be opened and a list prepared, arranged in order of price, for submission to the client. Any special conditions attached to the tender should be noted and entered against the tenderer's name in the list. If tenderers are required to state a contract period as well as a price, as is often the case, this too will be entered against each name. If the tenders are being opened by a representative of a public authority (often in the presence of an elected member), the same procedure will be followed for submission of the result to the council or committee concerned.

11.7.7   Reporting of tenders

In considering tenders, factors other than the price may be of importance. The time required to carry out the work, if stated on the form of tender, may be compared, as time may be very important financially to the client. The time stated by a reputable contractor may be taken as a reasonable estimate, having regard to the circumstances as known.

The architect, having considered these matters in consultation with the quantity surveyor, will report the tenders to the client or committee concerned. If there is any doubt, the case in favour of acceptance of one tender or another needs to be clearly set out for consideration. Other matters that may be considered are the proposed teams, quality and safety.

When tenders are invited from a selected list of contractors, the lowest, or potentially lowest, should be accepted. All go to a good deal of trouble and expense in preparing a tender, and the object of such tendering is to decide which amongst a number, all acceptable to the client, will do the work at the lowest price. Whether expressly disclaimed in the invitation or not, there is no legal obligation to accept the lowest or any tender.

However, when tenders are advertised and any contractor who can raise the required deposit and surety may submit a tender, the circumstances are different. One can justly say 'I didn't ask you and I don't want you', though even then, when the expenditure of public money is involved, there may be repercussions.

As soon as the lowest or any tender is accepted then all the tendering contractors should be notified (see section 11.7.10 below).

11.7.8   Examination of a priced bill

If the client decides to proceed with the work, the tenderer whose offer is under consideration will be asked to supply a copy of the priced bill (if it has not already been submitted with the tender). This will be examined by the quantity surveyor who will make an arithmetical check and will also look generally through the rates for any possible serious errors or omissions in the pricing. If there are no serious errors, and provided there are no other inhibiting circumstances, then the tender can be safely recommended for acceptance.

However, if mistakes are found, the tenderer must be notified. Then, if the JCT Practice Note referred to above has been adopted, one of two things will happen depending on the alternative provision advised in the invitation to tender: under alternative 1, the tenderer should be invited either to stand by the tender price or withdraw, in which case a commercial decision will need to be taken; under alternative 2, the tenderer should be given the opportunity to stand by the tender offer or correct genuine errors.

11.7.9   Reductions

Unfortunately, it is not uncommon for tenders to be higher than expected, sometimes due to overoptimism of architect and quantity surveyor at the approximate estimate stage or, more probably, because a full cost-planning exercise has not been carried out. If clients are not prepared to meet the higher cost, ways and means have to be found to get down to their figure, and at the same time meet their requirements as to accommodation, etc.

The architect will have to re-examine the drawings and specification with this in mind. Here, the help of the quantity surveyors can be useful as they may be able to suggest from the analysis that the priced bill has provided, where the architect's requirements are costly, less costly alternatives could be considered. A list of possible reductions will be prepared and valued in consultation with the quantity surveyors. They will prepare a bill of omissions and any counterbalancing additions, from which the tender sum can be adjusted.

For what sounds quite a simple reduction, adjustment on a bill of quantities may be lengthy. To take 150 mm off the length of a building (which may only mean a few broken lines and figured dimensions on the architect's drawings) affects a large number of items through many sections in the bill of quantities, from stripping surface soil to the paint on the walls and ceilings.

There is one cause of excessive tenders and consequent reductions which should be avoided: the inclusion of something which the architect wants, in the hope that the client can be persuaded to want it, when they discover that it is included in the tender. The architect may feel that it is easier to cut out such an item when tenders come in than to add it afterwards. Such conduct on the part of an architect may amount to professional negligence. Unless there is a reasonable likelihood of keeping within the client's price, it should not be included in the first instance. Reductions in a tender only make additional work for architects and quantity surveyors in altering drawings and specifications and preparing reduction bills and, moreover, involve the client in additional fees and expenses.

11.7.10   Informing tenderers

Preparation of competitive tenders is today a very expensive activity. Much time and effort and consequently money are expended and it is only reasonable that tendering contractors should be made aware of the result. The winner will want to know 'how much they left on the table', i.e. what margin there was between their bid and the next lowest. The losers in their turn will need to know, for future pricing and policy purposes, just where they stood.

Much is made of the need for confidentiality in competitive tendering and it is sometimes argued that publication of tender results breaches that confidentiality. Actual confidentiality is perhaps questionable; there are too many common contact points by way of suppliers, ready-mix concrete firms, etc., whereby it is not unknown for a tender list to become public knowledge. Once tenders are submitted, it is quite common practice for tender amounts to be exchanged by the competing contractors.

However, none of this alters the duty to publish the list and, with the confidentiality referred to above in mind, this can best be done by publishing a list of amounts without the firms' names being given. Each tendering firm will recognise their price and where they came. If in addition they are able to put names to sums, that is their business. An alternative is to publish the list of contractors in alphabetical order and the tenders received in order of value.

11.7.11   Negotiated tenders

All that has gone before in this chapter assumes that competitive tendering procedures are being adopted. However, in certain circumstances, where the contractors are known to either client or architect and for whom they have performed well in the past, or it is a further stage of a contract upon which the contractor has already worked or is still working, or perhaps due to pressures on time, a decision may be taken to negotiate a tender.

The procedures to be gone through are similar to those required for competitive tendering except that before the final tender is submitted, it will have been examined by the quantity surveyors, who may have been involved in the pricing themselves, and, if necessary, the tender prices will have been negotiated. Such negotiations can lead to several advantages referred to above, and although the price can be shown to be the right price, it can never be proved to be the cheapest. If the cheapest price is the criterion for letting the contract then negotiation has no place.

11.8   Preparing the contract documents

The duty of preparing the contract by completing the various blanks in the articles of agreement usually falls on the architect, although the quantity surveyor is commonly asked to do it. It may be necessary to add special clauses to the conditions of contract and to amend other clauses; if so, they must be written in, and both parties must initial the insertion or alteration at the time of signature. Any portions to be deleted must be ruled through and similarly initialled. All other documents contained in the contract (each drawing and the bill of quantities) should be marked for identification and signed by the parties, for example:

> This is one of the drawings
> or   This is the bill of quantities
> referred to in the contract
> signed by us this   day of   2010.

In the case of the bill of quantities, this identification should be on the front cover or on the last page and the number of pages can be stated. If the standard form is used (with quantities), the specification as such is not part of the contract and will not be signed by the parties. Where there are no quantities, the full specification is a contract document and must be signed accordingly. All the signed documents must be construed together as the contract for the project.

Contracts are either signed under hand, when the limitation period is 6 years, or, when 12 years is required, are completed as a deed. In the latter case, it is important to ensure that this is duly recognised, as failure to do so could have serious implications.

Case law exists that illustrates the importance of ensuring that all the contract documents are in agreement with each other. In one case, there was a discrepancy between completion dates set out in the contract bills and the completion date in the appendix to the JCT form of contract. Delays had occurred, and the question was which date was to be taken in calculating liquidated damages. The court held[4] that under the relevant clause of the standard form in use at that time (JCT 63 clause 12(1)), the date in the appendix prevailed, but the litigation would not have occurred if all the contract documents had been checked for inconsistencies. The equivalent clause in the SBC is 1.3. This decision has been upheld in a number of other cases.[5]

References

1. Willis, C.J. & Willis, J.A. (1997) *Specification Writing for Architects and Surveyors*, Blackwell Science.
2. JCT (2002) *Series 2: Practice Note 6: Main Contract Tendering*, RIBA Enterprises Ltd.
3. *Blackpool & Fylde Aero Club* v. *Blackpool Borough Council* (1990) CILL 587.
4. *M.J Gleeson (Contractors)* v. *London Borough of Hillingdon* (1970) EGD 495.
5. *Bickerton* v. *North West Regional Hospital Board* (1970) 1WLR 607; *English Industrial Estates Corporation* v. *George Wimpey & Co* (1973) 1 Lloyd's Rep 118; *John Mowlem & Co Ltd* v. *British Insulated Callenders Pension Trust Ltd* (1977) 3 ConLR 64.

12 Stages J and K: Mobilisation and Construction to Practical Completion

12.1 Contractor's programme

The value of a programme is that it will enable the contractor to plan ahead, give early and precise notice to sub-contractors, avoid the risk of overlooking the ordering of materials or fittings in good time, and enable adequate steps to be taken to reinforce or reduce the labour force as the occasion demands. Finally, it constantly signals to contractor, agent, clerk of works, architect and client whether or not the work is proceeding at a satisfactory rate.

On large contracts it is customary for the contractor to include in the programme the dates by which full details of the various parts of the Works are required from the architect or other consultants, together with instructions regarding the expenditure of provisional sums. Many JCT contracts now make provision for the architect to provide the contractor with an information release schedule which, if used, should render the practice obsolete. As the contract proceeds, it may be necessary to expand the programme to show in more detail the co-ordinated installation and commissioning of complex engineering services.

Although the provision of an information release schedule sounds like a good idea, it appears to have been devised by someone with little practical experience of either architectural practice or contracting. The schedule is intended to show when various drawings and schedules, required by the contractor to construct the Works, will be provided to the contractor by the architect. Essentially, it is a list of dates and descriptions of drawings. A major problem is that when the contractor is tendering, it needs to know when the drawings will be released, because a major factor in tendering in the case of many buildings is how the contractor will carry out the Works. A well-experienced contractor can secure a contract simply by clever planning of the Works. The contracts which include provision for an information release schedule are the SBC, IC and ICD. They provide that the schedules must have been produced by the time the contract is executed, but by that time, of course, the contractor will have submitted its tender. At first sight, a solution might be to provide the schedule at the time of tender. However, doing that would effectively amount to the architect dictating to the contractor the way in which it should carry out the Works. It is a brave, not to say foolish, architect who believes that he or she knows the order in which the contractor requires drawings during the construction phase. In any event, there is a general principle applicable to construction contracts that, in the absence of any indication to the contrary, a contractor is entitled to plan and carry out the Works as it pleases provided that it finishes by the date for completion in the contract.[1] It is possible that the architect and contractor could sit down together and try to agree the schedule after tendering, but before the contract is executed.

The question whether, in the absence of an information release schedule, an architect is obliged to provide information to suit the contractor's programme is often asked. The programme may well show a completion date earlier than that fixed in the contract. There is legal authority that, although the contractor is entitled to finish early, the architect is not obliged to provide information to suit the shortened programme. The architect's duty is simply to provide information at such times as will enable the contractor to carry out and complete the Works by the contract date for completion.[2] The SBC, IC and ICD now enshrine that principle in clauses 2.12.2 and 2.11.2 respectively. These clauses suggest that if the contractor is late, the architect may slow down the provision of information to suit. Architects are well advised not to slow down information for this reason. At a later date, it may be difficult to prove that the contractor's delay was responsible for the slow information and not the other way around.

Clause 2.9.1.2 of the SBC contains an optional requirement for a master programme. This is not a contract document, but the clause gives the architect the right to have a copy of the contractor's programme. The clause also requires the contractor to update the programme whenever the contract period is extended. That is quite unsatisfactory in practice, because the contractor may be in culpable delay and the architect may wish to see a revised programme. Unless an extension of time is given, the architect has no right to require the updated programme. The SBC has no provision to require the contractor to provide the update upon the architect's reasonable demand. With care, a suitable amendment could be made to the contract to achieve that result.

The master programme should be drawn up by the contractor before starting work and it should be monitored on a regular basis by both architect and contractor. It should be prepared so that all the information can be clearly tabulated and it should be placed in a prominent position in the site office. It must not be too complicated, but it should at the same time give a precise indication of the progress planned by each trade each week, together with the actual progress achieved.

The most common programme is the *Gantt* or *bar chart* on which proposed and actual progress can be indicated. A line is plotted in black (or any other chosen colour) against each trade or operation commencing at the week in which the particular work is due to start and continuing through the number of weeks that it is expected to proceed. This may not, of course, be a continuous line, as it may be necessary to suspend the particular work while some other operations proceed and then return for a second spell. The actual progress should be recorded by a line or lines in a different colour.

Other forms of programmes include network analysis, precedence diagrams and Performance Evaluation and Review Technique (PERT) charts. These show the planning of the work as a set of activities related to each other. The facility then becomes available to plan alternatives and variants to the critical, or chosen, path when for some reason or other there has to be a change to the planned path.[3] The architect is able to monitor the effects of delays to the work, especially where one of the many computer software programmes is used. Such matters as estimating extensions of time are much simpler and indeed, the courts appear to advocate extensions of time calculated by this means.[4] A programme in this form (showing resources) should always be requested in addition to the more common bar chart.

As an architect is not empowered under the terms of any JCT contract to give instructions to the contractor about the programme, the requirement to provide a programme in the form noted above should be made in the bill of quantities or in the specification if there is no bill of quantities. This will not create a conflict between the bills of quantities and the printed form, because there is no attempt to over-ride or modify what is in the form but merely to require something which is not already in the contract or, if there is a provision for a master programme, the item in the bills merely seeks to amplify the requirement.

12.2 Meetings

Every architect will be involved in meetings. There really is no escaping them although most people affect to consider them a waste of time. A meeting will be a waste of time unless there is a clear purpose and unless the participants are carefully selected and relevant to the purpose. A sensible way of identifying that purpose is to frame it as a question or a series of questions which the meeting must answer. It is useful to work on the basis that if the most effective meeting consists of two people, every extra person reduces the effectiveness in inverse ratio to the numbers attending. The meetings in which architects may be involved can be roughly divided as follows.

- Staff meetings
- Client meetings
- Design team meetings
- Site meetings
- Meetings for special purposes

12.2.1 Staff meetings

This is the kind of meeting at which all members of staff attend to talk about office reorganisations, expansion, contraction, etc. Many offices make a practice of having a regular staff meeting every month or 2 months to discuss points of interest to the whole office. It is a good way to air problems. How successful such meetings are depends on the maturity of the participants. In some offices, staff meetings may be called rarely to deal with major concerns. Some staff meetings are little more than a gathering of staff to enable management to tell them about changes and contributions 'from the floor' may be discouraged. How staff meetings are used, indeed whether they are used effectively at all, depends on the management styles of the partners or directors responsible.

12.2.2   Client meetings

It has already been said that the best meetings are one to one. A client meeting may involve one person other than the architect or the client may be a board of directors or local government committee. Meetings between the architect and a board of directors should be few. It is only really necessary when the commission is being set up and possibly when the architect is demonstrating the initial design proposals. At other times, the board should nominate someone with authority to deal with the architect on the boards' behalf, otherwise progress will be slow. Generally, the architect will initiate client meetings to make decisions, receive reports, view proposals and so on. Occasionally, there may be other professionals present. These may be the client's legal and financial advisors or the other members of the design team.

12.2.3   Design team meetings

In planning this kind of meeting, the architect should be guided by, but should not slavishly follow, the RIBA Plan of Work. Depending upon the size of the project, the personalities of the participants and the stage of the work, the client may be present at these meetings. In any event, all the consultants should be present. This meeting is necessary in order to co-ordinate the effort of the team and to create the right sort of enthusiasm which is essential for the success of any major project. Normally, these meetings are called at key points in the scheme rather than, say, 'every month just to make sure that everything is proceeding smoothly'. Such regular meetings for no good purpose are usually counter-productive as participants introduce various matters simply to justify their presence or make excuses for non-attendance.

The general rule about numbers is equally valid with reference to team meetings and the architect will often find it easier to work on a one-to-one basis with consultants as well as the key point meetings mentioned above. In practice, it is common to find that the necessity for full design team meetings ends at tender stage. After that, one-to-one meetings are the norm.

12.2.4   Site meetings

Architects commonly have regular fortnightly or monthly site meetings, although one school of thought considers that there is little to commend them. The purpose of site meetings is presumably:

- to measure actual against predicted progress
- to answer queries
- to provide information.

Progress is in the hands of the contractor, whose best interests will be served by a quick and workmanlike conclusion to the contract. The architect's principal role in assisting progress is to ensure that all necessary production information is provided at the proper time. The clerk of works, if appointed, can be asked to submit a weekly progress report in any format and incorporating whatever information the architect may desire. The contractor can be asked to submit a separate weekly report. Any problems with the progress of the project can be taken up directly between the architect and the contractor, in person, by telephone or, best of all, by correspondence.

The site meeting is not the correct forum for answering queries. Most queries arise between meetings and they should be answered immediately. In any event, it is best to answer queries and provide information in writing so that there is a proper record. Site meeting minutes are notorious as vehicles for what the architect wished had been said! Site meetings are always preceded by a site inspection but an inspection can be carried out without a site meeting.

A final point against regular site meetings is the number of expensive man-hours which are swallowed up. At every meeting there are many people in attendance who have an interest in only a small part of the proceedings. Indeed, in some cases, a professional may be there just in case, rather than for a specific purpose. This is a huge waste of resources.

Obviously, there must be a meeting for all interested parties before the project commences on site. Assuming that the contract has already been executed, this is usually erroneously called the 'pre-contract' meeting rather than the more accurate 'pre-start' meeting. After the first meeting to sort out procedures and deal with the many preliminary matters which must be resolved before work can actually start, site meetings should be reserved for specific purposes. Then, the meeting becomes an important occasion, not to be taken lightly. Before arranging a site meeting (or any meeting for that matter), it is useful to ask what the meeting can achieve which cannot be achieved in some other way, more effectively and at less cost.

12.2.5 Meetings for special purposes

There will always be the kind of meeting which cannot be properly categorised except under this heading. Meetings with local government officers, members of an amenity society or ministry officials fall into this group.

12.2.6 Conduct of a meeting

It should go without saying that every meeting must have a purpose and a clear idea of what it intends to achieve. A good meeting will be the result, among other things, of careful preparation. It is usual to prepare an agenda and to circulate it to participants together with any papers which should be read before the meeting. Provided that the date of the meeting has been agreed in advance, it is best to circulate the agenda and supporting papers no more than a week before. This gives people the time to read the information, but does not really allow time for it to be put on one side. The generally accepted format for any kind of meeting is as follows.

- Record of those present, including role
- Apologies for absence
- Agreement to minutes of the last meeting
- Any matters arising from the minutes of the last meeting
- Items for discussion
- Any other business
- Date and time of next meeting

An example of an agenda for a pre-start meeting is shown in Fig. 12.1 but this is only the merest outline, of course. Architects should not assume that the pre-start meeting is an opportunity to put restrictions on the contractor. By this time, the contractor should be in contract with the employer on clear terms. The architect has no power to vary those terms and if variations of work

---

Golf Club, Willow Developments Ltd

Agenda for Pre-Start Meeting

To be held on 15 January 2010 at 11.00am in the site office.

1. Personnel
2. Production information
   a) Prepared
   b) To be prepared
3. Contractor's copy of contract documents
4. Insurances
   a) By Employer
   b) By Contractor
5. Bond
6. Sub-contractors
7. Employer's licensees
8. Architect's instructions
9. Clerk of works' directions
10. Oral instructions
11. Queries and information requests
12. Further meetings and participants
13. Contractor's programme, form and updating
14. Progress reporting
15. Role of the clerk of works
16. Samples
17. Covering up work
18. Setting out
19. Services
20. Signboard
21. Consultants and their roles
22. Procedural matters not otherwise covered
23. Any other business
24. Date, time and place of next meeting if appropriate

Fig. 12.1   Example of a pre-start meeting agenda.

or materials are instructed during the meeting, there will be a price to be paid. This is no place to inform the contractor that certain parts of the site must be fenced off or that access is only possible at one, rather than the intended two, points. The architect may give such instructions, but they will certainly involve additional costs. The meeting is to give everyone the opportunity to meet and hopefully form the beginnings of a team and to remind everyone of the important points about the project. There will also be a certain amount of business to be carried on regarding insurance policies, bonds and the like unless these have been dealt with already.

It is usual, and desirable, for architects to chair their own meetings. This is a difficult task to do properly. The chairperson must lead the discussion and be prepared to silence the talkative. Minutes should be brief, recording decisions, not the perhaps rambling discussion leading to the decision. Minutes should be circulated within 24 hours to everyone attending the meeting or anyone who has an interest in the results of the meeting. Anyone receiving the minutes of a meeting should read them immediately and carefully in order to check for mistakes, omissions and sometimes insertions which should be reported in writing to the author of the minutes without delay. Such a letter or email should also be sent to all those people noted on the circulation list. It is fatal to wait until the next meeting to attempt to rectify a mistake; memories will have faded by then.

12.3   Site inspections

'Inspection' and 'supervision' are often confused. Architects are commonly referred to as being responsible for 'design and supervision'. That, of course, is quite wrong. Inspection involves looking and noting, possibly even carrying out tests. Supervision, however, covers not only inspection but also the issuing of detailed directions regarding the execution of the Works. Supervision is more onerous than inspection.[5] It can only be carried out by someone with the requisite authority to ensure that the work is performed in a particular way. That is the prerogative of the contractor.

Inspection is not something to be carried out lightly. Many architects simply wander onto the site with no very clear idea of what they expect to find nor indeed what they should be looking for. Before commencing an inspection of the Works, the architect must have a plan of campaign as follows.

- Inspections should have a definite purpose. They should coincide with particular stages in the Works. It is sensible for the architect to sit down beforehand and draw up a list of parts of the construction which must be inspected on that particular visit together with items of secondary importance to be inspected if possible.[6] The composition of the list and the frequency of inspections will depend on factors such as the employment of a clerk of works, the size and the complexity of the project. Comments can be made against the checklist as the inspection progresses. The list and the comments are for the architect's own files, not for distribution. Although an architect's inspection duties are quite onerous, he or she will be better able to defend themselves in court against an allegation of negligent inspection if they can show, by reference to contemporary notes, that inspections were carried out in an organised manner.[7]

■ Times of inspections should be varied so that a devious contractor cannot rely upon getting poor work covered up between inspections.

■ The architect should always finish an inspection by spending a few minutes inspecting at random.

■ Action should be taken immediately the architect returns to the office, whether or not any defects have already been pointed out to the site manager. It is wise to put in writing all comments regarding defective work.

■ During site inspections, the architect is bound to be asked to answer queries. It is prudent to give answers on return to the office when it is possible to calmly sit down and assess the situation. Many decisions made on site are either amended or regretted later.

12.4 Safety

The health and safety of those employed on a construction site are governed by Act of Parliament and subsidiary regulations. The principal Acts are:

■ the Health and Safety at Work Act 1974
■ the Factories Act 1961
■ the Offices, Shops and Railway Premises Act 1963.

The Construction (Design and Management) Regulations 2007, commonly known as the CDM Regulations, came into force on 6 April 2007. They replace the Construction (Design and Management) Regulations 1994 and the Construction (Health, Safety and Welfare) Regulations 1996 and apply to all construction operations except some minor works. The emphasis is on safety right through the construction process and including design. The principal object of the Regulations is to integrate health and safety into the management of the project and to encourage everyone involved in the construction process to work together. An entirely new discipline, that of CDM co-ordinator (formerly the planning supervisor), has been spawned by the Regulations. The preparation of a construction phase plan at the beginning and a health and safety file at the end of the process are important stages. All participants, including clients, have a responsibility under the Regulations. Standard form contracts have been amended to make failure to comply with important aspects of the Regulations a breach of contract. Many architects also practise as CDM co-ordinators but in any event, all construction professionals should be well briefed on the Regulations.[8]

Some relevant regulations are listed below.

■ The Notification of Accidents and Dangerous Occurrences Regulations 1980

- The Health and Safety (Consultation with Employees) Regulations 1996
- The Health and Safety (Enforcing Authority) Regulations 1998
- The Management of Health and Safety at Work Regulations 1999
- The Control of Substances Hazardous to Health Regulations 2002

The architect should have a reasonable knowledge of safety regulations and be on the lookout for any infringement on site. The architect should take basic precautions such as reporting to the site manager immediately on arrival, wearing a hard hat and other protective clothing as appropriate and conforming with all reasonable safety rules set up by the site management. Every office should have its own safety policy which should be clearly set out to all members of staff besides, of course, conforming to statutory safety regulations.

12.5   Architect's instructions and variations

Construction contracts generally give architects wide powers to issue instructions and they must adopt a systematic method for documenting all variations to the contract. In the past many architects have used standard forms for this purpose which were called 'variation orders' (usually abbreviated to VOs). The term 'variation order' itself does not appear in the SBC and its use is to be discouraged. The RIBA standard form for use with the SBC is entitled 'architect's instruction' (Fig. 12.2).

The SBC generally requires that variations are the subject of architect's instructions, but there are certain exceptions (e.g. clause 2.14.3) which are simply treated as variations. A letter or memorandum signed by the architect is actually sufficient authority for an instruction, but a form has the advantage of keeping the information complete and orderly for every instruction throughout the project. It will appear distinct from other correspondence and forms, especially if a coloured paper is used and all copies are filed separately. The following information should be on every architect's instruction.

- Name of project
- Name of contractor
- Date of instruction
- Serial number, each project starting with the figure 1
- Subject matter of the instruction or instructions
- Architect's signature

The last requirement is very important. Each instruction must be signed by the architect. It is also useful to indicate the distribution of all copies on the instruction. On the architect's and quantity surveyor's copies may be put the approximate cost of the variation and, if desired, a summary of the balance remaining from the contingency sum. It is not advisable to put any value on the contractor's copy, as such value for an extra will tend to be treated by the contractor as a minimum. However, if the quantity surveyor has been prudent,

Issued by: Smith & Jones Architects LLP
address: Design Studios, High Street, Notown, XX1 3BB

Architect's Instruction

Employer: Willow Developments Ltd
address: High Street, Notown, XX1 4RB

Job reference: 0055

Instruction no: 25

Contractor: Gerrybuilders Ltd
address: 10-12 Builders Way, Notown, XX2 2ER

Issue date: 25 March 2010

Sheet: 1   of 1

Works: Golf Club
situated at: Park Acres, Notown, XX3 1RR

Contract dated: 13 January 2010

Under the terms of the above-mentioned Contract, I/we issue the following instructions:

	Office use: Approximate costs
	£ omit ¦ £ add
ADD: Additional handrail to main entrance all in accordance with drawings nos. 0055/29 & 30	
	ON ARCHITECT AND QS COPIES ONLY

To be signed by or for the issuer named above

Signed _I. Jones_

Amount of Contract Sum	£
± Approximate value of previous Instructions	£
Sub-total	£
± Approximate value of this Instruction	£
Approximate adjusted total	£

Distribution

[x] Contractor   [x] Structural Engineer   [x] Planning Supervisor   [ ]
[x] Employer   [ ] M&E Consultant   [ ]   [ ]
[x] Quantity Surveyor   [x] Clerk of Works [ ]   [x] File

Fig. 12.2   RIBA architect's instruction (courtesy RIBA and RIBA Publishing).

it will reflect a maximum liability in terms of cost and complications could arise when it comes to agreeing the final account.

Where an instruction involves something quite different from the original requirements, a definite estimate may, of course, be obtained from the contractor and accepted by the architect on behalf of the employer as a firm price. Indeed, under the SBC, schedule 2, the contractor can be requested to give a quotation on receipt of an instruction (see reference to the priced statement in section 12.6.3 below). In such cases, however, it is the quantity surveyor who, before acceptance, will examine the detailed build-up of the estimate and ensure that proper credit has been given for balancing any relevant omissions.

When instructing variations, it is wise to mark each clearly whether they are omissions or additions to the contract and to give each item a subsidiary number within the overall instruction. A variation can be described in one of two forms, for example:

- For softwood door to Entrance Hall substitute oak to detail; or
- *OMIT*   Softwood door to Entrance Hall
  ADD   Oak door to detail.

It is not advisable to quote item reference numbers from the bill of quantities to define a variation nor to mention prices except when a definite quotation is being accepted. The architect will not be fully aware of what bill items other than those noted might be affected. It is better to specify the variation in normal terms and leave it to the quantity surveyor to look up the dimensions and see which items need to be adjusted.

Architects cannot generally delegate their powers or duties under the contract other than the customary delegation within a practice, and not even that without the client's permission if the architect has been appointed on a personal basis. Accordingly, an instruction signed by a clerk of works cannot constitute a variation within the meaning of the SBC. As has been stated earlier, duties of a clerk of works are solely that of an inspector. While certain inspection duties may be delegated, instructions to vary the contract must be given by the architect.

Some contractors keep a 'variation order' book on the site, into which the agent enters all instructions purported to have been given and the architect may be asked to sign them when visiting the site, afterwards receiving a copy. Remember that if a contractor confirms an oral instruction to the architect in writing, perhaps on a form titled 'Confirmation of Architect's Instruction', then this constitutes a formal notification under clause 3.12.2 of the SBC and, unless refuted in writing by the architect within 7 days of receipt, it will take effect as an architect's instruction.

With the named sub-contract procedures set out in schedule 2 of IC, it is open to the architect to give instructions regarding the expenditure of a provisional sum that work is to be carried out by a named person. In such an instance, the ancillary documents ICSub/NAM/IT (invitation to tender) and ICSub/NAM/T (tender) must be used. Attempts to name in an instruction without using these forms may well be unsuccessful.

One copy of all architect's instructions and revised or supplementary drawings should be sent to the quantity surveyor if one is employed.

12.6 Variations and their valuation

12.6.1 General

Most construction contracts include provision for changes in both design and construction. These can arise as a result of a change of client's requirements, revisions to the design by the architect or other design consultants or to address issues arising from construction activity on site. These changes are better known as 'variations'. Variations by their very nature can be both disruptive and expensive and architects need to think very carefully before authorising them. They must in particular adhere strictly to the terms of the contract and ensure that they do not act outside their powers.

The variation procedures under the JCT forms of contract are covered in the main by clause 5 of the SBC and IC. The JCT contracts draw a clear distinction between valuing variations (usually tied to rates in the contract bills or in the schedule of rates) and ascertaining loss and expense which may arise over and above the value of the actual variation. However, the SBC has provided, in schedule 2, for the architect to issue instructions requesting a quotation. The intention of this is to establish an all-encompassing price for a variation including direct loss and expense (see 12.6.3 below).

The procedures under the government form GC/Works/1(1998) are similar, in that facility is provided for the pre-costing of variations whereby expense for prolongation and disturbance are required to be included in the costing of variations; only such expense which arises from events other than variations is treated separately. This is also the case with the NEC Engineering and Construction Contract which provides for the submission and agreement of quotations for compensation events as the contract proceeds.

The line between the two is not always easy to draw in practice and, even if it were, there is the problem of reconciling costs which differ considerably from the rates in the contract. Clearly, the latter apply to variations but the question arises as to whether the client should have to pay costs which may greatly exceed rates simply because they rank as a loss and expense rather than an item to be valued. This dilemma can be partly resolved by listing the reasons that can give rise to such differences.

- Underestimate in the rate
- Remedial work
- Inefficiency and default
- Inflation
- Non-reimbursable costs (e.g. those caused by sub-contractors)
- Disruption caused by act, omission or default of the employer or his agent

12.6.2   Definition of a variation

A variation is defined as the alteration or modification of the design, quantity or quality of the Works as shown upon the contract drawings and described by or referred to in the contract bills (or specification if there are no quantities). The addition, alteration or omission of certain of the obligations or restrictions imposed by the employer also fall within the definition of a variation. In the case of the standard forms this includes:

■ the addition, omission or substitution of any work
■ alteration of the kind or standard of any of the materials or goods to be used in the Works
■ removal from the site of work or materials
■ changes to access to the site or part thereof
■ limitations in working space or hours
■ changes to the order of the Works.

12.6.3   Valuing variations

Items to be dealt with by valuing under SBC and IC clause 5 are:

■ variations
■ provisional sums both defined and undefined
■ the effect of variations on the remainder of the work.

Items to be excluded from valuation under these clauses are:

■ variations, the price of which is agreed between the employer and the contractor
■ disruption to regular progress and any items to which clause 4.23 (SBC) and IC clause 4.17, the loss and expense clauses, apply (except where a quotation has been accepted under the SBC – see below).

Factors relating to work which can properly be valued by measurement and which is varied by addition or substitution can be summarised as follows.

	Character	Conditions	Quantity	Basis of valuation
(1)	Similar	Similar	No significant change	The rates and prices in the contract bills
(2)	Similar	Similar	Significant change	As last but make due allowance for the change
(3)	Similar	Not similar	No significant change	Ditto
(4)	Not similar	—	—	Fair rates and prices

Other matters that need to be considered in the valuing of variations include the following.

- Work that cannot properly be valued by measurement is valued by reference to daywork. Daywork sheets must be delivered for verification within detailed timetables (SBC clause 5.7; GC/Works/1 (1998) Condition 42 (12)).
- Omitted work is valued at rates in the contract bills.
- Work that is not varied *per se* but is affected by a variation (including an omission) is valued as if it were the subject of a variation.
- Where work is valued by reference to bill rates, allowance must be made for:
  (a) measuring to the same rules (SMM) as applied to the contract bills
  (b) any percentage or lump sum in the contract bills
  (c) adjustment of preliminaries.

As bill rates form the key to the valuation of variations, it is important that any errors and/or inconsistencies are removed before the contract is signed. The CIB Code of Practice for the Selection of Main Contractors sets down appropriate procedures (see Chapter 11, section 11.7.3).

The above procedure for pricing variations could be described as the traditional route and applies to the valuation of variations under the government form when it applies to other variations or variation instructions where a lump sum quotation has not been called for. Under condition 42 the project manager, as has been stated above, has the right if so wished to call for a lump sum quotation. These quotations must include the cost of the work and the cost of prolongation and disturbance (if any), each to be separately identified. A strict timetable is laid down for submission of the quotation and, if called for, supporting documentation and for the subsequent acceptance or non-acceptance of the quotation. In the event of non-acceptance then the traditional route is reverted to.

As noted above, a similar procedure is set out in the SBC in schedule 2, which allows the architect to issue an instruction and, at the same time, to request a quotation. The contractor's 'Price Statement', a complex procedure which under JCT 98 and IFC 98 allowed the contractor to elect to submit a quotation (including loss and/or expense and extension of time) whether requested to or not, has been omitted from SBC and IC 2005 versions, thus considerably simplifying what was becoming a difficult procedure to manage.

The question often arises as to how work should be priced where there is an obvious inconsistency or downright mistake in the original pricing. Practice suggests that the fair solution is to hold the contractor to the wrong rate for the original quantity but to apply a corrected rate for any additional quantity. There is, however, case law[9] which lays down that a contractor can be held to the original rate irrespective of quantity. Although this was something of a special judgment, recent case law tends to support it.[10]

Although the contract does not require the parties to 'agree' the final account, it is obviously sensible to do so if possible. It is often the case that the quantity surveyor, on behalf of the architect, agrees a final account with the contractor and thereafter has to resist attempts by the client and/or the auditors, be they local or central government finance officers or (in the case of private clients) their professional accountants, to amend or challenge this. These attempts have to be resisted as these matters are decisions of the architect whose powers are expressly laid down in the contract. The remedy for an aggrieved client lies elsewhere in arbitration or through the courts.

12.7   Controlling costs

12.7.1   General

Possibly the most common criticism made by clients of their architects (and quite often quantity surveyors as well) is that they never keep them informed of how their money is being spent. They have in most cases signed what has been described to them as a 'lump sum firm price' contract and they have the greatest of difficulty in understanding why they are now being asked to pay a lot more money.

For this reason architects have a particular duty to watch the expenditure of their clients' money. When clients want changes made, not only must they be advised whether or not such changes are feasible but also what the cost is likely to be in terms of both time and money. Equally, they must be kept so informed when unavoidable changes have to be made for matters such as changed ground conditions or unexpected problems arising when an existing building is opened up. Finally, of course, architects must resist the temptation to change their designs to suit their own revised thoughts. If such architects' changes are envisaged then the client must be consulted and again advised of any financial effect on the total budget. If the financial effects are of any magnitude, the chances of the client agreeing to the changes being made are slim.

A running record of cost can be kept by having a valuation of each variation recorded and totals of omissions and additions to the contract sum made from time to time. Provisional sums must also be adjusted as and when instructions are issued for their expenditure. Such a record depends very much for its accuracy on the prompt issue of written instructions. Obviously if they are neglected, figures will be of little value. Price adjustment increases and payments made for loss and expense must also be taken into account.

12.7.2   Financial report

Ideally, a statement of the financial position should accompany each interim certificate so that clients when paying the contractors have in front of them a financial picture of the project. The statement needs to be tailored to meet specific client requirements. Certain clients will only require a summary statement of the current financial position (see example in Fig. 12.3), others will require a detailed report identifying the cost implication of each instruction, whether issued or anticipated. It is very important that the figures contained in such statements should be, if not completely accurate, then on the high side.

WILLOW DEVELOPMENT LTD		
GOLF CLUB		

COST REPORT NO. 6		
Date 21 July 2010		

SUMMARY	£	£
Contract Sum		2,168,328
Less Contingencies		65,000
		2,103,328
Adjustments for:		
Instructions Issued – Section 1	26,130	
Provisional Sum Expenditure – Section 2	5,263	
Anticipated Variations – Section 3	11,800	
Ascertained Claims	—	
	43,193	43,193
Anticipated Final Account		2,146,521
Current Approved Sum		2,168,328
Balance of Contingencies		21,807

Notes: Costs exclude VAT, Professional fees and direct client costs

Fig. 12.3   Financial statement.

There is nothing worse for clients than to be lulled into a sense of false security only to receive a bombshell at the end of the contract.

12.8   Workmanship and materials

Workmanship and materials are the very essence of a building and they should be specified by the architect in accordance with the design. Materials are inextricably bound up with the appearance and use of the building and specification of the wrong materials can ruin the concept and possibly leave the architect open to an action from the client for failing to take proper care. Examples would be if the architect specified an unsuitable roof covering which subsequently let in water or a floor finish which was inappropriate to the expected traffic and became badly marked or worn.

The specification of workmanship is less obvious and less clearly defined, yet poor specification in this area can be just as detrimental to the building as a whole. If poor workmanship is applied to the task of erecting the finest materials, the result will be worse than if less expensive materials had been erected with first-class workmanship. Good workmanship is difficult to define but easy to recognise. The specification of workmanship is more difficult than the specification of materials and reference is often made to the detailed guidance in published codes of practice. Certain aspects of good workmanship can be described, such as the way in which bricks are to be laid, but generally good workmanship is described by the result expected. Hence the practice of having samples constructed of various elements of work. A brick sample panel is constructed in order to have a point of reference for workmanship rather than for materials although, of course, it can serve for both. Thus, materials are the basic building elements, workmanship is the process which puts the elements together.

It is one of the architect's functions, and of the clerk of works if appointed, to check that the correct materials have been used by the building contractor and that the workmanship of the building is in accordance with the specification. Depending upon the size of the project, a clerk of works may spend a great deal of time checking materials and, for example, taking samples of concrete for testing in the laboratory. Under most standard forms of contract, the architect has wide powers to reject materials or work not in accordance with the contract. Under the SBC, clause 2.3.1, for example, the contractor must provide materials in accordance with the contract so far as they are procurable. That is a valuable protection for the contractor whose obligation seems to come to an end if the materials are truly not procurable. Of course, not procurable at a price or at a date the contractor considers reasonable does not fall within the meaning of this provision. Workmanship is to be to the standards described in the bills of quantity or specification if there are no bills. If no standards are described, the workmanship is to be to a standard 'appropriate to the Works'. That is fairly broad, but probably as good a standard as any in the absence of precise specification.

It is always open, and provided for in the contract, for the architect to specify materials or workmanship to be to his or her satisfaction, in which case the contract stipulates that they are to be to the architect's reasonable satisfaction. This is obviously intended to prevent the architect from insisting upon an inappropriately high standard. Whether the standard is inappropriate or not is something which, in the last resort, must be settled by adjudication or arbitration if the parties cannot agree. Architects must be sure that they inspect such work carefully, because the issue of the final certificate will be conclusive evidence of satisfaction in such instances (see Chapter 13, section 13.5). Clause 3.20 requires the architect to express dissatisfaction within a reasonable time of the execution of work which is to be to the architect's satisfaction. No doubt, some architects may be tempted to advise their clients to delete this particular clause as being a potential cause of trouble.

The SBC has elaborate provisions, in clause 3.18, to allow the architect to order the removal from site of work or materials which are not in accordance with the contract. The architect may also or alternatively allow the work to remain and make an appropriate deduction from the contract sum; or issue reasonably necessary instructions requiring a variation at no additional cost, no extension of time and no loss and/or expense; or require the contractor to open up or test the work to establish whether there is the likelihood of similar failure at no additional cost, but with an extension of time if the work examined is found to be in accordance with the contract. There are certain conditions which have to be satisfied before an instruction can be issued in connection with opening up and the architect should become familiar with them. The Intermediate Building Contract, IC and ICD have provisions which are less far-reaching but to similar overall effect.

The SBC, IC and ICD, in clauses 3.17 and 3.14 respectively, give the architect power to order opening up and/or testing of work or materials. If the work or material is found to be in accordance with the contract, the contractor is entitled to an extension of time, if appropriate, and whatever direct loss and/ or expense can be shown to have been suffered.

12.9   Certificates and payments

12.9.1   Responsibility for certificates

It usually falls to the architect under a construction contract to certify from time to time the amount of instalments on account to be paid to the contractor and to certify the total of the final account. It is generally provided that certificates shall include the value of work properly executed and unfixed materials, both on and off site, less a specified percentage to be retained, which is known as the retention sum or reserve.

Whilst the quantity surveyor (where appointed) will usually carry out valuations and recommend to the architect the amount to be certified, the architect is nevertheless responsible for the issue of the certificate,[11] the surveyor's recommendation being adjusted as necessary in respect of unsatisfactory work, delays in payment to sub-contractors, etc. A standard valuation form, for use with the SBC, is published by the RICS (Fig. 12.4) for completion by the quantity surveyor. Public authorities often have their own form for this purpose. If the architect is at all unsure about the valuation, it is a matter for the architect to request more information from the quantity surveyor.

12.9.2 Method of valuation

How valuations are carried out will depend on the size and complexity of the project. Provision can be made in the contract for the contractor to provide a detailed statement with each application which can then be checked.

On smaller contracts architects should quite easily be able to make their own assessment. Where there are no bills of quantities the contract schedule of works (if priced) can be used, or the contractor may ask for the original estimate to be used as a guide to the sub-division of the contract sum.

On contracts for larger buildings it is commonplace for a quantity surveyor to be appointed, who will go through the contractor's application (if presented) together with the bill of quantities or alternative pricing schedule and, taking each work section in turn, identify the work which has been done and its value. A total will thus be built up. Again, a suitable proportion of the preliminary items would be included together with any percentage addition made *pro rata* to any sums for insurances, etc. shown in the summary.

In the case of repetitive housing, it may be possible to fix values per house at each of half a dozen stages, say:

- damp-proof course level
- first floor joists fixed
- roof plate level
- roof completed
- plastering completed
- second fixing and decoration completed.

To this would have to be added the proportion of drainage and external works completed plus an allowance for the preliminary costs. As a valuation, this would only be approximate but would be sufficient for the purpose.

Another variant is payment in accordance with a predetermined stage payment chart or table, either provided as a tender document or submitted by the contractor at the time of tender. Payments will then be made at regular intervals based on the stated percentage. Allowances can be made to amend these percentages either up or down according to whether the contractor is ahead of or behind the programme.

Where the contract is based on a priced activity schedule, the assessment of the amount due in each interim certificate is the value of each completed activity adjusted to reflect the impact of any relevant variations. The valuation process tends to be easier than with contracts based on bills of quantities as

Valuation for JCT Standard Building Contract (2005 Edition)

RICS

Surveyor	Brown & Partners
	High Street, Notown, XX1 2CD

Works	Golf Club
	Park Acres, Notown, XX3 1RR

Valuation No:	3
Date of Issue:	9 April 2010
Reference:	123

To Employer's Agent/Contract Administrator

Smith & Jones Architects LLP
Design Studios, High Street,
Notown, XX1 3BB

Employer

Willow Developments Ltd
High Street, Notown, XX1 4RB

Contractor

Gerrybuilders Ltd
10–12 Builders Way, Notown, XX2 2ER

Contract sum £ 2,168,328

As at 9 April 2010 I/We have made, in accordance with the terms of the Contract, an Interim Valuation, the basis on which the amount shown as due has been calculated is clause 4.10 of the Conditions of Contract, and report as follows:

Gross Valuation
(excluding any work or material notified to me/us by the Employer's Agent/Contract Administrator in writing as not being in accordance with the Contract).

£ 845,390

Less total amount of Retention, as attached statement.

£ 25,362

£ 820,028

Less total amount of interim payments previously certified by the Employer's Agent/Contract Administrator up to and including Certificate No. 2 and any advance payment due for reimbursement by the date given below for the issue of the next Certificate.

£ 510,010

£ 310,018

Balance (in words)

THREE HUNDRED AND TEN THOUSAND
AND EIGHTEEN POUNDS

Signature Surveyor XXXXXXXXXXXXX / FRICS

Notes:
(1) All the above amounts are exclusive of VAT.
(2) The balance stated is subject to any statutory deductions which the Employer may be obliged to make under the provisions of the Construction Industry Scheme where the Employer is classed as a 'Contractor' for the purposes of the relevant Act.
(3) It is assumed that the Employer's Agent/Contract Administrator will satisfy him or herself that there is no further work or material which is not in accordance with the Contract.
(4) The Employer's Agent/Contract Administrator's Certificate should be issued on (see clause 4.9.2).

* Delete as appropriate

© RICS 2006

Fig. 12.4 Standard valuation form (courtesy Royal Institution of Chartered Surveyors).

there are usually substantially fewer items to consider and they are programme related.

Architects should beware that if they carry out work normally undertaken by quantity surveyors, they could find themselves without appropriate insurance cover (see Chapter 17, section 17.5).

12.9.3 Unfixed materials

Most forms of contract provide for interim payments to include the value of unfixed materials properly brought onto the site. The contractor should be asked to prepare a priced list of these at the date of the valuation, which can be checked by the clerk of works (if any) or by the architect. If verification of cost of any of the items is required, this can be asked for and at the same time assurances sought regarding retention of title to ensure that they are the property of the contractor and can safely be passed to the employer.

When these materials are paid for they become the property of the employer. Being the property of the employer, they must not, of course, be removed without permission, and in the event of the contractor's bankruptcy, they would not be an asset vesting in the trustee, but could be removed or, as is more likely, used by the employer.

A matter that needs careful consideration is the inclusion in a valuation of the costs of unfixed materials that are not on the site and so outside the physical control of the employer and agents (SBC clause 4.17). If the employer is prepared to agree to payment for materials off site, a list must be prepared at tender stage and, in due course, fixed to the contract documents. If materials or goods are not included in the list, they will not be included in certificates. Often a surety bond is required.

If payment is to be made for materials off site, the contract requires that:

- the items are in accordance with the contract
- reasonable proof of ownership and adequate insurance shall be provided
- the materials are set apart and clearly marked as to ownership and ultimate destination
- surety bonds have been provided.

12.9.4 Nominated sub-contractors

Under the earlier Standard Form of Contract (JCT 98), when issuing certificates architects were obliged to notify the contractor of the amounts included for nominated sub-contractors. It should be noted that the 2005 edition of the SBC does not make any provision for nomination.

12.9.5 Price adjustment

Where provision is made for price adjustment on account of fluctuations in cost of labour and materials, this must be taken into account in the valuation under the relevant contract clause.

Before any increased cost is included under the price adjustment clauses, the contractor should submit a statement showing the price adjustment formula computations for checking. If the adjustment is to be by way of wages and materials increases, the necessary information (backed up by time sheets, invoices, vouchers, etc.) must be produced. Increased costs (or in rare cases decreased costs) cannot be taken into account in interim certificates until they have been incurred and no profit is added (or deducted).

12.9.6   Nominated suppliers

Nominated suppliers fall into the same category as ordinary merchants supplying materials to the industry; the only difference is that they are nominated by the architect. Nominated suppliers are not included in the SBC but they are still available under GC/Works/1 (1998) although the relevant clause (63) is not as detailed as the clause 36 provisions which were formerly used in JCT 98.

12.9.7   Retention sum

In preparing certificates, architects have to take into account the sum to be retained under the contract. If the quantity surveyors have submitted a statement, the amount retained will be shown. The retention sums outstanding on various contracts constitute a substantial part of a contractor's capital. Whilst they are part of the financing which is expected of contractors, they should not be expected to do more than the contract requires of them. Architects should therefore see that, so far as they are concerned, there is no delay in releasing balances at 'practical completion' and at the end of the rectification period. To this end, they should be prompt in making their final inspection and in giving notice to the contractor of defects to be remedied.

The retention provisions of the SBC are set out in clauses 4.18, 4.19 and 4.20 and the contract particulars make provision for stating the percentage of the value of the work done and materials supplied that is to be retained. The default figure is 3%. In calculating the amount of retention to be held at any one time, the total value of the contractor's work and the value of materials on site (and sometimes off site: see section 12.9.3 above) must be taken into account when applying the percentage.

Clause 4.16.1 of the SBC indicates which work is subject to retention and which is not. The first category includes the value of work done, the materials on and off site and fluctuations computed under the price adjustment formula; the second category includes loss and expense claims and fluctuations adjusted on the rise and fall of labour rates and material prices. The requirements of the government form in this respect are slightly different.

The employer's interest in the retention sum is fiduciary as trustee for the contractor; the employer, unless it is a local authority, is required, if asked, to set the money aside in a separate account in the joint names of the employer and the contractor. This means that in the event of default or bankruptcy of the employer, the money is available to pay off the contractor and it is not lost in the general funds which may or may not remain. When the employer is a local authority, the same circumstances apply but there is no requirement for a separate bank account although it seems that a contractor could insist.[12] A trustee always has the obligation to keep trust funds separate.[13]

The purpose of clause 4.19 is to give the option of a surety bond from the contractor instead of retention.

A Statement of Retention Values form for use with the SBC is published by the RICS (Fig. 12.5) and provision is made in the RIBA certificate form for the retention details to be included (Fig. 12.6).

12.9.8   Final check

When the certificate has been completed, a careful check should be made to ensure that the figure shown as already certified is correct as a slip here can cause a serious error in the certification.

12.9.9   Release of part of retention

It is usually provided that half, or some other part, of the retention shall be released when the work is complete, the balance being retained until the end of the rectification period. Clause 4.20.2.1 of the SBC provides for this release on 'practical completion' of the Works, the architect being required to issue a certificate of practical completion under clause 2.30. It is not, therefore, necessary for the contractor to have completed the contract (see Chapter 13, section 13.2).

On a strict reading of clause 4.20.2.2, it is at least arguable that full retention in respect of materials and goods on and off site ('Listed Items') is to be retained until the issue of the final certificate. There was always a suspicion of that in the retention clause of JCT 98; the new form SBC appears to emphasise the position. In practice, most architects release half the retention on everything, including goods and materials, on issue of the certificate following practical completion and the balance on the issue of the certificate of making good.

12.9.10   Release of final balance

Under clauses 2.35, 2.39 and 4.20.2.3 of the SBC, the whole of the balance of the retention sum is to be released forthwith on the issue of the certificate of making good. Provision is made for adjustment later of any balance (either way) when the total of the final account is known. Release of the final balance may be delayed because the accounts are not complete. If the valuation of variations is progressively determined as the contract clearly envisages, the final figure should be available by the end of the rectification period and no further adjustment should be required.

Statement of Retention Values for use with the JCT 2005

Surveyor		Works		
Brown & Partners		Golf Club		
High Street, Notown, XX1 2CD		Park Acres, Notown, XX3 1RR		

This Statement relates to:
Valuation No: 3
Date of Issue: 9 April 2010
Reference: 123

	Gross Valuation	Basis of Gross Valuation	Amount Subject to:				Amount of Retention	Net Valuation	Amount Previously Certified	Balance
			Full Retention of 3 %	Half Retention of %	No Retention				
	£	Clause No.	£	£	£	£	£	£	£
Description of Works:	845,390		845,390	-	-	25,362	820,028	510,010	310,018
TOTAL	845,390		845,390	-	-	25,362	820,028	510,010	310,018

Notes:
(1) The sums stated are exclusive of VAT.
(2) See clause 4.20 for rules for ascertainment of Retention.

© RICS 2006

Fig. 12.5   Statement of retention values form (courtesy Royal Institution of Chartered Surveyors).

**Interim
Certificate**

Issued by: Smith & Jones Architects LLP
address: Design Studios, High Street, Notown, XX1 3BB

SBC

Employer: Willow Developments Ltd
address: High Street, Notown, XX1 4RB

Contractor: Gerrybuilders Ltd
address: 10-12 Builders Way, Notown, WW3 2ER

Works: Golf Club
situated at: Park Acres, Notown, XX3 1RR

Job reference: 0055

Certificate no: 3

Date of valuation: 9 April 2010

Date of issue: 14 April 2010

Final date for payment: 28 April 2010

Contract dated: 13 January 2010

This Interim Certificate is issued under the terms of the above-mentioned Contract.

Gross Valuation	£ 845,390
Less Retention as detailed on the attached Statement of Retention	£ 25,362
Sub-total	£ 820,028
Less reimbursement of advance payment	£ _____
Sub-total	£ 820,028
Less total amount previously certified	£ 510,010
Net amount for payment	**£ 310,018**

*All amounts are exclusive of VAT.
The Employer shall in addition
pay the amount of VAT properly
chargeable.*

I/We hereby certify that the **amount due** to the Contractor from the Employer is (in words)

Three Hundred and Ten Thousand and Eighteen Pounds Only

To be signed by or for
the issuer named
above

Signed _____

This is not a Tax Invoice.

Distribution	☒ Employer	☒ Contractor	☒ Quantity Surveyor	☒ File copy

F501A for SBC   RIBA CONTRACT ADMINISTRATION FORMS   © RIBA Publishing 2006

Fig. 12.6 Interim certificate (courtesy RIBA and RIBA Publishing).

12.9.11 Form of certificate

Certificates are usually issued in a standard form such as that published and sold in pads by the RIBA (Fig. 12.6). Each certificate form in such pads is in quadruplicate, the distribution being employer, contractor, quantity surveyor and file. Certificates need not be in any prescribed form, but they should use the words 'I (or we) certify', stating the name of the contract, names of contractor and employer, the amount certified as due and the date, and they must bear the signature of the architect. It is an obvious advantage if they are given a serial number. Provision is available for the amounts of advance payment reimbursement to be identified.[14]

Under the JCT contracts (of all kinds) as indicated above, the certificate is issued to the employer with a copy to the contractor. It is now no longer necessary for the contractor to present the certificate to the employer in order to receive payment.

12.9.12 Need for promptness

Finance is an important factor in the running of any business and contractors are no exception; like all businesses, they naturally want to reduce to the minimum the amount of capital they have tied up. The intervals at which interim certificates will be issued are usually dictated by the contract, and architects should see that certificates are issued at the specified intervals. If there is a delay in carrying out valuations and processing certificates, particulars given by the contractor quickly become obsolete and the time-lag between valuation and payment increases.

While it may seem that a delay of a week or two in payments of what may be relatively small sums of money may not be very important, the aggregate of such outstanding amounts can be substantial. Where the contractor has no significant margin, delays in payment may cause financial difficulties from which the employer may ultimately suffer. Quite apart from anything else, the architect would be in breach of contract for which the employer may be liable.[15]

12.10 Delays and extensions of time

Construction contracts usually take the form of an agreement that the Works will be constructed for a certain sum of money, or at least specify the way in which that sum will be computed. In addition, all contracts include an agreement as to the length of time that the Works will take to complete. Accordingly, either start and completion dates are stated or a set period is given. In either case, an end or *contract completion date* is established.

In many cases, for various reasons, a job over-runs and finishes on a date later than that originally set. This later date is the *actual contract completion date.* The fact that the contractor has to spend longer on site than they contracted does not necessarily mean that the original contract completion date will be extended nor that they will be entitled to reimbursement in respect of direct loss and/or expense.

To compensate the employer for late completion by the contractor, where the contract completion date is not formally extended, provision is normally included in the contract (for example, SBC, clause 2.32) for the employer to deduct liquidated damages at the rate stated in the contract particulars (normally at a rate per week). It is important that the rate included is a genuine pre-estimate of loss to the employer in the event of delayed completion, thus providing the contractor with a known amount prior to commencement of the contract. If this is not the case, actual damages would need to be calculated which could well be a protracted process.

The architect has a responsibility to certify the contractor's failure to complete the Works by the completion date and should calculate the level of damages that may be deducted and advise the employer accordingly. However, any decision to deduct liqidated damages rests with the employer.

In the event that the employer elects to deduct damages, they are deducted by the employer from the amount certified for payment by the architect. In certain circumstances, there may be an over-riding commercial reason for the employer not to wish to make such deductions.

Most contracts provide for architects to have the power to extend the original contract completion date if they are satisfied that the reasons for the overrun were those set out in the contract.

Certain contracts, the JCT standard forms in particular, set out very clearly the duties of contractors and architects in this respect. The contractor has to give notice as soon as it becomes apparent that delay has arisen or is likely to arise, to state the reasons and give an estimate of the length of delay. Architects in their turn have, within prescribed periods, to decide first whether or not in their opinion delay actually is going to occur and second what the true reasons are for the delay. To assist in the second of these requirements, what are known as *relevant events* are set out in the contract. In the case of the SBC the relevant events contained within clause 2.29 are as follows:

- variations
- architect's instructions
- deferment of possession
- approximate quantities, not an accurate forecast
- suspension of contractor's obligations
- impediment, prevention or default of the employer
- delay by statutory undertaker
- exceptionally adverse weather conditions
- loss or damage occasioned by a specified peril or perils
- civil commotion, use or threat of terrorism
- strike or lock out

- act or statutory power by government
- *force majeure.*

It will be seen that these 'relevant events' fall into two categories: those which are neutral, i.e. the fault of neither the employer nor the contractor; and those for which the employer or his or her agent is responsible. They have been rearranged in the SBC and IC to reflect this.

Once architects are satisfied that the delay due to one or more of these relevant events affects the completion date, then they are empowered to fix a new contract completion date and the threat to the contractor of the implementation of damages is lifted for that period. While an architect has to state the events taken into account, there is no requirement to give separate time allocation for each event. In the event of the full over-run not being awarded as an extension of time then the contractor is in what is known as a *period of culpable delay* and remains liable for the specified damages.

Other JCT contracts have similar clauses. The provisions of IC clause 2.20 are identical to the SBC. MW does not list events, other than architect's instructions, and relies upon a broad 'reasons beyond the control of the Contractor' phrase. Under CG/Works/1 the project manager has the power to grant extensions of time for any matter which is considered applicable in clause 36(2), with the notable exception of weather conditions, which are specifically excluded.

When questions of extensions of time arise architects must study carefully the particular contract clause and act accordingly. Certain basic facts have to be borne in mind.

- Unless the contract includes an acceleration clause the original contract completion date cannot be improved upon, i.e. there is no facility to shorten a contract period.
- A contractor has a duty to make every endeavour to prevent delay arising short of expenditure of significant sums of money. The obligation is to continue to work regularly and diligently. However, once delay has arisen there is no requirement that time lost must be recovered.
- Extensions of time provisions are to preserve a completion date and provide relief from the damages provisions. They can also be, as pointed out below, of benefit to the employer.
- No question of additional costs being paid arises at all.[16] These are matters dealt with elsewhere in the contract (see section 12.11 below).

Extension of time provisions are inserted in construction contracts for the benefit of the employer as much for that of the contractor. As far as employers are concerned, they protect their right to receive liquidated damages. If such provisions were not included and contractors were caused delay by the employers or any of their agents then the right to recover damages would be forfeited and the contract would become (as the lawyers say) *at large*, i.e. the only obligation on the part of the contractor would be to complete within a reasonable time.

12.11   Financial claims

The word 'claim' as such is not used in the JCT forms of contract at all. What has come to be known under the generic head of claims is in fact an entitlement to reimbursement of direct loss and/or expense, to use the exact terminology of the contracts. Before considering claims at all, it is necessary to define the differences between the two types of claim that the law recognises: common law claims and contractual claims.

Common law claims are claims for breach of contract when the claimant must prove a breach of contract and is then entitled to recover damages calculated on common law principles. These claims have to be pursued by way of litigation or arbitration and the architect has no authority to deal with them unless expressly authorised to do so by the employer. Any resulting payment must be made outside the terms of the contract.

Contractual claims arise because some provision in the contract entitles the contractor to payment for 'loss' or 'expense', made and settled under machinery provided by the contract itself. In some cases events which give rise to such a claim will also be breaches of contract and as such will give rise to a common law claim. In other cases they will not: for example, the issue of a variation order may give rise to a loss and expense claim even though it is authorised by the contract itself. In both cases the burden of proof lies with the claimant.

Before considering claims at all it is also necessary to define what the phrase 'direct loss and/or expense' means. Perhaps it is easier to say what it does not mean. It is not the difference between what the contractor thought the costs would be and what they actually were. This fallacy is a common belief among some contractors; it overlooks the possibility that the initial estimate might have been optimistic. It is what it says it is: direct loss and expense. The word 'direct' in this context means 'close to' or 'appertaining to the event causing the disruption'. 'Expense' means 'actual disbursements'. 'Ascertainment' means 'find out': not, as many claimants appear to think, 'work out'. In several cases, when considering JCT contracts, the courts have held that loss and/or expense is subject to the same principles as are applied to common law damages.

Claims, to use the generic term, in the construction industry fall into two categories: extensions of time, and loss and/or expense for disruption to the regular progress of the Works. Claims for extensions of time are covered in section 12.10 above. Claims for loss and expense can be sub-divided into prolongation and disruption elements, and while the JCT forms of contract do not recognise any distinction (each being treated as part of the whole), it is necessary to consider the difference when it comes to the computation of a claim.

A *prolongation claim* arises from delay in completion of the contract works beyond the date when they would otherwise have been completed. Such a claim is sometimes erroneously called an extension of time claim.

A *disruption claim* is one that arises from the effect of an event upon the contract works which does not in itself necessarily involve a delay in the completion of the Works. A popular misconception is that there cannot be disruption without prolongation. This supposition is quite false and it is no defence for an architect to say that no extension of time has been granted and therefore there can be no claim for loss and/or expense; there certainly can be.

The subject of financial claims and their ascertainment warrants textbooks on its own and indeed, various books deal with the topic.[17] Suffice it to say that architects will from time to time have to make judgements by way of ascertainment and occasionally have to be judge and jury on their own misdemeanours.

In making these decisions architects must bear in mind two main principles.

- Can any wording of the contract, though not specifically mentioning it, be reasonably applied to the point?
- The value of the claim should not affect a decision on the principle. If the claim is very small, however, whichever party is concerned might be persuaded to waive it, or it may be eliminated by a bit of 'give and take'.

Some claims may be due simply to misfortune which neither party could have foreseen, and it may be reasonable for the employer to meet the claim *ex gratia* to a greater or lesser extent.

References and notes

1. *Greater London Council* v. *Cleveland Bridge & Engineering Co Ltd* (1984) 8 Con LR 30.
2. *Glenlion Construction* v. *The Guinness Trust* (1987) 39 BLR 89.
3. Keane, P.J. & Caletka, A.F. (2008) *Delay Analysis in Construction Contracts*, Wiley-Blackwell.
4. *John Barker Construction Ltd* v. *London Portman Hotels Ltd* (1996) 12 Const LJ 277; *Balfour Beatty Construction Ltd* v. *London Borough of Lambeth* [2002] BLR 288.
5. *Consarc Design Ltd* v. *Hutch Investments Ltd* (2002) 84 Con LR 36.
6. Jamieson, N. (2009) *Good Practice Guide: Inspecting Works*, RIBA Publishing.
7. *East Ham Corporation* v. *Bernard Sunley & Sons Ltd* [1965] 3 All ER 619; *Sutcliffe* v. *Chippendale and Edmondson* (1971) 18 BLR 149; *Brown & Brown* v. *Gilbert Scott & Payne* (1993) 3 Con LR 120; *Alexander Corfield* v. *David Grant* (1992) 59 BLR 102; *Bowmer & Kirkland* v. *Wilson Bowden* (1996) 80 BLR 131. The most recent and comprehensive advice on the topic of inspections was given in *McGlinn* v. *Waltham Contractors Ltd and Others (No. 3)* (2007) 111 Con LR 1.
8. Summerhayes, S. (2008) *CDM Regulations 2007 Procedures Manual*, 3rd edn, Blackwell Publishing; Health & Safety Executive (2007) *Managing Health and Safety in Construction: Construction (Design and Management) Regulations 2007: Approved Code of Practice*, Stationery Office.
9. *Dudley Corporation* v. *Parsons & Morrin* (1967) unreported.
10. *Henry Boot* v. *Alstom Combined Cycles* (1999) 90 BLR 123.

11. *R M Burden Ltd* v. *Swansea Corporation* (1957) 3 All ER 243; *Sutcliffe* v. *Thackrah* (1974) 1 All ER 889.

12. *Rayack Construction Ltd* v. *Lampeter Meat Co Ltd* (1979) 12 BLR 30.

13. *Wates Construction* v. *Franthom Property Ltd* (1991) 53 BLR 23.

14. Three helpful guides to completion of all kinds of contract administration forms and other useful hints are published by RIBA Publishing in respect of SBC, IC and MW. They are entitled *Contract Administration Guide: completing the contract and administrative forms.*

15. *Croudace Construction Ltd* v. *London Borough of Lambeth* (1984) 1 Con LR 12; *Penwith District Council* v. *V P Developments Ltd* (1999) unreported.

16. *H Fairweather Ltd* v. *London Borough of Wandsworth* (1987) 39 BLR 106.

17. Chappell, D., Powell-Smith, V. & Sims, J. (2004) *Building Contract Claims*, 4th edn, Blackwell Publishing; deals with the legal principles and their application across different forms of contract.

13 Stage L: Post Practical Completion

13.1 Termination

Most forms of building contract provide that either party can bring the contractor's employment to an end on the occurrence of certain events. The contract itself is not ended, because it is important that the contract continues in existence to govern the situation after termination. The act of bringing the contractor's employment to an end must never be taken lightly by either employer or contractor. The provisions are intended to be used as a last resort, which indeed they are so far as those contractual parties are concerned.

If there were no termination provisions in building contracts, termination could only be achieved under the general law. In that case, the contract itself would come to an end. There are four ways in which a contract can be ended.

- By performance
- By agreement
- By frustration
- By breach

13.1.1 Performance

Most contracts end in this way, when both parties have carried out their obligations properly. The contract then ceases to have a purpose and comes to an end.

13.1.2 Agreement

It is open to the parties to a contract to agree at any time that the contract should be ended. In theory, all that is necessary is for both parties to agree to walk away. In practice, because human nature is sometimes frail, it is wise to record the agreement in writing. For the agreement to have binding effect, it must either contain consideration from both parties (i.e. both must gain and/or lose something) or it must be completed as a deed (see Chapter 6, section 6.4.1). In practice, completion as a deed is the surest way.

13.1.3   Frustration

This is a term with a specific legal meaning in relation to contracts. When an event completely outside the control of the parties results in the contract becoming fundamentally different from that contemplated by the parties at the time the contract was made, the contract is said to have been frustrated. It is not sufficient simply that the contract has become more expensive to carry out than the contractor intended.[1] A good example of frustration would be if a contractor was unable to carry out a refurbishment contract because the building burned down before the date for possession. There are less extreme examples such as a government order which restricts the work.

13.1.4   Breach

An unjustified failure to carry out contractual obligations. If it is a serious breach, it may entitle the other party to treat their own obligations under the contract as ended. The breach itself does not discharge the contract, it has to be accepted by the other party. The innocent party may either treat their obligations under the contract as ended and sue for damages or may treat the contract as continuing (referred to as 'affirming' the contract) and to sue for damages. Such a breach is known as 'repudiatory', because it is a repudiation of the contract.

The difficulty is knowing whether a breach is sufficiently serious to allow acceptance as repudiation. It is often said that such a breach must go to the root of the contract. If a party wrongly accepted a breach as repudiatory and refused to continue with the contract, that party would then be the one in breach. As a general guide, a breach will be repudiatory if it is clear that, by the breach, a party demonstrates an intention not to be bound by the terms of the contract. Great care must be taken, however, because it has been held that where a contractor in breach of contract suspended work, that was not a repudiatory breach. Far from indicating an intention not to continue with the contract, the word 'suspension' indicated only a temporary cessation of activities.[2] A clear case of repudiatory breach would be if a contractor simply walked off the site before practical completion, vowing never to return, or if the architect's client said that fees would no longer be paid in accordance with the agreed instalments, but only at the end of the project when the client was entirely satisfied. These are very clearcut examples. Less obvious is the situation when an employer fails to pay a contractor sums due under a building contract. Although it is fairly clear that continued non-payment can amount to a repudiatory breach, it has been held that refusal to pay a substantial sum can itself in some circumstances be held to be repudiatory.[3]

13.1.5   Termination under the contract

The conditions which have to be satisfied before the contractor's employment can be brought to an end under the contractual machinery can be far less onerous than those required under the general law. Typical grounds for termination by the employer are as follows.

- If the contractor completely or substantially suspends the Works.
- If the contractor fails to proceed regularly and diligently. This concept has caused some trouble in the past. It really has to be clear and unambiguous.[4]
- If the contractor refuses or neglects to rectify defective work and the Works are seriously affected as a result. There are usually other more suitable contractual remedies.
- If the contractor does not observe the provisions of the assignment and sub-letting clauses.
- If the contractor does not comply with the CDM Regulations 2007.
- The contractor's insolvency.

Since termination is such a draconian step, the courts are likely to look very closely at the procedure. The party wishing to terminate must comply strictly with the contractual terms governing termination. If the contract stipulates that notice must be given by special or recorded delivery or delivery by hand, other forms of communication such as email or facsimile may not suffice although facsimile has been held to be the same as actual delivery.[5] In the SBC, for example, although the architect is to give the prior notice of default, the notice of termination (if given) must be issued by the employer. There is no substitute for carefully reading the particular contract being used.

Where the contract requires that a certain number of days notice must be given before termination, the termination will not be valid if attempted even one day early. In such a case, the contractor may be able to sue for damages for repudiation, although much depends on the extent to which the employer has relied on the contract provision, even if mistakenly.[6] As the person charged with administering the contract, the architect has important duties to administer the provisions carefully after termination. The best drafted contracts expressly provide that the contractor must give up possession of the site after termination. Although it may seem obvious that the contractor must leave the site, there could conceivably be problems if the contractor disputes the termination and tries to keep possession of the site. Substantial time and legal costs may be wasted on gaining possession.

Most standard form contracts provide that the employer has the right to make use of the contractor's plant and engage others to finish the Works, taking over contracts for the supply of work and/or materials. Generally, the employer will not be obliged to make any further payment until the Works are complete, even if a certificate has been issued (see, for example, SBC clause 8.7.3). It will then fall to the architect and the quantity surveyor to take all the expenditure into account, including additional professional fees (some contracts include provision for including the employer's loss and damage in the calculation) and certify a final payment of the balance either to employer or to contractor.

If the contractor terminates, the situation will be very serious, not to say catastrophic, for the employer. The architect should make every effort to prevent such an occurrence. Many contracts provide that a contractor who terminates may claim the loss of the profit which would have been made had the contract continued.[7] Quite apart from that, the employer will have to shoulder the burden of completing the Works using another contractor at increased cost of building and fees and to an extended time scale. There are several danger areas which cause problems.

- The employer's failure to pay certified sums within the period stated in the contract.
- Interference by the employer in the issue of any certificate.
- Failure to comply with the assignment clause.
- Failure to comply with the CDM Regulations 2007.
- Actions, inactions or defaults by the employer or the architect causing suspension of the Works for a protracted period.
- The employer's insolvency.

Many contracts provide for termination by either party for such things as prolonged suspension of the Works due to causes outside the control of either party. Normally, the consequences are simply that the contractor is paid up to date and the parties have no further liabilities to each other. Of course, the employer still has the problem of paying extra and waiting longer to complete the Works.

A contractor has nothing to gain and everything to lose by terminating employment as a result of suspension. Having said that, the contractor cannot wait forever and the architect should attempt to obtain some agreement if it seems that suspension will last long enough to allow termination to take place. A most important provision is that the termination notice must not be given unreasonably or vexatiously. That provision must be interpreted in the ordinary commonsense way.

13.2   Practical completion

Practical completion is a term used in the JCT series of contracts. The ACA Form of Building Contract (ACA 3) uses the phrase 'fit and ready for taking over'. The Engineering and Construction Contract refers to the project manager certifying 'completion'. This almost certainly means the same as 'practical completion'.[8] There are conflicting views regarding the meaning of practical completion, but it is certainly not when the building is totally complete.

> 'I take these words to mean completion for all practical purposes, that is to say for the purpose of allowing the employer to take possession of the Works and use them as intended. If completion in [the possession and completion clause] meant completion down to the last detail, however trivial and unimportant, then [the liquidated damages clause] would be a penalty clause and as such unenforceable.'[9]

There is much sound commonsense in that view.

It has also been said that the architect may certify practical completion when her or she is satisfied that the Works are reasonably in accord with the contract with no obvious defects, even though there are some minor things left to be done.[10] This is probably the best view and receives support from an earlier leading decision of the House of Lords.[11] The minor things left to be done are at the discretion of the architect, but in exercising that discretion, it is suggested that the architect must consider as 'minor' only those items which can be subsequently carried out by the contractor without seriously interfering with the employer's use of the building. The golden rule must be that architects must not certify practical completion before they are of the opinion that practical completion has taken place. The certificate is a formal demonstration of the architect's opinion and, therefore, not something to be taken lightly. The architect is not entitled to certify practical completion merely because the employer or the employer's solicitor has instructed the architect to do so.

A vexed question concerns the extent to which an architect is justified in certifying practical completion, because the employer has retaken possession of the Works. Certainly, practical completion is not to be certified simply because the employer has occupied the Works.[12] The brief extract quoted above does not support that approach. Often an employer will retake possession long before the building is complete simply because the delay in completion is proving to be far longer than expected. However, it has been held that if the employer takes partial possession of the whole of the Works, it is deemed to be practical completion.[13] In those circumstances, it seems that the architect has no obligation to issue a formal certificate of practical completion, but merely a written notice of possession as detailed below.

Although practical completion is something which the contract generally leaves to the opinion of the architect, it can be seen that in reality the architect has very little discretion. Practical completion is very largely a question of fact in each case. Following the introduction of the CDM Regulations 1994 (now 2007), the JCT contracts set two criteria before practical completion may be certified. They have little changed in the SBC.

- Practical completion of the Works must have taken place in a physical sense as usual; *and*
- The contractor must have sufficiently complied with the obligation to provide the health and safety file to the CDM Co-ordinator.

The perhaps unexpected result is that the certificate may be withheld for weeks, because the health and safety file is not complete. The contract provisions allow the employer to deduct liquidated damages until the date of practical completion in such circumstances. The only glimmer of light is that the contractor must have 'sufficiently' complied with its obligations to provide the health and safety file. This no doubt allows the certificate to be issued when there are some outstanding pages missing from the file. However, the question whether liquidated damages would become a penalty, because practical completion has been delayed due to a few missing pages, has yet to be resolved. At the first site meetings, architects should stress to contractors the importance of completing the file before practical completion can be certified.

The contractor will be anxious to see the certificate because it marks a very significant date. In most contracts it marks the date at which:

- the contractor's liability for or damage to the Works and goods intended for the Works ends
- the contractor's insurance liability ends
- liability for liquidated damages ends
- half the retention must be released
- liability for subsequent frost damage ends.

Most contractors will notify the architect when practical completion is about to be achieved although it is rare for a contract to have a provision to that effect. A contractor will often serve notice prematurely. Architects must be on guard against this tactic which is possibly designed to suggest that the architect is being very unreasonable when certification is withheld. The contractor may well write to the effect that it is 2 months since practical completion was achieved and still the architect refuses to issue a certificate. Such manoeuvres are highly reprehensible, of course, but also it must be said that some architects can be slow to certify.

The architect should inspect the building and, if it is not complete, write a very firm letter to the contractor pointing out that, at present rate of progress, it seems to be … weeks from practical completion and that practical completion had not been achieved on the date suggested by the contractor. Figure 13.1 shows an example of a form of certificate of practical completion for use with SBC.

There is nothing wrong with and much to be said for architects who point out defects to the contractor. But architects should not be persuaded to carry out detailed inspections of every part of the building and prepare long lists for the contractor – so-called 'snagging lists' beloved of clerks of works. A danger with such lists is that the contractor will rely on the architect and clerk of works to do what the contractor's site supervisory staff should be doing. Another danger is that the contractor will frequently consider that when the listed defects are rectified, practical completion will be certified. In fact, the architect may well carry out another inspection 2 days later and add further items to the list. The architect is perfectly entitled to do so, but it does not make for good relations with the contractor. Far better to get the facts straight at the beginning, i.e. it is the contractor's obligation under the terms of the contract to construct the building strictly in accordance with the contract; the architect has no duty to point out defects. The contractor will no doubt want a list of defective work before practical completion and, if so, it should prepare such a list itself.

It has already been noted that the employer may try to persuade the architect to certify practical completion before it has really been achieved so that the employer can move into the building. Of course, as one of the parties to the building contract, it is open to the employer to agree with the contractor to

<table>
<tr><td colspan="2">

Issued by: Smith & Jones Architects LLP
address: Design Studios, High Street, Notown, XX1 3BB

</td><td>

Practical Completion Certificate

</td></tr>
</table>

Issued by: Smith & Jones Architects LLP
address: Design Studios, High Street, Notown, XX1 3BB

Practical Completion Certificate

Employer: Willow Developments Ltd
address: High Street, Notown, XX1 4RB

SBC / IC / ICD / MW / MWD

Job reference: 0055

Contractor: Gerrybuilders Ltd
address: 10–12 Builders Way, Notown, XX2 2ER

Certificate no: 1

Issue date: 29 November 2010

Works: Golf Club
situated at: Park Acres, Notown, XX3 1RR

Contract dated: 13 January 2010

Under the terms of the above-mentioned Contract,

I/we hereby certify that in my/our opinion

practical completion of the Works has been achieved

*Delete if not applicable

* and the Contractor has supplied the specified documents and drawings relating to the Contractor's Designed Portion

* and the Contractor has complied with the contractual requirements in respect of information for the health and safety file

on   29 November   2010

To be signed by or for the issuer named above

Signed _I. Jones_

Distribution			
☒ Employer	☒ Structural Engineer	☒ Planning Supervisor	☐
☒ Contractor	☐ M&E Consultant	☐	☐
☒ Quantity Surveyor	☒ Clerk of Works	☐	☒ File

F553   for SBC / IC / ICD / MW / MWD   RIBA CONTRACT ADMINISTRATION FORMS   © RIBA Publishing 2006

Fig. 13.1 RIBA Certificate of Practical Completion (courtesy of RIBA and RIBA Publishing).

take over the building at any time. However, it has been seen that the architect has no power and, therefore, it would be very unwise to issue the certificate before practical completion has actually been achieved. If the employer takes over the building before practical completion, the architect's duty depends on the form of contract. Under the provisions of the SBC or IC, if the employer takes possession of any part or parts of the Works with the contractor's consent, the architect must issue a written notice on behalf of the employer identifying the part taken into possession and the date.

Many contracts have provision for such partial possession. The idea is that where there is just one date for completion in the contract, but during the progress of the Works, the employer wishes to take possession of some part of it before practical completion of the whole, this can be achieved provided that the contractor agrees. It is important to remember that the provision does not enable sectional completion to be achieved. Where it is known at time of tender that sectional or phased completion is desired, care should be taken that the appropriate form of contract is used. JCT contracts now incorporate provision for sectional completion.

It is not usually sufficient to put a list of handover dates in the specification or bills of quantities if there is only one completion date in the contract form. In such circumstances, the architect will be unable to insist on sectional completion under JCT contracts due to the priority clause in the contract[14] and will be unable to give extensions of time to individual sections of the work and the liquidated damages clause might well become a penalty and thereby unenforceable. Where there is provision for sections, a section completion certificate must be issued at practical completion of each section. On practical completion of the last section, the architect must also issue a practical completion certificate for the whole of the Works. This is to avoid uncertainty and deal with the situation where the sum of the sections does not, by some oversight, equate to the whole of the Works.

13.3 Rectification period

Most forms of building contract provide for a period of time after the practical completion of the Works during which the contractor will be liable to make good defects which appear during that period. The usual period is 6 months, but 12 months is commonly specified in respect of mechanical services to allow the system to be exposed to the full yearly cycle. This is incorrect, because the contract does not allow differing rectification periods to be specified. The solution is to specify 12 months for the rectification period for the building as a whole.

The reason for the period is often misunderstood. It must be remembered that, during the contract period, the contractor is said to have a licence to be on the site (the employer's property) for the purpose of carrying out the Works. It is generally understood that the licence allows the contractor to remain on the site until the Works are completed. If the contractor were to stay on site or allow equipment to remain on site beyond that point, it would amount to trespass for which the employer could mount an action for whatever damages could be proven. Moreover, if there was no rectification period, the employer could simply notify the contractor of any defects, but arrange to have them corrected by another contractor and charge the original contractor with the cost. The rectification period allows defects to appear and provides for the architect to give a schedule to the contractor with a requirement to rectify them. The contract gives the contractor a licence to enter the site again to make good the notified defects. The provision is for the contractor's benefit who, therefore, has a right under the contract to rectify those defects.[15] Were it not for this clause, the employer would be entitled to engage another contractor to carry out the work and charge the cost to the original contractor (after due notice and time to inspect, of course).

This is a very valuable right to the contractor because the cost to the contractor for doing the remedial work will be very much less than the cost to the employer of getting in another contractor to do the same work. Some contracts allow the employer to decide not to allow the contractor to make good the defects and to make 'an appropriate deduction' from the contract sum. This sum is not the cost of engaging another contractor, but what it would have cost the original contractor to do the work.[16]

Another misconception is that at the end of the rectification period, the contractor has no further liability for defects. We suspect that a major reason for the change of name in JCT contracts from 'defects liability period' to 'rectification period' was precisely to avoid the misconception which may have been partly engendered by the former name. The contractor is liable for all defects (i.e. work not in accordance with the contract) until the expiry of the limitation period (see Chapter 6, section 6.4.1). Thus if it was discovered that 3 years after the end of the rectification period a contractor had omitted a number of wall ties specified to be used in the cavity walls, a legal action could be successfully brought against the contractor for the cost of making the defect good. Not just what it would have cost the contractor, but all the costs involved in getting another contractor to do the work.[17] A contractor is liable beyond that period, but the Limitation Act operates to allow a contractor faced with an action in respect of breach of contract to escape the consequences after a period of 6 years from the date of the breach (or 12 years if the contract is a deed). The starting date is usually taken as the date of practical completion. It is a basic principle, of course, that if the employer wants to recover the cost of making good defects from the contractor, it is essential that the contractor is first given notice of the defects and afforded the opportunity to inspect.

Most forms of contract provide for the architect to issue a certificate to the contractor when all the listed defects have been made good and, in some standard forms, there is then provision for the second half of the retention to be released. The retention acts as a safeguard to the employer if the contractor fails to make good the defects. The contractor should make good the defects within a reasonable time after notification by the architect. What is a reasonable time will depend on many factors. It is not possible to fix a period which applies to all circumstances. The criteria to be taken into account include the complexity of the work, the size of the project, the number and type of defects and the difficulty of making good.

If the architect is of the opinion that the contractor is not attending to the contractual obligations with reasonable expedition and does not respond to pressure, the architect should seriously consider giving notice on behalf of the employer that if the making good is not commenced/completed within 7 days, the employer will engage others to do the work and charge the full cost to the contractor. That would normally amount to making a deduction from the retention fund.

Some contractors and even some forms of contract refer to the 'maintenance period'. The term is quite misleading and it should never be used because it suggests an obligation to keep the Works in pristine condition rather than an obligation to correct defects. The only kind of defects which most forms of contract require the contractor to make good are those which are due to the work not being in accordance with the contract or to frost occurring before practical completion. Clearly, ordinary wear and tear is excluded as are the consequences of inadequate specification.

13.4   Adjustment of contract sum

It seems to be the fashion for architects to leave the calculation of the final account entirely in the hands of the quantity surveyor. In most instances, the result will be no less than satisfactory. Architects should remember, however, that they are the contract administrators and that when the final certificate is issued, it will be conclusive (under most JCT contracts) that all the clauses which provide for adjustment of the contract sum have been correctly operated. The consequences of a failure in this regard could be quite serious. The only safe process is to check through the contract and make sure. To take the JCT SBC as an example, it contains no less than 27 different instances which permit or require adjustment of the contract sum. They are summarised in Fig. 13.2. Each clause should be carefully considered and a positive decision should be made that the matters referred to in the clause have been dealt with.

Architects should not leave everything to the quantity surveyor, they should check through the material provided by the contractor. Although it is probably inappropriate for architects to attempt the kind of financial reconciliations which are the province of the quantity surveyor, architects can usefully see what sort of information has been sent by the contractor and the work categories concerned. Architects who do this may spot errors which the quantity surveyor has missed because the quantity surveyor was not so closely involved with the carrying out of the work. Needless to say, the quantity surveyor must have a full set of all the instructions issued by the architect during the course of the project. Included should be not only the standard architect's instruction forms, but also any instruction given by the architect in any other way.

Clause	Adjustments
2.10	Levels and setting out.
2.14.3	Errors in the contract bills.
2.16.2	Discrepancy in CDM documents.
2.17.2.2	Divergence between contract documents and statutory requirements.
2.18.3	Emergency compliance with statutory requirements.
2.21	Fees legally demandable under Act of Parliament.
2.23	Patent rights – instructions.
2.38	Defects.
3.11	Non-compliance with instructions.
3.14	Instructions requiring variations.
3.16	Instructions on provisional sums.
3.17	Inspecting – tests.
3.18.2	Work not in accordance with the contract.
4.3	Adjustments to the contract sum
4.25	Loss and/or expense.
5	Variations.
5.5	Adjustment of the contract sum.
6.5.3	Insurance payments by the contractor under clause 6.5.
6.15	Joint Fire Code.
6.16	Joint Fire Code amendments/revisions.
8.7.4	Consequences of employer termination.
8.8	Employer's decision not to complete the Works.
8.12.3	Consequences of contractor termination.
Schedule 2	Variation and acceleration quotation procedures.
Schedule 3, option B.2.1.2	Contractor insuring if employer defaults.
Schedule 3, option C.3.1.3	Contractor insuring if employer defaults.
Schedule 7	Fluctuations.

Fig. 13.2 Adjustment of the contract sum under JCT Standard Building Contract 2005 (Revision 2 2009).

If the contract is small and no quantity surveyor has been engaged, the architect will be responsible for checking the account in detail. Where appropriate, all invoices of sub-contractors and suppliers should be requested and they should be checked against entries in the account and the amounts allowed in the contract. All extra items should be authorised by architect's instructions and where there is no contractually precise method of valuation set down, care should be taken that prices are in accordance with any agreed pricing document or that they are reasonable. Finally, the mathematics of the account must be checked.

When the final account has been sent to the contractor and, hopefully, agreed, it should be sent to the employer. It is usually best to do this in a simplified version. Under most standard forms, the contractor's agreement is not required. The employer, of course, has the right to see the full final account and any other papers, but unless the employer has some professional expertise, a simple version will be appreciated. It is appropriate for the architect to prepare the simple version. It should not miss out anything important nor attempt to whitewash over difficulties. An example is shown in Fig. 13.3. Where architects are dealing with local authorities or companies who have

Willow Developments
Golf Club, Park Acres, Notown

Summary of Variation Account

Item		Omissions £	Additions £
1.	Preliminaries	—	3,704.10
2.	Substructure	5,282.40	8,921.50
3.	Concrete frame	7,828.74	8,184.25
4.	Floor finishes	2,501.67	4,601.35
5.	Fitted furniture	4,559.02	8,103.12
6.	Sundry variations	—	5,826.39
7.	Provisional sums and contingencies	130,000.00	73,260.09
8.	Dayworks	—	10,678.05
		150,171.83	123,278.85
	Ascertainment of loss and/or expense	—	14,000.00
		150,171.83	137,278.85
			150,171.83
	Net omission carried to statement		£12,892.98

Statement of Final Account		£
	Amount of contract sum	2,168,328.00
	Net omission as summary	(12,892.98)
	Amount of final account	2,155,435.02

Fig. 13.3   Example statement of final account to client.

their own technical staff, they will almost certainly require the full accounts to be submitted and they will equally certainly have a great many queries which must be answered.

The architect should have kept the employer up to date throughout the contract with the assistance of the quantity surveyor. It should have been made clear that changes from the agreed scheme will inevitably result in extra cost. Any instructions from the employer to the architect should be confirmed in writing by the architect so that at final account stage, there is no doubt about which costs have been incurred by the employer. Architects should never give instructions to the contractor which involve variations and extra cost unless so instructed by the employer. It sometimes happens that, towards the end of the contract, the architect may make savings which could usefully be spent on improving some aspect of the building. In such instances, the architect may never instruct the contractor without first seeking appropriate authorisation from the employer.

Architects should always keep in mind that no matter how experienced the employer nor how firm his or her views, it is for the architect alone, assisted by the quantity surveyor, to carry out the function of settling the final account. It is helpful if the contractor agrees the figure, but if not and if the architect and quantity surveyor are of one mind on the matter, they should simply inform the employer that there has been no agreement with the contractor. It is always open to the employer to come to some special agreement with the contractor as the two parties to the contract. This has nothing to do with the architect and the quantity surveyor and in such an instance, the architect will not issue a final certificate, because the architect cannot certify a sum of money unless he or she is of the opinion that it has been calculated in accordance with the contract.

13.5   Final certificate

It is worthwhile looking at the conclusiveness of the final certificate in some detail.

At one time, when the architect issued the final certificate, it was considered to be a statement that the whole of the Works were complete in all respects in accordance with the contract. That was certainly the position under some early editions of the JCT 1963 form of contract. In later editions of JCT 63 and under JCT 80 and IFC 84, the position was substantially modified.

Some forms of contract made the issue of the final certificate conclusive about certain things. Other forms did not state that it was conclusive about anything, not even the amount finally due. The final certificate under the JCT Minor Works Building Contract (MW and MWD) and the ACA Form of Building Agreement (ACA 3) were, and are, examples of the latter category and, therefore, these comments, relating to the conclusivity of the final certificate, did not, and do not, apply to MW, MWD or ACA 3. At the other extreme, JCT 80 made the final certificate conclusive in four instances. CD 81 (With Contractor's Design), JCT 87 (Management Contract) and IFC 84 (Intermediate Form) had similar wordings.

When a final certificate is said to be 'conclusive', what is meant is that if neither party has entered into adjudication, litigation or arbitration before the issue of the certificate nor so enters within a stipulated period (usually 28 days) after its issue, the certificate is conclusive (i.e. unchallengeable) evidence in any such proceedings in regard to the stipulated matters. Thus, if a final certificate is said to be conclusive in regard to the amount of the final sum certified, it will not prevent an aggrieved party from seeking satisfaction by way of arbitration if the sum is considered to be wrong.[18] However, the other party has simply to produce the final certificate for the matter to be at an end. Certificates under JCT 80, CD 81, JCT 87 and IFC 84 were conclusive in respect of the following.

■ *That where the quality of materials and standards of workmanship are to be to the reasonable satisfaction of the architect, the architect is so satisfied.* This referred back to an early clause (2.1 in JCT 80) stating the contractor's obligations and it was a failure to realise what this meant which gave rise to many misconceptions. Part of the contractor's obligations was to ensure that if the architect had stated that certain things were to be to the architect's satisfaction, such things were to his or her satisfaction. Note that the architect *must first have stated* (presumably in the specification or in the bills of quantities) that certain things were to be to the architect's satisfaction. This may have been done by stating that specified items must be 'approved' or 'to the architect's satisfaction' or some other form of words to the same effect. When the final certificate was issued, it was conclusive evidence that the architect was satisfied with any matters which were so specified whether or not the architect had in fact specifically expressed approval or even looked at the item in question. It will readily be appreciated that to insert some such phrase as 'All workmanship and material, unless otherwise stated, must be to the architect's satisfaction' was opening the door to the blanket conclusivity of the final certificate again. It was the business of the architect's satisfaction which gave rise to all the problems and it will be considered in detail below.

- *All the provisions of the contract requiring adjustment of the contract sum have been complied with.* The mechanics of this were covered in section 13.4 above, but the final certificate was conclusive evidence that all necessary adjustments had been properly carried out. Claims by the contractor after the appropriate period had elapsed from issue of the certificate that the figures were wrong would be fruitless. The only exceptions were if there had been accidental inclusion or omission of work or materials, fraud or if there is an obvious arithmetical error. This sub-clause still applies unchanged.

- *All due extensions of time have been given.* This was to prevent the contractor raising the question after the final certificate when the employer may have deducted liquidated damages and all financial matters appear to have been settled. This sub-clause still applies unchanged.

- *That reimbursement of loss and/or expense is in final settlement of all contractor's claims in respect of clause 26 matters whether the claims are for breach of contract, duty of care, statutory duty or otherwise.* This was a very widely drawn clause intended principally, like the previous clause, to ensure that the final certificate really did spell the end of the financial road. It should be noted, however, that the conclusivity was effective only in respect of the clause 26 (loss and/or expense) matters. It did not operate to prevent the contractor from making claims in regard to breaches of contract outside this parameter. This sub-clause still applies unchanged.

The effect of the issue of the final certificate, especially in regard to the architect's satisfaction with workmanship and materials, was considered by the Court of Appeal.[19] Much to the concern of architects, the court decided that the final certificate under JCT 80 was conclusive that the architect was satisfied with the quality and standards of *all* materials, goods and workmanship. The consequence was that the employer found it very difficult to take subsequent action against the contractor for latent defects. Various ruses were promoted to avoid the effects of the decision, but none of them were effective.

When the Court of Appeal considered the effect of the final certificate and came to its decision, it was not making new law. What it was doing was telling everyone what the terms of the contract meant even though until that moment perhaps no one (including the Court of Appeal) had realised it. What the parties intend to do when they enter into a contract is, of course, important, but only in so far as they give effect to their intentions by the written terms they agree in the contract. In turn, the court can only interpret their intentions by looking at the contract terms. Evidence as to their intentions outside a written contract is normally inadmissible. The court's interpretation of the contract term was very much in the contractor's favour, but that is what the parties agreed in law when they signed the contract.

As far as the contractor was concerned, nothing had changed. The terms of the contract required architects to issue final certificates within specific timescales. If architects did not so issue they, and through them probably the employers, were in breach. The architect's position was straightforward if he or she had been engaged on the usual (then SFA 92) terms of engagement or similar. During the progress of the Works, the architect must carry out inspections with reasonable skill and care. There is a duty to issue the final certificate in accordance with the building contract. If subsequently a latent defect was discovered, the employer may have been unable to recover the cost of remedial work from the contractor. The employer might then have turned attention to the architect. If the employer was to have been successful in recovering the loss from the architect in negligence, it would have to be shown that the architect failed to carry out administrative duties, including inspection, with reasonable skill and care. That would not have been very easy, but perhaps easier than most architects would have wished.

It was common, in former times, for architects to be so concerned about the conclusiveness of the final certificate that they often neglected to issue a final certificate at all, leaving a minute sum of money outstanding in the knowledge that the contractor would not seek arbitration in respect of such a small amount. By this method, it was hoped that the matters otherwise made conclusive by the final certificate would be left open and the employer would not be precluded from obtaining redress from the contractor if any latent defects appeared. Of course, it had also to be borne in mind that, if successful, such a ploy would effectively deprive the employer of the conclusive benefit of the other three matters. The courts have put an end to any likelihood that an employer could proceed against the contractor if the final certificate was not issued at the proper time. The court's view was that if the failure to issue was a breach of contract, the employer cannot take advantage of that breach.[20]

Following the *Crown Estates* case, the JCT issued amendments to each of the affected forms of contract which were intended to remove the effect of the Court of Appeal decision by rewording the sub-clauses relating to the conclusivity of the architect's satisfaction. Essentially, therefore, the position was restored that the final certificate was conclusive about the architect's satisfaction only if the architect had specifically stated in the bills of quantities or specification that some item of goods, materials or workmanship was to be to his or her satisfaction or approval.

The 2005 series JCT forms (SBC, IC, ICD and DB incorporating Revision 2 2009) incorporate the amendment. The current position is dealt with under clause 1.9.1.1 in the SBC, IC and ICD. It provides that the final certificate is conclusive evidence that if the contract bills or drawings or any architect's instruction or further issue of drawings states clearly that particular qualities of materials or goods or particular standards of workmanship are to be to the architect's approval, the particular quality or standards are to the architect's reasonable satisfaction. However, the final sentence makes clear that the final certificate is not conclusive that any of those qualities or standards or indeed any other materials, goods or workmanship comply with any other requirement of the contract. Therefore, even if the architect has inadvertently specified that something is to be to his or her satisfaction, it will not prevent an employer seeking redress for work or materials which do not comply with the contract documents in other ways. The DB contract contains clause 1.8.1.1 which is to similar effect except that it refers to the final statement instead of the final certificate and to the employer rather than to the architect, for obvious reasons. The current position under MW, MWD and ACA 3 is still unaffected, because the final certificate is still not conclusive under those contracts.

The main thing which can be said of the final certificate under all building contracts is that after the architect has issued the final certificate, he or she is said to be *functus officio,* having no further powers under the contract. The architect, for example, cannot then issue further extensions of time. An example of a final certificate for the SBC is shown in Fig. 13.4.

13.6 Review of project performance in use

This used to be termed 'feedback' and it is a most important stage of the building process. One of the most valuable references is an architect's own experience. Memory grows dim, however, and often it confuses facts. Records of projects become increasingly valuable as the numbers of projects completed increase.

At the end of each project, a routine should be established to extract the maximum amount of useful information. Ideally, records should be building up during the running of the project. In practice, everyone connected with the project will be so busy during the construction process that they will put off doing anything which does not seem to be urgent. An architect does not simply come to a conclusion on one scheme and then the following day start work on another. The reality is that work on one project overlaps work on another. Depending on size, an architect may well be working on several different schemes at once. Finding time to carry out a feedback and appraisal exercise is not usually a priority. It has to be done, however, if the practice is to develop.

Final Certificate

SBC

Issued by: Smith & Jones Architects LLP
address: Design Studios, High Street, Notown, XX1 3BB

Employer: Willow Developments Ltd
address: High Street, Notown, XX1 4RB

Job reference: 0055

Date of issue: 20 October 2011

Contractor: Gerrybuilders Ltd
address: 10–12 Builders Way, Notown, XX3 2ER

Final date for payment: 17 November 2011

Works: Golf Club
situated at: Park Acres, Notown, XX3 1RR

Contract dated: 13 January 2010

This Final Certificate is issued under the terms of the above-mentioned Contract.

Contract Sum adjusted as necessary .... £ 2,155,435.02

Sum of amounts already stated as due in Interim Certificates
plus amount of any advance payment .... £ 2,071,272.00

Difference between the above stated amounts .... £ 84,163.02

All amounts are exclusive of VAT. The Employer shall in addition pay the amount of VAT properly chargeable.

I/We hereby certify the sum of (in words)
Eighty Four Thousand One Hundred and Sixty Three

Pounds and Two Pence

as a **balance due**:

*Delete as appropriate

* to the Contractor from the Employer.

* ~~to the Employer from the Contractor~~

To be signed by or for the issuer named above

Signed _____

This is not a Tax Invoice.

Distribution			
[X] Employer	[X] Contractor	[X] Quantity Surveyor	[X] File copy

F552A for SBC   RIBA CONTRACT ADMINISTRATION FORMS   © RIBA Publishing 2006

Fig. 13.4 RIBA final certificate (courtesy RIBA and RIBA Publishing).

If all parties can be gathered around the table for an appraisal session at the end, so much the better. Theoretically, all parties are terribly frank with each other and the contractor takes part. There is no doubt that such a session would be very useful, but the chances of achieving it are remote. By the end of the project, all parties probably know what they think of each other. They may not be on speaking terms at that stage and in a minority of cases, regrettably, arbitration or litigation may be in the air and adjudication may have taken place.

Architects can produce quite a lot of useful feedback information simply by consulting the files and by spending an afternoon going through a prepared agenda and discussing among the design team within the architects' office just what was done and whether it could have been done in a more effective way. It is important that the discussion is carefully structured or it will achieve nothing. The first thing in preparation is to record the key dates and other information. Some suggested, but by no means an exhaustive list of, items may be:

■ dates of commencement of each Plan of Work stage, i.e. when was the first contact with the client?
■ projected and actual dates for commencement and completion of the contract on site
■ the cost history. Estimates of cost from inception until tender stage, then accepted tender price, contract sum and final certificate figure
■ project type, construction system, services
■ procurement method and form of contract, amendments.

This is a useful starting point for discussion which should attempt to answer the question 'why?' in relation to each item. Other matters which should be examined are:

■ drawings preparation and issue
■ architect's instructions, content, pricing, reasons for issue
■ site meetings and minutes
■ cost control
■ claims
■ communications within the design team, with the client and the contractor
■ client's brief compared to finished building, compared to building in use
■ appropriateness of materials, including reviews at set time periods
■ appropriateness of details, including reviews at set time periods
■ areas where improvements can be made.

Some architects consider that the client should be involved in the process and a questionnaire can be sent inviting comment on specific issues. Others think that to do so would be inviting trouble, rather like asking the client to consider whether it is appropriate to pursue an action for negligence. That is perhaps to take a rather gloomy view. The client should appreciate that the architect is simply concerned to give a good service and always anxious to improve.

Whether the client is involved or not, it is certain that architects will get much out of a thorough feedback exercise. Among other things, it promotes the questioning of long-established but possibly ineffectual practices. Many architects would be astounded to realise just how many times they have issued revised versions of certain drawings, just how long it took them to provide the answer to certain queries from the contractor or just how many people-hours were spent on site meetings.

One final point: the feedback exercise is intended to help all concerned. It is not intended to be a witch hunt to discover the culprit behind failed details or exceeded cost targets. If it is used as a method of apportioning blame by an office, there will only ever be the one exercise. One of the authors recalls an office where a senior architect falsified his own timesheets, spreading what appeared to be excess time on one project onto other projects. It was pointed out that accurate timesheets were an invaluable aid for estimating the likely costs of carrying out future similar work and that inaccurate timesheets were worse than useless – they were actually misleading. It emerged that the architect falsified the sheets because in the past he had been taken to task, on the basis of submitted sheets, for spending too much time on a particular project. An office which does not have an ethos of admitting errors of judgement without blame will have nothing on which to base future action (see Chapter 14, section 14.1).

References

1. *Davis Contractors Ltd* v. *Fareham UDC* [1956] 2 All ER 145.
2. *F Treliving & Co Ltd* v. *Simplex Time Recorder Co (UK) Ltd* (1981) unreported.
3. *C J Elvin Building Services Ltd* v. *Peter Noble & Alexa Noble* (2003) CILL 1997.
4. See the courts' views in *Greater London Council* v. *Cleveland Bridge & Engineering Co Ltd* (1984) 8 Con LR 30 and particularly *West Faulkner Associates* v. *London Borough of Newham* (1994) 11 Const LJ 157.
5. *Construction Partnership UK Ltd* v. *Leek Developments Ltd* [2006] EWHC B8 (TCC).
6. *Woodar Investment Development Ltd* v. *Wimpey Construction UK Ltd* [1980] 1 All ER 571.
7. *Wraight Ltd* v. *P H & T (Holdings) Ltd* (1968) 8 BLR 22.
8. *Emson Eastern Ltd (in receivership)* v. *EME Developments Ltd* (1991) 55 BLR 114.
9. *Salmon LJ, Westminster City Council* v. *J Jarvis & Sons Ltd* [1969] 1 All ER 1025, CA.
10. *H W Neville (Sunblest) Ltd* v. *Wm Press & Son Ltd* (1981) 20 BLR 78.
11. *Westminster City Council* v. *J Jarvis & Sons Ltd* (1970) 7 BLR 64 HL.
12. *BFI Group of Companies Ltd* v. *DCB Integration Systems Ltd* (1987) CILL 348.
13. *Skanska Construction (Regions) Ltd* v. *Anglo-Amsterdam Corp Ltd* (2002) 84 Con LR 100.
14. *M J Gleeson (Contractors) Ltd* v. *Hillingdon Borough Council* (1970) 215 EG 165.
15. *City Axis Ltd* v. *Daniel P Jackson* (1998) CILL 1382.

16. *William Tomkinson and Sons Ltd* v. *The Parochial Church Council of St Michael's and Others* (1990) 6 Const LJ 319.
17. *Pearce and High* v. *Baxter* (1999) 90 BLR 101.
18. *P & M Kay Ltd* v. *Hosier & Dickinson* (1972) 10 BLR 126.
19. *Crown Estates Commissioners* v. *John Mowlem & Co* (1994) 70 BLR 1.
20. *Matthew Ortech Ltd* v. *Tarmac Roadstone Ltd* (1998) 87 BLR 96.

Part 3
General Office Matters

14 Management Principles

14.1 Objectives

There are broadly two kinds of objectives: the objectives of the firm and the objectives of the individual. As a rough guide, the most successful firms are those in which the objectives of the firm and its employees most nearly correspond, because they can all go forward together without jostling for advantage.

The objectives of an architectural practice might well be to enjoy and to produce fine architecture, contribute to the environment, and make a reasonable profit. The architects in the practice will have joined because they have similar objectives and they are also, perhaps, looking for career advancement. A good manager will ensure that these personal goals are capable of satisfaction within the overall framework of the practice objectives.

Many large organisations have problems because the members of staff have rather different objectives from those of the organisation. It is not uncommon to encounter the kind of individual who considers that his or her objective is achieved if the pile of papers in the 'IN' tray can be transferred to the 'OUT' tray by the end of the day. In the context of that firm, the objective may be valid, but everyone should ask the question 'Is what I am doing assisting in achieving the objectives of the organisation?'. Sometimes, it is difficult to see how particular tasks are helping to achieve objectives. In such cases, the employee should ask the manager for an explanation (see section 14.5).

Objectives, of course, for both individuals and organisations may be long or short term. A short-term objective for a practice might be to complete a particular project. In the shorter term, completing a stage, such as the client's acceptance of outline proposals, may be crucial. Longer term objectives are probably associated with expansion, specialisation, movement to better premises, etc. It is clear that the longer term objectives can only be achieved if the shorter term objectives are secured first. Personal objectives have similar structures.

Achieving objectives can involve admitting mistakes, indeed must do so. Whoever first decided that it was a weakness to admit mistakes was very misguided. Everyone makes mistakes and it is only by acknowledging a mistake that progress can be made. For example, it is essential to know how to put a cost on a project so that appropriate fees can be charged. In order to achieve this objective, careful historical records must be kept to indicate just how well the practice's own cost and time targets are achieved. An essential part of these records are staff time sheets. It is not unknown, however, for some architects to put down a proportion of their time to other work when they begin to see that they are in danger of exceeding the budgeted figures. The only clear result is that the practice builds up a set of unreliable records and it will continue to underestimate time periods, project after project, until the laying off of time against other projects ceases (see Chapter 13, section 13.6, and Chapter 16, section 16.15).

Every practice should have a policy of admitting mistakes, including those of the partners or directors, so that something can be done about them. Once a mistake is admitted, there should be commiserations, lessons should be learned and then the mistake should be forgotten and the concentration should be on objectives. Every architect should learn to take decisions on the basis of the practice objectives; if a mistake is made, an admission will save much time and files of internal memos. Architectural practices who try this approach experience team work, often for the first time. There really is no place for a practice with an infallible sole principal and six frightened assistants. Common objectives should eliminate this problem.

If the objectives are clear, the best route towards them may be difficult to find. If the objectives are not defined, everyone will be setting off in different directions.

14.2 Leadership

Architects are called upon to practise leadership in different ways. In a small way, it is required in chairing a meeting. A principal, partner or director has to exercise leadership. If the office is large enough, a group leader is aptly named.

In the long run, the best leaders are low profile. There is much inconsequential verbiage written about leadership. A good leader really has only two functions:

- to decide objectives for those being led
- to set the pace.

The importance of objectives has already been discussed. Deciding objectives is a clear function, if difficult to carry out. Setting the pace is more complex. How a leader sets the pace depends on many factors, including the objective to be achieved, the circumstances, the personalities of others and, not least, the personality of the leader. This is what is sometimes referred to as leadership style. Some architects with large outgoing personalities like to lead from the front, building up an office image which is essentially their own image. This is not necessarily, or even usually, effective. It results in a practice which is essentially one person plus helpers. In the absence of the leader, things tend to slow or even stop.

The real art of leadership is to appear to be following, hence the phrase 'leading from behind'. A good partner will ensure that everything is in place to make it as easy as possible for project architects to carry out their tasks. A good leader must also be a good facilitator, prepared to do the things which would distract the architects from their essential tasks. Good leaders put forward their ideas in such a way that the project architects think they are their own. The true measure of successful leadership is the performance of the leader's staff who do not realise they are being led.

14.3   Communication

Communication is the most vital aspect of management. Ineffective communication will render the most splendid ideas useless. Communication is a two-way process. Many of the problems associated with building contracts result from failure on both sides. The general principle is that if a message is misunderstood, it is the fault of the originator. It is in the nature of the profession that architects can only get their concepts realised if they communicate them effectively. So architects must be excellent communicators. Good communication involves:

- clarity
- certainty
- brevity
- comprehensiveness.

14.3.1   Clarity

Architects should look at their drawings, specifications, reports and letters as though they were the recipients. Many architectural drawings need second sight to decipher. Preparing production information (see Chapter 10, section 10.3) requires the application of a mind which, having analysed the problem, can synthesise the solution to produce easily digestible information. It is not easy. Eccentric and flamboyant drawing styles do not help matters. One of the advantages of CAD is that it eradicates strange drawing styles.

14.3.2   Certainty

This quality goes arm in arm with clarity although there is a distinction. When the architect communicates with the contractor, there should be only one interpretation possible. Very often a message, which may be a model of clarity in itself, may be capable of two meanings when read in context with other messages or with the project as a whole. The architect should take care, therefore, that any communication, drawn, written or spoken is incapable of mis-interpretation. The message may be uncertain in itself, of course, as in such phrases as 'as soon as possible' or 'when convenient' or 'quality'. It has become fashionable to talk about 'quality products' or a pub serving 'quality food'. Such phrases are meaningless. 'Quality' is a characteristic or an attribute. Unless it is qualified, it means nothing. But *'good*-quality food' or *'poor*-quality products' gets the message across. Even if a time period is specified, uncertainty may still exist, as in 'You have only 7 days to respond'. Does that mean 7 days from today's date, or from the receipt of the letter, or from some other date which may be implied when the phrase is read in context with the rest of the letter? However, 'You must respond by close of business on 3 September 2009' is difficult to misunderstand.

14.3.3   Brevity

It is difficult to be brief. Extra words are added to a sentence or clause and extra lines are added to a drawing, intending to make the meaning clearer. Often they make the meaning more obscure. This is, in part, because it is more difficult to read, but also because the multitude of documents means that people get tired of reading and give most attention to short, easily understood messages. The popularity of emails is testimony to that. To be brief in a written document involves writing out the message as clearly, certainly and briefly as possible, then carefully editing out the superfluous, doing some re-arranging, then writing it out again. It will take the architect longer to prepare the document, but it should save time in the long term, because the contractor should be able to act on the document without any, or too many, questions. Hence the comment: 'If I had longer to write it, I could have made this letter shorter'.

14.3.4   Comprehensiveness

It is very common to assume that a recipient knows more than actually is the case. The golden rule is to assume that the recipient knows very little and to proceed accordingly. This will involve more time in preparation but again, it should save questioning time and it is also useful when drawings or other documents have to be consulted long after they were produced. Brief messages in the style of 'Got your message, and agree your suggestion' are unfortunately quite common. The only thing one can say is that they encapsulate in one document an ignorance of three of these principles, thus making the fourth, brevity, another fault. Messages of this kind are not the hallmark of the busy executive architect, but careless almost to the point of negligence.

These principles hold good not only between architect and contractor, but between architect and fellow consultants and between the project architect and the other architects in a particular group. Regrettably, architects' drawings are not always good examples of communication documents. The eminent architect Sir Edwin Lutyens once said that a drawing should be like a letter to the builder, telling him exactly what is required, not a pretty picture to impress an idiotic client. Not very complimentary to his clients, but very true for all that.

14.4   Delegation

It is common to hear architects say that the architect above them in seniority does not know how to delegate. Grumbles of this sort usually indicate that the architect in question insists on keeping an eye very firmly on everything that is going on. That architect, however, will probably say that since he or she takes the responsibility in the end, such close supervision is justified. That kind of response puts the cart before the horse. Delegation is a key function of management and the art of delegation is to know what to delegate, when and to whom. Of course, the senior takes overall responsibility; that is one of the reasons for the larger salary cheque.

The rule is to delegate work to the least qualified/paid person who is capable of doing the work. It is important to understand the principle properly. It does not mean that work should always be delegated to the least paid or least qualified. The important criterion is that the person should be capable of doing the work. Therefore, if the quality required is of a very high order it might well be that the person capable is actually the best qualified and highest paid. If there are three people who can do the work adequately, the least qualified and least paid should be chosen. To do otherwise is to squander talent and money.

Delegation encourages people to take responsibility. Architects in control of staff may be reluctant to delegate because they think that the task will not be carried out properly. What they really mean is that it will not be carried out precisely in the way they would have tackled it. In fact, it could be carried out with greater efficiency.

An example will make this clear. There may be a meeting scheduled at which an important client will meet the contractor to settle some crucial matters relating to a large contract. The senior architect may well feel an obligation to attend even though there is a very competent project architect dealing with that contract. The truth is that if the senior architect delegates the attendance at that meeting, the preparation for it and report after the meeting will receive the kind of attention the senior architect is unlikely to be able to give it. The senior architect should delegate attendance to the project architect (with reasonable notice) with the message that whatever he or she agrees will be backed. The project architect will appreciate the confidence and is likely to spend long hours, not all of them office hours, in preparation to make sure of achieving the best possible outcome. The senior architect will be freed to do non-delegable work.

Another important rule is not to delegate work and then interfere. A manager who does that has lost his or her nerve. Architects in positions to delegate work should pick the right persons and then demonstrate total confidence in the delegation. They will rarely be disappointed. If they are, it will usually reflect their own bad judgement.

14.5 Motivation

Motivation comes in two parts: motivation of self and motivation of others. Self-motivation is very complex. It may depend on the solving of a problem or the desire to improve an already satisfactory situation. The desire for status, money, power, social position, security, happiness, acknowledgment, service, etc. falls into either or both of those categories. Without a strong motive, little is achieved. A common term for a person with a strong motivation is 'self-starter' which describes the situation very well. Most professional activity is motivating for the participant, possibly none more so than architecture. It offers challenge and the opportunity to rise to the occasion.

An unmotivated architect will probably stay in the same office for the whole of a working life, maybe doing unrewarding work and progressing slowly, if at all, at the whim of others. If such a person changes offices or progresses more quickly, it will be as a reaction to some external pressure. To that kind of person, the professional challenges which motivate others may simply be depressing, particularly if they are beyond that architect's capabilities. Of course, not every architect who stays in the same office is unmotivated. The motivation may be to achieve some personal objective in that office.

A self-starter will determine his or her goals in life, long and short term, and create the appropriate internal pressure required to attain the goals. In fact, the unmotivated architect noted above is not really unmotivated; it is just that the motive is not the accepted kind. It may be to drift along to retirement with the minimum of fuss because the architect in question has some extra-office activity to which work is just a necessary interruption. Self-motivation in this context, however, is generally taken to mean the ability of an individual to drive him or herself without the necessity for any external pressure.

The motivation of others is very difficult. The secret is to discover the individual goals of team members. Motivators are generally seen as achievement, recognition and advancement. Whether an individual acts in particular circumstances depends largely upon whether the action is seen as resulting in the desired outcome. The art of motivation, therefore, is to let the individuals see that their actions are achieving the desired end. The carrot is more effective than the stick. The golden rule for motivating others can be summarised as follows.

- Find out what they want.
- Show them how to get it by doing what you want.
- Ensure they are not disappointed due to your fault.

15 General Office Practice

15.1 Introduction

There are certain basic skills which every architect should have in addition to specific professional skills. This chapter addresses the basic office skills which are essential to everyone who works in the office environment. Architects are usually left to acquire these skills as part of the practice experience. That is not the best way of learning. All architects should have a thorough understanding of good office practice before they enter the office in which they are to work and in which very bad office practice may be the order of the day. What follows is simply an outline of the key areas in which the architect should be proficient in the office. Some are relevant only to architects, some are of wider application.

15.2 Telephone, facsimile (fax) and email

A telephone is essential. There is sophisticated equipment available today which will allow virtually any installation appropriate to the office organisation. Installations may range from a single line to any number of separate lines incorporating facilities for inter-office communication, conference calls, answerphones, speakerphones and video conferencing. Where offices are spread over several buildings, it is possible to have the telephone system set up so that callers to the central switchboard are re-routed to the appropriate building. Sole practitioners can divert all calls to another telephone or to their mobiles when they leave the office. Mobile telephones are now in general use and they can be used for texting, taking photographs and videos. It is also possible to access the internet and to send and receive emails. The more sophisticated hand-held wireless device has improved capabilities for carrying out all kinds of functions as well as the ability for excellent wireless internet access.

Telephone calls should be made and answered promptly and they should be kept as brief as consistent with the object of the call. This is always important, because telephone calls can be costly, but it is particularly important if there are few lines and there may be a risk that outside callers cannot communicate with the office. A competent telephone operator with a good voice and manner is a boon to any office. Such a person is the firm so far as telephone callers are concerned. If the first impression is not good, they will not call again.

There are some basic rules for good telephone management. They include never keeping anyone waiting and keeping a record of incoming calls and messages if the recipient of the call is unavailable. Architects should always keep a written record of telephone calls. The degree of detail in the record will depend on the importance of the call, but the minimum must be the name of the caller and the time of the call. Most telephone calls will warrant more detail than that. Virtually all office telephones now incorporate voicemail facilities as a matter of course, although most people would still prefer to leave messages with a human receptionist.

A particularly annoying habit, so far as the recipient is concerned, is to have a secretary or the switchboard place a call. At the very least, it sends a clear message that the caller is much busier than the called and his or her time is much more valuable. An excuse often given for the practice is that telephoning and getting a busy number or discovering that the particular person is out is time consuming and much better carried out by someone who is costing the firm less than the architect. At first sight, there seems to be some merit in that argument, but it is axiomatic that when the switchboard has eventually made contact with the required person and got that person waiting on the telephone, the original caller has vanished from their desk and cannot be traced for several minutes, if at all. Before indulging in such annoying one-upmanship, the architect should judge the likely reaction of the person receiving the call, which might be to hang up.

Except when returning a call, the person telephoning is doing so with an aim in mind, a particular reason for calling. Courtesy requires that such a person must do the waiting, not the person called.

Although mobile telephones are a real boon to the single-handed practitioner, they must be used with consideration for others. Under the right conditions, listening to one side of another's animated mobile phone conversation may be a source of amusement to while away a tedious train journey, but usually such things are merely irritants. Save for the most pressing of reasons, there can be no excuse for leaving a mobile phone switched on during a meeting. Even then, the permission of the chairperson must be obtained and not assumed. To leave the phone on in normal situations shows the most flagrant disregard for the time of others. It sends everyone a message that the offender believes that he or she is the busiest and most important person present. Some companies arrange important meetings away from the office precisely because they do not want the participants interrupted by telephone calls or urgent consultations. To take a mobile telephone into that environment defeats the object.

Although the telephone has provided a means of transmitting the spoken word for many years, other means are available which enable the user to send letters, pictures and drawings almost instantly from one side of the world to the other. The facsimile (fax) machine has been in use for many years now and it revolutionised the way business was conducted. Sketches could be faxed directly to site and there was no longer any excuse for a delay before the architect confirmed oral instructions.

More recently, email has replaced faxing in large measure. Unfortunately, the ease with which an email can be sent encourages the sending of messages about the most trivial matters. Despite the cautions at the end of many emails to think carefully before printing, it is as essential to retain print-outs of all emails, which are other than trivial, as of other correspondence. Email is really valuable for the transmission of large quantities of text and diagrams, drawings and scanned letters from one place to another. The system is especially useful, because the recipient can make alterations to drafts and return them quickly by the same means. Large quantities of text can be transmitted by fax, but it cannot be amended without retyping or, if the text is very distinct, by scanning.

An architect should remember that an email sent is essentially the same as a letter. It is, when printed out, documentary evidence of something. Too often, emails are considered to be the equivalent of the spoken word of which, of course, usually there is no record. The sender of an email should take as much care as if composing a letter to be sent through the post. There is a growing practice of sending letters by email and by post. If urgent, there is good reason to send a letter by email. If not urgent, the letter should be sent by post. It is usually wasteful to do both.

15.3   Information technology

Many architectural activities that were formerly paper based are now replicated or replaced by computer applications. Although it is beyond the scope of this book to describe them, or indeed information technology generally, in any detail, the architect should be familiar with them and they warrant a brief mention.

Email and computer-aided design (CAD) are described elsewhere in this chapter, but there are other common applications. Word processing software is used by most practices these days. The key advantages are that everyday typing is more efficient, corrections and edits are readily made and standard documents of all kinds can be electronically stored for amending and issue. Word processing packages today are becoming more and more sophisticated with the facility to manipulate text in a variety of ways, to check spelling and grammar and to reference text. Crucially, it is possible to search thousands of files within seconds to find a particular word or phrase.

Spreadsheet programs allow arithmetic and logic operations on numeric data to be performed and they are now available for a wide variety of tasks. Databases are effectively computerised filing systems, which enable data to be manipulated and produced in many different ways to suit different purposes. Therefore, records can be stored for retrieval against different designated criteria. Project planning software is a boon for architects who have to decide the appropriate amounts of extension of time. It allows logic links to be inserted with lead and lag times and the appropriate resources for each activity. This method of working out the amount of extension of time due to the contractor has received judicial approval[1] and every architect's office should have the software. It is also useful to monitor progress as the work progresses.

The quality of printers available now allows inexpensive documents of excellent quality to be produced. For improved presentations, there are easy-to-use desktop publishing and presentation programs available.

15.4   Letter writing

The object of writing a letter is essentially to convey what is in the mind of one person to the mind of another, although the writer may not always wish to be entirely frank and open in the communication, and at the same time to make a permanent record of the communication. The other person is obviously not present to be addressed orally and therefore the writer must convey what would be clear from facial expression or tone of voice by the skill of combining words. Without embarking on a full exposition of the subject, a few suggestions may be made.

- Be sure that the points made are clear.
- Be as brief and simple as possible. Do not use two words if one will do. Avoid long words and convoluted phraseology.
- Start a new paragraph whenever a new point is to be made even if the paragraph is only two lines long. Do not split a point into more than one paragraph.
- If the letter becomes very long, consider whether it might be better to put the contents in the form of a report or schedule with a short covering letter.
- Be sure to write with the reader in mind. Technical terms may provide a useful shortcut when writing to like disciplines, but they should be strictly excluded when writing to non-technical persons. Despite what some architects may think, trying to impress a lay client with difficult words and concepts does not succeed.
- Avoid commercial and business clichés, journalese, Americanisms, slang and jargon.
- Avoid spelling mistakes and bad grammar. They give a poor impression to the reader.
- Avoid the impersonal. 'It is regretted' means nothing. Regret is a personal sentiment; if regret is felt, say 'I regret' or 'We regret'. It may or may not be prudent to say 'the Board' or 'the directors' regret.
- Be definite. Do not say 'this appears to be correct'. If satisfied that it is correct, say so.
- Standard reference books are available which can prove useful in ensuring that well-written letters are sent out.[2]

Some care should be taken over forms of address. Traditionally, men have been addressed as Esquire and women as Mrs or Miss. Today the mode of address is more likely to be Mr, Mrs, Miss or Ms. Whatever form is adopted, qualifications and honours should not be forgotten. When opening a letter, the usual form is 'Dear Sir' or 'Madam' and the ending 'Yours faithfully'. Depending on how well the parties know each other, these forms may become less formal, but in a business letter it is unwise to go beyond Mr, Mrs, Miss or Ms.

Unfortunately, it has become almost the norm for people to write to each other using first names only. At one time such a mode of address was reserved for friends. The use of first names in a business environment can mislead some participants as to the nature of the relationship. If it is purely business, it is better to keep it that way. Remember that letters sometimes end up in court and too much familiarity may come to be regretted.

15.5   Reports

The architect may be specifically asked to write a report, or may decide to do so when a letter looks like becoming long-winded. The art of report writing is a considerable subject on its own, but a few words of guidance are offered by way of assistance.

- Remember who is going to read the report. If it is to be a technical person then technical phraseology is quite acceptable, probably inevitable; the reader will understand what is being said. If the reader is to be a non-technical person or a lay committee, they will be completely at sea unless the report is written in language they can understand.
- Plan the structure of the report. There is nothing worse than a report which is clearly the thoughts of the author just as they have arisen, put down on paper without any consideration as to logical order, often called a 'stream of consciousness'.
- A report should start with an Introduction setting out the subject matter and, if appropriate, who the writer is and his or her qualifications. Then follows the body of the report: it is most logical and effective to note the facts first before going on to matters of opinion. The report should end with a conclusion and usually a request for instructions. It should be signed and dated.
- Adopt a simple and consistent system of numbering. For example:

  1.00 *Introduction*
  1.01 My name is ... etc., etc.
  1.02 I am asked to report on ... etc., etc.
  2.00 *Extensions of time*
  2.01 Extensions have been granted as follows:

- Take care with the English, the punctuation and the spelling. A good report reads well; bad English, poor punctuation and a plethora of wrongly spelled words give the worst possible impression.
- Report on that which has been asked for. Cut out all unnecessary verbiage; it may add to the bulk of the report, but it adds little or nothing to the

content. Better a short, pithy report than a long rambling version, which runs the risk of boring the reader and thus never being read.

■ Read over the final version very carefully; much may hinge on your efforts.

There are several useful books available on the subject of report writing.[3]

15.6 Filing

15.6.1 Correspondence and reports

Once the letters and reports have been written, the office copies together with letters, reports facsimiles, etc. received have to be filed.

The secret of good filing is to ensure that any document can be found quickly. Much time and cost, to say nothing of frustration and temper, can be expended in trying to trace a wrongly filed document.

The complexity of the filing will depend largely on the complexity of the project. A simple project will probably warrant a single file. More complicated ones may require a series of files for, say, architect, client, contractor, quantity surveyor, engineer, etc. Other files will be required for special matters such as partners' personal file, insurances and professional bodies.

As well as letters, the files should contain such things as reports, telephone messages and internal memos. These will help to complete the history of the project and they may prove to be invaluable later, particularly in legal matters where the side with the best records is going to be at a great advantage.

Typical files for a medium-to-large project might be:

■ correspondence: client, funder, etc.
■ correspondence: statutory undertakings, planning, building control
■ correspondence: consultant quantity surveyor
■ correspondence: contractor
■ mechanical and electrical services
■ structural
■ landscaping
■ clerk of works' reports
■ site meetings
■ architect's instructions
■ certificates, valuations
■ financial reports.

Another system which should not be overlooked is electronic data storage. There are many advantages to storing all data this way and only one of these is space. Obviously, enormous quantities of information can be stored on hard disks, floppy disks, zip disks, CD-ROM and memory sticks. Technology has advanced to the stage that documents of all kinds can be scanned onto disk very rapidly. The document can be retrieved and read on a monitor in an instant. Moreover, the system can be arranged to search for and display all documents of a particular kind or documents which deal with a particular topic. In short, it is easier to find a piece of correspondence after it has been stored electronically thaN before. The material can be guarded so that 'read only' access is available, or it can be manipulated in any convenient way.

There are some warnings. Electronic data are much more ephemeral than something on paper. It is essential to keep back-up copies of the data, because disks, even hard disks, can corrupt without warning and it is also possible to corrupt a disk physically, for example, by trying to remove it while the computer is trying to read from, or write to, it. Even though documents may be scanned and consigned to disk in some form, the original documents should not be destroyed straight away. There are some documents which must never be destroyed, such as contracts and various statutory permissions. It could be argued that ordinary documents, such as correspondence associated with administering a building contract, should never be destroyed. There is always a risk that a document will be needed many years after the building is completed. Most architects, however, would probably feel comfortable destroying original correspondence 6 years after the issue of the final certificate if the contract was executed under hand and 12 years after if the contract was executed as a deed. The fact that copies are still held electronically should suffice to deal with any queries after that date. Nowadays, there is no excuse for destroying all trace of any document.

Although electronic storage of documents is very useful, particularly when the project is finished and all the defects made good, architects should beware of the paperless office concept which has been advocated by many people. Although in some instances it may be feasible to have all incoming and outgoing correspondence and all other documents and drawings on disk with no paper print-outs, it is a dangerous practice. Computers may cease to function at any time and electronic files may be lost.

15.6.2 Drawings

The common use of CAD has led to a decreased use of drawings in hard copy in the office where all work and examination of drawings are done on screen. However, it is still easiest to examine a drawing in hard copy rather than on a screen and many small practices are not prepared to forsake traditional methods. Where drawings are still used in hard copy, drawings in current use should be filed flat in plan chests or vertically in cabinets. They should not be folded or rolled. Negatives, office prints and specialists' drawings, if possible, should be kept separate. Rough sketches which are probably prepared on pieces of paper of various sizes can be folded and kept in large paper envelopes or box files. For site use, especially where small contractors are concerned, drawings in hard copy are essential. Larger contractors will receive their drawings by electronic means and only if absolutely necessary will drawings be printed out.

When a drawing has been revised, the out-of-date print should be clearly marked 'superseded' and filed separately. Large paper envelopes can be procured for filing such drawings which, of course, can be folded if necessary. All drawing cabinets, box files or envelopes which are used for storing drawings should be marked with the appropriate number or reference.

Drawings which are removed from the plan chest should be returned as soon as possible, and in a large office it will be necessary to devise a form of register in which a record can be kept of any drawings which have been taken out with the names of the borrowers. In some large local authority and government offices, the filing and registration of drawings are undertaken by a clerk who is solely responsible for ordering prints, loaning drawings and keeping them in safe custody.

For convenience, except in a very large office, the drawing cabinets will be kept in the drawing offices, so that quick reference can be made to drawings of current jobs. It should be part of the daily routine to put all drawings away at night; they should not be used as dust sheets or the reverse for rough sketches. In the modern architect's office, the sight of a drawing is becoming something of a rarity, except perhaps when pinned up on the wall for reference purposes.

When a job is finished, the drawings should be brought up to date, removed from the drawing office and suitably filed. That is a counsel of perfection, but it will pay dividends later if it is observed. Unless a large amount of storage accommodation is available, only the electronic format or the negatives of hand-produced drawings need to be retained, as it will be more convenient to order new prints if they are subsequently required.

Traditionally, old negatives were filed in metal tubes which were stacked in racks. A tube 150 mm in diameter will store about 200 drawings. An alternative method of storage was in large paper envelopes which had the advantage of storing the drawings flat. These envelopes could be stacked vertically or clamped with wooden strips on one edge and slung from a bar rather like a coat hanger on a rail. An index should, of course, be kept of all old drawings in store.

However, even the smallest businesses can microfilm important information. Saving as it does tremendous space and being easily catalogued and retrieved, microfilm and microfiche is probably the best method of storage for architectural drawing records. Drawings produced by CAD will obviously be stored electronically with separate copies of each revision.

15.7   Office-based meetings

See Chapter 12, section 12.2.

15.8   Drawing office practice

Although the use of computers to produce drawings is widespread (see section 15.9 below), some practices still rely on hand drawing at least for some drawings and it is comparatively rare to find an architect's office which does not contain one traditional drawing board. Every architect should study the relevant British Standard on drawing practice whether using computers or the traditional method.[4] Where, as in the construction industry, clear communication is all-important, there is no room for an architect who employs exceptionally personalised drawing techniques. One of the byproducts of CAD is to eradicate idiosyncratic draughtsmanship although some might regret its passing. Many of the mistakes which occur on a construction site undoubtedly stem from a misreading of drawings and any attempt to co-ordinate symbols, hatching and representational methods of all kinds is to be welcomed. In some cases an exception may be made for drawings which are purely for the purpose of explaining the proposals to a client. It is not proposed to dwell especially on this type of drawing, because this is one thing which architects quickly learn to do very well.[5]

Certain basic information must be included on every drawing.

- Firm's name
- Address and telephone number
- Project title
- Drawing title
- Drawing number with revision number and description if appropriate
- Scale
- Date drawn and dates of revisions if appropriate
- Name or initials of draftsman
- North point on plans

It is common for a practice to have a set of standard sized drawing sheets pre-printed with the basic information and firm's logo, if applicable. Alternatively, it can be incorporated into the CAD information. Where grid lines are used to position structural elements or for modular purposes, they should be carefully referenced. It is usual to use numbers along one axis and letters along the other. Vertical positioning is best done by levels referenced to a datum. Such horizontal and vertical references must be used consistently, not only by architects but by other consultants also.

If all parties creating or using the drawings stick to this system of referencing, the chance of errors due to ambiguous descriptions will be minimised and time saved. Thus the vague: 'wall next to splayed abutment opposite general office on second floor' becomes more simply and accurately: 'wall between refs R4 and 5 on floor level 10.600'. The 'general office' will be unidentifiable during building operations (and perhaps after practical completion) except on a drawing and what constitutes a 'splayed abutment' is anyone's guess.

Time and clarity are served if symbols are used to show such items as WCs, washbasins, kitchen units, etc. rather than having them drawn out in meticulous detail.

Some offices adopt the practice of using standard details. This can be very useful for items which recur, such as access panels, cills, lintels, eaves, door frames and casings, windows, architraves, skirtings, etc. Although the same standard details will not be suitable for every project, architects should resist the temptation to design a totally fresh detail for everything on every project, bearing in mind that standard details should evolve over the years to represent the very best detail which that office can produce for a particular situation.

When a drawing is amended, it should be obvious from a numbering change (e.g. No. 1/103 to No. 1/103A) and a note on the drawing should state precisely what change has been made to the drawing.

15.8.1 Dimensions

Dimensions form one of the most important items of instruction to the quantity surveyor and later to the contractor. Incorrect dimensions are a constant source of problems on site.

A block plan must give overall dimensions of the building, setting out dimensions for all foundations and walls, together with their thicknesses. In practice, many architects do not understand what information a contractor needs in order to be able to set out properly on the site, yet most standard form contracts make the architect responsible for producing that information and probably such responsibility would be implied if not expressed. The contractor needs to be able to locate at least one, and preferably two, base lines on site. To do that, each point at the end of the base line must be securely fixed, by triangulation, from an already established known point (see Fig. 15.1).

If a building has a steel or reinforced concrete frame, the setting out of the centre lines of stanchions should be shown on the foundation plan. The contours of the site should be shown and the levels of foundation bottoms, with positions of steps indicated. Levels should be referenced to an established datum. A key on the drawing should make clear the difference between existing and proposed levels. A simple system is to put each existing level in a small box or show it in a different colour.

Floor plans should show levels, detailed dimensions of rooms, corridors, thicknesses of walls and partitions, widths of openings, etc. Care must be taken that dimension lines are not capable of confusion with lines representing part of the building. It is usual to show the extremities of each dimension by a clear arrowhead, cross, dot or other symbol. Figures must be clearly printed or written, particularly the stop separating the metres from decimal parts.

In a new building, the quantity surveyor and the contractor should have no doubt about the exact heights of, and dimensions between, walls in both directions of all rooms, including all recesses, cupboards formed by partitions, passages, etc. Where working between existing walls, it may be necessary to leave one of a series of dimensions to be verified on site, but all others should be given.

The finished floor and roof levels should be shown on the plans as well as on the sections, and it should be clear what allowance the contractor is to make for the difference between structural and finished surfaces. All doors and windows must be referenced so that they can be easily found in appropriate schedules.

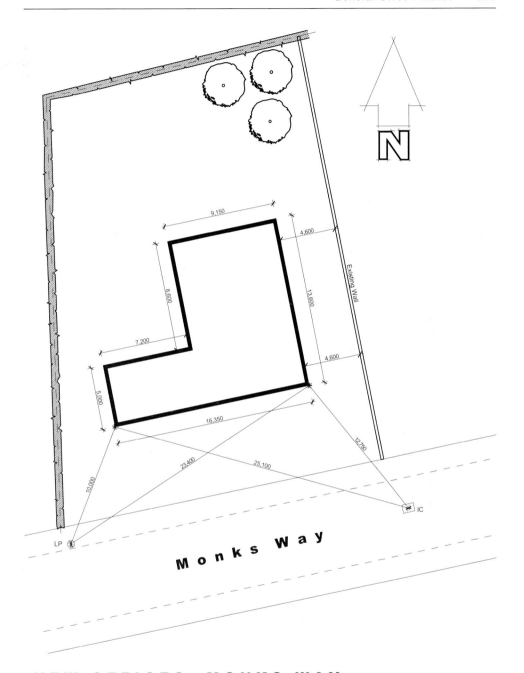

NEW OFFICES - MONKS WAY
PURLINGHAM

Fig. 15.1   Setting out plan.

Sections should be drawn through portions of the building where floor or roof levels vary, at the intersection of parts of the building, through staircases and any other places which are not shown elsewhere. To explain really difficult parts of the construction, isometric and planometric views should be used. The position at which sections are taken should be clearly marked on all floor plans. Floor levels and heights of rooms should be shown and on 1:20 scale sections where the walls are to be constructed in brick or block, it is a good idea to incorporate a brick/block scale, so that the levels of lintel, cill, wallplate, sole-plate, floor bearings, etc. can be properly related to courses. It is also helpful if the materials in the larger sections are indicated by appropriate hatching.

The elevations, besides indicating the external appearance of the building, the different materials used and the finished ground levels against the building, should also show the floor and basement levels dotted on and dimensioned, the levels of damp-proof courses, the opening portions of windows, external flashings and weatherings, vent pipes, rainwater pipes and the stepping to foundations. Windows and doors can be numbered on elevations as well. The golden rule of never showing anything on one drawing that can be found elsewhere may save a little time, but it sacrifices the very useful extra check provided by the inclusion of such details.

It is sensible to include a note on each drawing that figured dimensions are to be followed in preference to scaled measurements. The need for figured dimensions can be reduced considerably if grids are used to represent not only locations but also standard dimensions. 300 mm is a common grid measurement.

15.8.2   Lettering

An advantage of CAD is that lettering is clearly printed. It is essential to choose a style and size of lettering appropriate to the drawing and to remember that the purpose of the drawing is, usually, to show the contractor what is to be done in order to produce the building on site. Architects still have to produce drawings by hand from time to time. Neatness and clarity in lettering are essential and, to achieve the best results, the letters should not too large and should be evenly spaced out. The lettering should be kept as simple as possible and individual styling should be eschewed. Italic script, for example, can be very attractive in a letter and when carefully executed, but at the hands of many hard-pressed architects, it can become neat but unreadable. Stencils can be used, but they are never so quick as good hand lettering. Another option is the typed adhesive strip (the typescript must be dense) or the rub-off transfers which can be used for other parts of the drawings as well as lettering. However, CAD has replaced the need to produce drawings in the traditional way in most circumstances.

15.8.3   Negatives and basic layout drawings

The preparation of drawings by electronic means and the ability to transmit such drawings between consultants have all but removed the need for negatives. This process enables architects to provide the same basic information to various consultants to enable them to work it up into various forms. For example, the basic floor plans may be sent out before notes and additional information are added so that separate drawings can be provided for heating and electrical layouts, floor and ceiling designs, duct layouts, etc. based on the same constructional layouts.

Before such drawings could be produced by electronic means, they were prepared on translucent material, so that several copies could be obtained for distribution; it was common for drawings to be printed onto plastic sheet rather than being drawn directly on it.

There are various grades of tracing paper, still generally being used for sketching and scribbling initial design ideas. It is well worth while using a good, stout quality of paper, as not only will it stand up to frequent handling much better, but it will allow quite a lot of ink erasing without falling to pieces. Many architects still prefer detail paper for sketching. Plastic sheets are available, although less used, which have a very good ink surface, more transparent than stout tracing paper and better able to stand handling and erasing.

A frequent problem is that when the contract documents are to be prepared, the architect finds that the drawings on which the contractors tendered and which must therefore, with agreed amendments, become the contract drawings, have been altered and updated. Problems of this kind can be avoided if a set of drawings is stored electronically at tender stage especially for the purpose of preparing the contract documents in due course.

15.9 Computer-aided design

Most offices now use computers for the production of drawings, but there are few offices in which computers are the only design tool and there are still offices which do not use CAD at all. Some systems are easier than others; it is generally agreed that working in CAD is slower in the initial stages of producing the drawings, but that it is far easier to make amendments to the drawings and the way that the system works means that amendments to one drawing are reflected throughout all related information. This clearly removes the old problems of trying to remember every drawing affected when amendments were carried out on one.

The only way to learn to use CAD and to understand the possibilities is to sit at the computer and experiment after the initial period of instruction in the particular system. At the current state of the art, computers are not capable of thinking for themselves. The old adage 'rubbish in, rubbish out' is still true. The computer will only do what the operator instructs. It is unlikely that computers will ever replace the pencil and paper approach of the designing architect who wants to scribble around testing various design approaches but they are very useful for testing a design once produced. They can reveal the design in three dimensions from any chosen viewpoint, and they can be programmed to produce a virtual reality impression of a walk through the building if sufficient data are input into the system.

If basic design information is put into the computer at an early stage, it can eventually form the basis of computer-drafted production information. Computer images can be combined with programs which allow investigation of acoustics, heating, insulation, day lighting levels and so on. There is also the benefit of being able to plot all services and reproduce perspective views to identify possible conflict areas.

Computer-aided design is moving forward very quickly and highly sophisticated software enables full interrogation of designs at an early stage. No architect can afford to ignore these developments.

15.10 Presentation

The way in which architects present proposals to clients is largely a matter of personal choice. The truth is that whatever works is right. A client's capability to understand a scheme should never be overestimated. Many otherwise highly intelligent people find difficulty in understanding plans, sections and elevations, which is why models, perspectives and virtual reality productions are so popular. Despite the fact that computer programs can produce all kinds of interesting images, most clients still like to see a model. They like to be able to take it away and get a real understanding of the three-dimensional qualities of the building. It is useful for architects to get into the habit of producing simple working models. Models which clearly explain the scheme at the stage it has reached are worth any number of drawings to a client.

When making a presentation to a client, a model should be the basis so that the client can quickly get an idea of the scheme. Then plans can be used to elaborate and freely drawn perspectives used to show what it will actually look like. Sections and elevations are little use to a client. A building never looks like its elevations and sections are too complex for the average client to understand. It is easier to make a quick sectional model to explain any complex parts of the building and many times more effective. The virtual reality walkthrough, mentioned above, can also be invaluable to a client who may have difficulty visualising the building with all its floor, wall and ceiling finishes by means of drawings and models alone.

Plans should be clearly drawn with the room name printed in each room. The use of a key at the side of the drawing together with a number in each room can be irritating. It is helpful to include a drawn scale on the drawing and also one or two dimensions. Any part of the building which is especially important or which needs particular consideration should be drawn out to a larger scale and a separate model prepared, if possible.

Some architects produce highly intricate drawings and involved renderings to impress the client. The client may well be impressed and also confused. If the client fails to understand the drawing, approval could be given for something which may be a source of disappointment and aggravation when built.

15.11   Reproduction

It is becoming uncommon for drawings to be reproduced on paper. They are usually consulted solely on the computer screen and exchanged electronically between consultants, contractors and sub-contractors. If drawings in hard copy are required, they are usually produced by computer print-out. In the now comparatively rare instances where drawings are produced in the traditional way on a plastic negative, prints are produced by using light-sensitive paper on which the image turns black. Many practices used to have their own print machines, but now specialist printers will provide a service. Small drawings, up to A3, are often printed by photocopier which tends to give a clearer, crisper image than normal printing.

15.12   Work programming

Programming of any kind is a difficult business. Programming a project in an office is complex because there are so many imponderables, yet there is a need to programme such work, otherwise when the client asks, 'Will it be ready to go out to tender in 2 months?', the architect has no way of answering.

The basis for planning any project should be the RIBA Plan of Work. The stages usefully split up the work to be done. The next thing is probably to decide whether the project deserves one, two or more people working on it for any or all of the stages. For example, it is quite possible that a project may need only one person in the early stages and expand to require more people at stage D. The question, of course, is how many people and for how long.

The only safe way of getting to this answer is to consult historical records and look at the fees. In most cases, the fee will depend on how long the architect estimates involvement. Every office should have time sheets for this very purpose. Only by looking at the time needed to carry out a comparable project can an estimate of future time requirements be formulated after adjustment to take account of any differences. Work programming is a serious matter where failure can result in disaster for the practice. All members of staff, including partners, must realise that the accurate completion of current time sheets is essential (see Chapter 16, section 16.15).

References

1. In *John Barker Construction Ltd* v. *London Portman Hotels Ltd* (1996) 12 Const LJ 277; *Balfour Beatty* v. *London Borough of Lambeth* [2002] BLR 288.
2. *Concise Oxford Dictionary* (1999) 10th edn, Oxford University Press; Gowers, E. (1987) *The Complete Plain Words*, 3rd edn, Stationery Office; Allen, R. (ed) (1999) *Fowler's Pocket Modern English Usage*, Oxford University Press; Palmer, R. (1992) *Write in Style*, E & F Spon; Chappell, D. (2008) *Standard Letters in Architectural Practice*, 4th edn, Blackwell Publishing.

3. Chappell, D. (1996) *Report Writing for Architects and Project Managers*, 3rd edn, Blackwell Science.
4. British Standards Institution (2008) *BS 1192: 2007 Collaborative Production of Architectural, Engineering and Construction Information. Code of Practice*, British Standards Institution.
5. Hill, M. (1999) *Guide to Drawn Information*, RIBA Publications.

16 Finance and Accounts

16.1 Introduction

The subject of finance and accountancy is now part of most undergraduate courses. It is a practical form of economics and as such is important to the architect in general. It is also useful to have an elementary understanding of the subject. Larger practices and companies will have finance and accounts departments with specialist accountancy staff, whereas within smaller organisations all financial matters are dealt with by senior management.

16.2 The accounts

The primary purpose of keeping accounts is to provide a record of all the financial transactions of the business, and to establish whether or not the business is making a profit. The accounts will also be used:

- in determining the distributions to be made to equity shareholders
- in determining the partners' or company's tax liabilities
- to support an application to a bank for funding
- to determine the value of the business in the event of a sale
- as a proof of financial standing to clients and suppliers.

All limited companies are required under the Companies Acts to produce accounts and to file them annually with the Registrar of Companies in order that they are available for inspection by any interested party.

The principal accounting statements are the profit and loss account and the balance sheet.

16.3 Profit and loss account

The profit and loss account records the results of the business's trading income and expenditure over a period of time. For an architectural practice, income will represent sales in the form of fees received for the supply of architectural services; expenditure is likely to include such items as salaries, rent and insurance. After adjustments have been made for accruals (revenue earned or expenses incurred that have not been paid or received) and pre-payments

Profit and loss account for the four months to 30 April 2009		
	£	£
Income		
Fees received – Sales		300,000
Expenditure		
Salaries	150,000	
Rent	50,000	
Others	30,000	
Depreciation	20,000	250,000
Profit for the period		£50,000

Fig. 16.1   Example profit and loss account.

(advance payments for goods or services not yet provided), an excess of income over expenditure indicates that a profit has been made. The reverse would indicate a loss.

The preparation of the profit and loss account will enable the business to:

- compare actual performance against budget
- analyse the performance of different sections within the business
- forecast future performance
- compare performance against other businesses
- calculate the amount of tax due.

An example of a simple profit and loss account is shown in Fig. 16.1.

16.4   Balance sheet

The balance sheet (Fig. 16.2) gives a statement of a business's assets and liabilities as at a particular date. The balance sheet will include all or most of the following:

- *fixed assets:* those assets held for long-term use by the business, including intangible assets
- *current assets:* those assets held as part of the business's working capital
- *liabilities:* amounts owed by the business to suppliers and banks
- *owner's capital:* shareholders' funds (issued share capital plus reserves) in a limited company, or the partners' capital accounts in a partnership.

The various types of asset and liability accounts are considered in more detail below.

Balance sheet as at 30 April 2009

	£	£
Fixed assets		
Fixtures and fittings		200,000
Less: Depreciation		20,000
		180,000
Current assets		
Debtors (fees receivable)	60,000	
Cash at bank	60,000	
	120,000	
Current liabilities		
Creditors	50,000	
Net current assets (working capital)		70,000
Net assets		£250,000
Capital		200,000
Retained profits		50,000
		£250,000

Fig. 16.2   Example balance sheet.

16.5   Assets

The term 'assets' covers the following:

- *intangible assets,* which include goodwill, trademarks and licensing agreements, usually at original cost less any subsequent write-offs
- *fixed assets,* which include land and buildings, fixtures and fittings, equipment and cars, shown at cost or valuation less accumulated depreciation
- *current assets,* which are held at the lower cost or net realisable value. Current assets include cash, stock, work in progress, debtors and accruals in respect of payments made in advance.

Depreciation, referred to above, records the loss of value in an asset resulting from usage or age. Depreciation is charged as an expense to the profit and loss account, but is disallowed and therefore added back, for tax purposes. Depreciation is recorded as a credit in the balance sheet, reducing the carrying value of the firm or company's fixed assets.

16.6 Liabilities

Liabilities include amounts owing for goods and services supplied to the business and amounts due in respect of loans received. Strictly it also includes amounts owed to the business's owners: the business's partners or shareholders. It should be noted that contingent liabilities do not form part of the total liabilities, but will appear in the form of a note on the balance sheet as supplementary information.

16.7 Capital

Sources of capital may include proprietors' or partners' capital or, for a limited company, proceeds from shares issued. Capital is required to fund the start-up and subsequent operation of the business for the period prior to that period in which sufficient funds are received as payment for work undertaken by the business.

The example in Fig. 16.2 identifies an initial capital investment of £200,000; however, this investment is soon represented not by the cash invested but by various other assets and liabilities, as shown.

To illustrate the movement of cash in terms of receipts and payments, a simple example of a cash book summary is included in Fig. 16.3. This summary is produced periodically, usually monthly, and is the source of the cash postings to the other books of account.

16.8 Finance

There are several ways in which a business can supplement its finances. The most common way is by borrowing from a bank on an overdraft facility. The lender will be interested in securing both the repayment of the capital lent and the interest accruing on the loan. The lender will therefore require copies of the business's profit and loss account, balance sheet and details of its projected cash flow.

Receipts	£	Payments	£
Capital introduced	200,000	Salaries	150,000
Fees received	240,000	Rent	50,000
		Other expenses	30,000
		Fixtures and fittings	150,000
		Balance carried forward	60,000
	£440,000		£440,000

Fig. 16.3 Example cash book summary.

16.9   Cash forecasting and budgeting

It is necessary for a business to predict how well it is likely to perform in financial terms in the future. Budgets are therefore prepared, usually on an annual basis, based on projected income and expenditure. Once a business is established, future projections can be based to a certain extent on the previous year's results.

As mentioned above, if it is the intention to borrow money from a bank then the bank is likely to request a cash-flow forecast for the next 6 or 12months. The preparation of a cash-flow forecast is a relatively easy process and in practice a computerised spreadsheet package or accounting software will be used to project the likely phasing of receipts and payments.

The example cash-flow forecast in Fig. 16.4 illustrates the starting up of a professional business. It identifies the initial introduction of capital, the borrowing facility requested and the projected effect of expenditure and receipts over the period. It can be seen from the forecast that an additional £10,000 of funding will be required in April and a further (£25,000–£10,000) = £15,000 in May.

This cash flow is typical of a business start-up, when substantial sums are spent in advance of income being received. Provided the business is run profitably, the outflow should be reversed before too long.

	January	February	March	April	May	June
Capital introduced	200,000	—	—	—	—	—
Fees received	60,000	180,000	50,000	110,000	100,000	200,000
Asset sales	—	—	—	—	—	—
Receipts	260,000	180,000	50,000	110,000	100,000	200,000
Salaries	75,000	75,000	75,000	75,000	75,000	75,000
Rent	25,000	25,000	25,000	25,000	25,000	25,000
Equipment	100,000	50,000	20,000	30,000	—	—
Others	15,000	15,000	15,000	15,000	15,000	15,000
Payments	215,000	165,000	135,000	145,000	115,000	115,000
Movement in cash	45,000	15,000	(85,000)	(35,000)	(15,000)	85,000
Balance brought forward	—	45,000	60,000	(25,000)	(60,000)	(75,000)
Balance carried forward	45,000	60,000	(25,000)	(60,000)	(75,000)	10,000
Borrowing facility	50,000	50,000	50,000	50,000	50,000	50,000
Additional requirement	—	—	—	10,000	25,000	—

Fig. 16.4   Example cash-flow forecast.

16.10 Books of account

The underlying books of account are likely to comprise the general ledger (which will include all general items such as salaries and rents), and totals from the subsidiary ledgers such as the sales ledger (fees or other income receivable), the bought ledger (accounts payable), the cash book (a record of the bank transactions) and the petty cash account. Other books, such as fee and expenses books, may also be kept.

In addition to the books of account, businesses must retain vouchers such as receipts, invoices, fee accounts and bank statements to support the accounting records. These are required by businesses' auditors and for VAT purposes.

16.11 Fee invoicing

Fees are the lifeblood of all professional organisations and their payment at the earliest opportunity aids cash flow and limits the need for borrowings. It is prudent therefore to make provision for the payment of fees by instalments at regular intervals or, as is becoming more common, relative to achieved milestones.

Fees can be in the form of lump sum(s), a percentage of the construction work, reimbursement of time expended at agreed rates or a combination of these, all depending on the basis of the agreement entered into (see Chapter 6, section 6.3).

Fee accounts can be raised either as VAT invoices or as applications for payment which have different implications with regard to VAT, as described in the next section.

A schedule of all raised fee accounts should be kept in order to monitor payments, pursue outstanding debts and for accounting purposes.

16.12 VAT

VAT is a UK tax collected on business transactions in the form of output and input taxes. Output tax is the VAT due on taxable supplies, which in relation to professional consultants is charged on the fees for the provision of services to clients. Input tax is the VAT charged on most business purchases and expenses.

The time of supply of the services is defined as the 'taxpoint'. In respect of the provision of professional services, this is generally the date of issue of a VAT invoice. Such invoices must include specific information including the VAT registration number and separately identify the fees invoiced exclusive of VAT, the rate of VAT and the value of VAT charged.

Within the construction industry, an alternative to issuing VAT invoices is the use of 'authenticated receipts', which can be used for the supply of goods and services made under contracts which provide for periodic payments to be made. They must include the same relevant detail as a VAT invoice, but their use has the effect of delaying the tax point to the time when payment is received and the authenticated receipt is issued.

Up-to-date VAT records must be kept for completion of VAT returns and to enable HM Revenue & Customs to readily check the figures. Tax returns are sent to HM Revenue & Customs together with any tax due, i.e. excess of output tax over input tax during the tax period concerned.

16.13   Computerisation

Accounting functions have become less time consuming through the use of computers for the regular and routine entries and calculations that are necessary. Entries can be allocated to different accounts, and up-to-date information can be retrieved quickly and efficiently in a variety of formats to meet particular needs. This greatly assists in the financial management of a business.

16.14   Annual accounts/auditing

At the end of a business's financial year, 'end-of-year' accounts are prepared, bringing together all the previous year's financial information in the form of a profit and loss account and balance sheet as described earlier.

In most circumstances, accounts will be audited by an independent accountant; indeed, this is a requirement for all larger limited companies under the Companies Acts. Audited accounts will carry more authority with HM Revenue & Customs and are also useful to prove to third parties, including prospective clients, that the financial status of the business has been independently scrutinised.

16.15   Staff time records

It is necessary for detailed records to be kept of the time worked by each member of staff. The purpose is twofold:

- as a basis on which to build up an account for fees for services that will be charged for on a time basis
- to establish the cost for each particular project. Such costs will be used primarily to establish whether a particular project is making a profit or a loss, but may also be used to estimate a fee to be quoted for similar future work.

The RIBA Standard Form of Agreement for the Appointment of an Architect (SFA/99 (updated 2004)) clause 5.9 and the RIBA Standard Agreement 2010 clause 5.13 commit the architect to maintaining records of time spent on

Weekly TimeSheet

| Name | | | | | | Grade | | Wk Ending | | |

Project Description	Mon		Tues		Wed		Thurs		Fri		Sat		Sun		Code	Project No.	Rate
	Basic	O/T	Basic	O/T	Basic	O/T	Basic	O/T	Basic	O/T	Basic	O/T	Basic	O/T			
Office Administration																	
Training/Study Leave																	
Public Holidays																	
Annual Holidays																	
Sick																	
Other																	
TOTAL																	

Fig. 16.5 Sample timesheet.

services performed on a time basis. These records must be produced to the client on request. Even without this stipulation, it is difficult to see how a time charge could be made without timesheets.

Unless the means is available for an office to monitor its progress in a methodical way and assess performance at the end of a project, project planning remains pure guesswork. Although practice varies, the filling in of timesheets is usually restricted to technical staff, with secretarial and administration costs being treated as overheads, as it is difficult to allocate such time to projects. For the same reason, principals and partners rarely complete timesheets for the whole of their time. Of course, partners must keep a record of their time if it is intended to charge a client on this basis and indeed, it is good practice for partners to keep proper timesheets in order to check how time is allocated against each project.

Most offices have their own ideas about recording time and costing, but a typical procedure is as follows. Timesheets are completed at the end of each week and collected. All hours worked are then input into the accounts system and when costed out, it is possible to determine whether the project is financially on target, from a business point of view. Graphs can also be plotted to show the relationship between forecast and actual expenditure. Time charges to the client become simply a matter of extracting the hours for each member of staff and multiplying them by the appropriate rate.

It should never be thought that it does not matter whether the timesheet is filled in accurately or not. It is common for architects to be lax in filling in timesheets, often leaving them until the end of the week when it is possible that inaccurate records are set down.

It is important to log every time a different project is worked on and therefore the timesheet should be kept to hand at all times (or, as more likely nowadays, be readily accessible on the PC) and be filled in throughout the day. Most solicitors work in this way and there could be a lesson in that! It is equally important not to become overly scrupulous about timesheets, but common sense should be used.

Prompt and accurate feedback to the architects responsible for each project is an indispensable part of the system. If it can be seen, at an early stage, that the allocated time will over-run, steps can be taken to deal with it. If a particular project is taking up too much time, all attempts should be made to recover the situation, but this should not include allocating time to other projects. This undermines the whole purpose of keeping accurate time records. Furthermore, the reason why a particular project is over-running may be because the original estimate of time was low or because the client changed his mind at an important stage and should be charged extra fees. If the timesheets are fabricated, a nonsense is made of the office records on which future estimates will be made.

An example of a timesheet is shown in Fig. 16.5.

17 Insurance

17.1 Introduction

This topic is included because it is important for every architect. Insurance is a contract between the insurer and the insured. Some kinds of insurance, however, are more important for some architects than others. For example, the insurance of premises and public liability rests firmly with the partners or directors, but professional indemnity insurance affects every architect. What follows is of necessity a brief summary of the main kinds of insurance which an architect meets with during a professional career.

Insurance is very complex and an experienced broker should always be consulted. There are, however, two important principles which should be understood by anyone taking out insurance.

- *Uberrimae fidei*: of the utmost good faith.
- *Subrogation*: standing in the place of another.

Uberrimae fidei

The basic principle is that the party seeking insurance must disclose all material facts whether the insurer specifically asks for them or not. Failure to make such disclosure can render the contract voidable. Thus, an architect must reveal all circumstances in the past which might lead to a future claim, etc. when seeking professional indemnity insurance.

Subrogation

If an insurer pays out to a third party in respect of a claim against the insured, the insurer has the right to stand in the place of the insured for the purposes of recovering against any other person who may be liable in respect of the claim. A simple example will make this clear. Where a firm has professional indemnity insurance (see 17.5 below), an employee may perform a negligent action which leads to the firm being sued for negligence by its client. If the insurer pays out in respect of the claim, it is entitled to stand in the place of the firm and take action against the employee to recover the full amount paid out. To avoid this distressing situation, most professional indemnity policies contain a waiver of subrogation in favour of the firm's employees. In other words, the insurer agrees not to exercise rights of subrogation against any employee whose negligent action lay at the root of the claim against the firm.

17.2   Premises and contents

Loss or damage of the office and contents is potentially disastrous for a practice. The first thing to decide is the beneficiaries under the policy. In the case of a partnership, all the partners may own the property jointly or one may own and lease to the rest. Alternatively, the premises may be leased from a landlord and the practice may be only one of a number of tenants in the same building.

It is essential that the policy should provide protection for the partners or directors and the possibility of the insurance company exercising rights of subrogation should not be ignored. Thus, in the case of a tenant responsible for fire damage to the landlord's property, the landlord will be able to claim from the insurers, but they may subsequently take action to recover from the negligent tenant.

The basis of insurance will usually be 'full reinstatement', i.e. the insurers make no deductions for dilapidations. Care must be taken that sufficient cover is purchased and that the appropriate perils are included. If the premises are underinsured, the result will be that in the case of loss, the insurers will only pay out a proportion of the amount claimed.

The contents of an architectural practice are particularly vulnerable to damage, consisting as they do largely of paper and electronic material representing many hours of work. It is essential that a practice takes a proper inventory of the contents of the office and updates it regularly. So far as drawings are concerned, their value for insurance purposes must include the estimated cost of redrawing them after total destruction. Expensive pieces of equipment such as computers must receive special consideration and if equipment is to be used outside the office, for example laptops, the insurance must cover such use.

17.3   Public liability

This insurance must be taken out and maintained to cover the liability of the practice to third parties for injury or death or damage to property as a result of the negligence of the partners or one of its employees. The insurance does not cover professional negligence (see 17.5 below). A large indemnity limit should be specified (£2,000,000 plus) and it should be upgraded at regular intervals, because if a court gives an award in excess of the insurance cover, the additional amount must be borne by the practice. Where the practice becomes involved in other activities, such as social events or car parking facilities, etc., the insurance cover should be appropriately extended.

17.4 Employer's liability

A practice is required by law to take out insurance to provide an indemnity against its liabilities to its employees.[1] The indemnity should be unlimited. The policy is to cover death or injury and it includes sickness provided that:

- it arises in the course of employment; and
- the employer has legal liability.

Examples of such liability could be employer's breaches of the Factories Acts or Employer's Liability (Defective Equipment) Act 1969, unsafe systems of work or the negligent acts of other employees or an employee being attacked while going to the bank.

17.5 Professional indemnity

This is probably the most important area of insurance for all architects. Every practice should have an adequate level of insurance to cover the possible negligence of its staff. This is a requirement of the ARB Code of Professional Conduct and Practice (Standard 8). Failure to take out and maintain appropriate cover will render the architect liable to severe penalties.

Although no architect likes to contemplate the possibility of facing a claim for professional negligence, few practices escape such a claim or the threat of such a claim at some period. The insurance is for the benefit of both practice and clients. It ensures that there is a fund to compensate a client if the architect is found to have been professionally negligent and it also protects the practice against the chance that it is held liable in respect of a large sum which the practice would otherwise have to find from its own resources. Although one might hope that a client would not press a claim to the extent of making all the partners bankrupt, it does happen and the good nature of a client facing a huge bill to correct the consequences of an architect's negligent design could be overstretched. The subject is complex and a specialist text on the subject should be studied.[2]

There are certain important points to bear in mind regarding professional indemnity insurance.

- Premiums are high.
- The scope of professional activity carried out must be declared. The information provided must be accurate, because anything which is not declared may not be covered by the insurers.
- It is difficult to decide upon the amount of cover required, because the value of commissions actually being carried out is no indication of the likely maximum amount of any claim.
- Insurers prepared to provide the necessary cover are relatively few.
- The cover is only effective on a yearly basis, for example in respect of matters notified during that year. Thus if cover is not maintained, perhaps

because a practice has fallen on hard times, a claim made during that period cannot be referred to the insurance company even though cover may have been in place for 10 years before. This is why it is important for an architect to ensure that run-off cover is available for the years following retirement. Seven years seems to be a popular period for run-off cover although it cannot be guaranteed that there will be no claims after that period.

- The policy normally covers the amount of any damages awarded against the insured together with the amount of legal costs up to the limit of indemnity noted in the policy. It should be noted, however, that all policies carry excesses which may be substantial.
- Insurers usually claim the right to defend any claim. Alternatively they may decide to settle. Whichever course they take, it will be on the basis of sound business principles. This may not suit the architect. Policies should contain a clause which allows the insured to demand opinion from leading counsel and the insurers are obliged to proceed accordingly.
- Once cover is in place, the insured must immediately notify the insurers of any circumstance which may give rise to a claim. Failure may lead to the insurers repudiating liability.

It is possible to extend the cover to deal with certain other matters such as pursuing a claim for infringement of copyright, to provide indemnity in an action alleging libel or slander, etc.

17.6   BUILD insurance

BUILD stands for 'building users insurance against latent defects'. It was the subject of a NEDO report in 1988 which recommended that this type of insurance should be available for buildings. At first, the insurance was not available in the UK although it was common in many European countries. More insurers are interested in offering this type of insurance in this country. Some of its characteristics are as follows.

- It is non-cancellable for a period of 10 years from practical completion.
- Cover is generally limited to structure, weathershield envelope and optional loss of rent.
- Risk assessment is carried out on behalf of the insurer by independent consultants. This may necessitate amendments to proposals in certain instances.
- Policy is taken out during the early design stages and a single premium paid.
- Benefit to the employer.
- Waiver of subrogation against architect, contractor, etc. can be purchased for an additional premium.

If this kind of insurance becomes general or even mandatory by law, the burden of liability on the architect and other professionals could be eased.

However, there is little benefit unless subrogation is waived and that is usually quite costly. It is also unlikely that an employer would be prepared to pay an extra premium for this purpose. Even where subrogation is waived, it should be noted that the cover provided is fairly limited.

17.7   Other insurances

Some other common forms of insurance which a practice may take out include the following.

- Partnership – to cover the situation which may arise if a partner retires or dies and the practice loses a large slice of capital in consequence. A partnership will usually also insure the lives or all partners in favour of the others.
- Pensions – for the benefit of the partners and staff.
- Medical insurance – a popular benefit.
- Insurance of company cars.
- Personal accident insurance.

References

1. Employers' Liability (Compulsory Insurance) Regulations 1998.
2. Cecil, R. (1991) *Professional Liability*, 3rd edn, Legal Studies & Services (Publishing) Ltd is still worth reading although now somewhat out of date. See also the useful survey in *Architect's Legal Handbook*, 9th edn, 2009, edited by Anthony Speaight and Gregory Stone, Architectural Press.

18 The Architect as Employee

18.1 Finding employment

18.1.1 Self-assessment

Whether the architect is newly qualified and looking for a first appointment or an experienced architect seeking a change, obtaining employment is not easy. It is relatively easy to get a job (depending on the current economic climate), but it is not easy to get just the job required. To a large extent, the principles of getting a job are the same whether the person concerned is an architect, solicitor or a financial director. The field is known as professional and executive. But the aspirations of an architect are unique and demand a rather different approach to job hunting. For the most part, the principles of job seeking are widely known and widely neglected. In the last analysis the successful outcome depends upon the person and their particular talents, experience and personality; neglect of the principles will put the job seeker at a severe disadvantage. Most architects have experienced the interview at which the 'whizz-kid' gets the coveted job. Often, they fail to fulfil expectations and quickly whizz off to another, better position somewhere else. The common denominator is that this type of person knows how to set about finding a post, applying for it and making a good impression at interview. The art of finding employment is very much the art of self-presentation.

Just as a salesperson cannot market a product effectively unless they know all about it, architects cannot market themselves unless they know their strengths and weaknesses. Architects should be adept at the art of selling. After all, they are regularly called upon to make presentations of schemes to clients. The first step is to sit down and carry out a self-appraisal (Fig. 18.1) so that the prospective job seeker thoroughly knows the 'goods'. It is a good idea to do it in note form following the headings below.

- *Formal qualifications.* This should be easy: degrees, diplomas, certificates and memberships of professional bodies. Listing of minor institutes, which may give the right to certain affixes on payment of an annual subscription, should be avoided, because they tend to dilute an architect's principal qualification by giving the impression that the architect is scratching around to find something to put down.

- Formal qualifications
- Experience
    Most recent appointments
    Duties in each post
    Achievements
- Talents
- Personality
- Career objectives
    Job satisfaction
    Pay
    Advancement
    Responsibility
    Ancillary:
        Location
        Security
        Working hours
        Opportunity for initiative
        Personality of partners
        Type of work
        Design philosophy

Fig. 18.1   Self-appraisal.

- *Experience.* It does not pay to be vague. If qualification is recent, experience will be slim, but the most should be made of it. It is useful to put down experience as follows.
    - Most recent appointments (say during the last 5 years).
    - Duties in each post. This is not nearly so important as:
    - Achievements. This heading repays careful thought. It is an important selling point. Architects should consider whether they have played a major part in a really good building or brought a contract back from the brink of disaster or introduced a system which made the office more cost effective. In other words, whether they have ever done anything which makes them outstanding in a particular field. It is not uncommon to become quite depressed about this section of the self-appraisal. Architects may feel that they have achieved very little. What they are probably feeling is that they have not achieved as much as they would have liked – not the same thing at all. Architects who take it slowly, going through all the work they have done, are often surprised at the extent of their achievements.
- *Talents.* The things that the individual architect does best. To identify talents it is necessary to look at what one most and least likes doing.
- *Personality.* Relationships with colleagues, persons in authority and team members are important, as is the way in which an architect deals with contractors, manufacturer's representatives and officials of public bodies. An architect should consider his or her most vulnerable points. It might be age or youth and inexperience or difficulty in mastering some new technique or aspect of architectural practice. Some architects, for example, feel very exposed when they have to carry out a site inspection. It is impor-

tant to acknowledge such things at this stage so that the architect can be prepared if they arise during interview.

■ *Career objectives.* The next step is for the architect to decide what he or she really requires from a career. Presumably, an architect qualified in the first place because of a desire to participate in the creation and maintenance of a delightful, satisfying and durable environment for the benefit of everyone who will inhabit or pass through it. Ultimately, that should be the aim. All actions should be carried out with that end in mind. Efficient management and competent design work are not ends in themselves. Few people actually sit down and plan their careers, but it pays to do so even if things do not work out according to the plan. It is not unknown for architects to drift into satisfying, well-paid appointments, but it is not the norm. The following are a few headings to guide the thoughts.

— Job satisfaction. Most architects want this, but it means different things to different architects. What kind of architectural work is wanted? Very large or very small projects, mainly designing, contract administration, technology, new work or rehab? It is important to try to define one's ideal post.

— Pay. Thought should be given to how much money will be needed to justify a move. Sometimes an architect will be prepared to accept the same salary, or less, in order to secure just the right job. It is important to decide how much money is actually needed and what difference it would make if the job was 300 miles away. The two vital ingredients of a good job are job satisfaction and pay.

— Advancement. An architect must consider whether it really matters. Most people have a desire to progress, but not all. Usually, something must be relinquished to secure promotion. For example, an architect may have to stop active design work in order to concentrate on an entirely managerial role. Although the absence of good prospects may suggest that a job is not worth having, it is generally true that a good architect will create prospects.

— Responsibility. An architect who wishes to be completely responsible is aiming for the top of the tree. Such an architect must decide whether status matters more than the opportunity to practise particular skills.

— Ancillary. There may be many other things which an architect may include on the list of ideal job attributes. They may be important, but the question must be asked whether they are as important as job satisfaction and pay. If requirements are kept simple, securing a job will be easier. Among other things which might influence the job seeker are:

location
security
working hours
opportunity for initiative
office environment
personality of partners.

Completing this checklist should clarify the thoughts and, incidentally, reveal certain facets of the architect's character which were unacknowledged before. The complete self-appraisal is the unrefined raw material which must be used to find employment.

18.1.2   Opportunities

By this time, architects should have a clear idea of their own capabilities and the kind of post being sought. The next stage is to consider how to set about locating the sort of job vacancies required. It is always possible, of course, that someone will telephone unexpectedly and offer just the job required. Although this happens more regularly than might be thought, the main ways of locating vacancies are:

- reading advertisements in the professional, technical or local press
- making speculative approaches to potential employers
- by word of mouth, through contacts in other offices and recruitment consultants.

It is possible to persuade an employer that there is a need for just the kind of architectural expertise being offered. A number of architects have found their niches in this way. There are techniques to help job seekers achieve success.

18.1.3   Answering advertisements

This is probably the way in which most architects find employment. Besides looking at the obvious professional press, the less obvious construction journals should not be neglected. They occasionally have advertisements for architects and they may also advertise posts which are not aimed specifically at architects (see Chapter 3). National and regional newspapers are a fruitful source of jobs. Some small practices rarely advertise beyond regional level. Some large organisations have their own magazine or journal in which they advertise vacancies before they appear nationally. Local authorities, in particular, sometimes have a policy about advertising 'in house' as a first step. Of course, it is impossible to keep abreast of all such advertisements, but an architect with a clear idea of the post being sought will be rewarded by scanning as many relevant publications as possible. It should be remembered that advertisements on a national scale will almost certainly attract more applicants than regional advertisements.

Most practices and other organisations include advertisements for job vacancies on their websites. It is increasingly common for the first approach to be made to prospective employers through their websites. This is particularly true in the case of new graduates.

The kind of advertisement encountered will vary widely. Some give masses of information, others hardly anything at all beyond the job title. A salary may or may not be quoted. Large organisations commonly ask the reader to write for further details and an application form while private practices usually ask for a CV. The techniques for preparing these are discussed in section 18.1.6. The first rule of answering advertisements is to do exactly as they say. It is pointless sending a CV if they want an application form completed. It simply creates a bad impression. A firm which has its own application form usually does so because it always wants to see the information presented in the same order. Some firms still ask applicants to fill in forms or write to them in hand-writing. It may seem a trifle weird in the age of computers, but the instruction must be followed. Generally, employers are just trying to find out if the hand-writing is decipherable, but it is possible that they have retained a graphologist to comment on your personality. There are some employers who believe that character can be read in handwriting: a clear neat hand indicates a logical neat person, etc. Without passing judgement on such theories, all that can be said is that one's usual hand should be employed and care should be taken that it is legible. Otherwise, it is better to have the application typewritten.

If a CV is required, it should be sent with a covering letter. If there is an application form, it should be requested with a simple letter and returned when completed with a covering letter which should take the opportunity to briefly emphasise a couple of key points. If selection is to be by means of a completed application form, it makes little difference whether the form is returned immediately or just before the closing date, because usually all applications are considered together after the last date. Private practices asking for a CV will seldom state a closing date. It often pays to submit promptly.

Some forms invite the applicant to telephone for an informal chat. If the architect is confident of a good telephone manner and is quick thinking, it makes sense to telephone. Some posts are virtually secured on that basis, making the interview a formality. The architect telephoning a prospective employer should have some notes prepared as if for an interview, with questions ready. To approach the informal telephone chat casually can be fatal. It should be remembered that the telephone can magnify vocal mannerisms and the listener concentrates on the voice, because there is nothing else. There may be a bad line, the person on the other end of the telephone may seem abrupt and a thousand and one things can conspire to upset the friendly chat. In a face-to-face meeting, the participants can relate much better.

18.1.4   The speculative approach

It may be thought that writing to a firm of architects to offer one's services is a waste of time. Whether or not that is true will depend on the firm and its circumstances when they receive the letter. There are four possible scenarios.

- The approach may be rejected out of hand.
- The firm may be about to advertise a vacancy and they may decide to interview the writer before incurring the expense of inserting the advertisement in the press.

- The firm may be sufficiently impressed to create a post especially to suit the writer's expertise (this does happen quite frequently).
- The firm may be sufficiently impressed to interview the writer which may lead to a post in the future when they have the right opening. Firms do not enjoy the hassle of large-scale interview sessions. They do not like to waste the time and the money. If they have a post and they know of someone who can fill it, they will often contact that person.

The reason for making a speculative approach may well be that the architect knows the firm by reputation, admires their work and therefore wants to join them, even though they are not advertising any vacancies. There is nothing demeaning about a speculative approach. The recipient should be flattered. Some firms never have any need to advertise, because architects are anxious to join them.

Anything which looks like a mass-produced application should be avoided at all costs in these circumstances. Each application should be given an individual bias. At the very least, the letter should be addressed to the person in the firm who deals with staffing. This is easy to discover by means of a telephone call to the firm's receptionist. Even in this age of apparent informality, it is still prudent to address the letter 'Dear Mr/Mrs/Ms …' and finish it 'Yours sincerely'. It should be brief and to the point. There are no hard and fast rules about whether a CV should be included. Generally, it is probably better not to send a CV. The letter should give just enough information to convince the recipient that it is worth while meeting the writer. The sole purpose of the letter is to secure an interview. It is the purpose of the interview to secure the post. Therefore, the first few lines of the letter deserve a great deal of thought if quick despatch into the waste basket is to be avoided. Starting a letter: 'I am writing to enquire whether you have any vacancies for an architect' invites rejection in all but the most patient of recipients.

Speculative approaches should not be attempted by telephone. In communications, a telephone conversation is halfway between a letter and a face-to-face meeting. In a letter it is possible to say as much or as little as one wishes. It is impossible to be drawn into a hurried response. During a meeting, what is said can be moderated or emphasised by gesture or facial expression and silent signals can be received from the interviewer. In comparison, the telephone can be a very coarse instrument of communication. Its danger lies in the fact that it seems to convey a better picture of both parties whereas in fact it gives only a partial picture and that perhaps the worst part.

Speculative approaches should never be sent by facsimile or by email, because both are too often employed to send informal notes and memos.

18.1.5 Contacts

Everyone has contacts. Every architect has contacts in the architectural world and many elsewhere. If it becomes known that a talented architect is seeking another appointment, the results can be surprising. There may be an approach from a firm who had not thought of approaching previously, because the architect may have seemed settled for life. More often, a contact can sometimes tell of opportunities which have not yet been advertised, thus enabling a speculative approach to be made.

There are a number of other avenues for job seekers. For example, most universities, local authorities and large organisations have websites on which they list job vacancies. Recruitment consultants can be very effective, but it is important to keep up the pressure and to remember that their objectives are not quite the same as the architect's objectives. Some consultants are commissioned to search for and find suitable applicants. They may carry out the initial weeding out of unsuitable applicants. They collect their fees from the employers. They are always on the lookout for architects seeking new posts and they welcome approaches. The more people they can successfully place and the higher the salaries, the more money they make. There are many recruitment consultants who carry out their jobs with the utmost professionalism. Unfortunately, there are others who will try to place the architect in any kind of job so as to secure the commission. Other than by recommendation, it is probably safest to try those consultants who specialise in the architectural and construction markets.

18.1.6 Career history and CV

CV stands for 'curriculum vitae' – the story of a life. What most firms actually mean when they ask for a CV is a career history. They do not want to know about early childhood or anything which is not absolutely relevant to the application. Even though a career history may be submitted, it is diplomatic to head it 'Curriculum Vitae' if that is what is requested.

Ideally, the CV should occupy no more than one sheet of A4 paper. Most CVs take up more than one page, but long CVs become very tedious to read, particularly if the recipient is faced with reading, and trying to compare, several of them. The CV should be written to suit the post for which application is being made. The layout should be clear, it should be typed and the following should be borne in mind.

- If age may be a problem, the date of birth should be omitted. Employers often have a preconceived notion about a 50-year-old as opposed to a 30-year-old applicant. At 50, a person is less likely to move again, but experience and skill are evident and enthusiasm can be just as marked as in a much younger person. The only disadvantage with older persons is that they may be slower than their younger colleagues and that is by no means always the case. Age discrimination is unlawful.[1]
- Degrees and professional qualifications should be included, but not usually school examination results. The exception is if the school examination results show an aptitude for something which is not strictly architectural, but which could prove useful to a potential employer. An obvious example is an examination result which indicates proficiency in a foreign language.

- The current appointment should be described first followed by the next most recent and so on. Ten years ago is ancient history. Any posts held earlier than 10 years ago should simply be listed.
- Achievements must be emphasised rather than duties, and brevity is the watchword.
- Titles of some posts may be obscure and there is nothing wrong with amending them to make them more comprehensible to the reader. For example, 'Deputy to the Chief Architect', if true, is easier to understand and creates a better impression than 'Architect Grade ABC'.
- If the architect is currently self-employed, the prospective employer may wonder why the decision to change to employment. The thought may arise that the architect's business has failed. A convincing reason for giving up self-employment should be stated.
- Generally, however, it is best not to include reasons for wishing to leave the current or last post. If appropriate, reasons can be discussed at interview.
- It is a mistake to include details of present salary. Architects are worth an objective amount, not merely £1000 more than the last salary. They may have been underpaid.
- 'Additional information' should only include items which are strictly relevant. The fact that an architect is a keen fisherman is not relevant; it may suggest a loner. Involvement in local societies, however, indicates public spiritedness and possibly contacts which may be useful in the future.

This is only a guide and there may be good reasons to ignore some of the advice. The individual use of judgement is all-important. Applying for a new post should be approached with the same skill and care which is applied to any important task. There are few things more important than a career in view of the length of time spent working in it, but it is surprising how many applicants dash off an application in a few minutes. The recipient will probably give it the same sort of cursory treatment.

18.1.7   The application form

Many application forms are exceedingly badly arranged. The form should be used for the applicant's own advantage. It may sound trite, but it is important to read every bit of information about the post before starting to complete the form. All questions should be answered in the spirit of the information given, using the same words if possible. For example, if the information calls for an architect with a 'flair for design', the same phrase should be included in the application form. The form should be completed neatly, but it is important to fill the available space adequately. Additional sheets should be attached to detail experience if the space is too small (it usually is). Most application forms are straightforward, but some forms have one or more questions which are difficult to answer. A selection of such questions and outlines of possible answers are given below. The details, of course, will depend upon the individual.

What do you consider are your greatest strengths and weaknesses?

This offers both a chance and a trap. There is no place for modesty. Strengths should be clearly stated, whether they are the much sought after 'flair for design' or project management or the restoration of old buildings. If there is space, examples should be given. This is an opportunity for the architect to emphasise achievements. For example: 'I directed the design team on XYZ Building'. That can be very effective if XYZ is a well-known project. The second part of the question is a trap. It is an invitation for the applicant to give the firm a reason for exclusion from interview. On no account must such things as 'I tend to get bored with office work' or 'I dislike being told what to do' be put down. They may be true, but they will not help secure an interview. It is possible to turn such a question to advantage by stating as faults what others will probably see as good points. For example: 'I tend to concentrate on detail, but I am capable of seeing the broad picture' or 'I become frustrated if all members of the team are not pulling their weight. I tend to deal by face-to-face discussion with the person involved'. It is not suggested that these 'weaknesses' be invented, merely that the architect should take something about which he or she is a shade too fanatical, state it as a weakness (which it is) then say how it is overcome.

What has been your greatest disappointment?

Once again, this is a potential trap. It will be fatal to say: 'I have not got as far as I would have wished in my career' or 'I failed to solve the cladding detail on XYZ Building and there has always been a problem with water ingress'. The same technique should be used as for 'weaknesses' above. The perfectionist is always bitterly disappointed that a near perfect conception is not actually perfect. The architect's greatest disappointment might be that an award-winning design had a minor flaw or there was an absence of technology to achieve the whole concept.

Why are you applying for this post?

Another opportunity to relate achievements and show how they apply to the particular post. The aspects of the firm or organisation which are most appealing should be stressed, for example: reputation for good design, efficiency, new technology, etc. These points will impress the prospective employer who will be equally unimpressed if the reasons include nearness of office to home or the need for extra money.

What are the major ways in which you consider that you can contribute to the work of this organisation?

As above.

Reasons for leaving your present post

Being fired, made redundant or major policy disagreements with the boss are *bad* reasons. Anxiety to further a blossoming career in the firm to which application is being made is a *good* reason.

Which of your duties gave you the most satisfaction?

This is another opportunity to state achievements. Care must be taken to avoid the danger of appearing too much of a specialist, unless that is what the advertiser requires.

If you are offered the post, where do you see yourself in 10 years' time?

This is always a difficult one. It really is a silly question if taken at face value. But the totally honest answer that the applicant has absolutely no idea is probably a mistake. The safest way is to stick to generalities, stressing progress so far and concentrating on personal development as contracts administrator, designer, technologist, etc. which is seen as continuing in logical progression depending on the opportunities offered.

Describe, in detail, how your experience relates to this post

This question often appears in a very much longer form. It is not an invitation to submit a life story. It is important to be clear and to the point. Those achievements which relate most closely to the new post should be set out. Many architects ramble when trying to answer this question. 'In detail' simply means that the prospective employer wants actual examples to be quoted.

There are a few further points to remember about application forms.

- *Health.* Unless the applicant is disabled, health should be stated as excellent. Past operations and treatments, if successful, should be ignored.
- *Leisure activities.* The employer is looking to see that the architect is a well-balanced personality with the ability to mix easily. A brief statement regarding any involvement with a couple of sports and group pastimes is better than a complete list of all activities.
- *Interests.* This is the architect's opportunity to show involvement with local branches of the RIBA, RSUA, RSAW or RIAS and memberships of other societies. Private firms encourage members of their staff to develop a wide circle of acquaintances; it promotes work. All honorary posts or public duties should be included, such as Justice of the Peace.
- *Documents.* Drawings, photographs and diplomas should not be included with the application even if (rarely) they are requested. If appropriate, it should be made clear that these documents will be brought to an interview.

- *Projects.* The types and values of projects together with achievements should be stated.
- *Expertise.* Areas of expertise which are useful adjuncts of architectural practice should be stated, e.g. CAD, models, perspectives, expert witness, adjudications.
- *Referees.* Referees should be as senior as possible. It is a mistake to choose people merely because they are friends. The opinion of the person on the next drawing board is of little value. The most senior architect in the applicant's current employment, if well briefed, will be best placed to give a good reference. It is the kiss of death to include the name of a referee without permission, besides being grossly discourteous. Architects are sometimes afraid that they will get a poor reference, because of some incident in the past. The law provides some reassurance. The employer, in writing a reference, assumes responsibility and the employee relies on the employer's skill and care in its preparation. It is not sufficient that the employer believes what is said to be true. The employer must have exercised reasonable skill and care in checking the truth of any allegations.[2]

18.1.8 Before the interview

The whole purpose of filling in application forms, producing curricula vitae and sending letters to prospective employers is to obtain an interview where applicants can demonstrate to the employer that they are the persons most suited to the posts advertised. It is a matter of matching skills and experience to the employer's requirements. To be effective, applicants must be fully prepared.

The first thing to remember is that the employer must have been sufficiently impressed by the application to consider offering an interview. Finding the right post is a two-way process. Both parties should be finding out as much as possible about each other, because:

- something discovered may influence the applicant's decision to join the firm
- the applicant needs information on which to base questions
- an employer will usually be impressed that an applicant has taken trouble to do research.

Among the things which an applicant will want to know is the firm's policy on hiring and firing, how long the firm has been established, the ages and experience of the partners and the buildings they design. Apart from many standard reference books, the applicant should not neglect to enquire of past clients and employees, local chambers of commerce and the RIBA at local and national level. It is important to visit the buildings produced by the firm to get to know something about them.

A list of points needing clarification at the interview should be prepared. The chances are that most of the points will be covered by the employer, but experience shows that without a list of questions, the applicant often forgets

- Hours of work
- Holidays
- Salary and bonus
- Fringe benefits, car, mobile telephone, health scheme, insurance, pension, sabbatical
- Prospects for advancement
- Office organisation and range of disciplines
- Clarification of job description
- Particular office expertise
- Current workload
- Possibilities of working in other branches
- Initial programme of work for the successful applicant
- The design philosophy of the office. Do they believe in a house style?
- Use of computers
- Any particular method of working?
- Company policy about staff doing spare time work
- Is it a new appointment? If not, what happened to the previous holder?
- Any particular problems associated with the post?

Fig. 18.2   Checklist of points to clarify at interview (note that it is not possible to be specific because of the wide range of posts for which an architect might apply).

to ask something important. A checklist of such points is shown in Fig. 18.2. It should be used as a guide only.

Very little can be done about the timing of the interview. If one appointment only is to be made, there could be up to seven interviewees. It is common to take candidates in alphabetical order. A candidate whose name begins with either ABC or XYZ will probably be seen either first or last respectively, which are supposed to be the best positions. Sometimes other considerations affect the order, such as distance of travel. The middle of the list is supposed to be the worst place, because a candidate in this position becomes confused with other candidates in the mind of the interviewer. Someone in that position has to impress a bit more if they are to secure the post. Most architectural posts call for the architect to take along visual material. There are exceptions, of course, if the post is purely administrative or concerned with contracts. Some architects refuse to take examples of work to an interview as a matter of principle, presumably with the view that, being architects, they have no need to show their quality – it is taken for granted. That is a very mistaken approach. Whether or not requested, the architect should always take along visual material, to show not only competence but also that the approach to problem solving is what the firm requires. Some or all of the following may be taken.

- *Drawings.* Nowadays, a firm should accept drawings in electronic form, whether sent in advance by email or brought to the interview on disk. Whichever method is chosen, care should be taken that the office has the facility to read and display the material, otherwise the architect must bring suitable equipment. Drawings are still taken to interviews in hard copy. If so, they should be flat, not rolled, and prints, not negatives. Drawings should be chosen to suit the post. For example, if the firm does a lot of housing, the drawings should be domestic in character; if the post is for an architect to design warehouses and factories, industrial work should be taken. Unless the work is specialised, it is always a good idea to take along a brief selection of other work to show the breadth of expertise. The newly qualified will have to take one of two projects produced during training, but they must be prepared to face keener criticism of such work and they should have answers ready to the inevitable question: 'Why did you do that?'. Unless the post particularly indicates otherwise, only one or two production drawings should be taken, but they should be good. There is nothing wrong with taking drawings produced by others provided the architect makes that fact clear. The drawings may show the extent of a building on which the architect had an important role as leader or co-ordinator of the design team. An architect in that situation must be prepared for keen questioning.

- *Photographs.* They must be first-class large prints, but the architect will have to work hard to demonstrate a key role in the building if there are no supporting drawings.
- *Glossy brochure about the architect's work.* In theory, this is very good, but it does give the impression that the architect makes a career of attending interviews.
- *Complete file of correspondence concerning the post.* This must be taken. A copy of the career history or the application form must be included together with a list of points to raise and questions. Some architects think that it is bad form to take notes to an interview; they are mistaken. The interviewer will certainly use notes. An applicant who also uses notes will appear well organised and confident.

The above is merely a guide. There is no point in taking a portfolio of drawings if the last post was administrative and the application is for a similar post. One last thing which can be done in preparation for interview is to take along a 150 mm scale rule and a soft pencil.

18.1.9   The interview

The applicant should arrive about a quarter of an hour early. Any later, and there is little time to compose oneself. It is useful to arrive with a quarter of an hour in hand, if only to absorb the atmosphere. There are often examples of the firm's work on display in the reception area. If it is one of those interviews where it is necessary to wait with the other interviewees, it is always better to listen rather than talk so as to assess the strength of the competition.

Local authorities and large firms will have a special form for claiming expenses. Smaller firms are unlikely to have a form, but they will normally pay basic expenses, in which case it is usual to list expenses and leave them with the secretary. It is not something to bring up at interview.

There are two basic types of interview:

- one to one
- committee or panel.

The one-to-one interview offers the best chance to establish a relationship with the interviewer and, therefore, the best chance of obtaining the post. A committee interview can be very difficult. There is usually a chairman, and each member asks questions in turn. When answering questions, it is important to reply directly to the person asking the question. Although difficult, the applicant should try to remember the names of the committee as they are introduced and to use them during the interview. It is difficult to be sure of the relationships between members of a committee. They may be more interested in impressing one another than in the candidate. The interviewer will usually be an architect if a post as an architect is the subject of the application, but not invariably so. Other panel members may be personnel or managerial, related construction disciplines or, in the case of a local authority, councillors.

The RIBA *Handbook of Practice Management* sets out some useful guidelines for interviewing from the point of view of the employer. It also forms a useful guide for applicants, because they know the kind of things the employer is looking for.

Interviews may be structured or unstructured. The first follows a pattern set by the interviewer, the second rambles and gives the applicant the opportunity to set the pattern. The latter form of interview is very common, because interviewing is a skill which few employers bother to learn properly. A typical interview often runs as follows.

- The interviewer chats for a few moments to help the applicant relax.
- A description of the firm is given.
- A description of the post is given.
- The interviewer asks questions relating to answers on the application form.
- The applicant is asked half a dozen 'technical' questions.
- The applicant's portfolio is examined, with more questions.
- The applicant is given time to ask questions.

Arrangements vary greatly. The interview may take place across a desk or around a conference table or sitting in easy chairs with coffee. Quite a lot depends on the type of job for which the applicant is applying. An interview for a first post might well take place formally across a desk. Progression to more senior posts is marked by a steady decrease in formality, because the interviewer wants to get to know the applicant thoroughly. That is particularly true in the case of posts which may lead to partnerships. The applicant must:

- speak slowly and clearly
- look at the interviewer; do not look down
- resist any temptation to wave hands around to make a point
- be enthusiastic
- always pause to think before answering, not just after a difficult question.

Applicants should be wary of making a gift of their expertise. If asked to solve problems, they should try to show that they know how to set about solving it without actually doing so. Applicants should always open portfolios even if not asked to do so. A useful opportunity comes at the end of the interview when the interviewer asks for further points. It strikes a strong note to preface answers by 'yes' or 'no'. Answers should be elaborated, but not too much. No opportunity to display experience, achievements and skill should be missed. Although it is helpful to ask questions which show that the applicant has studied the firm's work, it does not pay to be too critical, unless the decision has already been made that the post is not wanted.

Interviews really are two-way affairs. They may not seem that way in practice, but they are. Applicants must decide whether they want the posts. If they are good at what they do, employers will be anxious to impress them. An applicant's approach should be positive, stressing achievements and interest in the post applied for.

Every interview contains awkward questions. The ability to deal with them depends on experience and confidence. The interviewer should always be humoured. It is never appropriate to say that a question is silly. If really at a loss for an answer, the interviewer should be complimented on devising such a difficult question and the admission should be made that the applicant is beaten. The device is particularly effective in a panel interview. Although awkward questions can never be entirely foreseen (that is one reason why they are awkward), the following is a selection of such questions which regularly make their appearance at interviews.

Why do you want to leave your present post?

Furtherance of career and joining the firm to which one is applying are acceptable answers; being fired, made redundant or seeking more money are not.

Do you think that you are too old/too young/too inexperienced for this post?

Given that age discrimination is unlawful, this is a naughty question. The answer to this is simply to stress interest in the post together with achievements and skills.

Given the opportunity, how would you reorganise this firm to make it more efficient?

This is a really silly question. The only reason for asking it is to see if the applicant is silly enough to attempt an answer. The only sensible response is to express delight in the question and ask for sufficient time to study the firm in order to give a worthwhile answer. This sort of question does give applicants an opportunity to explain how they reorganised some aspect of their present firm.

Who is your favourite architect?

It is important to be ready for this question and to say who and why. Jargon should be avoided. The why is more important than the who. It should not matter that the architect is not a favourite of the interviewer. Effective things to admire are attention to detail and planning.

Why did you stay so long at your last firm?

It is important to emphasise the additional responsibility taken on over the years and progress within the firm. It is unwise for the applicant to say that he or she was on the point of leaving many times, but stayed after being offered more money. Among other things, the current application could be seen as just a ploy to increase the salary yet again. This question inevitably leads to the one about reasons for leaving at this stage. The reasons can only be that it seems to be the right career moment. Be warned, however, that employers will want to know why such a long-serving member of staff does not warrant a partnership in the current practice. Only the applicant knows why, but it is unwise to directly criticise the current firm.

It seems to us that a person with your particular skills/ experience/qualifications should be ... (doing something else)

This is tricky. It may also be true. On the basis that an applicant for a job wants the job, the only answer is to say why the job is wanted and to emphasise interest in it.

Why do you think you are the person for this post?

Another opportunity to stress achievements in the previous post and to relate them to the requirements of the new post.

How would you motivate others?

Books have been written about this. It is useful to read one of them. Put very simply, motivating someone else involves getting them to want to do what the motivator wants by letting them see it is in their own best interests.

What salary are you looking for?

This is a question to be avoided if possible. It is up to the employer to make an offer, but in any case salary discussions should not take place until the end of the interview. As a general guide, it does not usually pay to accept less than desired for the promise of something indefinite such as promotion in 2 or 3 years time. Bonuses, too, have a habit of disappearing unless the percentage is written in as a definite part of the remuneration package. If there is no alternative but to state a salary, it is useful to state a range. If the applicant is confident of commanding a particular salary, it should be stated, but not tentatively.

The list of awkward questions is endless. In addition, applicants may be asked to sit what amounts to a short examination, spot mistakes in a drawing or undergo a psychometric test. It is important to co-operate fully with the employer's whims unless the applicant has already decided that the job is unsuitable. Remember, what may seem a silly waste of time may be something in which the employer puts the utmost faith. Of course, that itself may say something about the likely relationship with the future employer.

As in any other meeting, misunderstandings can arise during the course of an interview which can be the reason why the post is not offered. To overcome this possibility, it is sensible to ask a question at the end of the interview which exposes any reservations on the part of the interviewer. It can be phrased in different ways, but it should be something like: 'Did any points arise during the course of the interview which lead you to believe that I am not suitable for the post?'. The question is something of a trap for the interviewer. If the answer is 'No', the post should be secured. If the answer is 'Yes', the applicant has the opportunity to correct the misunderstandings. The employer cannot really refuse to give an answer, but if the answer is neither 'Yes' or 'No' but simply a confused mumble, it is usually because the employer is not going to give the post to the applicant, but does not want to say so at the interview.

18.1.10   After the interview

If all the candidates are being interviewed on the same day, it is common practice to announce the result shortly after the last interview is completed. In other cases, the result will be made known by post. No applicant should have to wait longer than about a week. If there is no word after 2 weeks it may be that:

- the post has been offered to another candidate and the employer is waiting for an acceptance before notifying the others; or
- the employer is unsure whether any applicant is suitable; or
- points raised during the interview have caused the employer to rethink some basic office policy.

It is not good policy to telephone to find out the situation. The employer may be embarrassed and forced into making a quick decision which is unlikely to be favourable. A carefully worded letter, on the other hand, which emphasises interest in the post and in the firm may just tilt the balance. Even if the post has been offered to someone else, it may be turned down and the letter pushes that applicant's name to the front of the list of alternatives.

18.2   Acceptable job titles

The use of the title 'architect', when applied to a person carrying on a business, is governed by the Architects Act 1997 (see also Chapter 2, section 2.4). Such a person must be registered and, therefore nowadays, qualified. The RIBA used to publish a Practice Note (No. 2) setting out job titles and descriptions which are acceptable and unacceptable. The note is no longer available, but the list is worth repeating here. The titles are as follows.

Acceptable titles

Chief Architect
District Architect
Principal Architect
Project Architect

Acceptable descriptions

Chartered Architect
Experienced Architect
Architect at B/C/D level of responsibility

Each of these titles or descriptions adds something to the basic 'architect' so as to indicate the status or job. The professional status, however, is not in doubt.

Unacceptable titles

Assistant Architect
Senior Assistant Architect
Chief Assistant Architect

Unacceptable descriptions

Registered Architect
Qualified Architect
Fully Qualified Architect

Each of these titles or description detracts from the status of the architect. The descriptions suggest that it is possible to be termed 'architect' while at the same time being unregistered, partly or wholly unqualified. To qualify 'architect' by 'assistant' indicates that the unfortunate title holder is somehow less than an architect. Some titles are of course unlawful, such as where a job advertisement calls for the post of architect, but the requirements are clearly for a person who need not be registered. Such phrases as 'architect at or about qualification standard' fall into this category. So do 'student architect' and 'trainee architect' as a matter of law.

18.3 Employment

18.3.1 Employed or self-employed?

The Inland Revenue have strict rules to outlaw the use of self-employment as a device when the situation is really one of employment.

The very first thing which an architect should be sure about is whether he or she is an employee. It is possible to work on an employed or self-employed basis. An employee enters into a *contract of service*, someone who is self-employed enters into a *contract for services*. The difference is very important.

- Employment law applies only to employees.
- Statutory rights apply only to employees.
- Duties at common law will be implied only in an employment situation.

It may seem obvious into which category a person falls, but that is not always the case. Often the situation is straightforward. An architect working for a client in return for a fee is self-employed whereas most architects working in practices for a salary are employed. A self-employed person is sometimes referred to as an independent contractor. If the matter comes before the courts, they will look at the actual situation rather than the title.[3] Thus a person referred to as a 'consultant architect' may be held to be employed while a 'project architect' may in reality be self-employed. In order to resolve the issue in situations where there may be some doubt, the courts have devised some tests which can be applied. Briefly, they are as follows.

Control

If the employer has control over the architect's method of working, the architect is an employee. The greater the degree of control, the greater the likeliehood that the architect is an employee.

Although this is quite a good test where the work is of a manual nature, whether skilled or unskilled, it is less satisfactory in the professional context where even an employee must have quite a lot of freedom to exercise his or her profession. The test is relative, therefore, and the amount of control exercised over a particular architect must be compared with the usual degree of control exercised in architectural practice.

Equipment

Architects who provide their own equipment are probably self-employed. The test is not definitive, because some practices may provide equipment for self-employed architects.

Integration

Architects who are integral parts of a business are likely to be employees. This test is probably more telling than the last as far as professional people are concerned. Thus it is easy to see the difference between an architect who freelances, self-employed, but working perhaps for a day or two a week for several practices, increasing or decreasing involvement to suit varying office workloads, and the permanent staff member. It used to be common for some self-employed architects to work permanently for one office. The situation was mainly for the benefit of the office, because there was seldom any long-term commitment on either side. An architect who carries out services for several practices is likely to be self-employed.

Risk

An architect who carries some financial risk is likely to be self-employed.

Multiple test

This is probably the best test. If the other tests are inconclusive, the questions to ask are: Does the architect work for an agreed salary? Is the degree of control such that there is a master and servant situation? Are the other provisions of the contract consistent with employment? For example, who is responsible for paying the architect's tax? Is there a company pension scheme to which the architect belongs? Who owns the drawing equipment which the architect uses?

Before the introduction of the stricter Inland Revenue rules referred to above, there was a growing tendency for architects to be employed on a self-employed basis. This was possibly because of the uncertain economic climate. The position used to be that an employer took less risk by using self-employed persons, because they were not protected by statute like an employee.

There are advantages to being self-employed. Architects in this situation pay tax on a different system and there is greater scope for claiming expenses against tax. In addition, many architects like the freedom which self-employment brings. It should also be noted that if a self-employed architect is negligent and the practice has to make a claim against the insurance policy, the insurer does not waive rights of subrogation, as is usual in the case of employees, and the self-employed may face the prospect of a personal claim from the insurer.

18.3.2   Employment contract

A contract of employment may be written or oral. The only problem with an oral contract is the problem with all oral contracts – the parties may have conflicting recollections of the terms. The contract can also be implied as the result of the conduct of the parties. Some firms, so it is said, still engage staff with a shake of the hand. There is nothing illegal in this and if the firm is equally relaxed about all aspects of its relations with employees, it may be the ideal environment for some. In general, however, a written contract of employment is an advantage, because both sides then know for certain the basis of the relationship, at least in respect of the main issues. In the absence of express terms between employer and employee, the general law will imply that the employer has a duty to:

- pay the employee
- provide work, if without work the employee would be unable to earn money

- reimburse the employee for reasonably incurred expenses in carrying out duties
- take care for the employee's safety
- provide a grievance procedure
- act in a spirit of mutual trust and confidence

and that the employee:

- must provide personal (i.e. not delegated) service
- must obey the employer's lawful instructions
- must take reasonable care when about the employer's business
- must show good faith in revealing to the employer that which should be revealed and in safeguarding confidential information.

In addition, there is much statutory law which governs the employer/employee relationship and which has now almost supplanted the common law for most purposes.

18.3.3 Written statement

The employer must give the employee a 'written statement' of the principal contract terms not later than 2 months after commencement of employment. The statement, however, is not the contract and, if appropriate, the employee can contend that the statement attempts to modify the terms of employment. The fact that the employee may be asked to sign a written statement is not thought to indicate anything other than acknowledgement of receipt of the statement. Many employers are slow to issue the statement because there is no effective sanction. An industrial tribunal may make a decision on the points in dispute, but that is all. The statement must be given to the employee personally, but it need not be issued at all if all the points have been covered already in a written contract of employment. It is not sufficient, however, for the employer to pin the statement to a notice board or to refer to standard conditions.

The statement must contain the following.

- The identities of the employer and employee.
- The job title.
- The date of commencement of employment and whether a previous period of employment counts as part of the period of continuous employment for statutory purposes.
- Rate of pay and interval between payment.
- Hours of work.
- Place of work.
- Holiday entitlement, including public holidays and the method of calculating holiday pay (see 18.11 below).
- Rules regarding absence from work due to sickness or injury and any sick pay provision. There is no right to sick pay under the general law, but most employers make some provision. An employer is obliged to pay statutory

sick pay for 28 weeks in any year after which responsibility for payment of statutory sick pay lies with the Department of Health and Social Security.

- Details of the pension scheme. The employee may be referred to another document.
- Whether a contracting out certificate is in force.
- The period of notice required to bring the contract to an end. The statement may stipulate any period, but if it is less than the statutory minimum, the statutory minimum will apply. If no period is stipulated, the statutory minimum does not apply and reasonable notice must be given (unless a fixed term contract is in force).
- Disciplinary rules and the grievance procedure. This is not necessary where the total number of employees is less than 20. The procedures are not regulated by statute, but codes of practice have been produced by ACAS which, if adopted, tend to demonstrate to an industrial tribunal that the procedure was reasonable. The names of the persons to whom the employee can refer grievances must be given.

If the contract is silent about any of these points, a note to that effect must be put in the written statement. If there is any change, a further written statement must be furnished by the employer within 1 month of the change.

18.4   Job description

Job descriptions are often included in job advertisements. They may be brief in the extreme, of the 'project architect with flair for design' variety, or they may be extremely detailed. Although in general it might be assumed that architects know what they do, there is a tremendous range of functions in practice, depending on the kind of practice, the kind of work, the position of the architect in relation to other members of the office. It is comparatively rare for a detailed job description to be included in a contract of employment for an architect.

The general rule is that the more senior the post, the less need there is for a job description. So the lowest paid member of staff doing relatively unskilled work might have a very long job description setting out the varied tasks which might be requested of that person. The highest paid member or senior partner will have no job description because, at that level of responsibility, the person writes his or her own description day by day. The job, for such people, is whatever they make it.

The employment contract should contain some description of the general nature of the work. Professionals cannot expect their contracts to spell out every detail of their duties.[4] Those duties, however, will not be held to extend beyond the duties normally associated with the proper performance of the functions indicated. Thus an architect cannot refuse to do something on the basis that it is not in his or her contract of employment if it is consistent with an architect's normal duties. From the employer's point of view, it is useful to include a general phrase requiring the employee to carry out other activities which are reasonably incidental to his or her principal job. Part of the job description in the employment contract may be that an architect is required to work at another branch office at the discretion of any partner. Without such a clause, the architect cannot be compelled to move.

A simple form of job description was pioneered in the 1961 survey *The Architect and His Office*[5] (Fig. 18.3). It graded all architectural staff in four grades: A, B, C, D. Each grade carried a brief description of the qualities required and the person's responsibility. Thus an architect seeing that a firm was advertising for a grade C post would have a good idea of the kind of person being sought. It also formed the basis of the salary structure. Some kind of job description is essential if the office carries out job evaluation (see 18.7 below).

18.5   Hours of work

The hours which an architect is expected to work should be detailed in the contract of employment although this is seldom the case. They must, however, be specified in the written statement (see 18.3.3 above), but there are no statutory provisions about the actual hours. There really is no such thing as 'normal' office hours. In London, the usual start is 9.30 am, elsewhere 9.00 am is common, the normal week being 35 and 37.5 hours respectively. On 1 October 1998, the Working Time Regulations 1998 came into force.[6] Essentially, they provide that a worker must not work more than 48 hours including overtime in a 7-day period. In order to arrive at the figure, an average is taken over 17 weeks. An employee can agree to work more than 48 hours, but the agreement must be in writing and the employee can terminate it on written notice.

It is very uncommon for any professional to keep strictly to the specified hours of work and architects are no exception. Whatever the appointed hours of work, architects will tend to work longer. More about this later (see 18.6 below). In many places, some form of flexible working hours is operated. There was resistance in some quarters, but it is the norm in many local authorities and it is becoming acceptable elsewhere. In principle, an employee is required to work during a 'core' period from perhaps 10.00 am to 3.00 pm each day together with other hours to choice or as agreed with the employer. The overriding rule is that the employee must put in an agreed minimum number of hours every week or month. There are obvious advantages for the employee and the practice may become more widespread eventually. The contract should state the office policy regarding the accumulation of hours into additional days leave.

An employee has a statutory right to request flexible working hours to care for a person. The right extends to male and female employees and covers caring for a child or an adult. Various criteria must be satisfied and a proper application must be made to the employer. The employer is obliged to consider any properly made application and to meet the employee no later than 28 days after the application. The employer's decision must be given to the employee

Type of work which can be handled	Knowledge and initiative	Influence on others	Responsibility
'A' level Perform simple jobs offering little or no alternative methods. Simple analysis of problems for which logical answers are readily obtainable.	No initiative required.	Able to understand and execute simple instructions. A minimum influence on the work of others.	Responsible for making minor decisions. All work closely supervised.
'B' level Perform work offering a limited number of alternative methods. Solve problems for which logical answers are not readily apparent and which will have some effect on the other aspects of the job.	Limited initiative required. Limited research into common technical literature required. Knowledge of the more common types of materials.	Able, to understand and execute instructions covering a limited field. Able to give simple clear instructions.	Responsible for making decisions affecting his work only, which must be reported to his senior. Parts of his work closely supervised.
'C' level Perform work offering a variety of alternative methods. Solve problems for which answers are not apparent and which will have considerable effect on other aspects of the job.	Initiative is required. Considerable research into all technical literature required. General knowledge of all types of materials.	Able to understand and execute instructions, covering a wide field. Able to give instructions to allocate work among and to control the work of, up to 5 or 6 others working as a team and to co-ordinate their activities.	Responsible for making decisions for all the work of his team within the framework laid down. Receives general supervision.
'D' level Perform work offering an infinite variety of alternative methods. Solve problems for which considerable thought is required to produce logical answers, the solution to which will have a profound effect on the whole design.	Considerable initiative is required. Considerable basic research is required into fields not normally covered by normal technical literature. Wide detailed knowledge of all types of materials.	Able to initiate a plan of working and check progress, able to convert plan into a practical method of working and give the necessary instructions. Able to control and co-ordinate the work of a number of teams working independently.	Responsible for submitting and agreeing design policy with the principal within the framework laid down by the office. Receives administrative supervision only.

Fig. 18.3 Grading table for architectural staff (from The Architect and His Office, courtesy of RIBA Enterprises).

6262464

no later than 14 days thereafter. A refusal, which must be substantiated, must be based upon a sound business reason.

18.6 Overtime

Attitudes to working overtime vary tremendously. Most architects will be expected to work overtime at times when there is a heavy workload or when there is a temporary crisis which demands attention. The way in which overtime is handled will depend on the particular office. Although, particularly in difficult times, it is better to be somewhat understaffed, it is not a good idea for anyone to work regular overtime. Everyone needs time to relax and recharge batteries otherwise tiredness becomes normal and mistakes occur.

Some offices repay overtime by offering time off in lieu. This can be useful to the employee, but if all members of staff exercise the option, there may be times when the office is seriously understaffed. In addition, those architects who work most overtime usually have difficulty in finding a space in their workload to enable them to take normal holidays, let alone time off in lieu. No architect should allow this kind of situation to develop. Overtime should always be paid with time off in lieu as an alternative.

Some offices do not pay for overtime and still the staff work extra hours. This reflects well on the commitment of the staff and badly on the practice. Overtime payment should be on a higher scale than normal, to reflect the unsocial hours and the fact that it is over and above what an architect can reasonably be expected to work. Fair rates are usually taken to be one and a third times the normal hourly rate to twice the normal hourly rate if the hours are especially late or during the weekend. It is not unknown for an office to pay only normal rates, however much overtime is worked. It has also been known for an office to stipulate that no overtime will be paid until the employee has worked in excess of a stated number of hours overtime on any one day. It is common for managers or senior staff not to be paid for overtime (except in exceptional circumstances), a reasonable amount of additional hours being expected as part of the role which is reflected in the overall salary package.

Some architects will work overtime without requesting payment in order to gain advancement in the firm. Whether that is a good idea will depend on circumstances.

18.7 Salary

Starting salaries should be settled at the time of interview. What should also be settled, and this is sometimes overlooked, is the frequency and timing of salary reviews. Every employer is obliged by law[7] to issue full-time employees with an itemised statement of pay setting out the gross salary, details of all deductions and the net amount payable. Remuneration is the 'consideration' which the employer gives for the employee's service.

In addition to the basic salary, many firms operate a bonus or profit-sharing scheme. If the term 'bonus' is used, it is possible that the employer thinks of it as an occasional, rather than a regular thing, something with which the employer can reward exceptional endeavour. In law, a contractual promise to pay a bonus as part payment for work done will be enforceable although the amount of the bonus will depend on the terms laid down. A profit-sharing scheme is probably the most satisfactory arrangement. What constitutes 'profit' should be clearly stated and the sharing may take place on the basis of a points system – a greater number of points represents a greater share. Points may be allocated for length of service, salary or status or in any other way deemed fair or set out in the contract of employment.

Job evaluation is a technique which is sometimes used to relate each post and its pay to every other post. There are two stages.

- Every post must be given a rank.
- Appropriate salaries must be attached to each post.

The system is said to have many advantages. It should produce a pay structure within the practice and an overall level of pay which is clearly recognised as being reasonable in itself and in comparison to external pay levels. In addition, the employees should feel secure from arbitrary changes in the pay structure and the practice has a method of fixing rates of pay for new posts.

It is quite difficult to grade the work of professionals. Job evaluation is usually based on a points system, which is most appropriate to manual work. Although there is no reason why such a system should not work when applied to professionals, a considerable amount of subtlety is required. It is the post and not the individual which is being graded. Points are normally given for effort, skill, experience, qualifications, working conditions, etc. It is open to a practice to establish its own criteria so long as they can be seen to be fair and reasonable when applied to all members of staff. A basic job description is described in 18.4 above.

18.8 Benefits

This is an important part of the remuneration package. Indeed, in some instances it may be a significant factor in determining whether an architect takes one post in preference to another. The most highly prized benefit is still a company car, particularly the more expensive kinds which architects may covet but be unable to buy themselves, even though the tax penalties are increasing, particularly for larger cars. Indeed, the tax disadvantages now make company cars less desirable. Firms have varying policies. In many practices, it is still quite rare for an architect below the status of associate to be given a company car. An alternative is the 'pool' car where architects may have the use of a car, but they must take whichever car is available on that particular day.

As an alternative, a firm may require employees to provide their own cars for use on firm's business and give an annual car allowance or monthly running and depreciation allowance together with a realistic mileage payment. In such cases, the employer may sometimes provide an interest-free loan facility. Problems can arise with this kind of provision. Employees who have major repairs to finance can find themselves in breach of contract if they are unable to afford the repair. If car use is essential, the car should be provided by the firm, either personally to the employee (as is common in other parts of the construction industry) or in a pool. Company-arranged car-leasing facilities for employees are becoming more common. It is also becoming usual for mobile telephones and laptop computers to be provided. Whether this last really is a perk is open to question.

Some firms automatically enrol all employees in a medical insurance scheme. This can have obvious benefits for the employees and the great advantage for the employer is that hospital procedures can be carried out quickly and, in the case of non-life threatening conditions, to suit the employee's office commitments. Points to note are that it is usual for these schemes to exclude cover for any illness even remotely connected with a previous illness in the same employee. For example, an employee who has had investigations for a stomach ulcer prior to enrolling on the scheme might well find that cover is excluded for any abdominal ailment. The actual extent of expense which will be reimbursed should be carefully checked. Such insurance counts as a benefit for tax purposes (see Chapter 17, section 17.7).

Parking is often a problem in centrally situated offices and a parking space is a valuable provision. An alternative is for the office to provide season tickets to local car parks. Some offices provide only minimal parking for the principals and a couple of visitors, and staff have to make their own arrangements. City centre parking on a daily basis is an expensive business. Many architectural practices have located in semi-rural areas to take advantage of, among other things, the easier parking situation.

18.9 Professional activities

All employees should be encouraged to take part in professional activities, but some firms are not supportive of such things and what should be regarded as commonplace has almost come to be regarded as an extra benefit. The degree of encouragement often depends upon the principal, and his or her mood on a particular day. The economic climate is also of prime importance. The following may be said to fall into the category of professional activities of varying degrees of importance.

Continuing professional development

Every employee should be allowed some time each year to go on courses either in or out of the office. Employers vary considerably regarding whether they are prepared to continue paying salary during days off for this purpose. The imposition of compulsory CPD by the RIBA on its members is particularly significant in this regard (see Chapter 2, section 2.2).

Examinations

Students require time off to sit their Part 3 examinations. They also need time for study and attendance at short courses during the period immediately before examinations. Employers must allow attendance at examinations; they should allow attendance at appropriate short courses, but pure study time is probably best left to the student to organise.

Sabbaticals and study trips

Sabbatical leave is recognised as an important constituent of some posts, particularly in education. It refreshes the mind and generates ideas. Above all, it plays an important part in the development of the employee. Study trips also assist the employee to develop a particular interest. It is rare for offices to allow such trips, except of course during the employee's own holiday period. Where an office does allow or even encourage such trips, the effect on salary payments should be clarified in advance.

Professional subscriptions

It is relatively unusual for an employer to reimburse an employee's subscription to a professional body. This kind of provision is generally regarded as a benefit for architects of high status such as associates.

Journal subscriptions

It is even rarer for an employer to reimburse professional journal subscriptions, but virtually all offices subscribe to a range of journals for the benefit of staff as a whole.

Attendance at branch meetings

Architects should be as active in the local professional branch as their other commitments allow. It is a way of keeping up to date, not only in regard to technical matters, but also as far as professional matters are concerned. Most branches have a series of sub-committees and they are usually desperate for members. It is a useful way of getting to know other architects in the area and of finding out what is happening in other offices. Most of these meetings take place in the evenings and, therefore, time off is not required. Where an employee is particularly active in the local branch, it makes sense for the office to allow time off to attend any special meetings during the day. Apart from other considerations, it is a useful piece of exposure for the practice and a means of keeping the practice tuned into what is happening elsewhere.

18.10   Expenses

Expenses are often linked to remuneration. That is wrong. Employees are not expected to make a profit out of expenses, but neither are they expected to make a loss. The intention should be that they are reimbursed – no more, no less.

The general law implies a term in every contract of employment that the employer will indemnify the employee against any expense reasonably incurred in the performance of their duties. Within that statement, however, there is considerable scope for differences in application. Thus, although there is not strictly any necessity for details of expenses to be set out in the contract of employment, it is worth doing so that both parties are perfectly clear at the outset. The key word is 'reasonable'. An expense will be reasonably incurred if authorised or, if prior authority is not possible, if it is justified by the circumstances. This latter category causes most trouble and there is much to be said for giving guidelines, if not in the contract itself, as soon as possible thereafter. The most common expense is travelling. The preferred mode of transport should be stipulated by the office: car, train, bus or taxi. Most probably, the type of transport authorised will depend upon the length of journey and whether or not a client is in the party. Where cars are involved, the mileage rate should be stated, as should the class where rail travel is involved. Taxis are normally reserved for transport between airport or station and office or hotel and for emergencies.

The employee must be reimbursed if he or she incurs expense in entertaining clients. In some offices, only partners are permitted that sort of expense account. The company policy should be made clear.

The type of practice and the location of its work will determine how often an employee may be away from his or her office base on business. The rates of subsistence payments in such cases should be sufficient to ensure a fair standard of accommodation and meals.

It is essential for employees to properly record all expenses so that the practice can recover from the client, if appropriate. However, the fact that an office cannot recover certain expenses from the client should not preclude payment to the employee. Expense repayments should be prompt. Some firms get the free use of money by making employees wait several weeks before payment. Expense repayments should ideally be *on demand* and there is no good reason why not *in advance* if the anticipated expense is likely to be more than the employee wishes or is able to advance from his or her own resources.

18.11   Leave

It used to be the case that there was no automatic right to paid holidays either in statute or at common law. An employee's holiday entitlement was, therefore, whatever was agreed with the employer. Legislation, however, now provides that all employees are entitled to 5.6 weeks paid leave every year.[8] Even part-time staff now have leave entitlement, in proportion to full-time employees.

Leave must be included in the 'written statement' (see 18.3 above), but it is preferable to have the details recorded in the employment contract. Holiday entitlement is often in excess of the minimum and commonly includes all public or bank holidays together with 20 or 25 additional days to be taken during the holiday year. This normally runs from January to December or from April to April (the financial year). It is generally stipulated that the holiday days must be taken within the holiday year to which they relate. Some firms allow a few days to be carried over to the next 'year' or give payment in lieu.

Payment in lieu of holidays is not generally encouraged by employers and it is not a statutory entitlement unless the employee is terminating employment, because it tends to encourage employees to forego holiday entitlement which every working person needs. It is better to allow a few days to overlap into the next period if pressure of work has prevented the taking of holidays at the appropriate time. Obviously, chaos would ensue if employees enjoyed untrammelled power to save their entitlement from one year to the next until perhaps they could take 6 months off to tour the world. Not that such an idea is bad in itself, but there are other ways of accomplishing that kind of ambition. The taking of holidays should be tempered by the need to keep the office running smoothly.

It is good practice for an office to have all the rules regarding holidays, as other things, clearly set out. There are few things worse than the office which is full of unwritten (and therefore, constantly changing) rules. Many offices close down completely from Christmas to New Year. Employers should make clear whether this period is included in or additional to the annual leave. Additional days are often added onto the annual holiday to reward long service with a firm.

In addition to holidays, there are other kinds of leave which may affect the employee architect.

- Maternity leave
- Paternity leave
- Compassionate leave
- Leave for public duties
- Unpaid leave and sick leave

18.11.1 Antenatal care and maternity leave

This is subject to statutory regulations which change from time to time. A woman expecting a baby is entitled to have time off to receive antenatal care. This right does not depend upon the length of service or the number of hours worked. A certificate of pregnancy must be produced for all appointments after the first. The employee is entitled to be paid as usual. A pregnant woman is entitled to maternity leave. To qualify for maternity pay and the right to return to work:

- the reason for absence must be pregnancy
- there is no qualifying period of work
- not later than the beginning of the 14th week before her estimated week of childbirth, she must inform the employer that she is pregnant and state the week the baby is expected to be born and when she wants her maternity leave to commence (she is not bound by this statement and can change her mind about the start date of her leave if she gives 28 days notice, unless it is not reasonably practicable)
- she must produce a medical certificate if required.

A woman is entitled to a total of 26 weeks maternity leave irrespective of length of service. Women who have completed 26 weeks of continuous service with the employer by the beginning of the 14th week before the estimated week of childbirth are entitled to take an additional 26 weeks (usually unpaid) maternity leave immediately after the end of the ordinary maternity leave. There is no longer any requirement to give notice of intention to return to work, unless the woman intends to return to work before the expiry of the full maternity leave. If that is the case, 8 weeks notice of return is required. The employer is not entitled to request written notice of intention to return to work.[9]

18.11.2 Paternity leave

To qualify for paternity leave:

- the man must expect to be responsible for the child's upbringing
- he must be the biological father of the child or must be the husband or partner of the mother. Leave may also be available to a female employee who is in a continuing relationship with the baby's mother
- he must have completed 26 weeks of continuous service with the employer by the beginning of the 14th week before the baby is due
- not later than the end of the 15th week before the expected week of childbirth, he must inform his employer of intention to take the leave, stating when the baby is due, whether 1 or 2 weeks leave is required and when he wants the leave to commence
- he must produce a self-certificate regarding eligibility on the employer's request.

The leave cannot be taken in odd days.[9] The man is not entitled to normal pay, but he is entitled to statutory paternity pay.

18.11.3 Parental leave

The Employment Relations Act 1999 gives employees with 1 year's service the right to take up to 13 weeks unpaid parental leave (18 weeks if the child is disabled). This applies to both natural and adoptive parents. Parental leave may be taken before the child's 5th birthday or, in the case of adoption, during the following 5 years or up to the age of 18, whichever is the sooner.

18.11.4 Compassionate leave

An employee has the right to compassionate leave (time off for dependants) of a day or two to deal with various emergencies. However, there is no right to payment; it is entirely at the discretion of the employer. The right may be exercised when a dependant dies, falls seriously ill, suffers injury, gives birth or when care arrangements break down. The right may also be exercised in the case of a problem with a dependent child during school hours.

Many firms lay down useful guidelines in their employment contracts and they will allow paid leave for such things as death, serious illness or accident to a close relative. In general, such leave is dealt with on an *ad hoc* basis depending on the particular circumstances. Some employers lay down a maximum compassionate leave allowance in any year. Such a provision is comparatively rare, however, because it can be considered by employees to be an entitlement which must be taken before the end of the year on sometimes flimsy grounds. Most firms are generous once they know that the need is genuine.

18.11.5 Leave for public duties

Legislation stipulates that certain persons holding official posts must be allowed time off from work to attend to their duties. A common example of this is the trades union official who is entitled to a reasonable time off with pay to attend to union affairs. In most other cases, however, time off must be granted, but it need not be with pay. Common examples are JPs and members of statutory tribunals, members of the local authority or other authority, members of tribunals, members of juries and school governors. Although, because it is a statutory requirement, there is no necessity to include references to such leave in an employment contract, many firms include a statement on the position for the avoidance of doubt. Employers can be quite generous in continuing to pay employees, less only any attendance allowance, for carrying out official duties. This may also reflect the recognition that it does the firm no harm at all to have one or more of its employees in the public eye (see Chapter 19).

Specific trades union members are allowed to have reasonable leave for all trades union activities (except industrial action). Unlike trades union officials, however, ordinary members must take the time off without pay.

There is a further situation in which an employer must allow time off with pay. That is in the case of an employee whose post becomes redundant. Reasonable time off with pay must be allowed for the purpose of seeking alternative employment.

18.11.6 Sick leave

Although the general law gives no right to sick pay, legislation fills the gap and most firms have quite detailed provisions of their own. If they are not in the contract of employment, they must be included in the written statement. The employer is obliged to pay statutory sick pay for a period of up to 28 weeks of sickness in any 3-year period. Certain procedures must be carried out and it is usual to make compliance with the procedures a condition of employment. This is because strict adherence to the procedure is necessary if the employer is to be able to reclaim any sick pay under the entitlement from the DHSS. There are some detailed conditions surrounding the entitlement to statutory sick pay which repay careful study.

An employer will often undertake to pay an additional amount to bring the statutory sick pay up to an employee's usual salary. Such payment is sometimes linked to length of service and commonly consists of 1 or more months at full pay and an equal number of months at half pay. The more generous schemes provide for an employee to be paid 6 months half salary if a period of illness occurs after a qualifying period of 2 years. Less than 2 years service gives rise to a reduced entitlement. This kind of provision is more likely in larger offices where the absence of a member of staff for a prolonged period is not likely to be more than inconvenient. The chance of several architects taking several months off for sickness at the same time is so unlikely as to be suspicious.

Subject to what may be included in the employment contract, there is nothing to prevent an employer terminating employment on the grounds of prolonged absence due to sickness. Some employers set out the relevant criteria in the employment contract, but this is rare. Where criteria are set out, they often include the right of the employer to ask for an independent medical examination of the employee after absence from work for a specified period or at the employer's discretion.

18.12 Disciplinary and grievance procedure

Every office should have a disciplinary and grievance procedure. There is no particular statutory requirement, contrary to popular belief, regarding the exact form of the procedure although where dismissal for any reason is contemplated, a standard procedure should be followed. ACAS has produced codes of practice which firms may adopt. The general principles are as follows.

- The procedure should be described in writing.
- The person who may operate the procedure should be specified.
- Possible action should be specified.
- Except in the case of gross misconduct, a first offence should not incur dismissal.
- The employee should be informed of the complaint and he or she is entitled to representation.
- There should be a warning procedure including at least one oral and one written warning followed by a sanction less than dismissal before dismissal actually takes place.
- There should be an appeal system.

The grievance procedure should state whom the employee should approach with a complaint and to whom appeal may be made.

The procedures may be contained in the office manual. Less commonly, they are spelled out in the employment contract. Some firms appear to be a trifle coy about this, as if admitting that a procedure exists is tantamount to encouraging disputes.

18.13   Notice and dismissal

Every employee must be aware of the period of notice required to end the employment contract. If the period is less than the statutory minimum, the statutory minimum will apply. Most firms give reasonably detailed terms governing the termination of employment, but it should be noted that such terms cannot over-ride statutory provisions. The statutory periods of notice which must be given by the employer range from 1 week if the employee has been continuously employed for more than 1 month but less than 2 years and, thereafter, 1 week for every complete year worked up to a maximum of 12 weeks. The employee, on the other hand, has a statutory obligation to give 1 week's notice of termination. If the contract stipulates a greater period, the employee will be in breach of contract if he or she gives less.

There is confusion between unfair and wrongful dismissal. The terms are often used as if they were interchangeable. There are in fact four circumstances in which employment can be terminated.

- Wrongful dismissal
- Unfair dismissal
- Fair dismissal
- Redundancy

Wrongful dismissal is a breach of contract, for example, if insufficient notice is given. Damages are available at common law. Unfair dismissal, however, is enshrined in statute and it refers to the situation when the correct notice is given, there is no breach of contract, but the reason for the dismissal is considered by statute to be unfair. In this case, the employee's remedies are prescribed by statute also. Fair dismissal is when the correct notice is given, there is no other breach of contract and the reason for dismissal is considered to be fair. Redundancy comes into a special category which lays down the particular statutory rights of the employee in such a situation. Dismissal will not be wrongful or unfair if the employee is guilty of gross misconduct or is unable to carry out the work properly. Some contracts attempt to set out precisely what may fall into these categories to avoid disputes later, but those contracts are rare in architectural practice.

18.14   Spare-time practice

Many architects engage in spare-time practice during the period they are employees. It may be a means of obtaining extra cash or a means of starting up in practice with a client nucleus. The general law will imply that an employee may so practise unless there is a term in the contract expressly forbidding it.

The employer's attitude, however, may be less than enthusiastic, either directly forbidding spare-time practice, in spite of the Code, or hedging it around with so many rules that it is not a practical proposition. Reasonable conditions are as follows.

- The employee must inform the employer in advance.
- The employee must have professional indemnity insurance cover appropriate to the spare-time work.
- The clients must be informed that the employee is carrying out the work in a personal capacity.
- The clients must not be existing clients of the firm.
- Private work must not be carried out in office hours or making use of office equipment or materials unless prior permission has been obtained.
- The firm's interests must not be affected in any way.

Many firms encourage employees to introduce work into the firm. Again, it is preferable if the policy is clearly stated. Very small jobs may not be welcome. Employees introducing work will expect something more than the usual salary for their trouble. Some employers reward the employee by a special payment related to the final profit on that particular project. Provided that the method of calculating the payment is known to all, it is a sensible way to proceed, because it associates the employees with the firm, it links the futures of firm and employee and paves the way for closer association in due time.

There is a great advantage to an employee in bringing all work into the office rather than carrying on spare-time practice. The employee will have the protection of the office professional indemnity insurance rather than having to go to the expense of obtaining personal cover (see Chapter 17, section 17.5). Private work is carried out at the employee's risk. If the employee is negligent in his or her own work, the client will look to them for damages. Such employees should carry their own insurance to cover their spare-time practice. The reality is that such cover may not be easily affordable. All may be well during the time the architect is employed and is not considered worth suing by clients. The situation may be different if the employee later sets up in profitable practice and earlier negligence results in a heavy claim for damages.

There are two matters which are closely associated with spare-time practice: copyright and confidential information. In general, copyright in work prepared by an employee belongs to an employer.[10] Employees should be aware that permission must be obtained from an employer to produce copies of their drawings to take to interview for the purpose of securing other employment. Employees, of course, retain copyright in work which they produce during their spare time.

Confidentiality is a difficult area. Information which an employee may gain in employment was considered in *Faccenda Chicken Ltd* v. *Fowler* [1986][11] to fall into three categories:

- information well known to people in the industry
- confidential information which becomes part of the employee's own skill and knowledge
- information of such confidentiality that it cannot be used lawfully to benefit anyone other than the employer.

Information in the third category can never be divulged by an employee even after leaving the employment. The second category of information cannot be protected when an employee leaves, but to reveal such information while still in the original employment would be a gross breach of trust and entitles the employer to damages. The problem lies in correctly identifying what information falls into which categories. It is probably for this reason that some firms purport to state the type of information which is considered to be highly confidential in the employment contract. An employee, of course, will be bound by such terms.

Some architects in employment, usually those with considerable responsibility and possibly access to information regarded by the practice as highly confidential, may have a restraint clause in their contracts. Such a term may try to restrict an employee setting up in practice within a certain distance of the previous employer for a period of time. Terms in contracts which attempt to restrict future employment are basically void at common law as being in restraint of trade but they may be valid and enforceable if:

- they are reasonable between the parties
  - (a) the restriction must protect the employer's legally recognised interest: protection of trade secrets; and/or protection of business connections
  - (b) the restriction must be no greater than necessary to so protect: in respect of the period of restriction; in respect of the geographical restriction
- they are reasonable in the public interest, for example, they do not deprive the public of special skills which the employee may possess.

Where a restriction is placed on ex-partners, the same principles generally apply, but it is considered reasonable to enforce stricter time periods and geographical areas.

18.15   Monitoring of telephone calls and emails

In general, interception is unlawful and possibly criminal if done without the consent of both sender and receiver of the communication. However, there are wide exceptions set out in the legislation. An employer may intercept and monitor calls and emails made on equipment belonging to the business in relation to that business. There is substantial legislation which affects the situation and with which architects, whether acting as employers or employees, should be familiar.[12]

There are many reasons why an employer may wish to monitor calls made by employees. For example, the employer may wish to ensure that an employee is not using business time and telephones to make private calls. The policy of a practice with regard to private calls should be clearly spelt out to all employees. It may be that an employee is away sick or on leave and the employer wishes to check that there are no important emails or voicemails lying unanswered. All employees should be notified in advance if telephone and email monitoring is proposed. Such notification is best done in the staff handbook, if provided, or otherwise in a written note. The Regulations set out specific circumstances where interception of communications by an employer is lawful:

- to establish the existence of facts
- to ascertain compliance with regulatory practices and procedures
- to ascertain or demonstrate employee standards
- in the interests of national security
- for the purpose of preventing or detecting crime
- for the purpose of detecting or investigating unauthorised use of the telecommunication system
- to ensure the effective operation, or as an inherent part, of the system
- to determine whether communications are relevant to the practice
- for the purpose of monitoring communications with confidential anonymous counselling or support services.

The Regulations prescribe various conditions which must be satisfied.

18.16   Discrimination

An employer may not discriminate against a person on the grounds of that person's sex or marital status.[13] The Sex Discrimination Act applies in cases of discrimination against trans-sexuals provided that the individual 'intends to undergo, is undergoing or has undergone gender reassignment'.[14] The Act has particular application to the recruitment of staff and to any benefits. Indirect discrimination is also unlawful, for example if criteria are laid down which favours one sex. An exception is made in the case of occupations where decency or physiology dictates that only a man or a woman can do the work.

Discrimination against a person on the grounds of race, colour or nationality or ethnic or national origins is also outlawed.[15] Again, indirect discrimination is also forbidden and the Act applies equally to fellow employees. Exceptions to the provisions are allowed – for example, if a particular racial group would have difficulty in doing certain work or if certain work could only be performed by a certain group. Stirring up hatred against an individual on race or religious grounds is a criminal offence.[16]

Regulations in force from December 2003 permit freedom of religious belief (or non-belief) and freedom in the expression of a person's sexual orientation (to an extent equal to that of a heterosexual) in employment. This is similar to, but not the same as, the position in regard to sex and race discrimination. Defences against harassment and victimisation are included.[17] In Northern Ireland, it is unlawful to discriminate on the grounds of religion or political opinion.

A woman may not be treated less favourably simply because of her sex.[18] Pay and conditions of service are covered. The Act of course does not apply where the reason for differences in pay is due to such things as differing job responsibilities.

It is unlawful to discriminate against disabled people in employment situations.[19] The Act applies to both mental and physical disablement. Discrimination is lawful only in very specific circumstances, for example to safeguard health and safety. Businesses of less than 15 people are excluded from the provisions.

It is automatically unfair to dismiss a worker for joining, being a member of, refusing to join, or refusing to remain a member of a trade union.[20]

Regulations against age discrimination came into force in August 2006.[21] They affect both old and young. A practice must not have any policies or rules which have the effect of disadvantaging persons of any age. Advertisements which state: 'Young, ambitious architect required' or 'A mature and experienced professional is sought' are equally unlawful. There are a number of sensible exceptions, including where a particular age group is most appropriate for certain kinds of employment or in relation to redundancy schemes.

References and notes

1. The Employment Equality (Age) Regulations 2006.
2. *Spring* v. *Guardian Assurance plc and Others* (1994) 3 All ER 129.
3. *Ferguson* v. *John Dawson* [1976] 1 WLR 1213.
4. *Sim* v. *Rotherham MBC* [1986] IRLR 391.
5. RIBA (1962) *The Architect and His Office*, RIBA Publications Ltd.
6. Based on the European Union Working Time Directive, the Young Workers' Directive and health and safety measures. The Regulations have been amended in 2001, 2002, 2003 (twice), 2004 and 2007.
7. Employment Act 1982.
8. Working Time (Amendment) Regulations 2007.
9. Employment Act 2002. Further information can be obtained from www.dti.gov.uk.
10. Copyright Designs and Patents Act 1988.
11. [1986] 1 All ER 617.
12. Data Protection Act 1998, Human Rights Act 1998, Regulation of Investigatory Powers Act 2000, Telecommunications (Lawful Business Practice) (Interception of Communications) Regulations 2000.
13. The Sex Discrimination Act 1975.
14. Section 2A(1) of the Sex Discrimination Act 1975 (an amendment).
15. The Race Relations Act 1976.
16. Race and Religious Hatred Act 2006.

17. Employment Equality (Religion or Belief) Regulations 2003. Reference for guidance should be made to www.acas.gov.uk.
18. Sex Discrimination Act 1975.
19. The Disability Discrimination Act 1995 as amended by the Disability Discrimination Act 2005.
20. Section 137, Trade Union and Labour Relations (Consolidation) Act 1992.
21. Employment Equality (Age) Regulations 2006.

19 Attracting Work

19.1 Active marketing

It is often, and correctly, said that the time to concentrate on marketing is when the firm is busy; which of course is the very time when no one has the time to give to marketing. The reason why marketing should be carried out when work is coming in and everyone is busy is that the effects of marketing usually take some time to show themselves. It can easily be a year after the event that a commission happens. If a practice waits until work is falling off, any initiative may be too late to achieve useful results.

The first thing for any architect to realise is that marketing any professional service is not like selling baked beans. An altogether different approach is necessary. Not very long ago, the only acceptable way for an architect to attract work was through existing clients. Apart from a brass plate with letters of a prescribed size, there were few ways the architect could advertise the existence of the practice. The situation now is vastly changed and a wide range of activities are allowed by the Code of Conduct.

Every practice must develop a unique marketing strategy for that firm. Very large practices may employ one or more full-time marketing people to keep the firm in the public eye and follow up particular opportunities. The majority of firms, however, must rely on the part-time efforts of their own staff. Some architects have the gift of attracting work. They can go to a party and come back with three new commissions. Such architects are worth their weight in gold and they need never do any architectural work themselves. They, however, are quite rare. Therefore, specific marketing objectives must be set so that all the staff in a practice are pulling in the right direction.

There are some very simple straightforward things that every practice can do.

- Chartered Practice scheme
- Architects' sign boards
- Lectures and articles
- Direct approach

19.1.1 RIBA Chartered Practice scheme

A practice can register as a Chartered Practice for a modest fee. At the time of writing, the subscription for a one-person practice is £110 per year, rising in stages to £395 per year for practices of more than 50 persons. Certain criteria must be satisfied before a practice will be accepted for membership. The criteria have been made much stricter than previously, but are little more than one might expect from a properly organised architectural practice in any event. Full details can be obtained from the Chartered Practice Brochure which can be downloaded from the RIBA website.[1] There are currently something under 3000 practices registered in this way. The decrease in numbers from the 4000 mentioned in the previous edition is probably a result of the stricter requirements and the current trading conditions.

Not only does RIBA Client Services promote architects in a general way, it also responds to over 7500 queries each year from prospective clients seeking an architect for a particular project. It is important to understand that the RIBA Client Services Team only nominates Chartered Practices. Whatever might be thought of this approach, the pragmatic response is to register as a Chartered Practice. Chartered Practices also have a substantial entry in the Directory of Practices which enables a practice to give its full details together with the kind of commissions it undertakes. It is available to be searched on the RIBA website. The scheme offers numerous opportunities for marketing the specific practice as well as the general advertising undertaken by the RIBA for Chartered Practices as a whole.

19.1.2 Architects' sign boards

Most practices have standard sign boards which are erected in a prominent position on new developments. If the development is of any size, the architect's board will be just one of many professionals' boards and there will be boards giving the particulars of the main contractor and sub-contractors. It must be remembered that such boards require planning permission (see Chapter 9, section 9.4) and the architect is usually responsible for approving, if not actually designing, the layout of such boards. The requirement for a board to be displayed on a site must also be included in the bills of quantities or specification for a project in order to avoid removing it in the case of a dispute.

An architect now has the right to insist that the practice is identified as architect of the project in any published material illustrating the building and to be credited with the design in permanent form on the outside of the finished building.[2] Although there may be isolated instances where the architect definitely does not wish to be remembered as the designer of a particular building, in most cases it is a valuable means of additional publicity, but the architect must assert the right for it to be effective.

19.1.3 Lectures and articles

Although it may be difficult for a one-person practice to find the time to give lectures or write articles, many practices contain members who can give short talks and others who can put together an interesting article on aspects of architecture in general and the work of the practice in particular. Many organisations, such as civic and amenity societies, chambers of commerce and the like have difficulty in finding speakers for lunchtime or evening meetings. There is nothing to prevent a practice from writing to such organisations offering a talk on architectural matters of interest. Although speaking in public can be daunting at first, practice makes perfect and provided a speaker is properly prepared with notes and possibly slides, the experience can be enjoyable for all parties. This is a good way of putting the firm's name in front of a wider public. An article is a more permanent record and likely to reach a wider audience provided it appears in an appropriate magazine or local paper. When speaking to or writing for people who are not architects, care should be taken to make the talk or article accessible in plain English and entirely devoid of 'architectspeak'.

19.1.4   Direct approach

Architects may now approach a client directly before there has been any initial enquiry. For example, an architect may hear that a company is expanding and looking for sites for additional factory production. There is nothing to stop the architect from writing to the company offering his or her services in finding a suitable site and designing the factory. Experience suggests that many commissions are obtained in this way. Some basic research is required before writing to ensure that another architect is not already commissioned.

19.2   Practice brochure

It has been suggested that a client will spend only 7 seconds flicking through a brochure.[3] This does not tend to promote confidence that a practice brochure will do much to assist in getting work. A practice brochure is not normally produced for wholesale distribution. Pressing a brochure on an unwilling client is counterproductive. The brochure should explain who's who in the firm, how long established and the kind of work carried out, preferably with illustrations. Special areas of expertise should be highlighted. Most importantly, however, the brochure should clearly explain the benefits to a prospective client of employing that particular firm. Although the brochure should be well designed in layout and typeface, it should avoid being too pretentious. It should be easy for a prospective client to find the way through to the information required (remember the 7 seconds – quite a long time actually). The brochure should be available in the waiting area of the practice office. It should be taken by a partner and left with a client after a presentation. In other words, it should be used selectively. It used to be the case that a practice brochure was very expensive to produce and print. It is now quite cheap to produce a full colour brochure printed on good paper, because it can be laid out on an office computer and copies printed only as required. Updating the brochure is simple.

It is a good idea for a practice to have two brochures: one, a full colour thickish document setting out everything about a practice and its projects for those times when a client asks for full details; the other, a folded A4 sheet setting out basic practice information, brief lists of projects and clients and evidence of the benefits that the practice can bring. The small brochure is useful for carrying around in a briefcase and for distribution before or after giving a talk.

19.3 Advertising

Advertising must be used with caution. Architects may advertise their services (since 1986), but whether it is wise to do so depends on circumstances. There is still a general feeling that advertising is not a very professional thing to do. It may be that it is worthwhile for a small practice to advertise in the local newspaper or in a magazine devoted solely to the subject of the practice's principal expertise. Obviously, a practice should ensure that it is included in every possible list, from Yellow Pages to local business directories, so that the name and telephone number are always available to anyone looking for an architect.

Viewed in a broad sense, advertising can be fruitful. That is the publicity a practice can get through the official opening ceremony of a prestigious building or for assisting in fund raising for a charitable building. The practice can get a high profile by offering to organise foundation laying or opening ceremonies or by becoming involved in the design of the commemorative brochure. A relatively poor client might want some assistance in putting together a fund-raising leaflet and the practice could well donate the services of a member of staff to draw a suitable pen and ink perspective for the front. Advertising can also be carried out by the setting up of exhibitions at galas, meetings and locations such as libraries and museums provided the subject matter is local and topical.

19.4 Contacts

This is probably the best method of attracting work. In the most basic form, the architect looks to relatives, friends and acquaintances to provide commissions and introductions to other sources of work. It is surprising how often one reads of old acquaintances achieving positions where they can be a useful source of work or further contacts. However, suddenly renewing an old friendship which has long since lapsed does not usually send out the right message. The answer is to cultivate as wide a circle of friends as possible. Those contacts are more a matter of luck than anything else, but the members of a practice can work to make contacts by attending functions and seminars and by joining clubs and organisations of a social, religious, sporting, civic or political nature. That is not to say that an architect should join a club for the sole purpose of getting work; there is nothing surer than that such an architect will not only get no work (his or her purpose will be obvious to all), but there will be no other enjoyment either.

Civic societies and conservation panels are a useful way of getting to know the local planning officers. Some architects make a practice of frequenting a local pub or club where solicitors, accountants and insurance brokers gather and sometimes a new commission will be obtained in that way. Not usually directly, but because when the solicitor is trying to think of an architect who can carry out a particular project on behalf of a client, the drinking companion may spring to mind.

19.5 Competitions

Competitions as a way of getting business should not be overlooked although they are not usually the first line of attack in this regard. Very often, the winning of a competition can be the start of a successful career for a young architect. Whether an office will enter for a competition depends very much on the volume of work in the office and the enthusiasm of its members. The RIBA website includes detailed information for architects thinking of entering a competition and for clients considering selecting an architect or a design by competition. The RIBA Competitions Office is based in Leeds. It organises competitions for specific client requirements. Two distinct types of competition are identified: finding the right architect and finding the right design solution. Under these broad headings, there may be several variations.

The various types of competition depend on the particular requirements of the promoters. In the first place, the competition may be single or two stage. In a single-stage competition, the competitors are required to submit fairly complete small-scale drawings sufficient to describe their designs, but in a two-stage competition, they are required to submit simple line drawings only in the first stage, indicating the broad outline of the scheme. From these entries, a shortlist is drawn up and the competitors on it are invited to submit a developed entry similar to the submissions in a single-stage competition. An obvious advantage of this method is that a relatively small number of entrants are expected to devote large amounts of time and effort. A variant is where the second stage consists of the competitors selected from the first stage together with a limited number of competitors specifically invited to submit schemes at the second stage. Persons invited to submit at the second stage only must be named in the conditions so that other competitors know the calibre of . persons they have to beat.

Another type of competition is the 'ideas competition', which is intended to solve particular problems. This kind of competition is sometimes set by manufacturers or the professional press as well as by clients, in order to air specific issues or to encourage rising architectural talents.

Competitions may be open or limited. Open competitions are those which may be entered by any eligible architect. Sometimes clients will promote a limited competition and invite architects of established merit, or entrants may be limited to architects from within a particular geographic area. Architects who are invited to submit designs or who are successful in proceeding to a second stage receive an honorarium. All winners should receive an appropriate premium and the author of the design placed first should be appointed to carry out the work. The premium is then subsumed into the fee for the project.

The assessors must be approved by the President of the RIBA and they are debarred from competing. Nor may an architect assessor take a commission to carry out the design in the event that no submitted entry is satisfactory.

There are opportunities for architects to compete worldwide in architectural competitions and international reputations have been made in that way. Such competitions are often advertised in the architectural press.[4]

19.6   Keeping clients and recommendations

The very best way of building a practice is to keep every client who is attracted enough to commission work. There is nothing so comforting as repeat business. It shows that the client is really satisfied and it provides a solid base from which the practice can grow. A satisfied client will recommend the practice to others and, in due course, there will be no necessity for a great deal of active marketing, because old and new clients will be anxious to commission work. Although such devices as regular mailshots, parties and regular correspondence on matters of interest help to show clients that their architect is concerned for their interests, the very best way of keeping clients is for the architect to give a first-class service.

References and notes

1.   www.architecture.com.
2.   The Copyright, Designs and Patents Act 1988.
3.   *Architects' Journal*, 13 December 1989, p69.
4.   Collyer, S. (2004) *Competing Globally in Architectural Competitions*, Wiley.

Table of Cases

Index

ACAS, 385

acceleration clause, 290

acceptable job titles, 369–70

access, 148, 216

Access to Neighbouring Land Act 1992, 216

accounts
  annual, 339, 345
  profit and loss, 339–40

accreditation of architecture courses *see* prescription of architecture courses

Achieving Excellence in Construction, 4

acoustic engineer, 11

active marketing, 392

activity schedule, 253

Acts of Parliament, 86

adjudication, 64–5, 115–16, 135, 136–7

adjudicator, 64–5

adjustment of contract sum, 303–6

advertisement control, 207–8

advertising, 395

agency, 9–7

agreement, 294

All England Law Reports, 88

ancient lights, 218

Ancient Monuments and Archeological Areas Act 1979, 228

annual accounts, 339, 345

answering advertisements, 356–7

application forms, 36–3

Appointment of a Consultant Architect for Small Works, Works of Simple Content and Specialist Services (ACA 98), 137

appraisal, 99

approved documents, 229–30

ARB Code, 32–8, 42, 43, 350

arbitration, 6–5, 135

Arbitration Act 1996, 135

arbitrator, 64–5

architect, 7–9
  appointment of, 3–5, 113–16
  education of, 18–28
  as employee, 353–91

architect's
  duties, 8–9
  instruction, 271–4
  services, 95–145
  sign boards, 393

Architect's Appointment 1982, 117

Architects (Recognition of European Qualifications etc and Saving and Transitional Provision) Regulations 2008, 48

Architects Act 1997, 28, 48, 369

Architects Council of Europe, 52

Architects Directive 85/384/EEC, 21

Architects Registration Act 1931–1969, 47

Architects Registration Board (ARB), 7, 18, 26, 29, 42, 47–51

Architects Registration Council of the United Kingdom, 47

architectural education, 1–28

architectural education, approval of programmes, 25–6

articles, 393–4

assembly drawings, 241

assets, 341

assignment, 126–7, 130, 142–3

associate, 71–2

Association for Consulting Engineers, 14

Association for Project Management, 13

Association of Building Engineers, 13

Association of Consultant Architects, 13

Association of Consultant Architects Standard Form of Agreement for the Appointment of an Architect (ACA SFA/08), 137

attracting work, 392–7